P9-DCU-032

WOMEN AND THE CITY

ALSO BY SARAH DEUTSCH

From Ballots to Breadlines:
American Women, 1920–1940
(The Young Oxford History
of Women in the United States, Vol. 8)

No Separate Refuge:
Culture, Class, and Gender
on an Anglo-Hispanic Frontier
in the American Southwest, 1880–1940

Women and the City

GENDER, SPACE, AND POWER IN BOSTON, 1870–1940

Sarah Deutsch

OXFORD
UNIVERSITY PRESS
2000

OXFORD
UNIVERSITY PRESS

Oxford New York
Athens Auckland Bangkok Bogotá Buenos Aires Calcutta
Cape Town Chennai Dar es Salaam Delhi Florence Hong Kong Istanbul
Karachi Kuala Lumpur Madrid Melbourne Mexico City Mumbai
Nairobi Paris São Paulo Singapore Taipei Tokyo Toronto Warsaw

and associated companies in
Berlin Ibadan

Published by Oxford University Press, Inc.
198 Madison Avenue, New York, New York 10016

Library of Congress Cataloging-in-Publication Data
Deutsch, Sarah.
Women and the city : gender, space, and power in Boston, 1870–1940 / by Sarah Deutsch.
p. cm.
Includes bibliographical references and index.
ISBN 0-19-505705-8
Women—Massachusetts—Boston—History.
2. Women in community organization—Massachusetts—Boston—History.
3. Women in public life—Massachusetts—Boston—History.
4. Spatial behavior—Massachusetts—Boston—History.
5. Urban women—Massachusetts—History. I Title.
HQ1439.B7 D48 2000
305.4'09744'61—dc21 99-34659

Map on page xii: U.S. Department of the Interior. Census Office. *Report on the Social Statistics of Cities.* Part I, *The New England and the Middle States.* Washington, D.C.: Government Printing Office, 1886.

Book design by Adam B. Bohannon

9 8 7 6 5 4 3 2 1
Printed in the United States of America
on acid-free paper

For Robert and Nancy Deutsch

Contents

ACKNOWLEDGMENTS

I have been working on this project for over a decade, and the list of those whose help I have been privileged to have is embarrassingly long. I would like to thank the staffs of Harriet Tubman House, the Social Welfare History Archives at the University of Minnesota, the Schlesinger Library at Radcliffe College, the Baker Library at the Harvard Business School, the Massachusetts Historical Society, the Boston Public Library, Boston University's special collections, the Goddard Library at Clark University, the University of Arizona library, and the Special Collections of the University of Chicago Library for their generous assistance. I would also like to thank the following people for their insightful comments and the gift of their time: Karen Anderson, Eileen Boris, William Chafe, Elisabeth Clemens, John Conron, Nancy Cott, Jackie Dirks, Gail Lee Dubrow, Faye Dudden, Cynthia Enloe, Elizabeth Faue, Ken Fones-Wolf, Maurine Greenwald, Susan Hanson, Nancy Hewitt, Robin Kelley, Sarah Henry Lederman, Joanne Meyerowitz, Martha Minow, Mary Murphy, Nancy Grey Osterud, Peggy Pascoe, Anne Firor Scott, Kimball Smith, Suzanne Spencer-Wood, Michael Spingler, Susan Traverso, Daniel Walkowitz, Richard White, and Karen Wigen's seminar. In addition I had the pleasure of learning from a variety of audiences who heard and responded to pieces of this work at Duke University, Boston University, the American Antiquarian Society, Clark University, Brandeis University, the Davis Center at Princeton University, University of Connecticut, University of Oregon, University of Alabama, New York University, University of Virginia, Northwestern University, University of California at San Diego, Southern Methodist University, University of Texas at Austin, University of Arizona, University of Washington, and

University of Vermont. The following undergraduate research assistants have my undying gratitude: Debbie Birnby, Nichole Dupont, Luella Gergen, Sheila Harris, Jennifer Mercier, Pamela Phillips, Carrie Siler, and Robert Wienerman. I have received generous support from the Southwest Institute for Research on Women at the University of Arizona, the Charles Warren Center at Harvard University, the Woodrow Wilson Center in Washington, D.C., and the National Humanities Center in the Research Triangle, in addition to M.I.T., whose Old Dominion Fellowship and Cecil and Ida Green Chair allowed me to take an early sabbatical to launch the project, as Clark University's generous sabbatical policy allowed me a final sabbatical to finish the project. And a special thanks to the extraordinary community of scholars, colleagues, and friends at Clark University for providing an exciting, vibrant home, sustaining me in difficult times and always challenging me, and to Reeve Huston for the generosity of his intellect and the pleasure of his company.

Sarah Deutsch, University of Arizona

ABBREVIATIONS

AFL American Federation of Labor
BCLU Boston Central Labor Union
BESAGG Boston Equal Suffrage Association for Good Government
BLWV Boston League of Women Voters
BWTUL Boston Women's Trade Union League
BYWCA Boston Young Women's Christian Association
DH Denison House
FS Fragment Society
GGA Good Government Association
IBEW International Brotherhood of Electrical Workers
ILD International Labor Defense
IWW Industrial Workers of the World
LWCS League of Women for Community Service
LWV League of Women Voters
MBSL Massachusetts Bureau of Statistics of Labor
MCL Massachusetts Consumers' League
MHS Massachusetts Historical Society
MWSA Massachusetts Woman Suffrage Association
NAACP National Association for the Advancement of Colored People
NRA National Recovery Administration
NWTUL National Women's Trade Union League
PSA Public School Association
UGW United Garment Workers
UTW United Textile Workers
WCC Women's City Club
WEIU Women's Educational and Industrial Union
WSC Women's Service Club
WTUL Women's Trade Union League

Boston in 1880

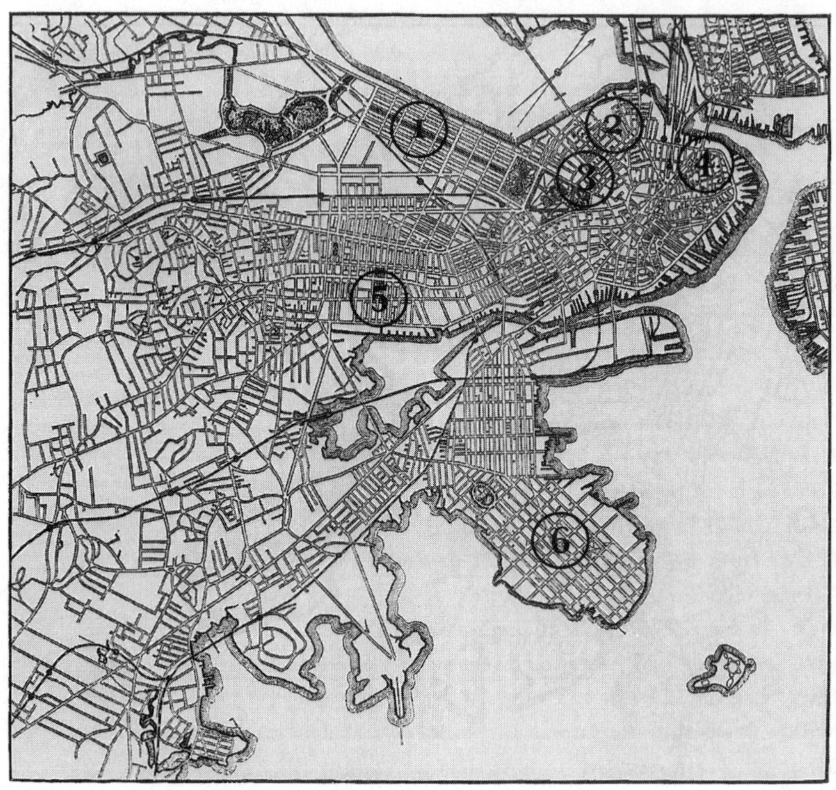

1 Back Bay
2 West End
3 Beacon Hill
4 North End
5 South End
6 South Boston

WOMEN AND THE CITY

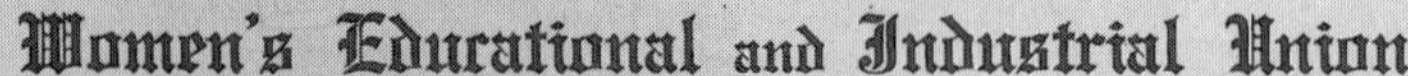

264 Boylston Street, Boston

LUNCH ROOMS

Boylston Street Lunch Room
Lunch, 11 A.M. to 3 P.M.
Afternoon Tea, 3.30 to 5.30 P.M.
Supper, 5.30 to 7.30 P.M.

Providence Street Lunch Room
Open 11.30 A.M. to 3 P.M.

Members' Lunch Room
Open 11.30 A.M. to 3 P.M.
For members and their friends.
Special Table d'hote Lunch, $ .35

New England Kitchen, 41-45 Charles Street
Open 7 A.M. to 6.30 P.M.
Breakfast, Lunch, Supper

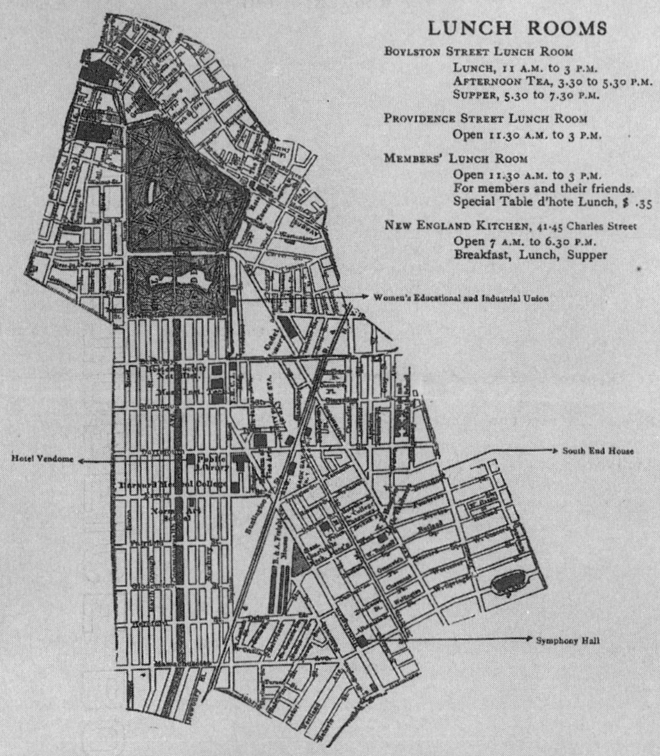

FOOD SALES DEPARTMENT

Food Specialties for light housekeeping:—Bread and Pastry, Cakes, Croquettes and Salads.
Catering Department:—Orders taken for Ice Creams and Ices of all kinds, for Teas, Receptions and Dinners.

HANDWORK DEPARTMENT

Exclusive models in Children's Clothes. Attractive Shirt Waists and Negligees.
Original Designs in Metal Work. Artistic and unusual Fancy Articles.

The WEIU's burgeoning satellites created a new map of the city for women.
Schlesinger Library, Radcliffe College

Introduction

Reconceiving the City

It was August 1893, in Boston. Times were hard. In the crowded dwellings of the South End, the onset of one of the worst depressions in the country's history would upset a precarious balancing act and tip many residents into poverty. Mrs. Scanlon was determined not to be one of them. On Wednesday, the twenty-third, Mrs. Scanlon buried her husband. By Saturday her thoughts turned to her own survival. She needed work so that she could keep her three children, and she needed child care so that she could work. She decided to look for a small tenement near a day nursery.[1]

Mrs. Scanlon's strategies and opportunities, like those of other men and women, lay rooted in a tangible environment. How close were child tenders? How far away was work? She knew the intimate relationship between her survival and the physical organization of the city. While some social scientists have turned their attention to these issues in contemporary cities, few historians have explored the relationship between the city's evolving structure and the choices and strategies of different groups of women. Sam Bass Warner's seminal work on streetcars did not deal with women; Stephen Thernstrom's quantitative studies also omitted women. Even those who have considered the sexual geography of the city usually focus on prostitution or the development of suburbs. Or they examine representations and symbolic uses of women, how women were placed in an environment created by others.[2] Ethnic and labor studies, such as those by Judith Smith and Ardis Cameron, have shown women's centrality in constructing neighborhoods, but have not attempted to demonstrate women's centrality in constructing the city as a whole.[3] Christine Stansell, Mary Ryan, and Kathy Peiss have broken new ground in giving women a more active role defining urban culture and geography. They show middle- and working-class women contending over the meaning of city spaces, such as streets and dance halls.[4] These historians have begun to see women as manipulating, if not shaping, urban space.

Women did more than respond to shifts in urban geography, however. They took a hand in altering the map of the city and in defining its meaning. No single pattern characterized the way Boston's diverse women approached the city, nor did their uses of the city follow a linear development.[5] But by their actions and their estimation of the city, women of all groups challenged the dominant, idealized sexual division of urban space and function between 1870 and 1940. Sometimes competing and sometimes converging with each other's needs and desires, they created a new set of relations and places. They changed the recipe of possibilities and even the urban infrastructure of schools and services, laws and landscape, for themselves and for men in the city. This book examines women's constant negotiations, alliances, and assertions in their struggle to survive at least in part on their own terms in a domain—the public space—in which their legitimacy as actors even today finds resistance.

Boston provides an ideal site for exploring these dynamics. It typified late-nineteenth- and early-twentieth-century cities in the U.S. with its female majority, expanding boundaries, relatively large female labor force, numerous female associations, ethnic and racial diversity, and political struggles between Yankee reformers and immigrant or ethnic political machines.[6] The city's spatial divisions—its working-class and elite territories, men's and women's spaces, public and domestic arenas—marked continuing relationships and negotiations rather than static terrains. Urban women's expectations and possibilities in the 1890s, for example, differed considerably from those in the 1870s or the 1920s. This book starts just after the Civil War, when women began to lay claim to public space in the city, and ends around the time of a woman's election to the Boston City Council in the late 1930s.

Although the 1890s appear as a pivotal decade in many of the chapters, with the rise of the college-educated "New Woman" and reform municipal government, I have ordered the book topically rather than chronologically. The first part puts at its center the politics of everyday life, or what James Scott has labeled "infrapolitics"—the "continent," of which organized movements, strikes, and candidacies are the "coastline."[7] It moves in four chapters through working-class matrons' struggles to make homes; middle-class and elite matrons' critique of those homes in favor of the primacy of their own; working girls' rejection of the purported safety of middle-class and elite or even parentally supervised spaces for their greater sense of safety among their peers; and, finally, female petty entrepreneurs' claims to ultimate autonomy.

In each case, the daily lives and domestic spaces of these women were intimately connected to the sorts of claims they made in and on public arenas. This is most clear in the case of middle-class and elite matrons, who based their claims to a new role in municipal governance on the purported superior morality of the domestic spaces they created. But the connection is equally intimate for the working-class women, as becomes evident later in the book, not only in the style of their kosher meat boycotts and labor strikes, but in the ways they mobilized allies. When working-class women recruited certain social service workers to aid them in labor disputes, for example, they did so within the pattern of daily interaction they had already established.[8]

The second half of the book follows women as they organized and institutionalized their efforts, from voluntarist to labor union to municipal party and electoral politics. Each chapter sets the shifting alliances by which women gained and lost power in the city against the ever-changing backdrop of urban governance and geography that facilitated or hindered them. The kaleidoscope pattern of their attempts to enter directly and shape the public arenas of streets, workplaces, and city hall demonstrates the complex ways in which the relationship between women and the public terrain is specific to class, ethnic/racial identity, and historical moment.

Space is not a character in this book the way land or water often is in environmental histories. Space does not have independent agency. Its meaning or power is determined by the way groups of people organize their social, political, economic, and other interactions.[9] This is a story of the constant interplay between different groups of people and city space. Urban spaces were designed, appropriated, or reappropriated by different parties. For all players, the ability to lay claim to certain types of space and the power to shape space—public arenas, housing, and so forth—was crucial to their ability to meet their basic needs and their often less basic desires.[10]

In a city neither designed for nor controlled by women, women had to reimagine or reconceive the city before they could create female-controlled public and semipublic spaces. At first I looked for those reconceptions where I had been trained to look for men's theories of city form, in explicitly theoretical texts or in sentences that started, "The city is. . . ." I did not find them. Instead women revealed their reconceptions of the city in the ways they wrote about moving through it, in the practices of their organizations, and in their daily lives.[11]

Reconceiving Boston

By the late nineteenth century, Boston had assumed its modern outlines. In a brief orgy of annexation, Boston brought within its borders Roxbury, Dorchester, and other outlying territories. At the city's center, the crowded elite of Beacon Hill swooped down upon the new blocks of the Back Bay, made possible by landfill. Impoverished immigrants continued to flock to the North and West Ends but also crowded into the genteel housing stock of the new South End, ambitiously developed but victim to one of the century's many depressions. The spread of the central business district crowded the poor still further into noisome streets, dank basements, and alley shacks. It spurred a move to the suburbs by those workers who could afford to flee the city, but it utterly failed to erode the understated dignity of the Back Bay and Beacon Hill. So successfully did these elite neighborhoods fend off commercial encroachment that their inhabitants remained anomalously, stubbornly anchored as the rest of Boston swirled about them. In the 1890s, four-fifths of the city's rich still lived in the city; cousins crisscrossed the tree-lined streets of the Back Bay. By contrast, almost half of the workers living in the city in 1880 were gone a decade later, and many times that number had come and gone in the intervening years. Amidst the flurry, the city retained its female majority, and women comprised one-third of the labor force.[12]

While the economy grew and its population rose rapidly in these decades from just over 250,000 to well over half a million, Boston failed to keep pace with the rest of the nation's major cities in either category and slipped further and further behind in the twentieth century. This relative loss, coupled with the increasing proportion of immigrant residents (one-third in 1880), the recurrent labor unrest, and the increasing visibility of ethnic Irish (a majority by 1890) made the tightly interwed and interbred elite anxious about their future. Henry James claimed of passersby on his 1904 visit to his old stomping grounds on Boston Common, "No note of any shade of American speech struck my ear. . . . [T]he people before me were gross aliens to a man, and they were in serene and triumphant possession."[13]

Those "gross aliens" may have shared the Boston Common with elite Bostonians, but their living quarters differed markedly. Each district had its own character. Though the West End, like the South End, had once been fashionable, by the 1880s its refurbished old buildings with bay windows, ornaments, bells, and speaking tubes housed the densest population in the city. Blacks, Jews, Irish, Portuguese, and Italians all had their sections.[14] In this labyrinthine district, alley led off alley; narrow passages emptied unexpectedly between high buildings or under them, and the only entrance to a tenement might be underground. Wooden walkways at different heights ran between the dark, crowded buildings.[15]

The dilapidated elegance of the West End and of the bowfront brownstones and avenues in the South End contrasted with the small, dark, cramped buildings that lined the North End's narrow, winding streets. With streets sometimes only six feet wide, sunlight rarely entered the buildings. In the back, buildings were even closer. Enterprising investors had filled the narrow tenement yards with more houses. Even the damp, noisome, and seeping basements had tenants. They suffered the highest death rate in the city. Scarlet fever, diphtheria, pneumonia, and whooping cough plagued the district. Stillbirths were common.[16]

To escape the close, dim interiors, men spent their time gathering in the streets and squares, women in the doorways and on the sidewalks. Mothers made lace, gossiped, and nursed babies on the stoops or at the open windows, and younger women promenaded through the neighborhood. Throughout the poorer districts, people jostled street performers and peddlers—and near the waterfront, sailors and dockworkers—and struggled to be heard over streethawkers' cries of "fresh fish."

In hot summer months, they slept on the rooftops, and in the winter, the men haunted the saloons and joined working women in the cafés and lodging-house restaurants, smoking, drinking, and talking politics and unions.[17]

In a semiautobiographical novel placed in the early years of this century, Vida Scudder, a professor of literature at Wellesley, tried to make sense of this landscape. Scudder had helped found several settlement houses in the 1890s and had resided in Denison House in Boston's South End. Settlement houses were homes purchased by members of the middle class or by middle-class institutions in working-class neighborhoods. Their founders' intent was to settle well-educated, middle-class people among the working poor, both to study the poor and to uplift them by their example of clean living and neighborliness.[18] The settlement house was both a social laboratory and a neighborhood center, and it often became an agitator for increased services and resources.

Scudder walked her heroine, on one wintry evening, across Boston from her uncle's home in the Back Bay to her settlement house in the South End.[19] This trek could be seen, and most often would be seen, as a journey not only through space, but also across class and ethnic boundaries. The Back Bay's straight broad avenues and relatively low density contrasted with the South End, whose sturdy housing stock was broken into ever smaller units to fit the pockets of immigrant workers who lived and lodged there.[20] So, too, did the Back Bay's old-stock Yankee Americans contrast sharply with the Irish, African Americans, Italians, Syrians, and Chinese of the South End.

Like most U.S. cities in the second half of the nineteenth century, Boston grew more and not less divided. It was still a walking city; Scudder's heroine could indeed cross the city on foot in an evening. But it was not undifferentiated space. The downtown became more distinct, with a greater number of quasipublic buildings: mechanics' halls, libraries, museums, and charitable institutions. And the Beacon Hill ladies from upper-class benevolent societies no longer found the objects of their beneficence on their doorsteps. Little directly connected the West, North, and South End working-class neighborhoods with Beacon Hill, whose residents successfully kept out the city's new streetcar system precisely for that reason.[21]

Later in the novel, Scudder's heroine walked in the opposite direc-

These pictures of Canny Place in the North End and Commonwealth Avenue in the Back Bay show the dramatic difference in light and space, and the appearance of order and chaos, available to working-class immigrants and the Boston elite. Top: Canny Place, from Dwight Porter, *Report Upon a Sanitary Inspection of Certain Tenement House Districts of Boston* (Boston: Press of Rockhill and Churchill, 1889); bottom: Commonwealth Avenue. Courtesy Bostonian Society/Old State House.

tion, and Scudder's language made clear the gulf between neighborhoods: as she walked, "dreary warehouses reared their immense sinister surfaces against the day"; a few minutes later, "the great artery of commerce" came into view. Then she crossed a bridge over the railroad tracks and greeted silence; "the dignified city of her youth rose about her—a city of prosperous and pleasant homes, of attractive churches, of noble public buildings, of tranquil sunny streets." Her heroine concluded, " 'Poverty and wealth, labor and luxury, connected, or divided, by commerce. . . . I have walked straight through our civilization.' "

The contrast between the orderliness of Scudder's Back Bay, sunny and tranquil, and the cacophony of the working-class districts increased to the point that in 1907 Louise Bosworth, a young woman investigating the "living wage," could describe her nightly exploration of the West End in language fit for a Dante-esque descent: "I gasped," she wrote her mother, "when we plunged straight for the west end, the worst part of the slum district":

> I had thought myself pretty brave to go down there in broad daylight but at night seemed even different. . . . The population was sprawled all over the street. Under the electric light all over the pavement and side-walks men were smoking, dragged out-looking women were nursing babies or watching the poor puny things asleep in the flar [*sic*] and noise, and the children—the swarm of children were playing, sleeping, shouting and tearing around everywhere.[22]

She entered a gloomy hallway in pursuit of an interview, and someone rushed by in the dark. Bosworth followed her up to the third floor where "in a stuffy little kitchen with children all around and a foreign mother, we found our girl. There were dozens of candles burning on the table, it was crowded with them, in brass candlesticks and broken cups and even pieces of mud shaped as holders. In the center was a beautiful branched brass candlestick." Afterward, she learned that bizarre ritual was Rosh Hashanah, the Jewish New Year.

Nothing in this landscape made sense to the middle-class Protestant Wellesley graduate from the Midwest—not the promiscuous mixing of men, women, and children living in the street, not the language, not the "foreign" mother and her candles.[23] It was just this sort of cleavage that the settlement house was invented to try to mitigate. The settlement house's middle-class invasion itself was an admission of the segmented class and ethnic geography of the city.

Yet Bosworth's and Scudder's writings reveal more than just their ideas on ethnic and economic geography. Their writings expose their place in a shifting urban sexual geography that was both ideological and physical. For a middle-class lady like Scudder to settle in a working-class neighborhood was already breaking the bounds of proper sexual geography. The gender ideology prevalent among the middle classes from the 1870s to the turn of the century increasingly separated work from home and saw the home as the opposite, rather than the microcosm, of the world outside it. This ideology placed women firmly in the home, creators of peace and light and virtue, and men in the harsh world outside, battling one another in the marketplace and fighting it out (often literally in the nineteenth century) at the polling booths.

The dominant ideology left little room for women who worked outside the home. They were neither "true" women nor "true"—that is, manly—workers. Nor did it encompass women working for wages in the home, doing piecework, and bringing waged labor into the domestic domain. And it certainly did not account for the contested employment relations between servants and mistresses.

It was, however, an ideology of space as well as function, and it defined working-class Boston as off-limits to middle-class women like Scudder. Working-class sections had "rough" men, those toughs smoking in the street. They had saloons and other "questionable" enterprises including dance halls, which to middle-class reformers were the feminine version of saloons. Young, single working girls went there and spent time in all too close proximity to working men. They also had kitchen barrooms, often Irish, where homebrew was sold in a congenial, homey atmosphere, which horrified middle-class observers as destructive of the sanctity and purity of the home, not only because it brought commerce into the home but also because men and women drank together in shirtsleeves, sometimes barefoot, and not bareheaded. And these neighborhoods had cheap theaters, where men and women watched other men and women pretend to be what they were not, and even places of prostitution, where there was little pretense at all.[24] Working-class neighborhoods failed to conform to the middle-class vision of sexually segregated civic virtue.

Middle-class men could enter working-class districts without endangering their status. Middle-class women, in theory, could not. Middle-class women, like Scudder and Bosworth, could not pass into such dangerous territory nor transgress these class bounds without risking their status as "ladies," without risking contamination.[25] Definitions of "class" in this way were gender specific as well as geographic, and definitions of womanhood were class specific.

In the late nineteenth and early twentieth centuries, however, women of all classes contested this gendered ideology of urban space.[26] "Streetwalker" and "women of the streets" were euphemisms for prostitutes. Yet not only was Scudder's heroine traipsing heedlessly along these same city streets, more and more women were working outside the home and frequenting the streets in their leisure time. Indeed, the line between prostitute and working girl was always a fine one in this period, in part because they both occupied the same space.[27] Scudder's character participated in this broader challenge to the city's sexual geography. Her cousin was scandalized to learn that the heroine had spent an afternoon at the Central Labor Union, "not a spot frequented by young ladies of his acquaintance."[28]

Scudder's novel challenged the division of urban space on another level, as well. When Scudder's character marched along the streets of Boston, she not only crossed class boundaries, but also headed from one female domain to another. She departed from her cousin's home, a feminine, domestic, private space in the Back Bay. The Back Bay was a women's space because by 1900 it was littered with women's organizations and because as early as the 1880s about 30 percent of the Back Bay's residential lots were owned by women and 60 percent of the area's residents (in contrast to 30 percent in the North End) were female.[29] From this feminine realm, Scudder's heroine headed toward a female-founded and female-dominated settlement house, just like the one in which the author had lived. In addition, the heroine, like Scudder herself, attended and taught at a women's college.[30]

The domain of the book is largely female, despite its urban setting. In the reality of a male-dominated city, Scudder had reconceived the city itself and turned it from a masculine entity—a place with no public space for middle-class women—into a feminine city—a parallel female universe. She did not create a world without men, but rather a world where men met on women's turf, a place where women empowered themselves in public affairs. This transformation was not simply a feat of the imagination. It had tangible implications for the way women interacted with the city's male political, economic, and social actors and with each other. The settlement house was both a concept and a physical institution.

As women like Scudder created new spaces for themselves in the city, in bricks and mortar as well as fiction, they diversified the character of women's places. The home had been the only acknowledged space for women in the Victorian American city. There were homelike aspects to both Wellesley and settlement houses, but they were not homes. Scudder carefully distinguished among them. She put them on a continuum, with the parental home on one end and Denison House on another.[31]

At the settlement house, the forces of the city all met: businessmen, workers, and the unemployed of both sexes; welfare workers and philanthropists; educators and doctors; journalists and ladies. They met in the course of their daily business, but in the reconceived city, they met on female turf. In Scudder's novel, the men at the settlement house observed and talked; the women alone acted. Conflict occurred on all sides in the settlement house as in the novel, both between and within classes and sexes. Settlement house workers and female charity association visitors bitterly opposed one another over the best methods of providing social welfare and relief and even over how to define the "needy" and the "worthy poor."

In the settlement house, businessmen, labor leaders, welfare workers, and others opposed one another over dinner. Unlike the strikes and political disputes that paralyzed the city, these disputes were domesticated and their impact controlled. Amid these conflicts, the settlement house continued to function: finding employment, educating, investigating, and organizing neighborhoods and unions. The settlement house used a domestic form to create a public, urban institution. It did not so much mediate between public and private for its female residents, as has been claimed, as eradicate the bounds between public and private—eradicate the notion of home as refuge from the world outside it and of women as limited in their proper sphere to the space within four walls. Living in the house itself was a public action. The settlement house was both part of a city reconceived and a vehicle for building a reconceived city.[32]

As in the novel, Wellesley and Denison House, the college and the city, were tightly bound. Emily Green Balch and Katherine Coman, like Scudder, were both Wellesley professors and Denison House residents. Jane Addams had shaped Hull House, the first United States settlement house, not only on the model of the English male settlement houses she had visited but also on her own female seminary experience. So, too, did the leaders and residents of Denison House use their female college experience to shape the House's urban vision and the institutional character. These were women whose primary duty was not homemaking for men, and the urban institutions they created reflected undomesticated priorities.

In contrast, Scudder described the late Victorian home of her heroine's mother. It was the perfect refuge from the world outside it, far removed from all the conflict and competition of American streets. The heroine's mother rarely set foot outside the home and insisted that no concerns from the world outside her parlor should enter it. To Scudder, the middle-class home was prisonlike; to the mother, it was a sanctuary. Its creation was a service she had provided before her widowhood directly to her husband and indirectly to civilization at large. The mother described how she "helped" her late husband in his social service work: "To help him was my highest privilege; but I tried to do it chiefly by making a lovely home to which he could return. . . . Our rooms were in a dreadful hideous street; but I shut the street out as well as I could with the draperies. . . . He used to wish to talk a great deal about his 'cases,' his work, but I never encouraged that. I felt he so needed relief." When her daughter asked whether she invited her poor neighbors in, as settlement workers did, her startled mother replied, " 'Oh, no!' "[33] She was the model Victorian keeper of women's sphere.

Scudder's rejection of her mother's privatized refuge for the different sanctuaries of Wellesley and Denison House posed the spheres as mutually exclusive. But myriad other middle-class women who crossed the boundary from private to public in late-nineteenth- and early-twentieth-century Boston moved daily from one domain to the other, blurring boundaries. They formed dozens, even hundreds of institutions, and many of these women wrote their organizations' correspondence while dandling grandchildren on their knees.[34] The development made quite an impression; the era's authors freely satirized it, one of them having a heroine declare, "I shouldn't be a true Bostonian if I didn't try to start some movement," and another proclaiming Boston "a mammoth woman's club."[35]

Women intended some of the institutions they formed to mediate between the privacy of the parlor and the public nature of the city. They created these as separate female spaces rather than female-controlled and feminized mixed-sex spaces. In the New England Women's Club, women practiced their debating skills on each other before venturing into a heterosocial city political arena.[36] The Women's Educational and Industrial Union (WEIU) bought buildings in the city's male-dominated center and created lunchrooms to provide space for working and other women safe from that perennial lothario, the traveling salesman. Other groups were also creating female urban space. Department stores arose in this era for the first time, and self-consciously fashioned themselves into women's spaces to attract customers; they, too, had lunchrooms. But the Boston women's organizations, in distinction to the commercial emporia, were controlled by women, and women set the rules of behavior and the values.[37]

Physically manipulating the city by buying or erecting buildings was clearly a strategy most available to middle- and upper-class women in this era—largely white, Anglo-Saxon, and Protestant—who had access to the resources necessary to participate in creating the city's structure. Once these groups had situated themselves downtown, it is not surprising that they launched, from their new physical proximity to the corridors of power, lobbying efforts at the city hall and state legislature for their own rights and to make the city a better place for women to live.[38]

These women's aggressive efforts to reshape the city were shared by members of the male middle and upper classes, who helped design parks and playgrounds and supported city missions and settlement houses. Indeed, the women of Denison House, like those men, seemed bent on redefining working-class neighborhoods. Women were never outside the city's power structure; they were always part of it, although their role changed.

The settlement house daily journals show the residents constantly coming into conflict with the local inhabitants over definitions of mutual service and appropriate behavior.[39] Some working-class women could be grateful for settlement house services and connections. Even in the vibrant, working-class ethnic neighborhoods of the North and West Ends, transience was high. In the South End, it ran rampant. The search for an adequate and affordable dwelling, frequent layoffs, and minimal wages forced so much movement that many women could not find or create fully sustaining communities. A German woman who tailored with her husband claimed that the Denison House visitor was the first person to come inside her rooms in the one-and-a-half years she had lived in Boston.[40] At the same time, both these women and women whose neighborhood networks did provide human support and jobs often found exasperating the obtuseness, condescension, and rudeness of their middle-class visitors, who always seemed to show up at mealtimes, who chased away customers, interfered in domestic quarrels, and who noticed every speck of dirt in the place.[41] It was not simply that the two sets of women had different standards of cleanliness. They had competing visions of the city.

Working-class women's voices come to us more often in fragmented and discontinuous form than those of the middle class and elite, usually filtered through the lens of middle-class social workers or other recorders. Piecing these fragments together provides some sense of working-class women's own perspectives. Middle-class and elite women, for example, defined kitchen barrooms as dens of iniquity. Yet their own descriptions of them and of conversations in and about them show that many working-class women and men saw them instead as bastions of working women's enterprise and as community centers that turned a hostile city into a neighborhood. In them—unlike in the commercialized, less personal, and much less familial male-only bars—local ethnic values and habits prevailed. According to the Irish neighbors of Denison House, Irish neighborhood police would not enforce liquor laws against local kitchen barrooms.[42]

Mary Kenney, an Irish Catholic working-class labor organizer, was twenty-eight when she arrived at Denison House in the early 1890s, beckoned by middle-class and elite women interested in working women's welfare. In her autobiography, she displayed the ambivalence that characterized cross-class relations. She called Denison House "the first open door in the worker's district in Boston" (ignoring the male South End House nearby).[43] Kenney was grateful to the elite women who gave the use of their homes for union meetings, providing safe space for women workers to organize, as opposed to the bars in which men often organized.[44] But at the same time, she noted the limited way in which the WEIU allowed a new mixed-class study group on industrial relations to use its building. She recalled, "They let us use their building, but the sign with gold letters of the Union for Industrial Progress must be put up at the back door on Providence Street and all literature intended for mills and factories must have the Providence Street address. That door must also be our entrance."[45] Within a year, she claimed, mutual understanding had grown, and the front door was opened to the group. Nevertheless, it was clear to working-class women that they could not rely on middle-class and elite women to reinvent the city on working-class women's own terms; rather those women might simply reinscribe class boundaries on new surfaces.

When Mary Kenney married Jack O'Sullivan, labor reporter for the *Boston Globe*, she created her own organizing space. "Our Carver Street home," she wrote, "was like the cradle of a new-born movement. And our life there expressed the joy of youth finding comrades in ideals, fighting for those ideals and of growing up to them."[46] In her home, as at Denison House, the representatives of the city—labor, welfare, elites—met over dinner. Wealthy Mrs. Glendower Evans did Mary Kenney O'Sullivan's ironing so that O'Sullivan could dine with Justice and Mrs. Brandeis, and when he was ill, conservative reformer Robert Woods spoke deliriously of "Mary O'Sullivan's mashed potatoes."[47]

On the other hand, working-class views of urban life and space reveal multiple and not united visions. Mary Kenney O'Sullivan condemned an elite social worker neighbor for interfering in cases of domestic violence caused by drinking, but proved less than tolerant of her own neighbors a few years later. When her Carver Street house burned, the O'Sullivans moved next door to Denison House. They did not stay long. She read in the *Survey*, a magazine of social work, that there were fifty-two saloons within three or four blocks of Denison House. Moreover, she explained, "I knew this neighborhood was not for us. Our rear windows were opposite of the Harrison Avenue tenements where men and women roomers got up at noon and smoked cigarettes till night, another picture I didn't want my children to grow up with."[48] When she was widowed, O'Sullivan became a rent collector and agent for various philanthropic landlords and their agencies while remaining a labor activist. In one case (in a neighborhood rough enough for her to keep a gun under her pillow), through agitation with the police and her own efforts she made the building a safe haven for professional women to live and a meeting place for the working women's organizations she continued to create, but she did it only by evicting seven illegal liquor sellers, empowering some working women by providing them with space at the expense of others.[49]

Those women of whom O'Sullivan disapproved had more in common with the younger, single, wage-earning women who also sought to create a city that met their needs. These women not only claimed the streets as their own, but also appropriated dance halls and working-girls' clubs. Moreover, by their work choices they demonstrated their desire to live in public, not simply in the private world. Overwhelmingly they chose factory work, even with low wages and appalling conditions, over domestic service. They rejected working in the home, even someone else's home. They rejected all the confining, irrational aspects of being at someone's beck and call and instead favored work that provided time for relatively autonomous leisure and working space away from family relations. And even domestic servants, who were largely Irish, refused to work in the suburbs where there was little companionship and no Catholic church.[50]

Like married working-class women, these unmarried working women greeted middle-class and elite attempts to aid them with some ambivalence. Despite myriad middle-class and elite attempts to provide supervised working-girls' clubs and hotels for vulnerable single women, the vast majority of women workers participated in neither. Bosworth, the living-wage researcher, admitted that a Miss Rider "has decided views upon all the various problems of the living wage, and seems to be hunting a solution to the lodging house question on her own account."[51]

Bosworth herself lived at the Hemenway, a model lodging run by Bertha Hazard. At first Bosworth was thrilled. In November 1907 she wrote to her mother that "[o]ur house seems like a tiny oasis in a big desert," and that living there with a shopgirl, teacher, stenographer, cook, stitcher, and other working women was "a grand opportunity for me of not only living cheaply and well and having an attractive home but of living with working girls." By May, she had had enough. Hazard, it seemed, was overly restrictive in her supervision, "so suspicious and narrow and exacting. But I find that is the type of woman who usually heads these houses and my room-mate says Miss Hazard is really better than most of them—for which the gods be praised!"[52] Bosworth found that successful model rooming houses were above the price range of most working women; the amenities that made them successful also made them expensive: a good table, good public rooms, little supervision.

Although some philanthropic homes for working-class women proved more flexible in response to their constituents, few such homes in Boston, including the YWCA in this period, accepted African American women. In 1904, a black branch of the Women's Christian Temperance Union (WCTU) in Boston, the Harriet Tubman Crusaders, created Harriet Tubman House in a rented South End brownstone as a residence for black women who, regardless of income, were excluded from the city's college dormitories and respectable rooming houses. In 1909, three years after the house incorporated, Mrs. Julia O. Henson, active in the branch and in the black Northeastern Federation of Women's Clubs, donated her own townhouse down the street as a permanent headquarters. The house provided fewer services than many white philanthropic homes, featuring only rooms, kitchens, and some recreation by the club women volunteers who raised money for the house. While settlement houses testified to the increasing class and ethnic divisions of urban geography; Harriet Tubman House testified to the continuing racial discrimination by white women.[53]

Black women, like white women, had multiple relations to urban space. Some created networks of support and kinship that were unrelated to physical proximity. Most black working women did live-in domestic service; through their kinship and visiting relations, they created networks of their own that overlay spacially those of the white women for whom they worked.[54] While there were also black neighborhoods in Boston, one on the "wrong" side of Beacon Hill and a more working-class area in the South End where black churches provided meeting places for a multitude of black women's organizations, Harriet Tubman House seems to have remained the only autonomous space created and run for and by black women until after World War I.[55]

It was not that there were no black club women who wanted their own space. Middle-class black women's challenges to women's place often resembled those of white women in form (for example, the creation of woman's clubs), but their meaning and possibilities differed. In *Woman's Era*, a Boston black women's newspaper of the 1890s, an editorial declared that "woman's place is where she is needed and where she fits in. . . . It is spurious womanliness that only manifests itself in certain surroundings."[56] Having claimed all space, the *Woman's Era* hoped also to create a discursive space to aid educated and refined "colored women" because these women in every state found it impossible to mingle "freely with people of culture and learning"; even "the most cultured colored woman" could not do so.[57] For these elite women, the newspaper would create a national community.

The editors recognized that Boston had a multitude of women's clubs "willing and anxious" to receive "colored" members. The paper's editor, Josephine St. Pierre Ruffin, herself belonged to the WEIU. In this setting, however, the Woman's Era club was still necessary, "not necessarily a colored woman's club," the founder's daughter declared, "but a club started and led by colored women." There were "so many questions which in their application to the race, demand special treatment, so many questions which, as colored women, we are called upon to answer, more than this, there was so much danger that numbers of women would be overlooked unless some special appeal was made to them."[58] While the club members felt charged not "for race work alone, but for work along all the lines that make for women's progress," they clearly felt they needed a space that empowered them as black women rather than just as women, a space in which they could articulate and act on their own interests.[59]

They made this reasoning even more explicit in their justification for having a black newspaper: they did not, they insisted, believe in accentuating race lines, but did believe in being "more accurately represented than we are or ever can be in any paper that has no colored man or woman on its editorial staff," and special contributors or reporters were not sufficient. *Woman's Era*, which included news about men as well as about women, was clearly concerned with gaining more control over the public representation of black people in Boston. At a time when black women were routinely presented by whites as immoral, and when female respectability earned with it crucial privileges of protection and influence, the importance of such control cannot be overestimated. But the Woman's Era club's ability to create a permanent imprint on the city's landscape was hindered by a lack of funds. Unlike white women's clubs and despite a building fund, the Woman's Era club and its newspaper remained ensconsed in the home of its president, Josephine St. Pierre Ruffin.[60]

Despite its limits, black women's access to public space in the North seemed vast compared to the South. Boston-born Harlem Renaissance writer Dorothy West described the experience of southern black visitors to Boston in the 1910s in her novel, *The Living Is Easy*: "The sisters went shopping every day. Charity and Serena were extravagantly thrilled to walk into any store, to take their turn at any counter, to try on any garment Cleo chose. The thrill got a very good start when they boarded the front of the trolley, expanded through their shopping spree, continued unabated when they ate their ice cream at the time and place of purchase, and increased, if anything, when they walked through the same entrance of the moving picture palace as anybody else who had paid admission."[61]

This relative equality in consumption, of course, was not matched by their status in production. Though Mamie Garvin Fields was a teacher in South Carolina, when she came to Boston to earn money for her trousseau, she worked first as a maid. She refused to allow herself to be redefined by her new setting in a white woman's home, referring to herself as "the teacher coming in with her chambermaid's uniform on."[62] Black women's class status had to float free of occupation and residence, given the limits imposed by racial discrimination. Instead it depended on community standing, social club and church affiliations, and education.

When Fields and her friend found, like many white domestic servants, that their "free time wasn't so free," they switched to work in a garment factory downtown, becoming the only native-born women in the plant. When, in addition, they opened their own dressmaking establishment, they did so, not downtown, but on the upper floor in the home of a friend in a black neighborhood of Roxbury.[63] Opening up a shop in one's ethnic neighborhood rather than downtown was a common strategy for women petty entrepreneurs of the time. In their own neighborhood, they could take advantage of kinship and neighborhood ties that they helped construct. Downtown relied on a more anonymous clientele.

To change those patterns of access required material resources. Josephine St. Pierre Ruffin's home was in the relatively elite Boston black neighborhood, in that part of the West End closest to the Back Bay and Beacon Hill; Harriet Tubman House lay in the less desirable and less expensive South End. Perhaps Ruffin and other middle-class black women were unwilling to settle for the South End as a clubhouse locale. When two black women's clubs did buy their own buildings, in 1920, they did so in the South End. By that date many West Enders had moved to that district, and some of the original Woman's Era club members were among the founders.[64]

There is little question that the power these women had to shape the city to their ends was limited and affected by class, race, ethnicity, and geography. Middle-class and elite white women could build downtown, immigrant and black women could open shops only in immigrant and black neighborhoods, and none of them controlled the shaping of streets, the conditions and locations of factories, and other fundamental aspects of urban geography. It is not surprising that they sought allies. Poor and working-class women were particularly vulnerable to shifts in location of workplaces and services, and particularly bereft of avenues to influence. Whereas working-class men had access to political machines because of their votes, working-class women had little to offer and little to hope for from political machines unless they had a large number of voting male relatives. Until 1920, when Boston women gained the vote, they often turned instead to those other voteless but more powerful and well-connected urbanites, the middle-class and elite women who were erecting their own social welfare machines in places like Denison House. In response to working-class women's demands, these middle-class and elite women established day nurseries and kindergartens. Often working-class women forced their hands, turning settlement houses into de facto nurseries simply by dropping off children there, altering the urban landscape by their practices of everyday life.[65]

Conclusion

Middle-class and elite white women creating safe space for themselves downtown and building launching pads for lobbying campaigns at the state legislature; black women creating residences, shops, and newspapers; and women workers creating child care and unions—all demonstrate women's active agency in shaping the city. Yet drawing a reciprocal relationship between women and urban space is not drawing an equation between women in public and women in power. Streetwalkers had been "public" women without being empowered by their presence in public. Women on the streets "were subject to intense male scrutiny," according to Mary Ryan, and the growing theatricality of the mid- to late nineteenth century, which Karen Halttunen has discussed, meant that "women's miles" (in the common parlance of the day) were not places where building after building housed women's organizations.[66] Instead, they were shopping streets that became promenades where women placed themselves on display in appropriate costumes.[67] In less fashionable districts, as Kathy Peiss has shown, working-class women also had a sense of themselves as costumed and on display in their off hours, in search of a squire and patron for dinner and a good time. Certainly it is important not to mistake this public appearance for empowerment.[68]

Even in the relatively new female spaces I have delineated here, spaces created by as well as for women, there were limits to female autonomy. Denison House bowed to external pressures at odds with its purported agenda. Its board managed to resist pressure to rid itself of its peace activist residents for two years during World War I, but ultimately asked the head resident to take a rest. In Scudder's settlement house novel the women alone were actors, the men were guests and marginal, but outside the settlement house, it was equally clear that the major actors were the male leaders of labor, industry, and church. In the novel, even her cousin's home was a battleground for those forces it purports to exclude, with its values shaped by her cousin's business sense. The women's spaces themselves were contested.

The spaces were also incomplete. In Scudder's novel there were no politicians at all. The settlement house did provide both working-class and middle-class women with an avenue of access to the powerful and influential that they did not otherwise have. But there were still vast realms from which women were excluded. "An American woman," wrote Scudder, "has few opportunities to agitate effectively for political reform."[69] Formal politics was on the agenda. Women lost the municipal suffrage fight in Massachusetts in 1895, but Scudder had her head resident claim that her house was now "ready to stand for larger activities in civic reform."

Mary Ryan has claimed that "the politics of the public streets divided women by race and class, and between the dangerous and the endangered."[70] But some women strove to invert that formula, to reimagine urban space and create places to bring women together—settlements and cross-class organizations. There were many things the settlement could not do, but it could create a space where women were not simply objects for male eyes. By reconceiving the city with public space for women, by creating new types of spaces—kitchenless apartments, kindergartens, day nurseries, Women's Trade Union League offices—women enhanced the possibility for their own political empowerment in a variety of urban sectors, from telephone exchanges to legislative halls.[71] Once they moved into the public sphere, women, like colonizers settling in to a new place, sought indigenous collaborators (in this case, powerful men); they could do so from a position of some power instead of simply as supplicants or the petitioners of an earlier generation. They had something to give back: services to provide to would-be voters, research organizations, constituencies and machines of their own.

Boston's women formed no unified bloc. But changing the notion of women's space, in an era when men and women shared few spaces on equal terms, was a crucial transformation of the city's structure. Women could not vote in Massachusetts until 1920, but using their new spaces, they were not powerless; they won strikes and day nurseries, government-sponsored school lunches, fresh milk, and legal aid; and attained appointed political positions by the 1910s. Women's experiences were shaped by the changing urban environment, but at the same time, women actively shaped their environment, reconceiving the city to redefine their place in it. In the early nineteenth century, women had largely filled urban spaces created for them. By the early twentieth century, they enjoyed urban spaces they had created themselves.

1
The "Overworked Wife"

Making a Working-Class Home and Negotiating Status, Autonomy, and the Family Economy

On August 21, 1893, a visitor from the Denison House settlement reported that Mrs. Scanlon's husband was to be buried the next day. Mrs. Scanlon had three children, all of them small. She had received help from Berkeley Temple and was now cared for by Rev. Mr. Dickinson and his people. Five days later, on Saturday, the visitor returned to 65 Chapman Street and found Mrs. Scanlon braiding her daughter's hair, hoping to find a small tenement near a day nursery and work enough to keep her three children with her.

I used Mrs. Scanlon's story in the previous chapter to point out the spatial awareness of working-class women and the intimate and vital impact of the city's geography on their daily lives. I also used it to demonstrate women's active engagement with urban space: Mrs. Scanlon, seemingly in dire straits, moved to take control of the geography of her life. Unfortunately, things went from bad to worse for Mrs. Scanlon, and her story illustrates not only the enterprising strategies of women of the working poor and the density of their local networks, but the limits of their ability to redesign or reappropriate urban space in their own interests.

By September 6, Mrs. Scanlon had given up on her original scheme. Now she sought a room for herself and planned to put two of her children in a mission home. Four days later she had put the two older children in a home and taken rooms at 83 Middlesex Street. She would, reported her visitor, be glad of work if she could put her baby in a day nursery. A nearby day nursery, at 64 Tyler Street, could take the baby the following week. Work, however, was scarce. The 1890s depression was reaching its height. In November, Mrs. Scanlon began to clean for Denison House.

On her own, with her baby, rooms, and a job, Mrs. Scanlon faced other worries. In January her baby boy fell ill. Mrs. Lucinda Prince, a Denison House resident, visited him at City Hospital and reported him no worse. Two months later, On March 9, 1894, Mrs. Scanlon came to Denison House, apparently no longer working there, to tell the residents that her baby had died that morning. On April 25, Helena Dudley, the head of the settlement house, visited one of the House's benefactors to arrange for Mrs. Scanlon and her son Charley, to quit the city altogether. She got Mrs. Scanlon work where she could keep her son with her, in West Lebanon, Maine, at three dollars per week.[1]

There are many noteworthy aspects to this case. First, Mrs. Scanlon's survival required geographic transience; she first moved within the city, and then left it, within little more than a year. Second, and most obviously, Mrs. Scanlon could not, despite her strategic deployment of no fewer than four social agencies—a home mission, a day nursery, Berkeley Temple, and Denison House—make ends meet as a widow with young children in Boston during the 1890s' depression. Third, whatever the aims of the Denison House visitors, Mrs. Scanlon had her own agenda for them; she made multiple use of the house's staff: housing agent, employment agent, employer, visitor, and neighbor. Fourth, Denison House's account makes no mention of help from neighbors (other than the settlement workers) despite the presence of neighbors in the Scanlon apartment surrounding Mr. Scanlon's death. Fifth, no one treated the death of family members as remarkable; they saw such occurrences as tragic but commonplace.

If to middle-class and elite women, working-class family life seemed a perpetual disorderly carnival of inappropriate mobility and behavior, to working-class women like Mrs. Scanlon, their lives had their own rules and resources. The networks and strategies of working-class matrons were often opaque to the middle-class and elite women who tried to aid them and who tended to mistake grim conditions—lack of running water, for example—for willful slovenliness. Scanlon's transience, economic vulnerability, mobilization of social agencies and neighbors, children's death, and struggle to preserve her own status formed the core of working-class life on the shifting terrain of late-nineteenth-century Boston. This chapter turns to such working-class women's experience of Boston and their daily informal attempts to map it, controlling or negotiating its spaces.[2]

Married Women and the Family Economy

Amidst the South End's faded elegance, where Irish and Germans, Chinese and Syrians, Eastern European Jews and southern black and rural white Yankee migrants jostled each other on the streets and in the new lodging houses; on the North End's dark and winding streets, in its damp and moldering tenements, and at its bustling Italian and Jewish street markets; and among the African Americans, Jews, Irish, Portuguese, and Italians of the densely populated refurbished West End residences, working-class matrons made their daily rounds. Unlike Scudder, they rarely experienced the city as a whole. They shopped, worked, and visited in the neighborhood.[3] They witnessed the era's rising tide of immigration, creation of urban infrastructure, and commercial and industrial growth on a distinctly local level: in the flood of relatives in their evermore crowded lodgings, the jobs that appeared and disappeared, the strangers hawking wares in raucous, barely intelligible accents outside their doors, and the ever-present urban grime and garbage-strewn streets.

The 1890s' depression helped make Mrs. Scanlon's struggle harder, as the recurrent depressions between 1870 and 1920 did for other working-class women, but her predicament was by no means new, nor even limited to depression eras.[4] The material conditions of working-class women's lives changed remarkably little during this period. People of all classes tended to assume that the prime earner in a family would be male, but for the working class, adult men were an unreliable source of support.[5] In his study of unemployment, Alex Keyssar found that though the annual unemployment rate in the late nineteenth century was only 8 to 10 percent, over the course of any given year 20 to 30 percent of workers had been out of work. In 1885 they spent an average of four months unemployed, in 1895 over three months. "Evidence is too clear," reported the Massachusetts Board to Investigate the Subject of the Unemployed in 1895, "that even in so-called normal times there is an amount of non-employment which occasions suffering."[6]

Even employed men usually made too little to support their families. A WEIU study of 500 immigrant women and children found only ninety-one wholly supported by others. A lone individual required at least nine dollars a week to survive. In the prosperous, busy winter of 1906/7 the average rate of pay of male relatives fell below twelve dollars per week.[7] Daughters and sons went early to work, not for "immediate economic independence," as one 1911 investigator noted, but because they felt they had to earn something. Working-class wives also did what they could to bring money into the home, particularly where the children were young and the husband's work unsteady.[8]

Married women often garnered the major part of the family income, particularly if they took in lodgers (who ate elsewhere) or boarders. Women's wage work, like men's, was unsteady. Lodgers and boarders could provide a steadier income than wage work, and married women with husbands present tended to take them in.[9]

These women were not necessarily desperate. Agnes Harrington, a thirty-two-year-old Irish wife of a police officer—a good, steady job in 1880—lived in the West End on Leverett Street with her five small children, two lodgers (male painters), a boarder (a dressmaker), a nephew at school, her niece who stayed at home and must have helped out with the considerable household, and her brother who kept a store, making fourteen in the house. While her household was unusually large, the other three women on this relatively prosperous block who took boarders or lodgers also took in relatives, housing seven or eight people in all.[10]

Thirty years later, in 1910, Boston's working-class neighborhoods had become even more crowded. In the West and North Ends, Jewish refugees from Eastern Europe and Italian immigrants had taken the place of the Irish. The worsening situation for Jews in Russia affected men and women differently in the United States. More children, brothers, uncles, aunts, nieces, nephews, grandparents, and in-laws squeezed into the same ramshackle wooden and brick tenements. With more children, fewer adult women went out to work, and with more relatives—largely

The multitude of beds in close quarters, typical of tenement dwellings, scandalized the middle class and elite, increased women's work, and lowered the rents of the working class. From Dwight Porter, *Report Upon a Sanitary Inspection of Certain Tenement House Districts of Boston* (Boston: Press of Rockhill and Churchill, 1889).

refugees from Russian pogroms—fewer took in unrelated boarders and lodgers. The average household size steadily rose. On Willard Street in the West End, four-fifths of the households took in relatives or lodgers or both; four households had eleven members each, and two additional ones had thirteen.[11] Taking in boarders and lodgers made an enormous amount of extra work for women in small tenements without hot running water, sometimes without even cold water or with a sink in the hall. With this housekeeping burden, only women who were widows or lived with their parents had occupations listed. The two exceptions were married women grocers.[12]

Women with lodgers lay mattresses on boards or boxes in the side room or kitchen for beds. One narrow three-story wooden tenement had a fruit store on the ground floor and sixteen Italian families with sixty-six people in all above it. Breathing space was in short supply. Health standards dictated 600 cubic feet of air per person; they got 250. In another wooden tenement whose foul-smelling walls crawled with bugs, three adults and two children occupied one small room, and two lodgers and two children another.[13]

Despite the crowding, boarders and lodgers appealed because they were more compatible with home duties than many other options. But married women also figured largely among laundresses, janitors (whose work was often done at night), small restaurateurs, and retail dealers. An early twentieth-century investigator was surprised to find a large number of female Italian merchants, but petty entrepreneurship within a neighborhood network of coethnics was a common earning strategy for many immigrant women (see chapter 4). Relatively few U.S.-born women, by contrast, were small dealers; instead (particularly if from rural areas) they, along with Irish and British-American women, dominated the formal lodging-house trade.[14]

Of all white immigrant married women, Irish women were the most likely to leave home for wage work. In 1911, 27 percent did so, as opposed to under 15 percent of Italian and Jewish wives. Faced with higher rents and lower-paying and unsteadier male jobs because of discrimination, more black than white married women worked for wages outside the home.[15] But none of those numbers should be taken as an index of income-producing work among married women. More Italian, Portuguese, and Jewish women than Irish informally took in piecework (seldom recorded by census takers) or boarders and lodgers, hauling extra water up the stairs to clean and cook for the extra income.[16] In short, most married working-class women of any ethnic/racial group worked at income-producing jobs.

They were part of a family economy whose support strategies continued over a lifetime. Boarding relatives moved out on their own and moved back in times of crisis. Unemployed sons moved in with former boarding relatives and sometimes went to work for them. The Brest-Shindler family interwove their lives over forty years. On Minot Street in the West End, Lizzie Brest had come to the United States two years after her husband, in 1887, and in 1900 at the age of thirty-six worked in the family grocery store while her husband Moses peddled dry goods. They moved five times over the next decade, always within a few steps on Minot Street. Their oldest daughter, Annie, sixteen, was a stitcher on white goods; one of their two male boarders—like them, Russians—also peddled dry goods. The other was a self-employed cobbler. Lizzie's brother, Joseph Shindler, twenty-four, was a watchmaker. The other four children were not yet employed.

In the ensuing years, the younger children got jobs, moving into department store and office work, and the daughters married men they met at work or in the neighborhood, leaving with them for the suburbs. Joseph Shindler married and moved out; when his wife died of cancer in 1916, his nephew, Israel, Lizzie's son, moved in until Israel's marriage. At this point, Joseph moved back to live with Lizzie and Moses. While the constant moving could seem to indicate instability, these interwoven lives manifested the emotional and material support the Brest-Shindler family provided its members for nearly half a century.[17]

The slim phrase "family economy" stands for more than cooperative housekeeping by multiple earners. It stands for a continual shifting of roles between men, women, and children or earner, caretaker, and housekeeper and a continual jockeying for resources, whether it be who would control the wages family members earned or who would seek what kind of assistance from public and semipublic institutions and agencies. It also meant a floating population of lodgers and boarders, often kin, and of children who might die from malnutrition, unsanitary conditions, epidemics, or poor treatment or who might have to be given up to an institution temporarily or permanently should any disaster befall wage earners—including drunkenness, incarceration, desertion, illness, or job loss.[18]

Moreover, while multiple-earner families provided mutual dependence and support, they could also be oppressive. Women's needs in particular, as wives or daughters, could be subordinated to those of men made more powerful by their higher earning-capacity and a legal system that privileged the rights of husbands and fathers, even though they were relatively disempowered immigrants. In 1894, a sickly Miss Daily turned down an opportunity to go to a convalescent home because her brother was unwilling to do without her services, "as he is working," reported a Denison House visitor, "and has no one to get his meals for him. . . . It is a pity as she needs the change."[19]

A more drastic case is one historian Linda Gordon tells of a Chinese American man who owned and operated a laundry in Boston with his Chinese wife and the help of his children. The rebellious oldest daughter, sixteen in 1920, worked from two until seven or eight in the evening after school, rolling collars, bundling, bookkeeping, and whatever else needed doing, but found the labor gave her no privileges. On the contrary, she submitted to her father's demands for sex in order to shield her mother and, later, to avoid being horsewhipped. "He says that I am still a slave to him. . . . I am willing to work," she told a social worker, "if he gives me my freedom to do the right thing." Her Sunday school teacher helped her leave home, but her social worker, also Chinese American, pressed her to return.[20]

In December, 1892, twelve-year-old Ephraim Marsh, of 62 Tyler Street, shared his views on marriage with Denison House resident C. M. Dresser. "Ephraim does not believe in marriage," Dresser recorded, "considers it a misfortune & when the advantages of a home life were presented to him, he said, 'You read about them but you never see any.' "[21] In these domestic working-class efforts to make ends meet, keep house, keep children, and so forth, it becomes clear that the tensions from industrialization, as Jonathan Prude has pointed out, were worked out most often in homes rather than at industrial sites.[22]

However oppressive family economies could be, women with small families were at a distinct disadvantage, and female-headed households, like Scanlon's, tended to be smaller than average. While multiearner families like the Brests were community networks in themselves, Scanlon was the sole support of her three children. Between 1880 and 1920, 19 percent, or nearly one-fifth, of all Boston families were headed by women.[23] When they could, widows lived with working sons, daughters, or mothers or took in lodgers. Catherine Nunin, at the age of forty-five, was typical. She kept one daughter at home, another worked for a dressmaker, and of her three sons, one clerked in a store, one worked in a brass foundry, and one had a broken arm. All were at least seventeen.[24] But almost 15 percent of widows, like Scanlon, could not rely on the earnings of adult children.[25]

Working-class men died younger than other men, multiplying cases like Scanlon's.[26] Insurance benefits, when they existed, usually lasted only a year. The widows had often worked before the husband's death and usually had worked before marriage. They returned to work as soon as possible. In 1910, Mary E. Richmond and Fred S. Hall reported from their study of Boston widows, "If the woman lives in a street where most of the women with husbands earn some money, or if the widow herself has earned before her husband's death, it becomes unnatural, in her eyes and those of her neighbors, to earn nothing.''[27]

The assumption of working-class matrons that they would earn sat uneasily with middle-class and elite women and men. It accorded ill with their notions of a domestic refuge and full-time motherhood. Most of the Boston Associated Charities district secretaries were ready to endorse one or two days' work per week for mothers with no babies at home and who could use a day nursery or the care of relatives or neighbors. But they were unhappy with the choices of many working-class women, particularly white ones, who kept school-age children at home or sent them out on the street to earn. Above all, they concluded, "it should always be kept clearly in the woman's mind that the main object in whatever she does is the bringing up of her children.''[28]

Few working-class women needed to be reminded that care of their children should come first, as they struggled to hold onto their children and their lives, but they did not always agree with their middle-class and elite benefactors as to methods or values. These women may have had jobs rather than careers, but so did their husbands. Neither had or aspired to middle-class notions of domesticity, though they did have their own aspirations: to own land, plush furniture, and perhaps a piano; to live in healthy, well-lighted apartments; to have all their children with them; to have stability and maintain kinship and community networks. Middle-class and elite men and women tended to want to "protect'' female heads of household, at least those they deemed virtuous, and provide for them as dependents—if not of individual men, then of philanthropies or, after 1913, the state in the form of newly passed mothers' pension laws. They were prone to see widows' engagement in wage work as an attempt to escape the boredom and confinement of home ("even in a tenement'' life could get dull), as a desire to conform to neighborhood expectations, or a desire to have a special hold on the children—as anything, in short, except a desire for relative independence from just such agencies and a recognition of the inadequacy of the few dollars a week such agencies offered.[29] Rather, working-class women determined to preserve their homes, such as they were, as relatively autonomous spaces rather than sites of dependency.[30]

Working-class women need not consciously have been trying to subvert dominant notions of women's dependence and passivity in order to fight for benefits without the constraints social agencies had to offer. They pursued their own agenda independent of, rather than in response to, middle-class prescriptions. They would take aid from lodgers, boarders, neighbors, relatives, lovers, private welfare agencies, and the state and earn wages from employers, but they did their best to retain the power to make decisions about their home and family, even about which sources of aid or wages they would approach and when.

The Nature of "Work"

Widowed or not, whether they struggled along on an inadequate male income or took in homework or lodgers, working-class matrons worked hard. But middle-class and elite visitors who controlled access to outside funds only recognized some of these forms of earning as legitimate work. The differences in perspective made the working-class home itself one site where working-class women negotiated status and autonomy with more elite women.

In a single week in January 1893, Laura Cate ventured forth from Denison House to visit two different families. At the Lees, on 24 Troy Street, the baby was sick and not expected to live. Mr. Lee earned only eleven dollars per week, from which the Lees paid three dollars in rent and supported their six children. Cate concluded simply, "overworked wife." She drew no such conclusion when she went to see Mrs. Duffy on Broadway. She found a "[d]runken man asleep in bed. Said he was her brother. . . . Pretended to support herself & 2 children on tailor finishing—6 cts. a coat. Work laid on dirty bed, beside drunken man. She earns 30 cts. a day; children do not go to school."[31]

Cate's suspicion of Mrs. Duffy clearly came from what she saw as poor housekeeping and parenting as well as poor company, but working as a finisher had to interfere with Mrs. Duffy's ability to keep a clean and tidy home. Keeping tenement apartments clean was itself a full-time job. Less than a decade earlier an investigator had found scarcely 1 in 500 tenement apartments had a bathtub or washbowl, and though these apartments might have a common hall sink, they had no running water. One-quarter of the houses inspected still had privy vaults instead of water closets, and one-sixth of the water closets were filthy, many beyond use. Dwellers resorted to an older system of buckets for their wastes.

These conditions contributed to the rampant spread of deadly but preventable diseases such as typhoid, diptheria, and scarlet fever—diseases responsible for 21,280 deaths in Boston between 1878 and 1887, two-thirds of them, like Mrs. Scanlon's children, under five.[32]

Cate's colleague Miss Mason trudged up the same two flights of stairs, through the dirty halls and across the ragged carpet, and came to similar conclusions. The second flight was absolutely dark. Slop pails, she recorded, were plentiful. She found Mrs. Duffy and a friend companionably working on coats from Simons, across the street. Mrs. Duffy's daughters, eight and eleven, were not in school; they lacked stockings and, ironically, coats. Mason, too, found the room and bed very dirty, and a good-looking young man sleeping off liquor on the bed. Dinner—beans, pie, milk, and bread—was not cleared away. Mrs. Duffy explained that her brother always came to her when drunk because it made his wife cross. "Things were queer," Mason concluded. "Woman appeared apprehensive, first floor blinds closed."[33] Unlike Mrs. Lee, who seemed to bring in no income, Mrs. Duffy was not seen as an "overworked wife," but as a suspicious character.

Even cleanly wives could come under philanthropists' suspicion, however. That same week, Lucinda Prince of Denison House went to visit the Flynns at 151 Albany Street. Both Mr. and Mrs. Flynn drank, and an Associated Charities visitor had "had them in hand some time. The conditions have improved and Mrs. Flynn does not drink so much as she did." Mr. Flynn earned only $7.00 per week at a junk shop, and Mrs. Flynn scrubbed and washed for a living. When Mrs. Flynn could get work, she put the two children, Mamie, five, and Hannah, two, in the Tyler Steet Nursery. Most recently, Mrs. Flynn had worked all day Sunday until 10 P.M. and Wednesday and Thursday from 7:00 P.M. to midnight cleaning at Jordan Marsh. The family lived in a single basement room for which they paid $1.25 per week. "Seems to need money," Prince noted in an evident understatement. Despite Mrs. Flynn's hours, lack of money, and crowded quarters, Prince found it "very bare & poor, but clean." The benefits of this cleanliness, however, were undermined by the lack of children's underwear, which seemed to scandalize Prince. She concluded that the mother was "very ignorant—seems to have no idea how to care for the children."[34]

To middle-class women accustomed to reading character from certain attributes of domestic space and bodies (including privatized sexuality: no drunken brothers on beds in "public," no beds in workrooms, no workrooms in homes, no beds in "receiving" rooms, and, very definitely, underwear), these two latter women, Mrs. Duffy and Mrs. Flynn, were failing in their proper "work."[35] Their paid labor could not compensate for the lapses in their true work of domesticity.

No one was more vulnerable to middle-class and elite judgments than impoverished widows like Scanlon and female heads of household, women lifted out of a family economy. Those who had no relatives in town, no insurance, and no close ties to coworkers because of the irregularity of work, had to rely on some combination of the city, charities, and employment because neither the city or charities nor employment provided enough money to keep body and soul together for their families. Widows in need did not hesitate to deploy the city's public and private agencies for help nor to use the agencies against each other. As agencies proliferated, rising to more than a thousand social welfare societies in Boston at the turn of the century, working-class women became more adept at mobilizing them, exploiting the overlap or competition between them.[36]

Gordon cites one widow in 1883 who earned her living doing garment finishing work. She had to travel to and from the jobbers' to pick up and deliver the bundles of clothes and to look for work. On one such trip, she got sick and went to a friend's home to recuperate. When she returned home, her children had been taken to the Chardon Street Home, a shelter run by the Overseers of the Poor. As an impoverished individual, she would have had little power in the case, but she went to another agency, the Massachusetts Society for the Prevention of Cruelty to Children (MSPCC), and asked them to use their influence to get her children back, receiving a letter from the MSPCC for the purpose.[37] Similarly, Molly Geary paid board for her two sons in the Home for Destitute Catholic Children while she spent sixty days in the House of Correction. If the home intended to place them out, she warned, she would take them instead to the Almshouse, where she could get them when she was able.[38]

As agencies professionalized and centralized, however, they became less amenable to the independent aims of working-class women. A minor request risked permanent separation from one's children. Letizia

Guarino had been brought to the United States in 1914 by the Central Italian Bank Steamship Agency for an arranged marriage. The ceremony turned out to be a fraud, with Mr. Guarino already married to another woman in Italy. When about five years later, his legal wife of twenty-two years arrived, Guarino deserted his new wife. Pregnant and with three small children, Mrs. Guarino went to the MSPCC. In return for providing aid, the MSPCC forced her to make a legal complaint against her pseudohusband and sent social workers to inspect her home. They found the mother working from 7 A.M. until 5 P.M. daily, neighbors looking in on the children, and the two rooms, without toilet or heat, "filthy" and unsuitable for children. Hoping for aid, Mrs. Guarino had disavowed all knowledge of Mr. Guarino though he, a pick and shovel laborer, sent her what money he could. The legal complaint led to nothing but bitter strife between them, and the MSPCC placed her children out. Only when her father hired an Italian attorney did she win them back.[39] Although agencies, particularly private ones without the coercive power of the state, were not omnipotent, they often had more power than working-class matrons.[40] They resisted matrons' attempts to manipulate them to ends other than their own. While the matrons caught on soon enough to the potential threat to family unity that disapproving social agencies could muster, need limited their options. The small sums from charities and welfare organizations could provide an essential margin, together with the promise of more aid in emergencies, which kept many impoverished women from altogether ignoring the agencies' strictures.

Mrs. N.'s husband, a meat carver, had died in 1901, leaving no resources. An African American, she found herself at age thirty-three alone with five children aged two to ten. She had sometimes supported the family when her husband had been unemployed, and for six months after his death she was able to earn enough money. After that, she had to go to the city for coal and groceries. In 1903, Mrs. N. was receiving $6.00 a month from the city to supplement her $3.50 in earnings. At one point, to make ends meet, she took in an unrelated male lodger, which led to a report that she was immoral. As a result, the city refused her relief "though," as Richmond and Hall record, "there was no corroboration." The official visitor and a church visitor did not believe the accusation, but nevertheless advised her to give up her lodger. Apparently the income from the city and the possibility of aid from elsewhere was worth more to her than the income from the lodger, because Mrs. N. followed the advice of the visitors.

But Mrs. N. moved to independence from the welfare organization as soon as possible. In 1905, she was able to find enough irregular work—day work and cleaning buildings—that she earned $6.50 per week; at that point she moved into a better tenement. Her neighbors provided child care and a volunteer made sure the children went to school and taught the older girl housework. By the time Richmond and Hall interviewed her, they found her "respectable and hardworking, keeps her home neat, and is ambitious to have her children well educated. . . . Mrs. N. has been practically self supporting for the last four years."[41] Need had enabled city officials to impose their own vision of public and private, family and work, virtue and immorality on Mrs. N. But as soon as she could, she disentangled herself from the coercive surveillance in favor of her own network. She re-created her home as autonomous not from all outside aid, but from middle-class and elite-controlled philanthropy.

Meanwhile, social service agencies became ever more tightly interwoven, until approaching one agency opened up avenues to all. Together, these organizations formed a dense network of possible support. On July 30, 1897, Miss Freeman from Denison House went to Mrs. Flynn's on a neighborly call; there she met the District Nurse, Miss Mumery. She promised Mumery to call on the Nickersons' baby. She also went to Dorothea House and found someone there to stay with Mrs. Flynn, despite the opinion of the Associated Charities visitor that "enough was being done."[42]

But the traffic on these avenues was two-way. As day nursery teachers made the rounds visiting the families of their pupils and collaborated with settlement house workers, they became links in networks of social agencies that provided not only care but surveillance, policing the work of working-class mothers.[43] Surveillance, in turn, could lead to the cessation of aid, as Mrs. N. had found. When a Mrs. Lowe came to Helen Cheever of Denison House for help, Cheever asked her permission to make inquiries about her at the Associated Charities, but Cheever also went to Trinity House Day Nursery, where the staff was ready to speculate at length on the family's character.[44] For impoverished women, going to any social agency, even one where they paid for services, provided them with valuable resources, but at the risk of enmeshing them in an informational net of what must have seemed like spies.

Friends and Neighbors

Most of these agencies—particularly the better-funded ones—were run by native-born Protestants. Other ethnic/immigrant, Jewish, and Catholic groups, however, ran their own philanthropic networks. They suspected Protestant prosletyzing in the name of "child saving," resented the condescension and intrusion, and worried about a rising tide of nativism.[45] By the turn of the century, both Catholic and Jewish organizations ran shelters for orphans and aged, working girls and the infirm, widows, and delinquents and destitute children, and they provided health care and aid in job searches. They offered a cradle-to-grave welfare alternative to that of the dominant Protestants.[46]

Even in non-Protestant philanthropic societies, ethnicity and class could be an issue. Irish-dominated children's philanthropic organizations celticized names—Kaminski became Casey, for example.[47] Boston's League of Catholic Women, founded in 1910, had only one Italian member of the executive committee, and she was related by marriage to the leader of St. Vincent de Paul. Yet the league was intent on serving Italian women, just as Boston's Jewish philanthropies were dominated by northern and western European Jews but often originated in response to the influx of eastern European Jews at the turn of the century.[48]

While working-class women seeking help could find such philanthropic institutions and societies as judgmental and intrusive as those of the dominant groups, they also found them, as historian Dennis Ryan has noted, a "physical as well as spiritual refuge." Around them, customary language and religious practices could be observed instead of condemned.[49] Such societies also seemed more sympathetic than those of the dominant groups to the need for temporary refuges for children and the desire of parents to be able to retrieve their children when they had regained financial stability. It was recent immigrant women of the North End who themselves created one such home, the Helping Hand Temporary Home for Destitute Jewish Children.[50] Moreover, unlike most groups, including the powerful Associated Charities, the United

Hebrew Benevolent Association and Federated Jewish Charities favored giving cash, not goods, to those in temporary need. And the workroom the Sewing Society women organized, unlike Denison House's, was geared to instructing women on machine sewing so that they could become self-supporting.[51]

That these philanthropies were more amenable to working-class women's desires demonstrated the reciprocal ties that bound women to church and temple societies. For many Irish women, particularly domestic servants, the church was their one formal, institutional affiliation.[52] For Catholic women, the church—and for Jewish women, the temple—although unequivocally male-dominated, provided a refuge, a site of organizing and female activism, and a welter of mixed messages.[53] With the church cast as a mother, that sacred space could combine maternalism and militance for women organizing in it.[54]

As an institution, Boston's Catholic Church stood firmly against feminism as threatening the family and undermining women's duty to the home.[55] Even women's religious orders owed obedience to male supervisors. Yet, the conventual orders also ran most of Boston's Catholic charities and schools, and their visibility as women living apart from men and as authority figures within those institutions, holding sway over male and female alike, sent as clear a message as their less visible subordination.[56]

While these relatively powerful women tended not to hail from the working class, they provided space for women who did. In 1911, they organized "retreat guilds" for married women, business women, and teachers; in 1912, for stenographers and secretaries and for domestics; and in 1919, for factory girls and telephone workers.[57] Like the settlement house clubs, these were subject to supervision, but at the same time provided collective space and services rarely available.[58]

So dedicated were Boston's Irish working women to the church that it was they who funded parish maintenance and Catholic charitable work. They pooled their resources to buy land for church buildings, and when the parish priest showed up at the back door of the homes where they worked, they gave to him from their savings. In philanthropic economic affairs of the church, they claimed equality. The report in the *Woman's Journal* of an 1886 fair that Irish women gave for Boston's Catholic charities noted, "In all this Catholic assemblage the women were equals of men, speaking and voting for its success."[59] According to historian Paula Kane, while the church hierarchy never interpreted female saints' lives in ways that endorsed women's autonomy, Catholic laywomen admired the activism of such saints as Joan of Arc.[60]

Little better illustrates the complex relationship of working-class Catholic women to the church than the annual Lenten play, "Pilate's Daughter," produced by Roxbury's Our Lady of Perpetual Help parish. A priest had written the play in 1901 "for the single women of the Archconfraternity of the Holy Family at their own urgent request." A man directed the play and served as the gatekeeper, keeping out aspiring but spiritually unworthy actresses. Only those could perform "actuated by the desire to bring souls nearer to God"; it was a "devotional exercise rather than a dramatic event." But despite its male author and director, women delivered this sermonlike play. Fifty women comprised the cast. The play itself consisted of female agents and heroines. Pilate's daughter, Claudia, uses a rose touched by Jesus' robe to bring a dead child to life; she inspires various conversions and disrupts Jupiter's feast. Finally she ends poisoned by a money changer's jealous daughter.

Each year many more women than could be accommodated wanted to participate in the play. The eagerness to be in it and attend it (as many as twenty-five performances were given in a single season), signifies the way Catholic idiom was a (perhaps *the*) language within which Irish Catholic women understood their lives.[61] It also demonstrates that although they did not protest the hierarchy that placed men in supervisory positions, Irish Catholic laywomen made room within that system to establish their own active authority.

On the other hand, such assertion was distinctly contingent. At that same church, in 1904 the leadership realized they had plenty of men's organizations but nothing for women and girls. They established a Guild of Our Lady, with female officers (all single) and priests as the "honorary president" and "spiritual director." They converted a large brick building into the "handsomest, most finely appointed clubhouse for Catholic women in the States." They enrolled women of almost every craft and profession, invited women speakers, and held whist parties and original dramas. But when the parochial school became overcrowded, the parish determined, "The children must be provided for. The Guild was not a necessity," and the distinct women's space and organization ceased to exist.[62]

Black women belonged to most white-dominated churches in Boston, but found few willing to return the devotion. The Irish-dominated Home for Destitute Catholic Children admitted some black children because one of Boston's few black priests, Father Healy, had been a founder and vice president and because the Daughters of Charity, founded by New York abolitionist women, staffed it. But black Bostonians found few other private philanthropies open to them. In 1860, Boston's four largest orphanages held 326 children; none of them was black. The Boston Female Asylum, which began admitting black girls in 1880, admitted only one or two at a time. In 1910 four of Boston's seventeen institutions for children barred African Americans altogether.[63] When John Daniels noted in 1910 the "small and declining extent to which the Negroes fall into the hands of public and private charity," it was at least in part because they had no choice.[64]

As a result, some groups, such as the Episcopal Sisters of St. Margaret, based in Louisburg Square, served exclusively black institutions, staffing St. Monica's Home for Sick Colored Women and Children. Black women worked to support such homes, but did not control them.[65] There were also a handful of white-sponsored settlement houses that served black individuals or rented rooms to black organizations. For a brief time, black women prominent in social service ran an independent employment service as a business out of Robert Gould Shaw House (a South End settlement house established by whites in 1908 primarily to serve blacks) and once a week held social evenings for black women in domestic service.[66]

In addition, black Bostonians formed their own institutions. Scarce resources and the unwillingness of landowners to sell to African Americans meant that they often lacked a permanent physical location, but they could be long-lived. The National Grand United Order of Sisters and Brothers of Love and Charity, for example, celebrated its 100th anniversary in 1932. In the 1910s, this lodge boasted approximately 600 members in six branches in greater Boston. In that decade, black lodges included roughly 3,500 of 13,564 black Bostonians. All provided sick relief and death benefits. These lodges provided many of the same benefits as the ubiquitous white ethnic mutual-aid associations did, but for a population with fewer outside options.[67]

With few resources because of job discrimination, impoverished black women could find the relief such societies had to offer even slimmer than their white immigrant counterparts. At the same time, the heavily migrant black Boston population had fewer of the "old country" links to bind them together than did white immigrant groups. While four-fifths of the Italian women in Boston married men from the same province in Italy, and three-fifths from the same town or village, over half of black Boston marriages occurred between people born in different states.[68]

To create sustaining links, black migrants, particularly women, filled the pews of black churches and the ranks of migrant societies. Church membership skyrocketed from 1900 to 1910 until four-fifths of the entire church membership was southern-born. The Zion African Methodist Church's 635 members were 90 percent laboring class and nearly two-thirds female. Despite their low wages, they assumed $59,500 in debt in 1903 to purchase a building in the South End. In addition to the debt, the annual expenses ran about $6,000, or $9.40 per member, plus debt relief for women making as little as $5.00 per week. Yet within the next ten years they managed to retire half the debt.[69]

In an atmosphere of discrimination and hardening race lines, black churches continued to provide both a refuge and a center of activism and community identification. Though historian Elizabeth Clark-Lewis has pointed out poignantly the difficulties live-in domestic servants had participating regularly in church activities because of the uncertainties of their days and hours off, black women, like Irish Catholic domestic servants, still managed to sustain the church's relief-giving functions, congregations, and ministers.[70] The church provided a visible manifestation of community for a dispersed population whose members had access to few other autonomously owned places and many of whom spent most of their time living in white-dominated neighborhoods and households.

Religious services at the more established black churches seemed to be converging in norms of decorum with their white counterparts. They abandoned what investigator John Daniels labeled "the dress-parade collection," where women walked up to the collection plate to show off their Sunday best. But churches still offered the best place to meet friends, exchange news, show off and inspect clothing, hear music, and gain emotional and spiritual sustenance.[71] Daniels read the stylishness of women's church wear and the sartorial splendor of black men at leisure on the streets as shallow showiness. As other scholars have pointed out regarding the South in the later twentieth century, however, many if not most of these men and women worked long hours in uniforms that signified them as subordinates at the beck and call of others. Many of the men were waiters or porters; the largest number of women would have been domestic servants. A black church was one place where they could signify themselves differently.[72]

That black women chose the church and men the streets for their signifying demonstrated the gendered urban geography of race. Black women's display on the streets would render them prostitutes in the eyes of whites and endanger their safety. In a black church, on the other hand, and on display for their own community, their virtue was doubly assured. In addition, for many black women, judging from their obituaries and the columns of activities in the black press, as well as the insightful work of Evelyn Brooks Higginbotham, social status came not from one's job but from church work, officerships in women's church groups, and so forth. The church became their society.[73]

It took about one-quarter of the columns of Boston's black newspaper, the *Guardian*, to record the tremendous activity of women's church groups, social clubs, and auxiliaries to fraternal lodges. Since they often lived in white households, black women had to sustain these ties across neighborhoods. Unlike white working-class women, their networks were not bound by geography.[74] "Distance and car-fares cannot keep them apart," Daniels reported, and the doings of such clubs as the "Fleur de Lis," "Longworth," "Waverly Outing," and "Blue Ribbon" "crowd the columns of the two Negro newspapers."[75]

Black women not only sustained relief-giving networks by such associations. They trained themselves "in the rudiments of combination," in running groups. And they trained themselves in other ways, too. In their clubs with "fancy and foreign names"; their daughters who studied music, art, or dramatics; and in the "bals masques, tableaux vivants," they literally enacted an identity unavailable to them in white representations of black Bostonians.[76]

False Friends?

Any woman in her right mind (not just the black working poor) preferred her own network of friends and kin to the city's organized philanthropies. Most working-class matrons of any racial/ethnic group never went to charitable institutions, and many who did so went only as a last and temporary resort.[77] Just as the residents of Denison House hoped to create a web of human relations through an endless round of virtually door-to-door visiting, to invent a neighborhood that centered on themselves as models, like the middle-class or small town neighborhoods in which they had grown up—taking jelly, for example, to Mrs. Houghton down the street at 134 Tyler Street, who was suffering from the effects of a fall—so black and white working-class matrons visited each other and expanded their maintenance of networks regionally. Daniels found "no end of visiting," among the black women he studied. They visited relatives and friends in Providence, Worcester, New York City, and various southern states.[78]

Earl Lewis has seen such visiting as "an integral part of the congregative character of urban living and the attempt by Afro-Americans to define their world." It not only maintained emotional bonds; it allowed visitors to "show the importance of these bonds."[79] It was a sort of conspicuous kinship. The constant publication in the pages of the black Boston press of who was visiting whom near and far, of the whist parties and recitals, of the welcoming and sending-off parties announced not only the activities and social status of those involved, but the networks themselves, making the web comfortingly visible and concrete.

Visiting was not entirely but was largely female among whites and blacks. Denison House women and the other visitors went to the homes specifically to find women; when they found men, they read it as a signal that something was wrong—the man was unemployed, drank, or was lazy. Visiting implied a kind of intimacy—the bonds of womanhood—for which these middle-class and elite visitors strove. Making intimates of working-class men would have had an altogether different connotation. While working-class women sometimes accepted and sometimes resisted these overtures, there was no male cross-class equivalent of nonsexual intimacy sought.

The working-class web of neighborhood relations overlay the physical map of the neighborhood with a different map. The physical neighborhood encompassed the familiar social institutions: the house of worship, those who lived next door or upstairs.[80] That map—the location of Denison House, the temples, the ethnic enclaves—was easier for outsiders to read. But not all physical neighbors were visiting neighbors. The complexity and multifaceted nature of race/gender/class relations encoded in visiting networks, the human microgeography of neighborhoods, the simultaneous intimacy and hostility, the mingling and segregation within a given block was more opaque. Adding to the difficulty, the human map was not fixed. The influx of new immigrants and new groups required constant negotiation and renegotiation of relations—who helped whom, who godmothered whom, who dined with whom and where.

Despite the neighborhood's transience and diversity, neighborhood support networks predated the advent of social service agencies, as Denison House residents found. "On the day of our moving in," noted resident Helen Cheever in late 1892, "three neighbors heated water for us on their stoves repeatedly, and sent it in by their little boys—So we became acquainted with Mrs. Flagan and Mrs. Quill and also with Mr. Sullivan, a door beyond, who is hard up, out of work, and desires to tend our furnace . . . and two of our neighbors refused pay for services declaring that they were glad to have such neighbors as we were, & to do for them."[81]

This friendliness came along with warnings from some, including a Mrs. Bremner whose little boy had recently died, that "it would be difficult for us to get acquainted with the people in the street as they were not naturally sociable and friendly." Bremner had lived on the street for several years "and had hardly a friend on the street."[82]

Neighborhood networks were built on trust and common interests, and rarely crossed class and gender lines. They closed quickly against distrusted intruders. A shoptender on Cove Street headed off C. M. Dresser of Denison House when she sought a Syrian peddler, Mary Joseph, and her five purportedly starving children. At first seemingly open, when Dresser returned, he changed his story. When she tried to find out why, she "could get nothing satisfactory. . . . He evidently did not wish me to come again." Other families refused to send their children to play, mothers claiming their husbands did not want the children to "be much from home."[83] Women would retain an air of affability, while keeping their would-be visitors at bay. On Shaving Street, "The woman seemed cordial and willing to talk although she did not ask us in. . . . The woman said that she had been working all the morning and had just come home to clean her house." In this case, since one would-be visitor, Mrs. Lucinda Prince, noted the dirt and disorder she observed through the doorway, it is perhaps not surprising that working-class women guarded their privacy and resisted spurious intimacy.[84] The suspicion, of course, was mutual. "I feel that we should be cautious about believing all these people tell us," wrote Prince, and Laura Cate felt she had learned a similar lesson, "to place not too great faith in the facts these people give me."[85]

Though Denison House residents hoped to enter and expand this dense neighborhood network, making thirty-five visits in a single week in January, they participated only on limited terms, as Protestants in a Catholic neighborhood, as wealthier women among impoverished families, offering to pay for and so turn into market relations what were assumed as nonmarket ones. When Denison House women brought food, they were welcomed. When they recommended the New England Kitchen (a philanthropic experiment offering low-priced prepared meals for home consumption), they found most of their neighbors thought it beneath them. Denison House residents' neighborly aid was never free of a judgment their neighbors felt keenly.[86]

Such interactions support historian Alexander von Hoffman's contention that the progressive urban reformers were trying less to break down an isolation, which did not exist than trying to control a system already in place, "to discipline the neighborhoods."[87] Indeed, Robert Woods hoped his settlement house in the South End would replace both ineffective charities and corrupt ward bosses.[88] The Denison House women hoped to teach their neighbors manners, starting with those easiest to access, the children, believing "the influence of ladies in their homes might be a good thing." They and their neighbors drew a distinction between the "ladies" of Denison House and the impoverished "women" of the neighborhood.[89]

Working-class women's suspicion of what they saw as false neighborliness could frustrate the intentions of middle-class and elite women they encountered. According to one Denison House resident, Mrs.

Crowley reported to her during a visit that she had heard through the papers that "we young ladies" intended to settle at 93 Tyler Street and devote themselves to the poor in the slums, "& added that therefore people felt like keeping away from people with such intentions." A few days later, Emily Balch received three women, including a tailoress and a member of a working girls club who displayed a sophisticated grasp of the economics of uplift, and who "said some among the girls were suspicious of it as either having ulterior religious motives or as an attempt to lower wages as working girls' homes are believed to do. A capitalist would give money to such a home & then get his employees for half wages."[90] While Denison House women determined to be "neighbors," their physical neighbors saw them in another category. Community was determined by social as well as physical "place."

Balch found that the working-class neighbors suspected insincerity on a personal level, as well. Her colleague Miss Cate mentioned that "she has met this suspicious spirit among working girls. They think that ladies take them up & drop them; would not want them in their homes. Would provide different sorts of entertainment &c."[91] The girls resisted becoming someone's hobby or being matronized. It was ironic that these middle-class and elite women visitors assumed they should be invited in, given their critiques of working-class life's lack of frontiers between public and private. In such encounters it became apparent that not only did the classes map public and private differently onto the urban landscape, but that they colored that map with other concerns.

While middle-class and elite social-service activists focused on what they saw as a "decent" interior space, such as those offered by settlement houses and philanthropic institutions, and "protection" for working-class women, working-class women and men acted on their preference for spaces that allowed them a sense of "independence," apparently from just such middle-class or elite interference. A Women's Municipal League report of 1909 claimed the great advantage of using schools over settlement houses was "their public character." Young men and women, the author claimed, would not go to settlement houses "because of some kink in their minds: they object to it either because it is a charitable institution, or because they are afraid there will be someone there to 'uplift' them (the settlements have been much written about). . . .

[M]any of them will come to such school buildings because they feel what they call 'independent' there.''[92]

Similarly, working-class women and men closed their homes not to one another or to business transactions or income earning, but to these social investigators coming in the guise of friends. Many, like the shop tender on Cove Street, refused to share information with these visitors, including as to the whereabouts of the people they sought. When trying to track down the Swisky sisters, Bosworth reported of the current inmate at their former address, "At first she seemed to know nothing about them," and then called her chum, Augusta, who said "why, what do you want with them?"[93]

To investigators who saw these working women as leading all too public lives, such a concern with controlling how they appeared in public and to whom came as a surprise. Middle-class and elite social service activists constantly asked working-class women to do things that offended their sense of propriety and often things the middle-class or elite women themselves probably would not have done. Mrs. Franks, for example, who had been ill, resisted using the New England Kitchen not only because she feared it was a charity but "also did not like to carry food through the streets."[94] "It seemed to me in approaching the girls that aggressiveness was fatal," Bosworth reported in another case. "The purpose should be stated simply as possible and then room left for them to ask questions."[95]

Hedged about by orders and authority at work, in their leisure and domestic spaces they resisted acting at the behest of others. Miss Jackson, who worked at a factory, impressed Bosworth with her "delightful little room with its canaries, its book-case and desk, center-table and couch, and she seemed a stout, healthy 'capable-looking' woman with obvious leaning toward 'sound common sense,' " but she still refused to gather girls to discuss their savings methods. She said "with impregnable finality, 'Yes, it might be very nice for those who have time for it, but I haven't.' " Libby Harrington, also a factory worker in Jamaica Plain, told Bosworth, "I've thought and thought and I can't see what it is to you," both in terms of her right to the knowledge and in terms of what the investigators gained from the study. When finally found, the Swisky sisters also resisted making definite arrangements to have Bosworth call monthly for the totals. Another confessed, "I'll tell you I don't like the idea of telling everybody how much I'm making, how much I'm spending and all that." Though Bosworth was often able to bring them round, with Harrington agreeing, "I do think it is about time somebody made some kick about women's wages," she "felt the necessity of a large amount of delicacy in dealing with them." Virtually all the domestic servants she asked unalterably refused to cooperate.[96]

Not all strove to hold settlement house residents at bay, however. Denison House residents exploring the neighborhood came on Yankee physicians who induced cures with magnets, German tailors, Yankee and Irish skilled workers in the building trades, Syrian peddlers, and Chinese restauranteurs, as well as impoverished laborers, largely Irish.[97] Emily Balch ventured forth from Denison House in 1893 to visit the Butlers, whom she found "very nice seeming." Her conversation there demonstrated the complexity of social status in the South End. Mr. Butler "spoke of his work of plastering; now at a job on Harrison Ave. where a Jew owns the contract for the work done and the weather so unfavorable that he will gain nothing by the work. . . . Talk ran on Jews, little sign of prejudice. . . . Nice Jewish people in house next but one (Kneeland Street side) to Day Nursery, Cohen; Mr. Butler spoke of a Jew would smoke cigar if given but would never buy one. Mr. Butler likes smoke 'like most workingmen'—(he said)—but would not working in nice rooms."[98] Miss Butler, the smoking workingman's daughter, attended the local Catholic church and "talked of her difficulties with a servant. Offered us use of her sewing machine."[99]

In Boston's rapidly changing working-class neighborhoods, including the South End, inhabitants could not rely on the location itself to indicate their social status.[100] Having established her family as one that could offer rather than receive help, one that hired rather than worked as a servant, as a family sustained by a particular kind of "workingman" (in her father's self-identification), a few days later, between showing Balch around the neighborhood and offering witch hazel to help the sore foot of Balch's colleague, Miss Butler responded to a query for local lodging houses. She mentioned that she herself let rooms and would be glad to take any Denison House friends. Helen Cheever noted of the Butlers, "I think they thought we had come to do some *other* people good and were glad of it."[101]

As the Butlers demonstrate—by distancing themselves from the impoverished, disorderly targets of Denison House's benevolence and the "foreign" Jewish newcomers to the neighborhood—such distinctions mattered. Denison House and institutions like it became sites on which not only its residents but its neighbors could define their class status. The house joined the constant relative jockeying for public social identity that characterized one facet of working-class life and led South Ender Mary Shea, for example, who rarely went out, to go with her sister to a "Poverty Party" in Charlestown at a cost of eleven cents, where a prize was to be awarded to the "raggediest costume."[102] Neighbors also took more aggressive action to define their relation to the house residents. Within three days in April 1894, two neighboring families named Denison House residents godmothers to their newborn children.[103]

Given the diversity of the South End, it is not surprising that some neighbors, like the Butlers, supported the settlement house efforts at surveillance. Mrs. Ellswell, for example, introduced by a local teacher, Miss Davis, to Helen Cheever of Denison House, knew the girls of the neighborhood and "spoke of Katy Sullivan. She thought she was worth saving and that the mother also had good in her. Of the Moriarty's she was less hopeful."[104] And Denison House residents began to distinguish among neighbors. When Miss Cate noted that one of the club girls had a death in the family, she wrote that they lived over a stable and that the father, an alcoholic, "has paid the price of his last spree" with his life. "The little mother," on the other hand, "belongs to the better class Irish-American" and kept a clean homey apartment.[105]

The jockeying for social identity was so complicated partly because there was no consensus on the rules. There were clearly differences in how the women saw the proper performance of urban femininity and masculinity. As Mr. Butler knew, workingmen smoked and drank.[106] Working-class women, as their neighbors knew, earned what they could to contribute to the household income, whether by running a kitchen barroom or doing piecework. By allying themselves with settlement workers, neighbors could differentiate themselves from those they put forth as objects of attention and enact/claim a kinship with the college women. Similarly, while working-class girls formed their own clubs, many also eagerly joined in those at the settlement house, not just for the entertainment but because of their social aspirations.[107] Settlement house women could become nodes in relation to which the local residents could define their status.

Conclusion

Scholars have sought working-class women's consciousness, politics, and modes of political expression in gender militance of labor movements, boycotts, and riots. Such expression also occurred, however, on the more daily level of demands for day nurseries, work, kitchen barrooms, and housing, as well as informal neighborhood and ethnic defense against middle-class "intruders." Kathleen Canning notes that working women's [and men's] work was imbedded in a family neighborhood community, where struggles occurred over pride and honor, gossip and respectability, bodies and sexuality, charity and tutelage "through which workers adapted to and subverted ordained locations within the factory regime," showing "complicity and resistance" and consciousness of their multiple-subject positions as workers/wives/mothers. And Elizabeth Ewen notes, "Daily life became a theater of cultural conflict. Work, family, shopping, personal appearance, and amusement were all in dispute."[108]

I find, however, that the fragmentation was more on the middle-class than the working-class side. The latter saw workers/wives/mothers not as multiple but as a single-subject position and often seemed less conscious of subverting or resisting than they seemed indifferent to a set of judgments that ordained a position for them; it seemed beside the point. For example, the continual complaints about the lack of underwear—which manifested middle-class notions of respectability, bodily control, privacy of the body, and bodily integrity—seemed to make no connection with the working-class women.

While not organized political movements, working-class matrons' actions were self-conscious demands to reorder space and power in their own interests in ways that did not fragment their lives into "work" and "home," "gender" and "class." Confronting a more powerful group of men and women who had different ideas about proper social/spatial ordering—domesticity, for example—these women, by their demands, conveyed another map of the city and of men's and women's lives.

By their elusiveness and refusals, as well as by their demands,

working-class women helped to shape the social services offered. Wellesley literature professor Vida Scudder spoke at the Emerson Society about Miss Weir's art class and found that "nine nice working-girls want to join, if class can be in evening."[109] Even agency records show poor women not as supplicants but as decision makers, snubbing case workers when the latter pried presumptuously into their sexual affairs, refusing degrading work, and retaining their own consumption priorities. According to sociologist Beverly Stadum, only their "ability to defy middle-class mores of feminine dependency in marriage" allowed them and their families to survive by taking in homework or working out. Working women were better than charity workers at conceiving ways to be independent of men or agencies—in part because independence, for them, was a goal. Through formal and informal networks—kinship, churches and visiting, philanthropies and social clubs—working-class women defined their own sense of the city and their place in it and created their own tools for survival. Such interactions determined, as much as the workplace could, their experience of what it meant to be working class.[110]

2
Work or Worse

Desexualized Space, Domestic Service, and Class

While working-class matrons struggled to create homes in relatively unvarying, if grim, conditions, middle-class and elite matrons found the sands shifting beneath their feet. They and their husbands worried over the ever-higher divorce rates. They became alarmed at the rising number of never-married women, some of them their own daughters, and outraged at abortionists.[1] They witnessed with dismay the burgeoning lodging-house districts. Their college daughters, like Vida Scudder, seemed not only to be turning away from but turning on the Victorian home and all it had stood for. Even worse, so did the daughters of working-class matrons. Middle-class and elite matrons watched, frustrated, as both Yankee girls and immigrants' daughters shunned domestic service for factory and shop work.

Besieged, they did not surrender. Instead, middle-class and elite matrons mobilized their forces and their allies in organized and individual ways to shore up the institution of the Victorian home, that putative refuge from the world of commerce, wellspring of civic virtue, and foundation of women's moral authority.

That shoring up involved them in an array of contests with the forces and groups they saw as threatening. They waged those contests in terms inseparably moral and spatial, as best revealed in three types of social investigations regarding women—exploring domestic service, moral purity, and wage work—that emerged at the turn of the century. All three spatialized concerns about women; they located public fears about changes in women's roles in particular parts of the city, particular homes, leisure places, and works. In one way or another, all three set up an opposition between the orderly middle-class and elite residential spaces of the city and its working-class spaces of factories, tenements, and commercialized amusements.

The construction of working-class spaces as sexualized and chaotic, so well described elsewhere, is not my focus here.[2] Rather I want to look at what these three types of social investigations reveal about the other half of that equation—the half we tend to take for granted and so assume does not need mention.[3] Just as the working-class spaces of the city were sexualized in this literature, the middle-class home was implicitly *de*-sexualized. That desexualization was equally essential to the moral, gendered geography of the city the investigative literature constructed—and just as artificial. When carried into policy, it directly affected not only its perpetrators but working-class women, including those domestic service women for whom middle-class homes were waged work sites.[4]

Reformers and Their Literature

The first of the three categories of social investigations concerned what the middle and elite classes labeled "the servant problem." As early as 1866, the Industrial Aid Society for the Prevention of Pauperism warned that "female domestics are becoming absorbed by the various manufacturing establishments and there is not sufficient emigration to Massachusetts to supply their places." The society hoped that southern black migrants might take up the slack, but they miscalculated.[5] Blacks never formed more than 3 percent of Boston's population in this period, and although over half of Boston's black female workers were domestic servants, as late as 1908 they had never comprised even 5 percent of Boston's domestic servants. Moreover, domestic employment agencies reported difficulty placing black servants. White employers did not want black servants, complaining of the "proverbial uppishness of Negro domestics." Nor did they easily accept the plentiful Irish Catholic immigrants who came to dominate the trade. They persisted in advertising for white Yankee Protestant workers, the very sort most likely to head for factories and shops. By 1910 such workers comprised only 12 percent of domestics.[6]

As the absolute numbers of servants rose more slowly than Boston's population, and their proportion of the female labor force dropped, middle-class and elite matrons looked with suspicion on their rival employers.[7] In the 1890s, a contingent of such matrons connected to the Women's Educational and Industrial Union went to their friend, Louis D. Brandeis, to discuss their dissatisfaction with the low wages paid women and girls in industry, stores, and laundries. Brandeis trenchantly suggested that they first get, literally, their own houses in order. Before the women tackled what Brandeis saw as a problem in the men's sphere (both outside the home and where men were the employers and supervisors of women), he advised them to turn to what he saw as a problem solely theirs, "woman's exclusive problem the domestic worker."[8] Brandeis rejected these women's claim to authority over women workers who were not in their own homes. At the same time, he recognized something they often did not: their homes were paid workplaces and bore examination as such.

As a result, the WEIU hired a college woman, Mary Dewson, to investigate. She reported on efforts to attract workers to domestic service and away from other forms of employment and on conditions of service in domestic work. The WEIU also maintained an employment bureau for domestic servants and opened a training school for servants and their mistresses. The WEIU investigators were, to some extent, applying new techniques of social analysis, "the scientific and careful consideration of present conditions," as they put it, to the "servant problem" (how to find them and how to ease tensions between them and their employers). By so doing, they, like Brandeis, lifted domestic service from the realm of a naturalized set of relations to a modern industrial social problem theoretically susceptible to solution.[9]

Despite all their efforts, however, they found that if at all possible, working women would choose any occupation before they would choose domestic service. One declared flatly that "she would not be a servant at any price." An investigator spoke to another, who ran a bookbinding machine for ten hours a day at six dollars a week and wanted to learn manicuring and massage, but lacked the means. "She had been a lady's maid," the investigator reported, "and when it was suggested that she should return to that occupation and save money to learn the other trade, her ambition seemed to vanish, and she decided to stay where she was."[10]

A second, and sometimes overlapping set of reformers, known as purity reformers, tackled the thorny question of urban vice. While prostitution was hardly a new urban problem, in each era the analysis of its causes changed. Starting around 1900, a new round of investigations in Chicago, Syracuse, Boston, and other cities began with the premise that the roots of prostitution lay in the increasing numbers of unattached young women and men living and working in the city. The lack of acceptable supervision coupled with the inadequate wages of the women was, to the investigators, a dire combination. Amidst growing fears of an epidemic of "white slave" trading, studies pointed out that young susceptible women could meet men, sometimes just as young and susceptible, other times older and with practiced air, in the lodging house, the boardinghouse, or at work. Sometimes those men, the studies alleged, were even their bosses.[11]

Despite their focus on the potential dangers of the nondomestic work sites, most found that, disproportionately, the largest number of prostitutes were drawn from the ranks of domestic servants. The studies offered little or no analysis of that connection. Their middle-class and elite readers and investigators continued to channel reformed prostitutes or "fallen women" into domestic service.

The third set of investigators focused similarly on whether the new occupations were safe for women. "Safety" here meant moral safety, not physical safety. Despite the presence of women in textile mills since the turn of the previous century, "new" turned out to mean anything that was not domestic service. In Boston, two investigations of working women and girls, Carroll Wright's for the Bureau of Statistics of Labor in the 1880s "to determine whether the ranks of prostitution are recruited from the manufactory" and Mary Conyngton's for the federal government in 1911, bracket this period.[12] Both investigators explicitly excluded domestic servants from their concern. Both, in addition, championed the morality of women's new occupations.

Like the purity crusaders, these investigators saw only nondomestic work as requiring investigation regarding its morality. It was working women's living and not just working outside the middle-class or elite home that made them subject to investigation. In the course of the nineteenth century, middle class and elites' ideology had posed an ever-widening gulf between the nature of "home" (nurturant, cooperative, female, affectional relations) and "workplace" (individualistic, competitive, male, monetary relations). The difference had come to define proper male/female identity and relations. In a related way, the separation investigators drew between domestic service and nondomestic service defined, for the middle-class and elite, working women's moral geography and appropriate space. Outside the middle-class or elite home, working women's virtue was suspect. Survival outside it required, as one female Boston lodging-house keeper explained to a Wellesley College investigator in 1907, "either work or worse."[13] Work, it seemed, was bad enough.

Wright defended the morality of working girls by focusing on their home life. To Wright, the new occupations were safe not because of conditions in the workplace or on the streets, but because he could locate the workers within a geography of domesticity. When Wright questioned whether factory or store work really led women to prostitution, he carefully did it within an acceptable moral geographic framework. "The fact that so many live with their parents," he argued, "is one which enters largely into the moral condition of the working girls."[14] Moreover, 85 percent of the working girls did "their own housework and sewing wholly or in part. No stronger evidence of the essentially 'home character' of the lives of our working girls could be adduced," Wright concluded.[15] Wright, basing his opinions on what he saw and heard from working girls, was sanguine about the moral nature of working-class families and even about boarding and lodging-house keepers, "as evincing a motherly interest in the welfare of the homes and those living with them." Wright clearly tied female morality to the evidence of domestic activity, and he, unlike others who followed him, was willing implicitly to position the working-class home as a moral alternative to the middle-class one.

By the time Conyngton did her investigation in 1908/9, herself an independent young woman, she no longer presented a world in which only domesticity guaranteed a woman's virtue. She started at the other end of the spectrum. She interviewed matrons at homes for unwed mothers and fallen women, prisons, and reformatories. Her approach inadvertently yielded an even more direct challenge to the moral superiority of middle-class and elite homes.

Like the investigators of prostitution, she found, almost universally, that a disproportionate number of the fallen women had been domestic servants at the time of their "fall." In bemusement, Conyngton commented, "The general agreement that the home and domestic service furnish the majority of the inmates [of homes for unwed mothers] is the more striking since most of the superintendents held strongly to the established opinion that domestic service is the safest occupation for women." For example, at the Door of Hope Mission, the assistant manager who had been there for five years and received 200 girls a year, "Questioned as to the relative safety of occupations, assigned domestic service as far safer for a girl than store or factory, but admitted that they got very few factory girls and very many domestics. Did not attempt to account for this." Similarly, at another mission receiving 240 unfortunate girls a year, Conyngton questioned the manager of ten years, "Asked as to dangerous occupations, Mrs. V. said at once she thought saleswomen were exposed to special perils. On further inquiry, said they rarely had a saleswoman among their inmates and she had seldom heard of a saleswoman going astray. Could not reconcile this with her views as to dangers of the occupations, but said she had never before thought of the matter statistically."[16]

Unlike the purity reformers and the reformatory matrons, Conyngton did try to explain the statistics. What did Conyngton conclude from these findings? Not that the middle-class or elite home endangered working-class women, but that domestic service attracted women of low morals. Recounting the cases of two prostitutes from Boston who, in domestic service at ages fifteen and sixteen were seduced by their employers' husbands, Conyngton deduced that neither of the young women seemed to have had any particular morality to begin with. "With each it seems probable," Conyngton concluded, "that she would have taken to the life sooner or later, unless guarded with a degree of care a working girl is not likely to receive."[17]

In short, if there was illict sex going on in middle-class and elite homes, it was the servants, not the homes, that she would sexualize. "In these cases," she insisted, "the connection [to occupation] is almost certainly incidental, not causal."[18]

These three literatures together, by their own criteria and logic, do not point to domestic service in a middle-class or elite home as a safe haven for working women, but as a breeding ground of prostitution and sexual exploitation, a last resort for working women. That conclusion, perhaps not surprisingly, was never the one reached by these investigators, despite the statistics at their fingertips and despite—or because of—the girls in their attic rooms. How and why, in the face of their own evidence, did elite and middle-class men and women maintain as a cornerstone of ideology about private and civic virtue that the middle-class/elite home was the safest moral space? What was at stake for the ideology's proponents? And how did the changing economy of the city, which called into being the image of the sexualized working girl, simultaneously call forth the desexualized middle-class or elite home so successfully that the one called for investigation while the other did not?

Sexuality, Labor, and Middle-Class/Elite Homes

I am less interested here in the extent to which domestic servants were actually sexually exploited by their employers than I am in the ways and reasons by which middle-class/elite women kept such an eventuality out of the discussion of working-class women's moral safety. Whoever was seducing, raping, or partnering those domestic servants who became prostitutes, what matters is that they made their move from the supposedly sheltering arms of domestic service more often than from the supposedly exposed occupations that so much more concerned the middle-class public. But it is probably worth taking a moment to address the issue of coercive sex in domestic employment.

Here the silence in the records echoes the silence in the investigators' reports. It is impossible to establish, by current social scientific standards, the extent of sexual exploitation of servants, the process by which servants entered prostitution, or the proportion of servants who entered prostitution. Even the kind of anecdotal evidence given above is scarce. Middle-class/elite families involved were unlikely to broadcast the affairs; workers tended not to leave records. I have searched the records of homes for unwed mothers and for fallen women and the records of the Boston Lying-In Hospital, a third to a half of whose maternity patients were unmarried in this period; all these institutions assiduously avoided naming the father in the records, or even categorizing fathers or seducers as a group.[19] The Boston Female Moral Reform society yielded only a few examples.[20] In addition, few scandals from private homes reached the courts.

Faye Dudden concluded from the dearth of court cases that "perhaps sexual conduct between employer and domestic was rather limited after all, or at least, flourished more in imagination than in reality," and that the lack of strong taboos against marriage between the employing and the servant population in New England, where approximately 90 percent of the servants were white, kept employers aware of potential risks to such action.[21] It seems to me, however, equally significant that court cases were notoriously hard to win. The age of consent in Massachusetts was only ten in 1885 and sixteen in 1900.[22] Moreover, Massachusetts never passed a seduction law, and the law seduced servants could have used included a "presumption of chastity" clause in which any evidence impugning the character of the female accuser led to the dismissal of the case.[23] As Marybeth Hamilton Arnold has argued, such proof of chastity, always defined in middle-class terms of passivity and seclusion, was virtually impossible for working-class and serving women who ran errands on boisterous streets and who often had no male relatives in the city to vouch for them and few resources with which to retain effective counsel.[24] Even wealthier women's resources seemed inadequate. When the respected WEIU's Protective Department wanted to take up bastardy cases, the minutes reported that purity reform leader Mrs. Kate Gannett Wells, former member of the Boston School Committee and president of the Moral Education Society, which housed unwed mothers, "came to the meeting for the purpose of protesting against it. . . . [the department] should need the best legal assistant to successfully carry on the work, that it was very difficult and expensive . . . that [the WEIU] had not means or reputation sufficient to undertake it at present."[25]

Joy Parr has noted that servants are psychologically positioned in a way similar to prostitutes by having their bodies at the beck and call of others. Indeed, that their bodies were available was the principal marker

of their lower and dependent status, and the totality of that dependence featured prominently in working women's reasons for rejecting service as an occupation. The WEIU found "an intelligent chambermaid whose surroundings are unusually good, and who works where there are several others employed, nevertheless feels that housework is slavery."[26] Another WEIU study found that, indeed, mistresses did deny dignity to their servants, and it labeled their behavior "feudal," a "survival of the belief that the household employee is a chattel to render personal service."[27]

"To be young, a servant, and a stranger was to be unusually vulnerable, powerless and alone," concludes Parr. The emigration society Joy Parr studied sent young English servants to Canada, participating in institutionalizing the idea that middle-class homes were the best possible workplaces for young women. Nonetheless, the society instructed the mistresses "not to leave the girl at night when another woman was not present in the house." As time passed, the emigration society had to provide an ever larger home for unwed mothers among its protégées.[28]

Piecing together the investigative reports with internal reports of refuges, it seems a typical pattern involved a young domestic servant finding herself pregnant, whether by the man of the house or by some other man. As soon as her pregnancy became evident to her employers, they fired her. Now bereft of lodging as well as work, she would pick up such other work as she could, as long as she could, and when she could no longer work, afraid to go back to her natal home even if it were near enough by, she would attempt to get into a Lying-In Hospital. Once the child was born, she would find it difficult to get domestic work where she could have her child with her and difficult to support her child on other wages. Within two years of the pregnancy, she would be on the streets, making far more than she could, though for a shorter span, given the ravages of disease, than in any other occupation open to her.[29]

While late-nineteenth and early-twentieth century middle-class women like Conyngton could explain such stories by the low and unsteady character of women who entered domestic service or by the entrapment of servants sent by employment agencies to brothels, middle-class and elite women had not always been so reticent about the seducer in the middle-class or elite home.[30] The stock character of antebellum moral reform literature, the wealthy man-of-the-house seducer, faded from the postbellum northern reform literature.[31] This fading came at the same moment as the concern over "the servant problem" reached new heights.[32]

The postwar world had brought not only increasing competition for working-class female labor, but a reemphasis on more elite women's moral authority. The rights discourse that Susan B. Anthony and Victoria Woodhull had used in the 1870s when constitutional amendments were redefining who had access to such claims proved less popular with the pulling back from radical change after Reconstruction. As a growing body of literature has made manifest, women wanting a public voice returned to older claims of women's moral authority as keepers of the virtuous home and instillers of virtue in others.[33]

In reform literature, the middle-class/elite domestic seducer was replaced with the (always male) lecherous or simply immoral nonhousehold employer or the city slicker, a stranger on the streets.[34] A true gentleman supported and protected women; that relationship was already transgressed by a male boss profiting from (being supported by) female labor. Economic and sexual language were conflated in notions that manufacturers and department store managers lured young women to work for them at less than subsistence wages and then either assumed they found other men to support them or pressured them into sexual favors for themselves.[35] "Heads of large mercantile establishments," warned the WEIU's president, "wax rich on the earnings of women working at pay unjustly lower than men's; pay so meagre that often starvation or shame is the only alternative. The work of reclaiming fallen women, so called, is zealously undertaken, but it is the well-to-do who own and support the disreputable houses and whose victims help to fill them."[36] In connecting sex only to the nondomestic workplaces and streets, such a scenario heightened the contrast between the middle-class/elite home and other workplaces.

Investigations of domestic service did provide a certain kind of critique to explain its failure to attract workers, but the exploitation deplored was strictly one of attitude, hours, and wages. In a somewhat odd turnabout, it now seemed that working-class women's labor exploitation might happen in middle-class/elite homes, but their sexual exploitation only happened outside them. Middle-class/elite female domestic reformers deplored the treatment doled out by their peers. The chief clerk of Boston's YWCA employment office asserted, "The attitude of the American employer is largely to blame for the dislike which immigrants have for housework. If employers were less haughty with their servants, and didn't make household positions so menial they would be more sought for." A WEIU employment committee leaflet chastised both employer and employee for "the unorganized effort of the employer to secure domestic ease and comfort—often in disregard to the principles of ethics and economics; and on the other hand, a tendency on the part of the employees, owing to the excessive demand, to control wages without regard to efficiency." The idea of sexual as opposed to labor exploitation never entered their public discourse in regard to domestic employment.[37]

After all, in the house it was women, housewives, who were the (fictive) counterpart to the male employers outside the house. Of course, in actual daily life, the men of the house (for whose comfort and refreshment, ostensibly, women managed the home) did intrude into the disputes over wages that female reform societies found themselves mediating. Yet, in these same societies' printed discussions of the servant problem, men were absent.[38] Despite the physical presence of men in the house and of back stairs, private bedrooms, servants' quarters, and other spaces where servants, resident around the clock, might encounter, alone, the men of the house, the reform literature regarding conditions of service presented the home as though it had no men at all. If middle-class/elite women were going to question the morals of the men of their own class, they would not do it in a way that would bring into question the efficacy of their own, female, moral authority in the home. They would criticize the men as factory owners or public rogues, not as an untamed domestic menace.

For middle-class/elite women's moral authority did more than provide them with a public role in urban reform and ideological power within the household. It also provided them with a claim to control working-class women's labor and to control female adolescents of all classes. In rejecting the trend away from live-in service to day work, which the servants seemed to prefer, a matron responding to a WEIU survey claimed, "The reason is simply a preference to have a good home under my roof for as many persons as possible. Also the conditions in most homes in which the girls otherwise live are not likely to be favorable

to their development as neat and efficient servants." Another wrote, "It is also far better for their own character to come under the influence of a good home," and another, "I think servants are much better off at service in a family; their health and food are better. They come in contact with a better side of life than they do in shops, factories, trades, etc. Good manners, charity, and other virtues are being constantly exercised in a family life and I think these things are worth much." Another matron made even clearer the missionary notion of live-in domestic service; regarding day work, she insisted, "I do not feel that it will be an uplift morally to employer or employee. Personally I feel a sense of responsibility for those under my roof." In the same vein, another wrote, "The mistress must watch over, love for, and feel a personal interest in the girls in her kitchen, and the girls must feel as much interest in their work and their mistress as if it were their own home. They must put themselves in each other's places therefore, to have the best results they *must* live together." Service under middle-class female moral guardianship, the women held, benefited the employee with moral uplift and benefited society, binding different classes into a single family, albeit unequal: "In my opinion the family bond which does exist, in greater or lesser degree between the two classes is worth maintaining."[39]

The matrons never lost sight of who held, as one put it, "the reins of government," and despite the familial rhetoric, the "personal responsibility" of mistress to maid was always limited by the stipulation "if she deserves it."[40] Hazel Carby's recent analysis of black reformer Jane Edna Hunter and her advocacy of domestic service training and employment for black women also applies to Boston's white matrons. Carby contends, "Hunter clearly tries to establish a maternal framework to disguise and legitimate what are actually exploitative relations of power. Exploitation becomes nurturance."[41] In an 1898 Massachusetts study, investigators found that of 245 servants, 91 had no day off in the first week of the study, and 80 had had none by the end of the second week.[42] One Boston matron inadvertently explained how such conditions could seem reasonable to maternalist employers, "Between right-minded persons a bond springs up when the same house is 'home' to both. . . . The hours of every woman who is desirous of promoting comfort and cheer in a home, mistress as well as maid, must be elastic.

The element of personal devotion is a greater factor in this work than in any other."[43]

While middle-class/elite women often sincerely desired to protect not only working-class women but the social order, they also needed both the presence of servants and their labor to retain middle-class status and their own freedom of movement. Late-nineteenth-century households still required tremendous amounts of manual labor and increasing displays both of leisure and of all-too-dust-catching, high-maintenance goods. Domestic servants were both part of the display and a vehicle for maintaining it. One WEIU investigation referred to Boston's matrons as participants in "a social system which makes the 'doing of one's own housework' the line of demarcation between those who are 'in society' and those who are not."[44]

Middle-class/elite matrons seemed to have no conception of a legitimate household without servants. "I desire servants in the house," wrote one, "to answer the bell in the hours when an employee by the day would have left, and for numberless conveniences, for attention in illness or emergencies, or small matters. With an elderly person, or small children, it seems to me indispensable to have servants in the house as residents." In cases of unexpected guests or illness, wrote another, "to be without them would be enough to give the average housekeeper an attack of nervous prostration." Rather than do without at least two houseworkers under her roof at all times, another confessed, "I should rather try to introduce economy in methods of living than change the character of home life for a typical family, i.e., father, mother and children."[45]

With increasing alternative demands for working-class women's labor, middle-class and elite women's claim on adolescent women, particularly of the working class, had heightened significance, but also met with heightened tension and competition. Turnover was high. Domestics averaged only a year and a half per job.[46] Faye Dudden pointed out the increasing social distance between mistress and maid that accompanied the growth in size of cities and the impersonal nature of employment bureaus. No longer the "hired girl" who ate at table with the employing family, such women were more and more strangers whose behavior was suspect, whose past was unknown, and whose employment required constant negotiation. Dudden reported cases where prospective female employers deplored the "self-assertion" of potential servants. Boston feminist Julia Ward Howe, known for being condescending, found herself facing an infuriated discharged servant she described as "a perfect demon" who, driving off "in a drizzle, . . . laughed and said, 'Women's rights!!' "[47] Their literal as well as moral authority over these women was part of what defined them—even to themselves—as at least middle class, but it was perhaps harder to maintain.

In their attempt to shore up the Victorian home and their own status, they demanded complete subordination from the workers in their midst. The matrons deplored not only the self-assertion but the independence of day workers, who would owe allegiance to some family other than the one that employed them, where "home duties" might keep them from punctuality. "I think outside help upsets the regularity of one's household," complained one matron, "They are more independent and are inclined to make the girls [live-in servants] think they are doing too much." Another exasperated matron responded to the survey testily, "There appears to be too much deference to the criticisms and opinions of uneducated servants."[48] They sought as ideal workers those most isolated, dependent, and alone: the same characteristics that made them vulnerable made them good servants.

When other work looked more attractive, these matrons had few incentives to expose the sexual dangers in their own homes. In this way, they became complicit in endangering women through their participation in an interconnected language, ideology, and set of institutions, in short, what many scholars call a "discourse" regarding sexuality that claimed that danger never existed in the middle-class/elite home, but was elsewhere ubiquitous.[49]

For the Good of the State

The description of working-class homes and families that prevailed in the reform literature was in striking contrast to the literature's depiction of middle-class/elite homes. Wright was exceptional in his approach. In other investigations, working-class dwellings were, in fact, not seen as "homes," their kin not as "families."[50]

As is evident from the last chapter, working-class families often lived in multifamily tenements. They often took in lodgers or boarders. Their children often spent much time on the streets, away from the small, crowded, and occasionally filthy rooms. On the streets, as Christine Stansell and others have shown, they gathered useful bits and pieces for their families and often picked up odd bits of change by performing occasional services, which sometimes included sexual services. Stories abounded in the welfare case and investigative literature of women running off with lodgers, single mothers sleeping with lodgers in return for help with support, children being abused by lodgers. The meaning and frequency of such relations clearly varied with the beholder. Faced with this alternative, working-class girls would be better off, investigators and matrons agreed, in the true homes and families of the middle-class. One matron summed up this line of thought in stating her opposition to servants who lived with their own relatives or on their own rather than with their employers: "Young women would be much on the streets, going and coming, and liable to be imposed upon and tempted to spend money for clothes to make a good appearance outside. They are deprived of the shelter of a home."[51]

Investigators and middle-class/elite matrons tied virtue (and, hence, legitimate female authority) not just to any home life but to middle-class/elite home life alone. In harmony with the claims of the middle-class/elite, investigators saw virtue as inhering in a particular spacial arrangement as well as in particular types of people. Increasingly, they connected virtue to "that privacy which," it now seemed, in contrast to the preindustrial or rural United States, "every human being requires," but which, within the city, only the middle class and elites had the resources to provide.[52] Edward Everett Hale, an activist on behalf of workingmen's homes, approvingly reprinted the findings of one investigating committee that condemned the common corridors and privies usual in tenements as "public nuisances, in as much as they encroach upon the family relations, tend to make them impure, and thereby sap the very foundations of the state."[53]

Sustaining the middle-class/elite family became something of a patriotic duty, an act for "the common good." Even the WEIU investigators concluded that to solve the problems of domestic service by boarding out, as one woman's husband in the study had, "is to do away with the home and strike a fatal blow at national, civic, family, and individual welfare." This sense of the primacy of the middle-class/elite family (including the servants essential to maintain it) in the nation state, as the only true family and the bulwark of civic virtue, also helps to explain employers' refusal to weigh as equally important the demands of servants' own families. In this line of reasoning, servants who refused the "personal devotion" to the employers' family were running counter to the national as well as to the servants' own welfare.[54]

More than in the domestic reform literature, men joined in this discourse. At stake was not only middle-class/elite women's authority, but the Victorian home and family that gave its men authority over all. While some were willing to see redeeming features in tenement life as "homes of families, such as they are," they condemned in toto the boarding and, particularly, the increasingly popular lodging houses, whose inhabitants were lifted out of nuclear families altogether. With men and women in adjacent rooms and easy visiting habits, Boston investigator Albert Wolfe wrote in 1906, time would "render immoral practices not only easy, but almost a matter of certainty."[55]

At first, it seemed that Wolfe's concern lay in the failure of the boarding and lodging-house keeper to fulfill the female role of guardian of household virtue. But on closer reading, it becomes apparent that the central problem to Wolfe was that, in contrast to the middle-class/elite matron who also had unrelated young women (servants) in her household, the boarding and lodging-house keepers were largely working-class women. Wolfe admitted "there are many landladies . . . who are above moral reproach in the conduct of their houses, and who are doing much for themselves, their lodgers, and the community." But the attributes that rendered them "above reproach" were largely also signifiers of middle-class status: memberships in women's clubs and philanthropic organizations, and "a dozen or more who are sending sons and daughters, nephews and nieces, through Harvard and Radcliffe. No suspicion can attach to the intentions of women of this type."[56]

Suspicion, rather than evidence, comprised most of Wolfe's opinion, yet his view of lodging houses as the seedbeds of prostitution and dangerous places for women became standard. The power of the accepted social framing of this issue to structure debate emerges clearly from Louise Bosworth's conclusions as to her investigation of living conditions among working women in Boston a few years later. Bosworth felt obliged to dismiss her own findings and her own experience as a single woman in the South End of Boston in the face of the strength of Wolfe's assertions: "Albert Wolfe, in his study of lodging houses of the South End, gives a comprehensive and searching view of the lodging house problem. The dangers to unprotected girls, as well as the temptations to seasoned lodgers are seen to be very real and far reaching in their effects. That the present investigator has not met with this problem may be explained in several ways still consistent with the existence of the evil."[57]

The discourse about urban sexual geography affected the way women like Bosworth negotiated the urban terrain. Geographer Gill Valentine has studied the differences between current women's beliefs about which city spaces are dangerous to them and police blotters' indications of spaces in which women have actually been endangered, as well as studying women's sources of knowledge about both.[58] "Women's fear is not aspatial," writes Valentine. "The geography of violence against women suggests that they should be more fearful at home and of men they know. . . . Yet, research has shown that women perceive themselves to be in danger from strange men and in public space." Valentine warns us against seeing women's perceptions as "natural" and advocates instead seeing them as the outcome of a process that requires analysis, a process by which women "develop images of certain environmental contexts as dangerous." Similarly, Elizabeth Wilson, in studying the city, has discussed the ways in which the city, so enticing as an arena of potential freedom for women, was constructed instead as a dangerous place.[59]

Valentine points out that for women, safety in the home is often economic and social, not physical. In line with what we have seen above and what Linda Gordon found in her study of domestic violence in the nineteenth century, Valentine concludes that despite the statistics women were encouraged "to perceive the home (private/residential sphere) as a haven of safety and refuge and to associate the public world where the behavior of strangers is unpredictable with male violence." In modern terms, she discovers that, "far from making girls aware of the greater risks of date rape and domestic violence, parents actively encourage them to seek the protection of one man from all men (perpetuating the ideal of the family)."[60]

In the same way, nineteenth- and early-twentieth-century middle-class/elite matrons, claiming to stand in loco parentis to working-class women, urged them into domestic service rather than into work and life among what to middle-class/elite women seemed a multitude of strangers. These women's own social and economic dependence on individual men and on a system that placed them in that position would have encouraged them, as Valentine puts it, "to suppress or deny violence committed by men they know in the private sphere," even had they no other reasons to do so. In turn, for these women, investigators like Albert Wolfe, lurid stories in the press, and rumors became sources of information for women of all classes trying to read urban geography. Bosworth and the *Massachusetts Report on White Slavery* in 1914 both reported investigating persistent stories of abduction, trickery, drugging, or simply unpleasant experiences in looking for rooms only to find that, in Bosworth's words, "first hand accounts are rare."[61]

These stories, spread avidly by both middle-class/elite and working-class women and men, coupled with women's daily experiences of verbal assault (comments or whistles from strange men) would affect women's sense of public security and encourage them to see public spaces as dangerous and "to adopt false assumptions about their security when in places falsely deemed safe for women, such as the home," according to Valentine.

When Wolfe and others claimed a social need to oversee working-class women's lives, they also claimed the right to oversee, protect, and, hence, control the physical whereabouts of these women. Their stories told of innocents in need of rescue, unsuspecting women who wound up in demoralizing boardinghouses, fraudulent employment agencies, or slovenly tenement families.[62] Acts of rescue, like chivalry, affirm the rescuers' power to protect, affirm their superiority.[63] They helped relegitimize the claims of moral authority (enacted through surveillance) on which middle-class/elite women, as stated earlier, based claims to a voice in public affairs.[64]

Institutionalizing

This conjunction of middle-class/elite needs and frameworks goes some way toward explaining why moral reformers of the time, far from condemning the dangers that middle-class and elite homes seem to have held out for working-class women, channeled reformed prostitutes back into those homes as domestic servants. According to Barbara Hobson, "Domestic influence and domestic training, the cornerstones of female penal institutions of the nineteenth century, reinforced the social, economic, and psychological dependency that brought the majority of women there in the first place."[65] Faye Dudden concluded that finding a woman a job as a servant was seen as the cure for all female ills: prostitution, poverty, or friendlessness, which no doubt explains why virtually every women's organization hoping to better the lot of their less fortunate sisters facilitated such employment informally or through formal bureaus.[66] And Barbara Brenzel, writing on the first reform school for girls in North America, found that trustees, administrators, and the state all believed in "middle class" virtues of respectability linked to domesticity and that "the haunting specter of prostitution loomed large for all three and resulted in the acceptance of an extremely narrow and conservative view of domestication as reform."[67] "There are a number of things I should like to do," a young woman facing parole said, "but there is only one thing I will be able to do, and that is to go back to housework."[68]

Other reformers built new asylums and prisons where they hoped to rehabilitate the criminal and insane through an orderly atmosphere, providing an external discipline for those lacking internal discipline. Middle-class/elite women already had such an institution ready at hand for their subjects. While women outside the home represented chaos, the middle-class/elite home represented civilized space. In short, that home held all that was necessary for "wild" girls to be "domesticated."[69] In this sense, the desire for independence on the part of the working women was itself, to these matrons, a problem to be managed.

As the domestic service solution met with a resounding lack of enthusiasm from the young women themselves, middle-class and elite women and men compromised sufficiently to create working-girls' homes where women could live in subsidized housing under the careful eye of approved matrons.[70] Such a solution encoded in space the gendered vision of these reformers. The goal of working women's housing was moral supervision; the ultimate goal of working men's homes was independence. While there were YMCAs to protect the virtue of young unmarried men in the city, there were no female counterparts to the single-family homes that constituted the plan for workingmen.

Roswell Phelps, a social-reform investigator at the turn of the century, was less than keen even on the collective workingwomen's homes because they would "concentrate in one district a large number of working girls under conditions which will counteract the decentralizing forces tending to encourage residence in the less thickly populated and less demoralizing sections of the city."[71] His preferred solution, like Hale's, was for individual homes headed and owned by male workers. Working women's boardinghouses, to Phelps, constituted a mixed blessing, keeping young women within moral bounds but making it even easier for them to continue to live outside of nuclear, male-headed families. It is important to recognize both the differences and the similarities in these visions: it was female middle-class supervision for the female reformers and paternal supervision for their male counterparts, rather than the presence or absence of family itself, that made for moral spaces.

Indeed, elite matrons took their campaign for moral supervision into the workplaces. As John Potter and Michelle Reidel have pointed out, Brahmin Fanny Baker Ames, a Massachusetts state factory inspector in the 1890s, like Wright, worried more over moral than physical safety. She argued for separate approaches to bathrooms lest working women be "brought into contact with men who were not their fathers, brothers, etc." "where crowding into the same lavatory or sink to perform their ablutions before leaving the mill, or meeting intimately at the common approach to adjacent water closets" would lead to "a coarseness of manner . . . that is, if not immoral, at least a condition of immorality." When one employer called her demand "fussy," she asked him to imagine his own daughter in the situation which led, she claimed, to his appreciation of "the full moral force of the law."[72]

By 1909, the matrons were ready to tackle the streets. The Boston Equal Suffrage and Good Government Association asked the police commissioners to appoint at least one woman officer "to watch and care for the girls on the streets and in the Common during the evening." "In view of the fact that many young boys and girls in the more congested parts of Boston are exposed to grave moral danger by their intermingling without previous acquaintance on the streets and Common during the evenings," their draft request read, "we the undersigned respectfully request that one or more police matrons or *street mothers* [my italics] shall be provided."[73]

All these solutions aimed at the endangered, isolated, kinless "woman adrift." But that construction excluded from concern single women without their own families who were living as domestic servants. Indeed, there is some evidence that these women, more often than lodging-house inmates, had no family in the vicinity. I do not mean to romanticize working-class families, which, like families of other classes, often involved violence and abuse. The point is that the women were no safer in middle-class or elite homes. And working-class kinship networks could and often did provide a measure of protection for workingwomen. Middle-class and elite reformers, on the other hand, defined "family" in particular ways, ignoring that dependence on a family of employers was not the same as having a protective nuclear family or kinship network. On the other hand, boarding or living with a working-class family, despite studies showing that the family often shared wages with their boarders in times of trouble, was not considered having a "family," but rather living in dangerously overcrowded quarters.[74]

The institutionalization of these middle-class prescriptions in the various reformatory and refuge employment programs, so that they became public policy, demonstrates the power of the middle-class/elite vision of sexual geography and virtue to affect the material life of working-class women. Certainly this vision of sexual geography and virtue helped organize middle-class and elite women's and men's thinking about what needed regulation and the way they tried to regulate wage working women's access to protection, rights, wages, and occupations through legislation, vocational training, and private and public social agencies.

In this way, factory, store, or office work and domestic service were conceptually organized as a set of oppositions, a set that reinforced the connection between female and home. It connected to the way that the nineteenth-century home itself took its ideal shape (so different from the economically productive colonial home) from being placed in opposition to the factory—home as not factory, not marketplace, not place of work. (Note, in this vein, Carroll Wright's exclusion of domestic servants from the term "working girls."[75]) The factory, the store, and so forth, in turn were not homes, not places for personal nurture and virtue. If women's work was to be regulated, then, it was less to bolster their role as economic players in the marketplace than to ensure that women's paid work would not interfere with their home functions.[76] Women's work in middle-class/elite homes, paid or unpaid, remained the normative, idealized, and unregulated standard in this discourse.

College Women

There was, however, a growing group of middle-class women who saw "freedom" not as dangerous but as desirable. The WEIU labeled these "college women" as opposed to "club women."[77] Increasingly in this period, middle-class female social investigators—college women—supported working-class women's desire for independence against the claims of middle-class and elite matrons who saw that desire as deviant and antithetical to the well-being of the republic. In this competing discourse, factory work, like the lodging house, was seen as "modern," "independent," and individualistic and domestic service as "anachronistic," despite the large numbers of domestic servants and the continuing demand for them.[78]

Wage work, rarely seen as liberating for men, could be seen as liberating for women—college or working class—only in contrast to an alternative total dependence on family or domestic employer, particularly since all studies showed that most wage-working women did not earn enough to support themselves. As Joanne Meyerowitz has pointed out, "dating, cohabitation, golddigging, and casual prostitution" were all part of larger economic strategies to make ends meet.[79]

This new breed of college-trained female social investigators identified not with the matrons, but with the workers. These were the women exasperated by the desires of middle-class and elite women to claim that their employees were part of the family, to demand their employees give up all desire for independence in deference to the maintenance of the middle-class home as the bulwark of national virtue. These "New Women" advocated putting housework on an industrial basis, with regular hours, wages, and explicit contracts. These women, like the servants themselves, wanted liberation from the confines of the privatized middle-class home and its supervision.[80]

Yet these dissenting voices did little to disturb the picture of the safe middle-class home. They were not interested in attacking that home, only in legitimizing women's nondomestic work—as were Carroll Wright in 1884 and Mary Conyngton in 1911.[81] They used their investigations of working women to try to redefine appropriate urban space for women, without challenging the sanctity of the middle-class home.

They, like Conyngton, could take a different tack because unlike the matrons their presence in the public sphere relied not on their moral authority as homemakers, but on their college degrees. These women created different kinds of vocational opportunities for working-class women and increasingly shifted the focus of employment bureaus such as that at the WEIU, away from domestic service. To these women, female independence from the home was not a mark of deviance and potential depravity, but a badge of citizenship. And it was these women who, by the 1910s, held more and more power to shape the urban structure of opportunity for women.[82]

Conclusion

Middle-class and elite matrons needed servants for labor, for status, and to enter (literally and ideologically) into the public realm as authorities. When other options proved more enticing to potential servants, middle-class and elite women and men, consciously or not, deflected and controlled criticism of their own homes as inadequate. Instead, they attacked their rivals. They denied the legitimacy of working-class homes and the authority of working-class matrons over their own daughters. And the women in particular, their compassion aroused, called attention to the very real abuses in nondomestic worksites, accusing male employers of nefarious practices and lecherous tendencies. In the process, they helped construct an urban geography of sexual danger that left them captains of the only safe vessels.

Their homes, like working-class homes, had waged work and strangers, unrelated men and women with free access to each other's bedrooms at all hours, and even unsanitary conditions (such as the use of slop buckets, as servants' quarters rarely boasted the modern bathrooms the employers enjoyed).[83] But middle-class and elite matrons interpreted the spaces differently. In so doing, they bolstered their authority by participating in a larger project of creating institutions and spaces that demarcated the normal and the abnormal, the virtuous and the deviant.[84] The middle-class and elite reformers' discourse on virtue reinforced their roles as surveillers and as those who chose what got looked at and what got overlooked. It also affirmed their position as producers of "virtue" itself and coproducers of the discourse about it.

As middle-class and elite matrons increasingly claimed public space, having been removed from it at its inception, they had to take part in this process of ordering, labeling, knowing, and redefining "public" and "private." Only thus could they create spaces for themselves. They drew a new map that delimited where they could go and where "others" should stay, and the routes along which it was possible to move. Their control over resources essential to working-class women in the way of jobs, training, and welfare increased, as became evident in the previous chapter, turning their ideology into material reality for those women. These club women could preside not just over homes, schools, philanthropies, and reformatories, but over factories and streets. Their college counterparts were even more ambitious. They redrew the lines between orderly and disorderly women and blurred the lines between themselves and the working girls to whom the next chapter turns.

3
The Moral Geography of the Working Girl (and the New Woman)

If I were you," Louise Bosworth told Grace Harvey in 1907, "some Sunday I would get up and have breakfast and cut out prayers and cut out church and cut out Sunday School and young people's meeting and get out in the country for a good time." Harvey, a resident at the YWCA, hesitated. She would like to, she said, but had no idea where to go or with whom. She did not want to go alone.

Bosworth saw Harvey as hiding a lack of funds. At five to ten cents a ride, carfares, she knew, loomed as an obstacle for any excursion beyond walking the city streets, particularly when one was trying to save money to buy winter clothes.[1]

But there were other dynamics at work in the exchange. Bosworth's letters often mentioned her discomfort and sense of danger in the working-class neighborhoods she visited while investigating women's wages. Even in her own and Harvey's South End neighborhood, she felt anxious about returning to her rooms at night.[2] Harvey, on the other hand, evinced anxiety about traveling alone to the country. Their geographies of danger differed.

Middle-class and elite matrons had constructed an urban moral geography that defined city streets, factories, department stores, and almost all spaces except their own homes as dangerous spaces for young working-class women, full of snares and temptations they themselves might be able to withstand, but working-class women could not. College women, including the numerous investigators, had demurred as to the danger of other workplaces, but largely concurred as to the dangers of the streets, lodging houses, and leisure haunts and to the unique moral vulnerability of young working-class women. Young working-class women, on the other hand, those between the ages of sixteen and thirty-five, dubbed the "working girl,"[3] had their own moral geographies, their own notions of safe and unsafe spaces, and what made them so. From elusive bits and pieces of evidence in reports of more elite investigators, contemporary working-class fiction, and the rare autobiographical writings, those different maps begin to emerge. As with the maps constructed by working-class, middle-class, and elite matrons, working girls' maps, too, were intimately connected to the claims they made to a place in the public realm.

Wild Girls

Whatever their motives, the middle-class and elite matrons had grounds for their anxiety on behalf of the working girls they increasingly saw on Boston's streets. Hours were long, wages were low, work was unsteady, and temptations were many. Not only had the number of self-supporting women risen precipitously since the onset of the Civil War, but most of the workers were young.[4] In Massachusetts, 80 percent of the girls left school between the ages of fourteen and seventeen, the majority to earn a living.[5]

The work they could find paid pitifully low wages. According to Carroll Wright, in the mid-1880s women workers needed at least $8.00 a week to maintain decent morals, but most of the 1,032 women he interviewed earned less than $7.00.[6] Twenty years later, little had changed. The laundries of Boston's South End still paid as low as $3.50 per week to their female employees.[7]

Department stores provided a relatively bright spot in the bleak picture. They were unusually sensitive to bad publicity, partly because their workers met face to face with middle-class and elite matrons. The stores offered a shorter workday than factories or domestic service and better benefits. Many department stores, like Filene's, voluntarily established a minimum wage of $8.00 per week. Its "junior workers," however, such as bundle girls, message carriers, cash girls, and others, received only half as much.[8]

Living-wage investigators learned firsthand about working girls' cost of living. In 1907, investigator Gertrude Marvin reported that working women could afford to pay at most $1.50 per week for a room that had to be walking distance to work. That sum usually bought a hall or attic bedroom without heat and with only a small window or skylight. Marvin rented such a room that summer, up three flights of a narrow, stuffy hallway. In her room, she struggled to light the gas jet. It had been covered with a hard substance, leaving only a parsimonious pinhole for a flame. It rendered just enough light to show the sheets were not clean. She fled to a good hotel, at $1.50 per night instead of $1.50 per week.[9]

Experienced factory women made higher wages and felt they had little in common with those who made less.[10] But such differences could be illusory or at best fragile. Jobs were notoriously unsteady.[11] Jordan Marsh and the Thomas G. Plant Company regularly cut as many as 2,000 workers each during their slack season.[12]

Any temporary job loss, unexpected illness, or family disaster could rapidly deplete savings and run up debt. Few jobs provided sick benefits or paid leave. In May 1908, Bosworth was spending her mornings at the Massachusetts free employment bureau and found the experience trying: "the people there are so wretched and miserable and their stories are so hopeless that I have come back at noon pretty much of a wreck. I have gargled and sniffed listerine and generally fumigated after each day of this sort, because the place is so crowded with sickly looking people and I have to talk to so many."[13] The slim margins that separated survival and destitution became apparent when the WEIU began to help women demand back wages from recalcitrant and unscrupulous employers. They were besieged by women seeking restitution of two dollars or less.[14]

But it was more than low wages that worried the matrons. It was the increasing scale of workshops, offices, and stores. In 1860, for example, the city's ten cloakshops employed 27 women each.[15] In 1908, a single clothing shop employed 100.[16] Many factories employed thousands.[17] Similarly, the number of clerical workers at thirty-eight Boston companies more than doubled between 1870 and the mid-1890s.[18] And by

1900, even smaller department stores had hundreds of employees.[19] Jordan Marsh had up to 5,000.[20]

Unlike factories, department stores and offices concentrated downtown. Factories continued to draw workers from localized, relatively homogenous immigrant enclaves.[21] But store and office work, requiring unaccented English, drew "American" workers. They came from the countryside or other parts of the city. They needed, like other workers, to live near work[22] and helped to create those notorious lodging-house districts, filling the rooms on the fringes of the central business district.

It was this new geography, the concentration of financially marginal women workers downtown, newly visible in vastly increased aggregations, streaming onto the streets during lunch and after work, taking over lodging houses and restaurants, visiting theaters and dance halls, that had fed the increased concern about women's moral safety. Unlike domestic servants, these working women shifted continually from workers to consumers, servers to patrons.[23]

Scholars have built a firm foundation for exploring the moral geography and economy of the working girl. They have depicted tension between middle-class and elite women's and men's preference for ordered leisure spaces that preserved personal restraint and bodily integrity (through lack of crowding and jostling), such as Olmsted's parks, and working-class women's and men's preferences for more boisterous amusements that provided them not with freedom from the city so much as freedom from restraint.[24] In these historians' accounts, immigrant parents often appear alongside middle-class and elite men and women attempting to control working girls who felt the effects of a new world of commercialized leisure. Peer relations appear as most typically governed by mutual exploitation between women and men in a range of sexual exchange from conversation to intercourse.[25]

The evidence for this picture derives largely from court cases, studies of girls judged "delinquent," and the investigations of middle-class college women adventuring into foreign and exotic terrain that they could use to explore the shifting meaning of sexuality and desire in their own lives and circles. Like the matrons, all these parties agreed that urban streets and commercial amusements were sites of sexual license, morally dangerous or not.

Without doubt, Boston had plenty of wild girls, or girls who seemed wild and incorrigible to their parents and to the investigators. But their proportion was not enormous and their sexual abandon not always clear. Their wildness was defined in part precisely by their frequenting those places designated as wild, leaving the putatively safe harbor of family or domestic service for the streets, lodging houses, and dance halls.

Only 3 women out of 500 immigrant women and children that the WEIU investigated in 1906/07, for example, seemed clearly "wild." All three displayed an entrepreneurial turn, exploring and exploiting the city's opportunities (including sexual ones) to make their fortunes and avoid a life of drudgery. Such women were the victims of neither isolation nor immoral home life. As the WEIU reported in some bafflement, "These three girls seem to have been associated with fairly prosperous, eminently respectable relatives or friends, kindly disposed towards them."[26]

Faced with daughters similarly aspiring to fun and freedom, parents who needed their wages might commit such pleasure seekers to the state industrial school. Swooping down on their daughters, police officer in tow, at "the low dance halls," parents committed from just over one-quarter to over three-quarters of the girls at the school.

The case records labeled these girls as "*inclined* to lewdness." That label covered everything from being out late and away three days, to seeking the company of boys and most tellingly, having no inclination "to yield to the wishes and instruction of her father and home government." Few cases of *actual* lewd and lascivious behavior, however, numbered among the industrial school's residents; they peaked at 10.1 percent in 1886. The real crime for most was rejecting the family.[27]

While these enterprising young women took flight with or without men to escape a home situation of dirt, labor, confinement, or even abuse, other women, not incarcerated, mentioned male "friends," whose precise relationship was hazy but who clearly subsidized their recreation. Parents did not always disapprove of these relationships. When one working girl "was out ill a few days last Easter . . . a 'friend' sent her an Easter lily in a carriage. Her mother rushed out thinking some one of her family was injured and when she opened the carriage door and saw an Easter lily for her Alice she was delighted."

But even when parents did not, investigators condemned these girls as showy, superficial, and a bit mercenary—"the butterfly type," wrote one.[28] The working girl who told the WEIU investigator Alice's story "would have nothing to do with poor men." A graduate of Nashua Business College and the daughter of a small country-store owner, she had "numerous 'friends' who are wealthy." The investigator concluded, "Is efficient, robust, both of which qualities are rather overshadowed by exaggerated hair puffs and floating veils." Themselves independent "New Women," the college women distrusted the focus on sexual attraction and the dependence on male "friends" for a good time.

If women like Alice and her friend—"Americans" with access to the clerical "business" education and better-paying office jobs—depended on men for recreation, women with smaller wages did so even more heavily.[29] Marvin repeated a story she considered "well substantiated," though not firsthand. Two sisters, the story went, waited on table at a Back Bay hotel that served its employees with leftovers and inferior food. Tantalized by what they served, they went out after work ended at 11 P.M. and hung around the streetcar stations until picked up by some men, "never a slow process," according to Marvin. They went with their gallants to a restaurant where they enjoyed a sumptuous supper, "then out on the street again,—at the first dark alley they would dart down it, and lose themselves on some side street, so suddenly that their escorts never caught them."[30] The story appeared in numerous other cities; given the women's clothing of the era, which makes it hard to believe a determined man could not catch up to any woman, it may have been, like so many of the white-slave trade stories, an urban myth. It clearly also struck the listeners as credible, however, and so revealed the sense of at least some young women of a cat-and-mouse game of working-class heterosocial relations.

Such stories were part of a larger revision of urban etiquette and gender roles debated daily in the Boston papers of the mid-1890s as unescorted New Women and working girls became familiar figures in public. Letter-writers and columnists presented opposing images: women as mobile athletes, bicyclists, and bloomers wearers and men as stationary office workers; wives spanking husbands and fathers beating daughters who stayed out late with strangers. Daughters asserted their right to party three to four nights a week at "respectable assemblies," while a secretary warned, "Remember, dear girls, it is easy to find a lover, but hard to find a [male] friend." A columnist asked, "Are American girls too ready to take advantage of mistletoe boughs and kissing games?"[31] Alongside older tales of urban seduction and abandonment, now almost entirely concerned with rural mill girls and immigrants, came spunky stories like that of Minerva Athens, who wrote of an evening encounter on a bridge in the public garden; "I dropped my glove, and immediately it was handed to me by a young man. 'Good evening,' said he. 'Beautiful night; isn't it?' " Unlike the girls in Marvin's story, she did not run, but rather drove him away with long words. She concluded, "Now, if every young woman was armed with a few sentences like the above, they could go through the world without molestation."[32] Finally, with growing respect, the paper covered young women strikers who took to the streets.[33] With women's increasing assertion of mobility and autonomy, clear markers distinguishing between respectability and wildness faded.

Amidst this chaos, the police launched a series of brothel raids. At just the moment that working girls and the more elite New Women claimed the streets as space for respectable women, the brothel raids threw Boston's five thousand prostitutes out to join them. In response, madams in the South End organized a "Landladies' Union" to promote licensing of brothels and to protest police raids that had put "thousands of girls into the streets of Boston without means of support, and no provision made for their support or maintenance by said officials, thereby spreading disease and destitution all over the city by driving this class into lodging houses, hotels and flats."[34]

While the raids led to a permanent association in the public mind of lodging houses with prostitution and certainly did nothing to enhance the status of the streets as respectable, they did not turn back the tide of young women with different ideas. Moreover, matronly white feminists well into middle-age gave distressingly violent advice for asserting the rights of women. "Shoot your betrayer," they advised a young Italian immigrant girl and those like her.[35]

It was in this context, too, that Josephine St. Pierre Ruffin sent out her call for a woman's convention to defend the moral purity of black women against aspersions cast by U.S. politicians and others, and she created an organization and a paper entitled, significantly, "Woman's Era." These black women did not, like the white women, endorse vigilante action. Indeed, they organized against lynching, exposing as false southern white claims of outraged womanhood.[36]

By the turn of the century, the debate over women's urban behavior in Boston centered on the South End. Not simply lodging houses, dance halls, restaurants, cafés, and amusements, but the entire South End had, in the eyes of the white middle-class and elites, become morally questionable terrain. The building of a streetcar line through the South End to the more affluent suburbs had cemented the South End's image among those who managed or owned the downtown offices (and among social investigators) as a moral no-man's-land, where they could stop on the way to the dry suburbs for a drink and even some illicit sex. The noise and dirt from the streetcar assured the district's undesirability, making it affordable to poorly paid women and men living on their own, to new immigrants, and to African Americans, all those designated by social investigators as inherently disorderly and disorganized in their living habits and family lives. The once grand mansions added to the sense of the district as degraded, even more than if it had originally been created as a tenement district. The growth of Chinatown and of a black enclave not accidentally coincided, as it did in other cities, with a policing of vice that tended to be more permissive in those districts already defined by the influential as less restrained and exotic.[37]

Boston's licensing laws strictly limited the number of saloons, for example, but the liquor trade in the South End was ubiquitous and gendered.[38] Licensing boards tried to concentrate legal bars on the main thoroughfares, to keep them from contaminating residential neighborhoods with vice. Tenement women, particularly Irish and Irish American women, took up the slack. In keeping with a long home-brewing tradition, they opened "kitchen barrooms" in their homes. A few men joined in the trade, but by and large it was run by women and patronized by men.[39]

Part of the problem with bars in middle-class, elite, and some working-class eyes was that while they purported to be male space, in fact they were mixed. Unlike German beer halls, which drew entire families, bars attracted men without their kin. Women who entered bars, even by discreet "ladies' entrances," were considered morally suspect, entering a commercial resort that catered to unattached men. Bars, like lodging houses, became associated with prostitution. Even the kitchen barrooms, according to investigator William Cole, were sites of assignation.[40]

Indeed, Cole found prostitution "much more deeply rooted in the South End than in any other part of the city." The district became, to him, one large sexual playground. He saw prostitution everywhere: "No section or neighborhood—one might almost say, no block—is free from it." He read signs of prostitution into massage, manicure, clairvoyant, and even millinery and dressmaking shops. "The line of demarcation which separates this class from the rest of the community is," he concluded, "of course somewhat indefinite." Similarly, Marvin found vice and lodging houses in the South and West Ends "intermingled so promiscuously that in many cases only experts can discriminate."[41] It is not clear what kind of "expert" Marvin had in mind. It is clear that she and Cole saw the South End, the epitome of the new urban landscape, as a minefield for the unwary.

Marvin made no comment on the fact that these districts also housed Boston's largest black enclaves, but the relation between vice, race or ethnic mixing, and perceptions of disorder could be intimate. Essays in Woods's *Americans in Process* (1903), not only labeled blacks as having a "natural tendency to immorality," but also condemned any interethnic sex. Interethnic sex in the Woods volume was always illicit, as in the claim that when a Jewish girl "does lose her virtue it is seldom or never through a man of her own race" and that households of multiple Italian men kept an Irish or American mistress under the guise of a "housekeeper." Licit sex, by contrast, only appeared intraethnicly.[42]

Racial/ethnic mixing in Boston as elsewhere was not uncommon, gender neutral, or timeless in its patterns and in the interpretations of observers. The West End, for example, had housed an intricate and often contradictory pattern of intimacy and segregation. In the 1880s, it had two facilities for aged women. In the Home for Aged Colored Women, twenty-one infirm or aged black women lived in the care of a black widowed matron and two black female servants. Nearby, in the Old Age Home for Women, lived eighty-six white New England natives. The staff consisted of nine white women—three New Englanders at the top (the matron, nurse, and housekeeper) and six Irish servants. Also serving were one black woman from Virginia and one white man from Maine.[43]

This stark segregation, with only a black maid, carefully subordinated, in the white home and no whites in the black one, typified most of the social services available to blacks in Boston. The inclusion of Irish women as servants and their exclusion from being served similarly signified the exclusiveness of Boston's white Yankee Protestants. While they did not seem to exclude the Irish from being "white," they did seem to see them as perpetually "un-American." They were not black, but they were not Yankees, either. Even impoverished Yankees would be kept apart from them. In the 1870s and 1880s, black Bostonians married whites—largely Irish women—at a higher rate than Irish Catholics married Yankee Protestants. In 1877, 38 percent of black marriages were to whites, the highest rate in U.S. history. It would not drop sharply until 1909.[44]

By the turn of the century, Boston Irish women were also marrying Chinese immigrant men, and, as with blacks, they shared occupations, neighborhoods, and sometimes mission churches. During an 1895 Knights Templar convention, a *Globe* reporter followed a segment of the group and their wives on several forays to Chinatown.

> Last evening, a rather good-looking girl rode around the block on a bicycle several times. She became an object of interest to a knot of Knights at the corner of Beach and Harrison avenue. There were one or two women in the party who wondered audibly who the girl could be, and why she rode around the block on the cobblestones, instead of spinning over suburban roads. They were about to move away when a Chinaman appeared in a nearby doorway.
>
> "Lil," he called; "come quick!"
>
> The girl reluctantly dismounted and with her wheel disappeared up the dark stairs after the Chinaman.
>
> "Whatever does it mean?" exclaimed one of the women in great surprise. She was still more surprised when informed that the girl was probably the Chinaman's wife, and that there were several of her kind in the colony.[45]

Cycling, with its enhanced individual mobility, epitomized New Womanhood, a sense of autonomy and adventure entirely compatible with Lil's marital foray into Chinatown.

On the other hand, it was not just elites who advocated racial separation. In 1872, at the Massachusetts Infant Asylum, a foundling home admitting both black and white infants, white wetnurses refused to suckle black babies, staging what approximated to a strike. According to historian Peter Holloran, the white Brahmin managers of the home had depended on more impoverished white mothers whom they paid just over the wages of domestic service to nurse the infants. As a result of the action, the managers had to hire a few black wet nurses, but also chose to limit the number of black children whom they admitted.[46] Racial boundary setting was clearly crucial to some at the low end of the spectrum as well, including those whose own social status, like those of the wet nurses, hung on a thread.

Twenty years later, tensions had only increased. The white factory workers—often Irish Americans in Boston—who joined working-girls clubs to enhance their respectability, resisted the attempts of their elite female sponsors to incorporate black or southern or eastern European immigrant women.[47] And when young Katie Murphy disappeared from the Denison House neighborhood only to be found a month later in November 1893, the officer who found her told Helen Cheever it was "a very sad story and a very bad story about her." The bad and sad story turned out to be "that Katie Murphy was at Faulkner Street, among negroes."[48] Murphy's transgression may have been sexual as well as racial, but by the 1890s, according to William Cole, simply living in mixed-race lodgings was grounds for moral condemnation.[49]

Indicative of both the continued interracial mixing and the increased tensions—and gendering and spatialization of such tensions—was the raid on Chinatown and its aftermath in 1903, the reporting of which differed drastically from the tone of matter-of-fact acceptance in the incident of the cycling wife nearly a decade earlier. The Chinese remained in the press, as investigator Frederick Bushee had portrayed them in 1898, people "who can never be in any real sense American." But by then, the Boston Irish women had become sufficiently "American" in some situations to engender condemnation of their mingling with Chinese.[50]

When the police and Immigration Bureau raided the city's Chinatown that year, surrounding the area and barging without warrants into busy restaurants, shops, clubhouses, and homes, they found, according to the *Boston Herald*, "some degenerate young American men, who by long and constant association with the Chinamen have come to look as yellow and to smell as strongly of opium as do the celestials themselves"; these men "found difficulty in proving that they are or were once Americans and did not require registration papers from the government." Some of them may have been among the whites who took "slumming parties through Chinatown" to watch opium smokers. Others were undoubtedly neighbors.[51]

While the white men risked their nationality and race in such associations, the white women risked their respectability: "white women, young girls in some instances, who frequent Chinatown and live among and with the Chinamen, came in for a fright which should be a warning to them in the future. Some were found lounging about the dingy dens of the half-civilized and semi-opium-drunk Chinamen. They were ordered to dress themselves properly and to leave the district at once for their homes." As historian K. Scott Wong has pointed out, these women could be rescued from what was constructed as a dangerous and homogenous space (which was actually a heterogenous working-class space) by the white male raiders, and unlike their male counterparts, they could be saved for (and sent home to) white civilization.[52]

Alternatively, "American" women could play saviors themselves. The paper reported the Chinese arrested "screamed for their white friends, their American wives, the Sunday School teachers, the missionaries and habitues of Chinatown." Among those coming to their rescue was Kitty O'Connell, who came to the Federal Building to verify the status of her husband, Charlie En Goon, who was dressed in "American clothes." Mrs. Wong came too, and with a heavy Irish accent, launched a tirade against the police. Bertha Crane, described as a "colored woman," provided bail for four men. A public protest demonstration at Faneuil Hall drew a "goodly sprinkling of women, some of them Sunday School teachers."[53]

It was no accident that the Chinatown raid happened just as Boston's political map was being redrawn, in harmony not only with the turn of the century's new set of gender but with a new set of racial/empire paradigms (embodied in the Spanish-American War and the rise of social Darwinism and its cousin, scientific racism). The new paradigms diminished the importance of differences among Europeans and European Americans and heightened the significance of differences between those groups and African- and Asian-origin peoples. It was in the mid-1890s that Boston redrew its ward lines and gerrymandered out of existence black representation in the city's government, that the South End began to surpass the West End as the home of Boston's largest black enclave, and that Irish politicians began to experience continuous victories in city hall. Simultaneously, the developments mentioned earlier, including the streetcar's arrival through the South End, converged with these other shifts to demarcate the South End as a black, Chinese, and white borderland, displacing the wharves in the North End as the focus of social anxieties.[54] As literal repositories of racial identity, women were key players in any borderland, both through their own potential disruptive agency and as potential bearers of mixed-race children.[55]

The debate over sex roles in the 1890s converged with the debate over race. Respectability was race and class (as well as space) specific, as the founders of Woman's Era and the working girls' club members knew all too well. White reformers' anxiety over the moral safety of working girls largely concerned white working girls; most dismissed black women as inherently immoral. While black reform women struggled to assert their own respectability and to work for the uplift of the race as a whole, nonelite black women, largely domestic servants and so excluded from the category "working girl," struggled simply to be visible. In her 1900 Boston novel, *Contending Forces*, Pauline Hopkins described a streetcar ride in which young black women "was a-trampin' onto the feet of every white man an' woman in thet car to show the white folks how free they was!"[56] Hopkins's streetcar riders could only be visible by subverting the rules of genteel decorum. They literally made room for themselves as autonomous figures, imposing on those most inclined to ignore them.[57]

To most middle-class and elite white observers, such behavior—like Katie Murphy's living "among Negroes" and the "promiscuous" mixing of unmarried women and men of various races in lodging houses, dance halls, restaurants, and streets was disorderly and subversive of the (usually unstated) racial/sexual order. They labeled the women who mingled this way "wild" and even if married, sexually loose, and the men as sexual predators.[58] To middle-class and elite authorities, white girls who negotiated an increasingly rigidly divided racialized terrain with relative autonomy risked wrecking themselves on the shoals of Chinatown and the South End. Their imputed "wildness" had as much to do with transgressing race lines and trampling parental authority, with mobility and modernity, as it did with sex.

Eating and Living Places—Not So Wild?

As much as the "wild" working girls' maps differed from those of the socially elite, so did they differ from that of Miss Harvey, the YWCA resident who opened the chapter. She may have distrusted the country more than the city, but her social world was filled not with urban commercial amusements but Christian Endeavor. If Harvey had been truly typical, the new commercialized amusements could not have survived, but other sources hint at a range of moral geographies, of rules governing the heterosocial world of working women and men, that lay between Miss Harvey and Alice.[59] Since most working-class young women did not come before the courts and since Kathy Peiss estimates the proportion of women enjoying the "cheap amusements" at only about 10 percent, it is possible that the "looser" part of this world has been overstated. Just as early writers on immigration who based their research on court records exaggerated the disfunctionality of immigrant families, the historians, like many of the turn-of-the-century investigators, have exaggerated or hypersexualized the heterosocial, youthful, working-class culture and its tendency to view human relations (including sexual ones) in market terms.[60] Even Conyngton claimed that the size of this group was usually exaggerated, based on the observation of looser behavior, language, and conversational style that investigators assumed indicated the women were having sex with their male counterparts.[61]

While the overwhelming proportion of working girls lived at their parental home throughout the period, in 1900 28 percent of Boston's adult working women, excluding servants and waitresses, lived as boarders or lodgers. Black women, white women with U.S.-born parents (labeled "Americans" in studies at the time), and clerical workers (sales or office—categories dominated by "Americans") were disproportionately represented among them. Though fewer factory women lodged away from parents, among a 1910 sample of Jewish garment workers 20 percent did so. These were the women generally seen as most at risk.[62]

Boarding and lodging marked a rearrangement of domestic life suited to the needs of women workers, but it was not a perfect system. Each year, as many as 51 percent of lodgers moved.[63] In less than a year, one of Bosworth's account-keeping groups "had evaporated almost completely."[64] Finding a satisfactory living space near enough to a satisfactory job steady enough to keep up with rent payments preoccupied almost all working women, as it did working-class matrons.

Young working women had their own notions of how to improve the system, but they lacked capital. In the mid-1890s, Vida Scudder, Wellesley literature professor and Denison House resident, took Misses O'Callahan, Skelligan, and Halley, who roomed and ate out, to the Massachusetts Fine Arts Museum and then to lunch, where they talked "eagerly of a little co-operative flat."[65] Without capital, however, they had to choose instead among a variety of boarding and lodging situations—from the more institutionalized petty entrepreneurship of professional boardinghouse keepers to nonprofit houses run by reformers to the informal family arrangements of the crowded immigrant and migrant households.

At best, they could be like the relatively prosperous Miss Kirby. She had a large room with two windows, a mantel, and in a recess, a marble basin with hot and cold water, on the third floor of an old-fashioned residence on a quiet side street in the South End. A large Wilton rug with a crimson background covered the floor; a couch with matching embroidered sofa pillows, two tables, a bureau, and plenty of comfortable chairs, magazines, a sewing bag, and a large dish of oranges filled out the room.

Less prosperous lodgers in the South End fared less well. Miss Becket's landlady "seemed a pleasant, rather slatternly woman," according to Bosworth. "Her house is the regular South-End type, on an extremely noisy corner with a cafe in the basement and streetcars and trams jangling by continually." Rooms, like Annie Green's (and Marvin's $1.50 venture), could be "small, close and crowded up two flights of dark stairway."[66]

Whatever the quality of rooms, despite Cole's concern, few boarding or lodging houses of any type took both black and white clientele. Most discriminated on further grounds as well. The YWCA, for example, took only evangelical Protestants. Unitarians need not apply.[67]

Lodgings did, however, often mix women and men, skilled and unskilled workers. In *Contending Forces*, Pauline Hopkins described Ma

Smith's respectable lodging house. Many of the lodgers, African Americans, came through her son's acquaintance at the hotel where he worked. But they also included a young student preacher, a stenographer (female), two dressmakers, and among the "respectable though unlettered people," a former cook and a housemaid who together ran a laundry business.[68]

Similarly, union activist and journalist Frank Foster in his 1901 novel, *Evolution of a Trade Unionist*, described a cheap, cheerless white South End boardinghouse in which his hero, Ernest Aldrich, lived. It was run by a Mrs. Jordan, like Ma Smith, a widow. Jordan's two previous marriages and twenty years in the boardinghouse business had left her pessimistic and ironhanded.

Though Jordan departed from the kindliness of Ma Smith, she housed the same heterogenous collection of Bostonians. Most of the boarders were manual laborers who, according to Foster, "fed rather than dined." But the boarders also included a machinist, an advertising canvasser, a spinster shopkeeper, two tailoresses, and a typesetter, along with a "lady boarder" married to a railroad clerk, "one of that not inconsiderable number of American women who 'detested keeping house.' "[69]

Single and married, manual and skilled workers, unattached women and men, the houses posed precisely the picture of blurred lines between classes, sexes, and private and public lives that so worried the middle-class and elites. Yet neither Foster nor Hopkins portray the sort of moral free-for-all of the social reformers.

In Foster's depiction, the mixing in the boardinghouse or elsewhere is precisely what made the site urban, modern, and even enlightening. Bosworth echoed this sentiment when, to save money, she moved into a model working-women's boarding house and found herself living with a teacher of cooking in a trade school, an invalid Wellesley alumna who worked as a secretary for the woman who ran the house; Elizabeth Wallace, a stout forty-year-old "who stitches in an awful hole in the back part of Hollanders [department store] from morning till night"; Carrie and Minnie Driscoll, Catholics, one working in a box factory at seven dollars per week and the other a shop girl at Filene's for twelve dollars, both of whom had worked since the age of thirteen, and whose father drank and gambled until he had died three years earlier; a stenographer for a publishing house, a department-store shop girl; and a teacher. She concluded that living there provided "a grand opportunity . . . of living with working girls."[70] For Foster and Bosworth, mixing, rather than dangerous or dubious, became an adventure in modern democracy and, in a sense, defined "American."[71]

Although investigators tended to see boarding and lodging women as isolated, few of them were without relatives or friends in the area. The Jewish garment workers in the 1910 sample, for example, boarded with relatives or friends and were considered part of the family. The "Americans" in the sample, while less likely to board with relatives, lodged with friends or coworkers.[72] Within thirteen months of their arrival, only 13, or 3 percent, of the 500 women immigrants interviewed in a WEIU study were living with strangers; 6 of them shared the experience with siblings, and several of the others chose to live with strangers despite the presence of family in the area.[73]

What distressed investigators, of course, was not simply women living alone in rooms but what they did there. Bosworth found entertaining a man in one's rooms a common practice among the women she interviewed for her living wage study. The women she met in such situations seemed not at all embarrassed or compromised, and there was little suggestion of sexual play. A high-waged Miss Flaherty with a "ruffled blouse and silk skirt," for example, "had a young man in her room so received us in the hall." Bosworth, clearly less at ease than Flaherty, noted, "We tried several times to get away and leave her to her caller but she said 'Oh he can wait. I like to talk,' and followed us out to the step still talking."

Bosworth asked Flaherty why she had left home for Boston, and Flaherty responded in a way that demonstrated the attractions of the vigorous heterosocial life Boston had to offer young women and men: "It's too monotonous there. It's a little country town and there's nothing going on. I like the theatre and dances and all this. But sometimes I do get awful homesick." Though shocked earlier in her study to find men so often in women's rooms, Bosworth now identified Flaherty not as loose or degraded, but as good-hearted.[74]

It was not only the sociability of men that such living offered. Apartments, lodging houses, and working-girls homes offered women a peer group, as well. Bosworth visited one group of longtime roommates. She was seeking a woman named Emma Goozey for the study. Goozey was not there, but those who were invited Bosworth in to wait. Miss Jones, a friend, was dressing to go out or to entertain a caller, and Bosworth "saw a man sitting in" Goozey's room. Five women shared the apartment and ate at a lodging house down the street. The rooms were attractive and comfortable, and "the girls good friends." Two were dressing for the evening, experimenting with their hair. The youngest of the five, nicknamed "Chicken," was at most sixteen, "with cheeks round as apples—so fat that her eyes were quite barricaded. Tremendous, frizzly pompadour, perpetual good-natured little pout made her quite overbalance her very fat short person. . . . The girls all spoiled her in affectionate, elder sisterly way." The eldest roommate, Dwyer, commented, "Me and Chicken used to board ourselves, but we ate so many sweet things that it made us sick—pies and stuff like that."[75]

These girls provided for themselves a surrogate family with no parents. It may be, as Joanne Meyerowitz found in her incisive study of women "adrift," that women had little to offer each other economically, but these women and many like them provided both emotional support and a safe environment in which to entertain men.[76]

While the white middle-class and elites tended to see boarding or lodging as a permanent break with family life and boarders and lodgers as a breed apart, particularly as fewer and fewer white middle-class families took in boarders, many working-class women moved in and out of boarding and lodging situations. After Mary Jane McGrath married, she and her husband roomed with her husband's doctor friend and his wife, who owned a rooming house. The Sheldons left after six months for their own place, where their first child was born. When their printing business fell on hard times around 1913, McGrath Sheldon got a larger house and took in roomers.[77]

For wage-earning women, boarding or lodging was not evidence of their depravity but of a life stage, not evidence of isolation, but of networks. When Bosworth tracked down the Swisky sisters, she found they had moved from 7 Poplar Street to 171 Leverett Street, a large, seven-story building with forty-nine families, but they still boarded at 7 Poplar Street. She found them "up to the elbow in the washtubs when I called" and the small kitchen "filled with soapy steam and clothes" because not only the three Swisky sisters but the two girls of the family with whom they roomed were also washing. In this homey setting, Bosworth found that the oldest Miss Swisky "looks indifferent and a little forbidding usually, but has a most illuminating and attractive smile which comes very unexpectedly."[78] The three made good wages, enough to live on their own. One of the sisters worked as a tobacco stripper, at eight dollars per week, and the other two as dressmakers, at ten dollars and eight dollars. That they chose to live as roomers testified to the benefits they derived from the human connections.

Even when they lodged in cramped apartments with private families rather than in rooming houses, working girls like the Swiskys often chose, and their landladies encouraged them, to dine elsewhere. A host of new eateries had arisen to serve the rising lodging-house population and the downtown women workers. They ranged from expensive restaurants to saloons offering free lunches, from second-floor temperance tea rooms to basement barrooms and cafés. The eateries saved landladies' labor and proferred more choices to working girls, expanding their autonomy and their physical mobility.

Eating in public was transgressive enough to the middle-class and elites, but the promiscuous mixing of solo women and men at the lunch counter or table, sometimes with alcohol available, seemed not only chaotic but a recipe for social breakdown. At least the boardinghouse table had been, theoretically, under the supervision of the parental-surrogate head of the house. No metaphorical family relations governed commercial eateries, and some, undoubtedly, were places of assignation.[79]

Accompanied by her predecessor in the living-wage study, Jane Barclay, Bosworth made a nighttime tour of the barrooms in Jamaica Plain. They found one barroom with "exceedingly pretty artistic little clubhouse effects with a 'Coffee-tree Inn' sign," diamond-paned windows with awnings, and window seats. There were tables and magazines and newspapers, "and doubtless much sociability and political gossip," she speculated.

Despite the attractive decor and the vision that seemed to have crept in unbidden of intellectual ferment, Bosworth found the barroom, perhaps by definition, morally degraded, and by association, its customers, as well. The cosy fires, she was convinced, were lit to entice homeless men; and women, too, could fall prey to the allure, "poor sodden things with nowhere else to go probably."

Yet, on the same tour, Bosworth admitted that they confronted exactly where else working girls might have to go.

> There is one "girls club" at Jamaica Plain, and the contrast struck us forcibly. It was a dark gloomy house in an out-of-the-way part of the town. We rang the bell three times before any answer came—no open doors and fire and cheerful lights here—and then a voice from up-stairs came down through the speaking tube "what do you want?" it said, and then inquired minutely into who we were, and where we came from. Then it said we might come Saturday afternoon and see the house. How's that for a counter-attraction to the bar-room?[80]

The nature of eateries the working girls frequented—even aside from barrooms—exposed the different expectations of middle-class female reformers and their targets. Bosworth tried out The New Waverly one day in October 1907. She found it a typical basement dining room of the South End, stuffy, with a certain odor, and long tables in the center and across each end, with two small tables against the wall. The wallpaper she termed glaringly green and scarlet, "the tables piled with food in no sort of order and the atmosphere thick with flies," the serving staff typified by an "indifferently clean waitress," and "the originally coarse and exceedingly soiled table-cloth was quite equalled by the silver which was worn down to the lead foundations of the spoons and forks." Offended by the shabby pretensions, the communal tables, and lack of order, Bosworth was also unimpressed by the food, which included a "fairly good" clam chowder followed by greasy fish, scant lima beans and potatoes, a choice of fish, beef, or pork, and a dessert of rice pudding.

That the restaurant's working-class clients may have judged the center table piled high with baking powder biscuits, lettuce, butter, vinegar, salt, and pepper and the rest of the surroundings differently was indicated by the fact that Miss Chisholm, one of Bosworth's less needy budget keepers, chose to board there. The whole meal cost only a quarter, which a friendly male proprietor took from behind a desk in the hall as the diners left, smiling and saying to each, "Come again ladies," an appellation with which middle-class and elite women rarely endowed them.[81]

Like the for-profit lodging houses, The New Waverly proved more respectful of its customers than did the nonprofit houses run by reformers, even beyond using the term "ladies." Bosworth noted that at The New Waverly, patrons were invited to seat themselves, as opposed to being seated by staff as they would be in the YWCA, a mark of disorder to investigators like Bosworth, but also preferable, perhaps, to the YWCA, whose headwaitress Bosworth herself found sat people with an attitude both dictatorial and rude.[82] Disorder to investigators was a different order to working girls who, in commercial restaurants as in lodging houses, became respected customers—ladies—in a position to order rather than be ordered.

Safety and Autonomy

Both the lodging houses and the cafés could, as Bosworth suspected, provide space for political discussions late into the night. In the 1910s, many of the leaders of the telephone operators' union patronized a basement restaurant on Beacon Hill owned by the mother of the department vice president. At its four candlelit tables, patrons stayed until after midnight "discussing many subjects from poetry to economics," according to an FBI agent. Patrons could buy socialist literature with their coffee, and it formed "a rendezvous for socialists and malcontents of every class, from the dynamite anarchists to the 'pink tea' socialists."[83]

Frank Foster's novel depicts a working-class youth culture compatible with this café scene, more heterosocial than the working-girls clubs, but less sexualized than the picture painted by the investigative literature, with freer women, independent of mind and money, who shared lodging houses, bicycle excursions, union picnics, ideas, teasing, and friendships with men. They met in cafés, at parks, or on the Common, where "sprucely dressed" retail clerks rubbed elbows with laborers in overalls and jumpers, cash girls and boys, typists and stenographers.

Foster's hero, Ernest Aldrich, meets the heroine, Vera Lermentoff, at the Workingmen's Educational Club, where the speaker holds forth on "Woman in Modern Industry." Vera works as a designer in a large establishment. Her father had been exiled from Europe as a revolutionary, and Vera, an anarchist, laughs at Ernest's plans for a peaceful overthrow of the social order, which startles Ernest, who despite his revolutionary fervor has conventional ideas on relations between the sexes. Nonetheless, he soon comes to admire Vera's "self-reliance" while valuing her "purity," having never before met with so "indomitable a will and clear an intellect, so great a capacity for self-abnegation." When he asks her to marry him, she refuses. He is not fully mature, she tells him, and adds, "My freedom is too dear for me to easily give it up." She suggests they simply stay good friends for the time being, an alternative for which the historians have not prepared us.[84]

In Foster's world, women's independence is valued, but so is purity, and marriage is still the expected lot of women and men. In the novel, Lizzie Bolton and Marguerite Wrenthem work in adjoining "frames" in a printing office. Marguerite says to Lizzie, "You've only four weeks more before you graduate," meaning before she marries. Lizzie replies, "Follow suit. . . . George only needs a bit of encouragment to remove you to your 'natural sphere,' as they call it." Even if "women's sphere" is treated tongue in cheek by his women characters, Foster assumes that they will "graduate" from wage work to marriage. "Graduate" implies that women workers are in a tutelary position, not quite mature and certainly a temporary state. Even Vera, that pillar of independence, five years after she heads off alone to Russia to further the revolution, returns to Aldrich.[85]

But it also implies that waged work is a crucial and a public stage for women. The working-class culture depicted in the book is both a *public* culture of cafés, speakers' halls, union meetings and picnics, streets, and lodging houses and a *youth* culture. The novel's working women and most of its men are young. Indeed, marriage has a privatizing effect on men as well as women. Lizzie's marriage not only removes her from the workplace, but it and the little cottage in West Roxbury modify her husband's radicalism.[86]

Foster's women may be independent and socialize with men, but they can still "fall," even if short of prostitution. There are several kinds of moral disapprobation available. One is reserved for young women who do not do wage work. Aldrich is eating lunch in a park with a friend when "two fashionably dressed young ladies, whose appearance denoted wealth, if not refinement, strolled up the broad path. . . . Both of the ladies drew aside their skirts, with a suspicious glance at the workmen, as though fearing contamination by contact." One of the young women exclaimed, "Disgusting creatures!" Ernest's companion cynically remarks, "The other half!" Ernest writes a poem on the greater worthiness of his life than theirs because he works and their life is more limited.[87]

But if he had no patience with leisured women, Foster also did not romanticize working-class women's lives. "How soon the bloom faded from the cheeks of the shop girls," he comments in setting the scene in a working-class neighborhood and "how the painted woman wrecks thronged the streets at night."[88] The juxtaposition of faded cheeks and painted woman wrecks implies an evolution as sure as the one from working woman graduating to wife. Even further lie the "nightbirds" and the occasional girl keeping in the shadows hovering around Bowdoin Square just past midnight, watching for a chance to ply their trade unseen by the law, as "belated citizens" await the Cambridge streetcar and Harvard freshmen work off their energy.[89] Regarding none of these women does Foster make even the mild sort of judgment he casts on the ladies of leisure, but it is clear he considers them unfortunate, victims of the economic structure rather than weak moral fiber.

Despite the threat of becoming a "painted wreck," parental guidance seems unnecessary, or more accurately, irrelevant. There are few parents in the novel. Working-class relations between women and men are governed by a kind of chivalry on the part of the men and an assertion of autonomy by the women. Indeed, the only working woman in the novel to be "ruined" is Mina Sassanoff, the one living with her parents. Sassanoff winds up seduced by a labor spy, whose rooms she visits and who has promised marriage.[90]

In Foster's morality tale, it is as important that Sassanoff is seduced by a labor spy as that she lives at home. Her home life left her unprepared for negotiating the public world of work and leisure. She dies, of course (the price of sin in Victorian fiction), but not before giving deathbed court testimony that exposes the spy and saves the hero from indictment for violence during a streetcar strike. Honest workers, male and female, behave with honor toward one another; autonomous women (unlike Mina Sassanoff) can tell the difference between honest men and dishonest ones. While others saw women rooming without their parents as adrift, Foster seems to see them strengthened in their independence, and dependent women, those living at home, as endangered everywhere.

With its conventional tropes, Foster's novel may provide as questionable a guide to the moral terrain of working-class Boston as court records and investigative reports. There are, however, a few other affirming sources. Mary Jane McGrath Sheldon's autobiography might have served as evidence or antidote to the purity reformers, who saw lodging-house waitresses as among the most morally endangered of all working women since waitresses relied heavily on their ability to please their male customers to earn their necessary tips.[91] Moreover, it was McGrath's second job. She arrived there from waitressing at Durgin Park, already tired, and worked until midnight among the strange men who lodged and boarded, vulnerable and alone.

McGrath described herself as "without family and home," though she lived with two of her sisters, having left an unhappy situation with her brother's family. And sure enough, lonely, and bereft of parents, McGrath struck up a friendship with a male customer. Together they rented a room for three years, while retaining separate lodgings. But what scandalized McGrath's family was not her keeping company with an unmarried man in a loft every evening while he worked his second-hand printing press and she sewed or entertained friends, but her elopement with him and their marriage outside the Catholic Church, after his business became established.[92]

McGrath's narrative gives no indication that she saw herself morally endangered or even on morally questionable turf at any point except the denouement—the precise point at which middle-class and elite narratives would have seen her as finally reaching solid ground, safely married, in a Protestant church no less. For McGrath and her peers, there was nothing inherently morally dangerous in the city's working-class restaurants, streets, and tenements and nothing inherently safe in living with family. In marrying out of the church and by elopement, McGrath had transgressed moral codes of loyalty to family and church. But at no point does she seem to have supposed that in simply keeping company with a man, unchaperoned, she had transgressed sexual codes.[93]

Louise Bosworth found similar clues to working-class moral codes. She found that romances might begin in basement dining rooms, but that acquaintance was seldom carried outside them. Men and women diners, she explained, did not feel obliged to speak on the street.[94] And when she attended her first melodrama at a South End theater in 1908, *Lottie, the Poor Saleslady, or Death before Dishonor,* she wrote her mother, "It was lovely. . . . I observed . . . what I have heard—that the lower type of audience the more pathetically applaud the high moral sentiments."

The theaters that showed such plays as *Death before Dishonor* were favorite haunts of Boston's young working women. Middle-class and elite observers might see them as immoral or at least unmoral, but shop women, restaurant workers, and even domestic workers, preferred going to the theater to going dancing, walking, cycling, on trolley rides, or excursions, in more or less that order.[95]

Theaters differed considerably. The South End theaters played a mix of variety shows (which went on all afternoon and into the evening), and plays and ballets, some vulgar, some meeting the standards even of the more elite middle-class sightseers.[96] Theater audiences also varied, from immigrant mothers nursing babies to the extremely rough crowd Mary Shea's sister found inhabiting "Niggers' heaven," as the second balcony at the Harvard Athenaeum was called. Demonstrating the racialized as well as classed and gendered nature of Boston's leisure spaces, when Shea's sister ventured up she found white men but "no ladies there—men spit down from balcony on to audience which apparently inconvenienced the ladies (and their bonnets) below."[97]

At her theater, Bosworth found an "audience of shop-girls and cheap 'sports.' " "When Lottie scorned the proposal of her villanous employer with a wild [cry] of 'No, Never! Death before Dishonor,' " she wrote her mother, "they stomped and whistled approvingly. And when she escaped unscathed from the gambling den of 'the woman in red' whither she had been lured by 'the woman' disguised in brown, they went quite crazy with joy. It was very exciting with the villain shot by the hero in the last act and still kicking when the curtain descended."[98]

The geography of moral danger in *Death before Dishonor* struck a familiar note for its audience. Gambling dens littered the major routes to work, and workplace sexual harassment was part of daily life. In the melodrama, the predatory male was the boss, not the coworker or lodging house neighbor. The heroine, like the independent women of Foster's fiction, survived "unscathed." Protection, such as it was, came from peers, not patrons or matrons.[99]

While workers applauded *Death before Dishonor,* in the daily discussions of working-class women and men the prescriptions were less clear. In 1893, Lucinda Prince went from Denison House to visit a young woman named Jenny on nearby Dover Street. Jenny was unmarried and pregnant, and Jenny's mother was "heart-broken over Jenny's condition." She talked in an offhand way until Jenny left the room, and "then broke down completely." Prince found her, "a capable, bright woman, overworked & not very well. She is determined to have Jenny married to the man before the baby is born, but she does not want Jenny to live with him afterwards. J. does not care for him, & the mother thinks his is the blame—Unfortunately there is not confidence between mother & daughter."

The mother could get Jenny to speak of the issue at all only "in a joking way." Prince herself made no prescription, but recorded two days later the advice of a visitor to Denison House, Miss Lillian Clarke: "She does not advise Jenny's marriage unless it means living together afterward. The man as her husband could give her much trouble. Miss Clarke's experience has shown her that girls in Jenny's condition, unmarried, living right lives afterwards, have a better chance of marrying respectable men and of leading happier lives."[100]

Death before Dishonor may have been the ideal, but in the reality of working girls' lives, one "mistake," while a matter of grave concern and even a tragedy to parents, did not a fallen woman make, provided, of course, it was not repeated and that the woman had familial support. How Jenny viewed the matter is unclear, except in her resistance to marrying the father of her child, which argues a certain degree of confidence that no marriage was better than that marriage and that her future did not require the marriage—whether because "respectability" at all was unnecessary in her eyes or because her future "respectability" did not hinge on being married at the birth of her first child. Like the ruined woman in Foster's fiction, Jenny lived with her mother; unlike the woman in Foster's fiction, she did not die to pay for her sins.

New Women

There was another set of working women, those for whom the term "New Women" was invented. Usually single and from white, recognizably middle-class backgrounds, sometimes having fallen on hard times, these were the women, who might take up residence at Denison House and seek music pupils or who had to invent some other place for themselves, as the creators of Denison House had, in the city. At times they invented careers, as they invented social work.[101] At times they were self-conscious both about the creation of careers and about the creation of a kind of female utopian urban space. Like the creators of Denison House, if they succeeded, it was often because they found more elite, moneyed women to fund their ambitions.

The younger generation of these women could trod paths already created: get jobs as social investigators for urban bureaus of philanthropic organizations (Bosworth found "lots of Wellesley people here [in the WEIU], a regular hot-bed, so it seems quite home-like"), adopt the more sexually expressive mores that had long been common among working-class women. The older generation, those born in the 1870s, like the founders of Denison House, opted for a more homosocial world that left their reputations intact, but still let them enter a public realm.[102] They became part of the new professional and managerial middle class. They took as their life's work Jane Addams's social housekeeping—creating order and stability in a city where they saw chaos—but simultaneously, by their very existence as self-supporting women in often invented professions, they were among those destabilizing forces. In Vida Scudder's Boston settlement house novel, two of the residents went to live in communal experiments with women of the same neighborhood, one went to join an anarchist press in Colorado, and only one married.[103] Such characters were not only fictional. Miss Cora Stewart, friend of a Denison House resident, came to the house in search of a neighborhood studio for her china painting in 1893. She wanted to be near the depot and a kiln, and "would like to be in house with girls, working girls."[104]

These were not would-be matrons. As Polly Kaufman has written, they created a "new kind of family unconnected by ties of kinship"; they lived together in "Boston marriages" (pairs) or in groups of self-supporting women, like the young women they often studied or for whom they ran clubs and services.[105] By claiming for themselves the right to define when society was healthy, claiming new sorts of legitimacy and authority for women (college education) and claiming access to a newly redefined "professional" status, these women shaped a world in which they played not the marginalized part of "spinster aunt," but a key role as social arbiter/social glue. They were more than the public face of private womanhood implied by the term "social housekeeping." They were often at odds with those they called "matrons" or "club women" in their analysis of social good. They were a new brand of middle-class womanhood.

Their increasing assurance made many of them less easily cowed than the young intern Louise Bosworth, whose response to conflicting assertions was to doubt the efficacy of her own evidence.[106] In 1914, the male Boston Overseers of the Poor complained about just such assurance in their annual report. The visitation of cases, they asserted, had been committed by the state board to "a group of comparatively inexperienced young women, appointed without civil service exam. These young women were very positive in their statements of the conditions and needs of the families visited and were upheld as a rule by the State Board, even when opposed by the judgment of experienced overseers of the poor. . . . it seems especially unfortunate that proper consideration should not be given to the opinions of experienced men of mature years," the overseers somewhat peevishly concluded.[107]

New women were also workers, usually on meager wages, as Louise Bosworth was, and they had to negotiate the status shifts that often entailed. Bosworth wrote to her mother that with her $9.61 fellowship a week (this in a study that would determine $9.00 as a living wage), "at the present high rates of board, rooms and everything is a problem. I must get a cheaper room." She sought one of those $1.50 to $2.00 rooms and tried to skimp on meals, allowing twenty cents for breakfast, fifteen for lunch, and thirty for dinner, "but so far I have been too hungry for that and even with breakfasting on fruit and crackers in my room and having no dessert I need plenty of what I do have." "I think I must room somewhere," she concluded, "where I don't have to pay car-fare."[108] In November, after explaining to her mother that she could not possibly afford to come home for Christmas, at a cost of thirty-five dollars each way, she declared, "Living is high and anyone who lives on less than I am getting doesn't have enough."[109]

Working as a single, self-supporting woman, even of professional status, quickly reduced the dramatic distance between Bosworth's life as a member of a male-supported, middle-class household and the lives of the working-class women she studied. "I think that it is good training for me," she confessed to her mother. "As Papa never gave me an allowance I don't know the first thing about planning and managing money." The hardest task, she found, was doing laundry after tramping the streets investigating the lives of working-class women, "But there too I never washed a thing in my life. . . . Working girls have to do that." At college, laundry had been among her greatest expenses.[110]

She slowly grew more adept at managing her money. In October, her expenses included candy, magazines, peanuts, cider, and church, and in November she gave fifty cents to a woman in Boston's Public Garden and spent a dollar to see Isadora Duncan.[111] In December, she spent her mornings posing at the art museum, perhaps to raise more money, and crowded her investigative work into the afternoons and evenings. Finally, in April 1908, she reported that she was living very comfortably on her $9.61 "now that I know how." She had saved enough for a new suit, not pretty but good and serviceable and had half a dozen shirtwaists made up for her by Mollie Stepanski in the North End for fifty cents each. "Isn't that pretty good for the living wage?" she queried.[112]

Women like Bosworth did not become "working-class," even when they earned the same wages. They were not in the same relation to production, having joined the men in the new managerial class. But also, they resisted that definition by themselves participating in defining who would be "working-girls" in their investigations and their interactions. Despite the ongoing relations she developed with the girls in her clubs, Edith Guerrier always expected to be called "Miss Guerrier" by them. She was well aware of the slim margins that separated her from them and rejected the impulse of "doing good." Impoverished when she ran her first settlement house club, she later thought perhaps she had been seeking "self respect by assuming a position of authority toward those who were supposedly worse off than I was." She shifted instead to work at a library clubhouse because it seemed a place where she could work together with—instead of supervise—young women. But simply having the choice between benefactor or collaborator placed her in a different position from them.[113]

They also chose careers that accorded ill with most working-class women's notion of a good job. When Denison House resident C. M. Dresser told Mrs. Connelly, with whom she was visiting, that she was "living in the neighborhood and hoped to find work to do very soon, perhaps some music pupils" in this rather impoverished part of the South End, Connelly, familiar with the struggle to earn a living and now ill and supported by her working children, "seemed interested and suggested that she knew of a position as a seamstress that I might be able to obtain." Dresser's rejection of Connelly's helpful suggestion (one Denison House residents routinely offered their neighbors) required an explanation that appeared to leave neither confident that she understood the other. "When I said I didn't sew well," Dresser recorded, "and had spent some time in studying music and therefore it would be better for me to do the latter, she said, 'yes, perhaps it would be'."[114]

The women of Denison House were all professionals who earned to support themselves, according to the original model of the settlement house. When the house was founded, the profession of "social worker" had not yet been invented, so the residents tended to be music teachers, college professors, artists, and so forth. Often, but not always, they had some small inheritance or other income that supplemented their salaries or wages. Such organizations began to offer more paying positions, but women like Louise Bosworth occasionally found that philanthropic organizations could not pay them a living wage. Marie Gullet explained her rejection of an offer as assistant head worker at the house, "It has always been a great joy to me to be one of the workers [i.e., resident but with salaried position elsewhere] of Denison House, but unfortunately, I am dependent upon my salary and cannot easily afford to accept."[115]

In any case, some young women rejected the life they saw their older counterparts living. Bosworth, impressed with the WEIU leaders' energy, power, and initiative, was less enchanted with their domestic life: "the Union is full of married women who seem to need some interest in life. . . . There is Mrs Moran superintendent of the lunch room. Her husband hardly sees her, it seems to me. On the first of May she goes to Squantum and lives with Miss Parton until December. She is very

In this futuristic cartoon, a female orchestra serenades lonely men. A letter from Jones Sisters, Attorneys at Law, lies on the ground. *Boston Globe*, August 11, 1895.

attractive and nice but I feel sorry for Dr Moran. Then Mrs Prince is forever busy and can't see her husband very much, the same is true of Mrs Young, Mrs Lincoln & loads of others up to Mrs Mary Morton Kehew the president. All these husbands are mere names to me. I have never seen some of them. I don't see the point in being married."[116]

Many of Boston's most active social reform women agreed. They abjured heterosexual marriage, often for deeply passionate lifelong partnerships with women. So common were such relationships that they became known as "Boston marriages." Several of the founders of Denison House ultimately engaged in Boston marriages, including Vida Scudder and Florence Converse, and Katherine Coman and Katherine Lee Bates. Hardly limited to Denison House and Wellesley, such partnerships included literary hostess and social reformer Annie Fields, who after her husband's death, set up housekeeping with author Sarah Orne Jewett, and there were many others. Such relationships meshed better with women's reform activities than the traditional marriage would have. They formed the domestic equivalent of the settlement house as an institution.[117] Just as younger women like Bosworth and her peers nurtured each other in hard times by putting on bloomers and going to the Municipal Gymn when depressed or by taking each other shopping or for meals and as as the working-girl roommates did by the intimate humanity of their relations, these women sustained each other at the same time they redefined and rearranged the connections between private and public lives and networks.[118]

Edith Guerrier epitomized these developments. She had come to Boston in 1891 in her late teens, well educated and needing to support herself and to find stability.[119] She worked as an aid to nursery schools supported by Pauline Agassiz Shaw, then conducted girls' clubs in several settlement houses, also supported by Shaw, maintained a reading room and Boston Public Library station at one of the settlement houses in the North End, and launched a career in librarianship.

Librarianship was still a new field for women, one that attracted upwardly mobile daughters of Irish Americans, like Marion Agnes McCarthy, as well as daughters of declining gentry like Guerrier. The disparity between their career trajectories, however, demonstrates the difference their class/ethnic origins made to these New Women. In 1900, at the age of twenty-three, McCarthy appeared in the manuscript census as living with her parents at 17 Minot Street, the only Irish American family on a Russian Jewish block. Marion was the eldest of four living children. Her father worked as a night watchman at the public library where she had worked as a clerk since 1895—a year in which Boston's Central Labor Union touched on the issue of "the low salaries paid the library employees." A brother, age twenty-one, was a drummer for a chemical company, the other, only sixteen, an errand boy at a "gents furnishings" store. Her youngest sister was still in school, and they shared their lodgings with a thirty-seven-year-old New England boarder who clerked at a wholesale grocery store. Thus far in the story, there is little to distinguish McCarthy from other working girls of her ethnicity heading into clerical jobs, little to place her nearer to Guerrier.

After thirty-nine years, McCarthy was still single, now living in Ward 21 at 92 Corey Road. She had no dependents and lived with her sister. Unlike the middle-class women who became professionals, Marion McCarthy had no high school. She had, however, taken various courses of college grade to further her career, beginning in 1918 with a university extension course on personal and business efficiency. Other courses she took over the following two decades included current history, English composition, American literature, modern Continental writers, the classics, psychiatry, and economics. In addition, beginning in 1919, she had taken Boston Public Library courses in bookbinding and repair, the history of the book, modern librarians and methods, fine and rare books, and reading under guidance. By July 1939, she was in charge of branch binding. She directed office assistants and traveling menders, and visited branches to check on the condition of their books. Her salary had reached $2,086.80 per year. She worked a thirty-seven and three-quarters-hour week and enjoyed twenty-four vacation days a year.[120]

Although McCarthy had risen within the system by taking courses after working at the library for over twenty years, the future must have looked less rosy earlier. Despite the status of the work and the education required, the average Boston Public Library worker in 1912 earned only eight dollars per week, below Bosworth's minimum living wage. With skill and some advanced education, workers could rise to twelve dollars to fifteen dollars per week. On such wages, innovation required outside capital and patronage, a route more open to a middle-class woman like Guerrier than to an Irish American woman with working-class roots like McCarthy.

Guerrier found a patron in Helen Osborne Storrow, a founder of the Women's City Club, a board member of one of Guerrier's settlement houses, and the wife of lawyer and Brahmin politician James Jackson Storrow. She donated the money and used her connections to create the branch library that Guerrier, the first woman supervisor of a branch library, directed.[121]

Like the women at Denison House, Guerrier was interested in reimagining urban industrial space for women. Influenced by the arts-and-crafts movement of John Ruskin and William Morris, she and her life partner, artist Edith Brown, decided to open a pottery that would provide a new model of industrial relations. They turned, again, to Storrow. In 1908 she bought them a building on Hull Street in the North End for a library, clubs, and the pottery, and in 1915 backed them in building a two-story pottery and residence in Brighton, near the Commonwealth Avenue streetcar line. By the time the pottery closed at the beginning of World War II, they had employed 200 women, providing an eight hour day, a woman who read to the other worker, and $10 per week. They sold their wares to Storrow's acquaintances and through a shop set up by one of Guerrier's girls' clubs downtown.[122]

With the advantages the cultural capital of their race/ethnicity and class gave them, Guerrier and Brown had been able to create a utopian urban space of which working girls—even the upwardly mobile McCarthy—could only dream. Unlike when middle-class and elite women took up the ideas of working girls to create cooperative housing, their sponsor imposed little or no supervision on them. Despite their own lack of financial capital, they, like the women of Denison House, could begin to create a new city.[123]

No matter how well educated, black New Women in Boston found discrimination closed many of these paths to them. They needed patronage not to create utopian spaces but simply to get hired in schools, libraries, and offices.[124] Prospective employers refused them outright, offered them domestic service jobs, or propositioned them. Pauline Hopkins, daughter of a Civil War veteran and descendent of the founders of the first black church in New England, needed not only excellent scores on the civil service exam but the recommendations of wealthy, influential Republican men to secure a job as a stenographer in the Massachusetts Bureau of Statistics.[125] Black New Women could revise Boston's black social scene as a "smart set," continue the work of uplift, and occasionally find work in the new Robert Gould Shaw settlement house built to serve blacks, but most either found themselves working in jobs for which their education was needless or taking an entrepreneurial turn.[126]

They lectured for fees to white and black audiences, as did Josephine St. Pierre Ruffin and Mary Wilson; taught music lessons or drama, as did Maud Cuney Hare; edited journals they helped create, as did Ruffin and Hopkins, or put together a more eclectic mix of occupations. Less often single than the white New Women, they sometimes worked during their marriages and other times only in their widowhood. As extraordinary as she was, Maud Cravath Simpson, in the structure of her life, was typical of black new womanhood.

Cravath Simpson had come to Boston in 1882, six years after graduating from high school in Rhode Island and two years after she had fallen in love at first sight with her husband. She trained as a contralto singer for seven years, making her debut as the first trained black contralto in 1891, and met with much success, culminating in a performance at Madison Square Garden. In Boston, she helped organize the Woman's Era Club and served as secretary for fourteen consecutive years, helped William Monroe Trotter organize the Equal Rights League, served as an original corporation member of Harriet Tubman House, organized the Massachusetts State Union of black women's clubs, serving as its first president, helped organize the Northeastern Federation of Colored Women's Clubs, chairing its antilynching committee, and was active in the Grand Army of the Republic ladies auxiliary. Despite all this activity and though she left the singing profession in 1895, she continued to earn. She not only had a public-speaking career, encouraged by her husband (who did the dishes and housework when she needed to write a speech), but by 1911 was advertising her services as a chiropodist trained at the Boston College of Chiropody, also offering manicuring, facial massage, shampooing, and general hair care.[127]

Unlike Guerrier, Simpson had no access to a patron like Storrow, and unlike McCarthy or Hopkins, she could not get skilled public sector employment. Simpson had turned to entrepreneurship to make her way, without ceasing her untiring work to remake the racial as well as sexual moral geography of Boston and society at large, to make it safe for black women as well as men to take their place in public.

Singer, clubwoman, civil rights activist, and chiropodist, Mrs. (sometimes referred to as Dr.) Maud Cravath Simpson remained publicly active for over half a century. *Boston Guardian*, July 29, 1939.

Reorienting the Moral City

All of these women participated in defining a new urban morality for women that did not require cloistering, but required reorganizing space and the meaning of space. Guerrier, McCarthy, and Simpson all worked to make room, literally, for women in the professions.

Like working-class matrons, working girls and New Women valued independence over protection, but many of them valued independence from family as well as from employers and elites.[128] The New Women, like the working girls "adrift," were part of the new urban scene, and their moral geography, like that of the working girls, was not just about a sexual and racialized moral order, but about the morality of human/ market relations.

When they could, working girls created spaces suited to their own moral geography—rooming and domestic situations where they could protect each other and themselves. The physical layout, with eating places distinct from living places, suited their needs, faced as they were with often irregular work and low wages, while wanting freedom from the restraints of a male-dominated family without isolation. That they now bought meals and domestic space on the market did not mean all their human relations were market driven. For the working girl, lodging and boardinghouses, restaurants, and workplaces were sites that simultaneously manifested and created community ties that enhanced their safety. The workplace and the streets were indeed morally liminal and dangerous to them, as they were to Lottie in *Death before Dishonor,* but in their view, independent young women had the tools to participate in them safely and were able to protect and assert themselves better than more dependent girls could be protected by others.

Distinctly peer oriented, they created their own notions of mutuality, sharing laundry, food, hair-dressing tips, and work. Parents, in their view, seemed ill-equipped, or perhaps simply irrelevant, for dealing with their peer-oriented world of work and leisure. Supervisory elites were confining and demeaning. If she wanted to live in public, the working girl felt safest surrounded by her peers.

4
The Business of Women

Petty Entrepreneurs

Edith Guerrier's utopian pottery venture had thrust her into the world of petty entrepreneurship. Like the heroine of Louisa May Alcott's *Work*, set in Boston almost half a century earlier, she hoped to redesign business relations as human relations.[1] Most businesswomen set their sights lower. They left the larger picture of commercial relations alone, but redesigned their own spaces. Well into the twentieth century, the majority of these women, like Guerrier, combined home and business. By doing so, they hoped to turn homes—associated with female economic dependence—into sites of not only social but economic autonomy.[2] It was the ultimate individual claim of women for autonomous space in the city scene—not just a room of one's own, but a business of one's own.

Female petty entrepreneurs were everywhere in turn-of-the-century century cities, and Boston was no exception. Highly fashionable dressmakers and milliners displayed colorful wares in elegant shops on downtown's Washington and Winter Streets; less ambitious needlewomen spread their wares in North, South, and West End shops or operated out of modest rooms. By 1900, women headed more than half the lodging and boarding houses that ringed the commercial center. They comprised as many as a fifth of Boston's grocers and dry goods dealers, a third of its fancy goods dealers and employment agency owners, half its variety shop owners, virtually all its milliners and dressmakers, and owned smaller numbers of Boston's bakery and confectionary shops, restaurants, clothing stores, and other businesses.[3] In addition, women professionals in healing and teaching opened their own schools, free-lanced music and art lessons, offered homeopathic care, acted as Christian Science practitioners in independent offices, or set up small maternity hospitals as paying concerns.[4]

To many working girls, struggling New Women, and overworked wives, self-employment was the ultimate desideratum. While at any given moment only a small proportion of Boston's working women were proprietors, a much larger proportion made the attempt at some point in their lives. Working women had a keen sense of career ladders. Even in domestic service, if one had the right chance or could spare time and money for training, one could become a highly paid cook rather than a lowly general houseworker.[5] In store work, though most employees worked as cash girls when very young and saleswomen when older, a few became superintendents of daily operations and policy making, and a number became buyers.[6] From these heights, the leap to entrepreneurship was possible. Cooks began catering businesses, and women who had worked for Jordan Marsh or R. H. Stearns for a decade or more set out on their own.[7]

But the greatest lure were the needle trades. In 1903/4 the WEIU reported its evening dressmaking and millinery classes filled with young women in domestic service and its morning classes with those who, after leaving school or college, could not find work.[8] Garment workers, who only learned to make pieces and never the whole garment at the factory, eagerly signed up for dressmaking classes not only at the WEIU, but at Wells Memorial and working-girls clubs. They even created their own, as when in 1891/92 working girls in suburban Boston rented a room and hired the WEIU teacher, convinced they could get enough custom work after their lessons to pay the expenses.[9] Not only former domestic servants but better-off women such as Miss Davis's sister—Davis taught at the public school opposite Denison House—were proud to ply their trade as dressmakers.[10]

In 1890/91, the WEIU *Annual Report* remarked of the wide variety of pupils in its dressmaking and millinery classes, "At present there seems to be no element of caste."[11] Not everyone, however, had equal access to the dream. Even in fields with low costs of entry, such as dressmaking, many could not afford to serve an apprenticeship. Contrary to popular opinion, these were not skills women learned at mother's knee.[12] Dressmakers demanded apprentices serve three months to two years, usually without pay, and milliners at least two seasons. Families with steadily employed skilled or petty bourgeois fathers, husbands, or siblings, proved surprisingly supportive of women's ventures. R. G. Dun's credit records are full of family start-up loans. But about half the apprentices left the business, wanting or needing to earn more money sooner.[13] Visiting the Fitzgeralds in 1893, Denison House residents found the mother just up from an illness, unable to go out but ready to take in washing, and the daughter who cared for her earning by sewing. The daughter wanted to learn dressmaking, they reported, "but can hardly afford to serve her time."[14]

For these reasons, entrepreneurship, by and large, was not an option for the very young. Most working women did not have fathers, brothers, sisters, husbands, or mothers who could provide backing. The single women would-be capitalists who dominated the needle trades had to work long years at slowly rising pay to save their seed money.[15] They rarely entered self-employment before their thirties. The married women who dominated the neighborhood shops were also older. They usually became sole proprietors only in widowhood.[16]

These patterns changed in slight rather than dramatic ways from 1870 to 1940. The proportion of women running businesses out of their homes, for example, steadily declined from just under three-quarters in 1870 to just over half in 1920. And while ready-made shirtwaists, simpler styles, and large department store workshops undermined independent dressmaking and millinery beginning in the 1890s, independent beauty shops vastly increased.[17] What remained were the underlying structure of female entrepreneurship, the sex-segregated nature of most petty entrepreneur fields, and the marginality of women in business. There was not even a language to describe them, as by the 1910s and 1920s the term "businesswoman" meant a stenographer, typist, or clerk, not a petty entrepreneur.

Amelia Baldwin

Amelia Baldwin, an interior decorator, lived from 1876 to 1960, covering almost the whole span of the period under discussion. Her pro-

This portrait of Amelia Muir Baldwin, dashingly dressed, dates from the period of her interior decorating shop. Schlesinger Library, Radcliffe College.

fession rendered her unusually articulate about space, and her rare collection of papers provides us with insights as to the tensions, dynamics, and vulnerability of the business of women. No women and only two men were listed in the 1870 *Boston City Directory* as interior decorators, and even in 1920 only seventeen firms, all male, appeared. All of the five women in the field that year, including Baldwin, were among the eighty firms listed under simply "Decorators." By 1930, Baldwin was one of twenty-one women listed among approximately 110 interior decorators.[18]

While Baldwin's profession made her atypical, her lower middle-class roots were less unusual. Her father was a small businessman. The family fell on hard times, and though her uncle was, at the time of her birth, president of the YMCA in Boston, he seems never to have provided any aid.[19]

In high school in the 1890s, Baldwin's peers, with whom she had close and affectionate relations, saw her as bossy, diligent, and ambitious for an artistic and social career. They wrote her a verse proclaiming, "She's gone in for erudition and she's got it mighty bad./ She's got the *Transcript* [Boston's society newspaper] habit and the social circle fad."[20] After high school, amidst the 1890s depression, a long silence falls over Baldwin's records, a silence that represents her period of frustrated aspirations. She worked at plebian jobs, taking commercial courses at Simmons, doing clerical work, which she clearly despised, and finally taking courses as a special student at Radcliffe, which enabled her to lay claim to that institution as her own.[21]

She emerges from this period, in her own records, only when she has become a successful interior decorator. Like many of her female entrepreneurial peers, it was in her late thirties that she gained her own shop. By this time she also had connections to the elite Massachusetts Woman Suffrage Association through the highly visible suffrage bazaars she designed for them from 1913 through 1917 at Boston's Copley Hotel. For Baldwin, the significance of suffrage seemed less its potential empowering of a female political bloc than its connection with society women, the people with whom she sought to identify. Her suffrage bazaars received notice (with attribution) in the society pages of the *Boston Transcript*, achieving all her youthful aspirations. To her, this, too, was empowering.[22]

The scale of her triumph in achieving her own shop is revealed in part by a 1909/10 study conducted for the WEIU's Vocational Guidance Bureau. Though the WEIU investigator insisted repeatedly that interior decorating was "woman's work," her view did not prevail in the city. There was no formal training available in Boston, and openings for women in established firms were almost as rare as training. Once in business, women decorators complained that the wholesalers and importers, almost entirely male, never kept them informed about the condition of their stock.[23]

What saved the women decorators, as it did Guerrier and many female entrepreneurs, was elite patronage, largely female. The three women the WEIU investigator interviewed who had succeeded, like Baldwin, in entering the field, all had the benefit of elite connections. Miss Celeste Weed Allbright had half a dozen years of art training, but was only able to begin work because several women "were interested in her," including Mrs. Alice Freeman Palmer, president of Wellesley College, under whose patronage she had rented a studio, sent out cards, and gave talks that generated business. Misses Harlow and Howland also ran a small firm, based on Harlow's art history knowledge and, undoubtedly, Howland's Radcliffe connections. Despite their lack of experience, they had many large orders as soon as they opened.[24]

But elite patronage could not rescue them from the vicissitudes of war. World War I brought an end to Baldwin's promising start, and, ever resourceful, she closed up shop and applied for war work. During the war, she worked under Dr. James Ford, professor of social ethics at Harvard and division manager of housing work, for which she was paid between $1,600 and $1,800 a year as the only woman field agent.[25]

By the war's end, she had come to favor more government action in housing and registration of rooms for women during peace as well as war. Indeed, she seemed about to launch herself into a classic Progressive female career. Such careers in social reform, though they drew largely by this time on college-educated middle-class women, also proved unusually open to intrusions by other groups, usually labor union women with reformer connections, of whom Mary Anderson is perhaps the best-known example. For an upwardly mobile woman like Baldwin, such a career provided middle-class and even elite identification and society. On the heels of her investigation into safe living space for working women and with her new credentials in social welfare, Baldwin endured an extremely brief stint working for Russell Sage investigating recreational space in New York.[26]

Baldwin soon reverted to type, however. She rejected the altruistic career in favor of a more individualist one. She wanted her own space, her own studio, and her own business, and she returned to Boston. There she picked up a position in the Statistics Department of the National Industrial Conference Board at 15 Beacon Street while she prepared to reopen her business.[27]

Her tie with the Industrial Conference Board tempted her to give full rein to her ambitions to redesign the world from the inside out, combining what she had learned in her recent stint in social welfare with her decorating training, in short, combining social engineering with drafting.

Like other decorators and architectures in the 1920s, Baldwin believed that interior decoration could create harmony between the forces and pace of the outside world and the self.[28] She considered interior decoration a form of expression comparable to writing, expressing the "emotions which have grown out of the instinct for shelter." Her sensibility was modern: "the more abstract a design is, the more restful it is." She lauded the "beauties which reside in efficiency."[29] But she cautioned against shaking off traditions altogether, favoring a creative transformation of them in line with order and beauty, logic and emotion.

She hoped, in 1919, "to improve the interior of factories," to harmonize the physical surroundings with the conditions of work and the desired mentality of the employees, a sort of artistic version of social control. Such a transformation would be effected "not by window boxes or colored prints, but by emphasizing structural parts of the building and natural articulations made by processes of work, using colors inducing moods desired." The aim in particular, for Baldwin and other like thinkers, was to make the factory a more enticing place for women workers, just as through this planning, Baldwin was aggressively seeking a shaping place for herself in the male-dominated world of industrial entrepreneurs.[30]

She found, however, that factory owners were less than interested in such experiments.[31] They were afraid her colors would be expensive; that grey, white, and black would get tiresome; and afraid, period, of the "very light greens." Perhaps, they suggested, it would be better to leave the doors mahogany.[32] Baldwin found them "rather hopeless in the matter of receiving new ideas." Though she still insisted that "an artist has something to contribute to our present industrial problems," this episode seems to have ended her personal attempt to blend social work and entrepreneurship.[33]

She brooked no such hindrance in the creation of her studio, on fashionable River Street, the margin between the Back Bay and Beacon Hill. Thrilled to have her own space to design and control, she spent over $2,000 on improvements before moving in.[34] She redid the place inside and out, apologizing for changing her mind so often on the exterior, as it was her "first garden." Women's historians have long realized how important space has been to women on this personal level; space dedicated to women as their own for their own ends, after all, was absent in the conventional home of the period.[35] Interior decorators had a particular need to fit their studios beautifully, to impress their clients with their taste.[36] But this sense of exultation in spatial autonomy (not only Baldwin's interior but her garden) must have been common among women petty entrepreneurs, who worked so hard and took such risks to achieve an autonomous space.

The industry, however, had gotten no friendlier to women. In 1923, a Miss Morse, a Smith graduate (class of 1892), was the only interior decorator in Boston "holding partnership with men." "Women as a rule," one interviewee for a second WEIU study indicated, "can do better in a firm of women or by going into business for themselves." And a Miss Sacker, whose shop was reputed the best in Boston, explained that successful decorators still had to do extracurricular activities—voluntarily staging philanthropic plays, and so forth, like Baldwin's suffrage pageants—to meet potential clients.[37]

Baldwin took all these steps, but there was trouble ahead. Harlow and Howland, still in business, complained that conditions had declined steadily since 1917, with Boston's deteriorating status as a port hurting their access to imported goods and the Chamber of Commerce's ruling against retail houses giving discounts to decorators hurting their profit margins. When the Paine Furniture Company practically shut them out of buying, the partners found themselves forced to take on the higher and riskier overhead of keeping their own stock.[38]

In such conditions, fiscal conservatism seemed a good policy. But though Baldwin had grown up in a household that maintained meticulous monthly accounts, including such items as tobacco and cigars, carfares, paper, magazines, and ice, as well as clothing, rent, medicine, and provisions, she clearly never learned the art.[39] Apparently her spending in the creation of her own space resulted in bankruptcy at the outset, in 1921.[40] Though she admitted that her financial troubles dated back to the war, she claimed the current mess was unforeseen. She fell victim to her own ambition as well as the 1921/22 recession and the changing terms of trade.

It is through Baldwin's financial troubles, which continued ever after, that we glimpse the strategies and contests over power and position that formed part of daily life for women who wanted to break conventional bounds without rebelling against conventional ideologies and who had entered an arena where they had little direct access to instruments of power: credit or wealth. Particularly for Baldwin, from white Yankee petty bourgeois roots with social aspirations, a conventional language of genteel femininity became not a hindrance but a tool to deploy selectively both for staying in business and for maintaining status.

Baldwin's contracting tended to be informal and couched in a language of personal rather than business relations. In a bill dispute with her architect, each side made claims based on what the other had "said" rather than written, and Baldwin claimed that only the desire to be "courteous" had made her place incidental contracting through his office. To Frank Bourne, the architect, such a word ("courteous") was inappropriate; labor was labor and a bill a bill, not a question of manners or favors.[41]

The bankruptcy proceedings also brought Baldwin into conflict with her new landlady, like herself an unmarried petty entrepreneur. The landlady, Miss Rebecca R. Joslin, relied on her rents. Unlike Mr. Bourne, Miss Joslin's correspondence was framed in the same terms as Baldwin's. She set the rent high in return for paying for more improvements in order to feel she could evict Baldwin if need should occur, and still, in her words, be "fair."[42] In response, Baldwin wrote a male friend that Joslin was "one of the old fashioned type of landlord, who does as little as possible for her tenants" and still charged top prices for rent.[43] But Baldwin used a different language in her business dealings with Joslin. When dunned for her rent, Baldwin was "hurt."[44] When Joslin finally had her lawyer send an eviction notice, in January of 1922, Baldwin admitted that Joslin herself had remained very pleasant. Joslin, unlike Bourne, used the same language Baldwin did. Her language to Baldwin was unfailingly maternal and conciliatory. "I have been very lenient" she wrote, "because we have both had mutual troubles on which to sympathize."[45] When the time for lenience had gone, a few weeks later, Joslin wrote, "My dear Miss Baldwin, . . . you force me to do most disagreeable things!"[46] This personal and maternal rather than commercial language between the two women rarely if ever referred to their respective, hard-nosed instructions to their lawyers.

Though the immediate crisis of the postwar depression passed, the later correspondence was full of letters from Joslin demanding rent and excuses from Baldwin. In 1925 came another eviction notice, and another in 1926, neither of which resulted in Baldwin's ouster. By 1928 Baldwin was eight months behind in the rent. With the onset of the Great Depression, Joslin and Baldwin's relationship hit a new low. By 1930 Baldwin was eleven months behind. She asked for a retroactive reduction in rent. Joslin explained that she, too, had been hard hit by the Depression and yet all her bills were paid promptly and she never charged Baldwin interest on back rent. In May of 1933 Baldwin had made no payments for the year. In reminding Baldwin of this fact, Joslin apologized, "Regretting that I am obliged to be so stern, I am," she claimed, "very truly yours."[47]

Faced with another crisis, Baldwin again reminded Joslin of their human relationship: she admitted Joslin's unusual patience, reminded her of her long tenancy and the cumulative rent of about $15,000 over twelve years, hoped that "we might see the depression through together," and told her how the "several times [you] wished me luck . . . lightened the burden on my mind." She was uncertain where she could go if evicted and asked to see Joslin face to face. She could not, she realized, "ask a new landlord to wait for the rent. . . . I did think I could ask you to wait, in view of the long time I have been here." And, "in any case I do not want to have any hard feelings or an interview with a lawyer. I shall have no hard feelings and do not want you to have any."[48] In May of 1934 Joslin finally evicted Baldwin, who owed her in the neighborhood of $4,000.[49] Joslin died, an old woman, later that year.

In order fully to understand this correspondence, it is necessary to look more closely at Baldwin's material reality as well as how she interpreted it in this period. Was Baldwin simply fiscally irresponsible? Thrift was seemingly not one of her virtues. Her bankruptcy case from 1921 reveals that in addition to the $2,000 she spent on the apartment, she had bought four dresses that year, costing over $100 each, and two suits for $150 and $200, in addition to other clothing expenditures. She owed her employees their salaries, ranging from $30 to $200, and for six years had owed almost $500 to one creditor for materials.[50] In a similar fiscal vein, and in the same years, Boston's Society for the Decorative Arts hired Baldwin to make their shop a going concern and then found her so expensive, as she quickly spent twice what they had in mind, that they decided to abandon the enterprise.[51]

Yet Baldwin displayed no inkling that any of this behavior was in the least questionable. Indeed, she later expressed a sense of personal injury when an employee, who by 1934 had worked for Baldwin for ten years, dunned her for back pay.[52] Baldwin retaliated by labeling her "somewhat unbalanced," her favorite code for anyone adamantly insisting on her money. Baldwin supported her judgment by citing the behavior of the former employee who, unconstrained by the gentility Joslin and Baldwin showed one another, had verbally abused Baldwin in the presence of the latter's maid, repeatedly insisting that "labor had to be paid first." By her verbal abuse, particularly in front of the maid, the employee had breached Baldwin's attempt to maintain a status indicated by language and behavior as well as consumption. (Apparently the irony of Baldwin's continuing to employ a maid failed to strike either woman.)

While Baldwin pulled out the excuse that business was bad, she also admitted that she had not paid her employees on time even during good years. Two other employees collected from Baldwin only by trusteeing her bank account, and this one, Grace, threatened to do the same. To Baldwin, such behavior seemed ungrateful. After all, even when hard pressed Baldwin had, purely from a sense of duty, kept Grace on at the same salary of $125/month; she just hadn't paid it. It might appear to some people, she claimed, "that I had done a good deal for Miss Grace, who has had no other permanent position except with me."[53]

It may be that this apparent gross fiscal irresponsibility was a financial strategy of Baldwin's own—a way, with no capital, to maintain a luxury business within the realities of the day. At the same time that she begged her landlady for lenience, she admitted to her unabashedly, indeed as a point in her favor, that she had maintained a payroll of $300 a month in addition to outside or part-time workers, and that all along she had planned to pay what bills she could to keep her credit good and only when none were pressing, pay her landlady everything above her living expenses.[54]

In this context, the female language of affectional bonds takes on an additional significance, as male creditors are paid first. Most businesswomen, like Baldwin, operated in sectors where the employees and customers also were women. They existed largely within a female world, as a female economy with relatively few interfaces with a male economic world apart from occasional visits from tradesmen and suppliers, R. G. Dun investigators, and creditors. The female economy was not without its conflicts, however. On the contrary, what power these women had was shaped in part by the endless contests among them, like those between Baldwin and Joslin. The class-bridging Women's Educational and Industrial Union found that after the largest part of their legal aid bureau's work, getting middle and upper-class women to pay their domestic servants, came the next lump of cases—still almost half the caseload—consisting of women dressmakers dunning women clients and dressmakers' employees struggling to get their wages from their employers.[55] As was typical in this female economy, Baldwin, too, was having trouble collecting her bills from other women.[56] In turn, she had to bring suit against her customers.

But this contest must be seen in a context of general relative economic powerlessness, and as has often been said of academia, the battle was so heated because the stakes were so small: livelihood to the dressmakers, their employees, and domestic servants, but a pittance to middle-class and elite matrons. In domestic service relations, the silent participant in the discourse over wage disputes was the omnipresent master of the house, ultimate controller of the purse strings. Like the silent actor in domestic service disputes, the men to whom Baldwin owed money were outside of her vision of a female economic language, and they determined her relations and language with those within that female world.[57] Their assumed lesser flexibility and greater power put greater pressure on the economic relations between women. Baldwin's language of personal relations, which made her delinquency more a matter of sisterhood than of power, thus obscured relations of subordination and hierarchy in which she was enmeshed at the very time she wanted to lay claim to independent entrepreneurial status. The affectionate language of these women that purported to put human relations above accounting not only legitimated their place as distinctively middle-class female entrepreneurs by denying that their economic activity rendered them "unwomanly." It also obscured to a certain degree the very lack of the independence they sought.

The marginality of the whole female economy showed clearly in the Dickensian finale to Baldwin's bankruptcy case of 1921: the creditors received nothing as the available funds were eaten up in court costs.[58] Yet in 1934, evicted and in debt, the indomitable Baldwin wrote, "To many people at my age [58] it would seem a total eclipse, but I do not feel that I have not a good many days ahead of me."[59] To Baldwin, as to other women in small business, this reversal was business as usual. It was her age alone that made things worse.

The 1930s and 1940s were long years of struggling to find a job. With amazing persistence, Baldwin tackled one possibility after another, taking training courses to teach Americanization at a settlement house and ship drafting for war work. She found her age worked against her until the labor shortage led Washington to lift the age ceiling for federal war jobs. By 1941 she was sixty-four, and the ceiling was fifty-three. "Some people say I look twenty years younger than I am," she claimed, "I am still vigorous like Winston Churchill, and not quite so old as he."[60]

She lived from pillar to post, moving from River Street to Lime Street, evicted from Lime Street for failure to pay rent, and keeping on the move to avoid creditors. To her horror a creditor found her rooms in 1936, and she moved yet again, this time to Myrtle Street.[61] She saved face and her business by writing her letters and receiving them at the elite Women's Republican Club in the Back Bay, a female refuge, as her actual residence slipped further and further down the back slope of Beacon Hill. Finally she got a job with Arthur D. Little Company in November 1942 making charts for $1,600 a year, the same salary she had made over twenty years earlier, in World War I.

Simultaneously, she moved into Elizabeth Peabody House, a settlement house in the West End, an arrangement facilitated by some of her former female customers. Baldwin served the settlement by teaching Americanization and worked on the sets and costumes for theater productions. Historians have seen settlement houses as the ultimate female refuge in a male city, a female-dominated autonomous world and a launching pad for female activists. But by the 1940s, the settlement seemed a different animal, and ultimately it would fail Baldwin as a last refuge. In 1954, after fourteen years, the settlement house evicted her, now seventy-eight, insisting that the settlement was for professional social workers and academics to study social problems and not a permanent residence for anyone.[62]

As often happened with other female entrepreneurs, throughout her career it was to two men, her lawyer and March Bennett (the only two men she called by their first names), that Baldwin turned in her deepest troubles. Bennett lent her money and gave her mortgages on her merchandise and furniture. It is not clear exactly what her relationship was to these two, other than as old friends. She did pay "Billy," her lawyer, bills as high as $900, but there is no evidence she paid Bennett anything. On the contrary, by 1935 she owed Bennett $6,067.[63]

Baldwin seemed to cultivate no female networks outside her business connections. She did not have the neighborhood networks of small shopkeepers nor the kin networks of domestic women. In seeking autonomy, downtown white women petty entrepreneurs like Baldwin did not create a power base for themselves the way middle-class women did in their clubs and associations or the way matrons, including shopkeepers, did in their neighborhoods. The enterprise itself was individualistic, but female entrepreneurs still strove against that isolation by the language of relationships used in their business correspondence with other women. Baldwin's attempts to humanize relations with Joslin through the language of their business dealings may be seen in the light of trying to extend these commercial bonds to social bonds, as well as attempting to paper over divergences in the roles (business/lady) Baldwin hoped to fill. It may be that Baldwin's language with Joslin helped stave off eviction for twelve years. And, in the end, this female commercial network did come to the rescue: the same woman customer and patron who got her into the settlement house created a job for her doing secretarial work for a philanthropic organization.[64]

The General Case

At first I believed Baldwin, with her wildly expensive wardrobe and her self-serving economics, was unique and even marginal in her sanity as well as in every other way. Yet all surrounding evidence for the period confirms that she is simply the best documented rather than the most bizarre example of women petty entrepreneurs.

Fictional presentations of women in small businesses at the turn of the century tended to depict them as William Dean Howells did, as gentlewomen in distress.[65] As historian Wendy Gamber recently pointed out, such a depiction allowed women's entrepreneurship to look like a last, desperate resort, rather than a choice at odds with the dominant gender ideology. Certainly the number of Civil War widows, women with disabled husbands or fathers, and unwed women in the skewed sex ratio of Boston at the end of the nineteenth century seemed to provide support for the view. The problem was that while widows, divorcees, and even single women may have been working because they had to, nothing said they had to risk capital, leave the hearth, and open their own shops.[66]

There was no question but that small shopkeepers were, even if precariously, middle and lower middle class in status, and as such, should have partaken of the ideology of domesticity that rendered women homebodies, oriented to the private sphere, to be pious, emotional, dependent, and self-sacrificing. Nothing could have been more at odds than the competitive market-oriented, coolly rational, independent, public, and fractious life of a marginal small business.[67] But like Mamie Garvin Fields, who set up a dressmaking shop with two friends after her stint in a garment factory, these women preferred being their own bosses.[68]

When the women who owned or ran shops other than millinery and dressmaking—ranging from the common dry goods, fancy goods, and groceries to restaurants, hardware stores, apothecaries, funeral parlors, newspapers, and "gents" clothing—inherited the business, they stayed there, rarely hiring a male manager even when the business could support it, and if they remarried, they continued to be active in the business operations after marriage.[69] Many, like Mrs. Brest from chapter 1, had probably helped operate the businesses before they inherited them; there were few other ways they could get the training required to run such businesses or the capital to open them. Once in business, some succeeded well enough to pass on the businesses to sons and, rarely, daughters.[70]

The autonomy these widows and matrons sought probably differed from that of which working girls and New Women dreamed. Single female proprietors were more likely than other single women to live alone, aspiring to a comfortable independence.[71] Gamber uncovered a *Demorest's Monthly Magazine* discussion in which the editor of "Talks with Women" admitted, "The fact is, when women have once tasted the charm of an honorable independence achieved by themselves it is very difficult to persuade them to marry."[72] Widowed proprietors, by contrast, often lived with children, even adult children, and married proprietors with husbands and children. They may have sought autonomy not from family, but of family, autonomy from employers, and, among the black female entrepreneurs who joined the Bookerite trade association in Boston, from whites.[73]

The risks were enormous. More often than not, the records for women entrepreneurs in R. G. Dun's credit investigation business closed with the entry "out of business." Reversals could be swift and devastating, as they were for Baldwin. In March 1874, Mrs. Mary E. Saunders, newly widowed, took over her husband's variety store. She was said to be worth about $9,000, owned the house and store where she lived and did her business, and owned the house adjoining, and she cared for her three children. R. G. Dun's investigators labeled her an honest, reliable woman with a snug, safe enterprise. Six months later she was out of business.[74]

While small businessmen also suffered from frequent bankruptcy, they survived, in most trades, at about twice the rate of women. Over one-quarter of all grocers survived from 1900 to 1910, for example, but fewer than 10 percent of women grocers did. Most women's businesses perished far more quickly. A hard-won attempt to open one's own shop might last only a few years. In the 1880s, according to recent studies, women's businesses lasted on average three to six years.[75] Thirty years later, few female bakers could aspire even to that. Of forty-seven female bakers in 1910, only fifteen remained in 1912. Even in sectors women dominated, survival was precarious. In one sample of eighty dressmakers in 1910, only sixteen remained two years later.[76]

The laconic investigators for R. G. Dun recorded one insolvency after another, and a number of women determined simply not to get involved in credit lines even when R. G. Dun rated them as worthy.[77] More often Dun recorded them as "of no account" whether because of their lack of capital or because of untrustworthy relatives. One husband, for example, was uncharitably described as a "dead weight"; another was described as "a serious drawback" and "a poor shiftless husband" of an "honest worthy woman" who "could do well enough, if her husband did not spend it." This woman still managed, in the course of a dozen or so years from 1864 on, to accumulate $12,000; but by 1882 she, too, was out of business.[78]

The R. G. Dun investigators, always men, tended to admire good businesswomen for their sparkle as well as their acumen, and noted their heroic struggles against such odds. Only very occasionally, as when one worthy shopkeeping widow married an expressman and continued in business, did they give equal admiration to the husbands of enterprising wives. Perhaps it too greatly offended their notions of "manliness" that these men's wives were at least as enterprising, if not more so, than their husbands.

That R. G. Dun would recommend little if any credit in most cases said much about the possibilities of these women's businesses. Some women did have family backers, which provided a safety net, or male or female patrons (Baldwin was by no means alone in this) who could take out mortages on stock and expect no rapid repayment; some men similarly turned to female relatives for funding. But among women on their own in uninherited shops, such backing was the exception, not the rule. More often, like Baldwin, after a dozen working years, they had poured their life's savings into the venture. When that nest egg was gone, there was no more.

As women, even in an age of newly minted married women's property laws, they had little access to credit or to capital.[79] Even middle-class women's organizations (see chap. 5) had to create advisory boards of men when they wanted to borrow money to build a building; these women of working and lower middle-class background trying to enter business, without such advisory boards, had limited possibilities for realizing their dreams for expansion or even weathering minor reverses.

Their strategies could differ with their situation. As opposed to dressmakers and milliners, who often served a middle-class or elite female clientele, the women who ran small shops, dry goods stores, groceries, and fancy goods stores, were often of immigrant origin and often had been or were still married.[80] They were less likely to look to elite patrons than to neighbors. Milliners and dressmakers who were immigrants often found it expedient to change their names, from "McCluskey," for example, to "Delavenue," or simply to substitute for the mundane "Miss" or "Mrs.", the Continental "madame."[81] But such shifts would have been counterproductive for dry goods proprietors and grocers, who relied on their commonality with their neighbors for their custom.[82] They relied on face-to-face relations with the neighbors to bring them regular business and to ensure the payment of bills come payday. And their shops became meeting places for women of the neighborhood where they could find their own language spoken.

This dichotomy reflected two distinct types of female petty entrepreneur geography: neighborhood and city center. In the neighborhood shops, despite the continual motion of many working-class residents, moving from tenement to tenement within the neighborhood and as many as half gone within a decade, shopkeepers and customers related to each other not simply on commercial terms but as neighbors, co-ethnics, and often as kin.[83] In the city center, women petty entrepreneurs had commercial relations only, and the networks they created, and their language, as with Baldwin's, differed as a result.

Moreover, businesswomen's social marginality varied with ethnic and racial group and over time. According to evidence in the turn-of-the-century black Boston women's newspaper, *Woman's Era*, for example, at least some black dressmakers and businesswomen belonged to elite black women's clubs as members and officers rather than as employees, unlike their white counterparts. That eclecticism, however, would deteriorate in the 1920s when a critical mass of black college women could make sorority membership the sine qua non of social acceptance in their set.[84] In the 1930s, few black women entrepreneurs, particularly if they had started their enterprises on their own rather than inherited them from brothers and if they had no college, were invited to join the most elite of Boston's black women's associations. Nor were they asked to serve on the boards of Boston's cross-racial agencies. But black businesswomen did serve as officers along with men on the Boston Trade Association, a black equivalent of Boston's white Chamber of Commerce (which did not include women in the same way).[85] They also founded their own social clubs and trade associations, and were acknowledged social leaders in the press.[86] And more established black women's businesses, such as

Mrs. Estelle Forrester's Ancrum School of Music, could successfully rally the support of the neighborhood when bankruptcy threatened.[87]

Women seeking upward mobility along avenues usually considered male, wanted some of the same things society encouraged in men but considered transgressions in women: they wanted autonomy and independence. They risked their all to be independent and gain or maintain middle-class status, leaving behind the workshop and the factory, as well as the kitchen. Baldwin's World War I study of landladies in Boston found that the landladies would have been better off financially if they had worked downtown or in a factory, but the chance to have a home and be independent as to time kept them in the relatively unremunerative business.[88]

While women in business presented a challenge to the orthodox gender ideology, they did not challenge everything. As a recent study pointed out, these women were not necessarily crusaders on behalf of women's rights.[89] Proprietorship offered them a way to improve their status that did not depend on winning the vote. And, after all, most of their work stayed within a recognized female sphere of activity, even when it left the home. As with many of women's professions, women in business served mainly other women in pursuits that could be seen as extensions of the sewing room and the kitchen. In the most common women's businesses—millinery and dressmaking—as with Baldwin's decorating business, the activity was a professionalized version of something women did in the home. And many dressmakers worked by spending a week at the home of their employers.

In a similar way, neighborhood variety and grocery stores functioned like public kitchens in their produce and sociability. Proprietors moved often, but business women and men usually moved, like working-class matrons, within the neighborhood.[90] Localized relations empowered them; it was the neighborhood and kin networks that supported these stores, not some impersonal working out of the invisible hand. Women were chief creators of neighborhoods, and women petty entrepreneurs who stayed in the neighborhood reaped the benefit of the networks they helped to create.

Moreover, it was not just in this sense that the geography of the female economy fit into acceptable patterns that gave women some, but limited, economic autonomy. Until 1930, many if not most women, like Baldwin, operated out of their apartments or homes. Women shopkeepers lived above or across the street from their shops. Women dressmakers and artists often lived in their shops. Such a spatial arrangement of living in the store, on the one hand, blurred distinctions between public and private space in a way that made private space (the parlor/shop) public, but on the other hand, it moved women only into a sort of halfway world, a limbo in their market activity; it moved them into a semipublic space not totally divorced from the home and its associated dependencies or at least associated ideology.

Small businesswomen found the dominant ideology of womanhood provided no vocabulary in which to wage the contest to survive and still be "ladies." This may have mattered little to most working-class employees, like Grace, or to immigrant and neighborhood shopkeepers, but it mattered much to upwardly mobile entrepreneurs like Baldwin, who had to create a new vocabulary to weld an older women's culture of domesticity to a masculine culture of business efficiency, had to create a new language to legitimate simultaneously their activities and their desired status.

The result was a woman's business culture different from that of both the dominant business culture and the dominant middle-class woman's culture. In epistles redolent with the language of nineteenth-century morality and sentimental notions of women's character, women ruthlessly dunned each other or defaulted on bills.

This language, as well as the behavior of women petty entrepreneurs, also reveals a self-conscious female class structure that existed independent of the men to whom women were related, a female class structure largely ignored or hidden in the historical record. Women petty entrepreneurs fit squarely between the wage-working women they wanted to leave behind and the more elite women to whose company they aspired. They found their upwardly mobile path strewn with obstacles. With virtually no access to credit and no resources of their own, women in business survived by their wits when they did survive, and Baldwin's fourteen-year survival is little short of amazing.

Baldwin had worked her way up from a rug shop and clerical work to owning a prestigious decorating and needlecraft shop. As an interior decorator on fashionable River Street, on the margin of Beacon Hill, she dressed the part. Her dresses, her address, her maid, her connection to the elite woman suffrage movement in Boston and to the Women's Republican Club were essential and highly visible badges of status. These badges, in turn, helped sustain not simply her claims to middle-class membership, but her business among an elite clientele. And despite all her reversals, she survived, retaining her shop/apartment and her maid (though not her shop assistant) even through much of the Depression.

These women lived on the precarious margin in every way: the margin of solvency, the margin between classes, and the margin of the business world as petty entrepreneurs. These margins were reflected geographically. Women petty entrepreneurs lived and worked in the public world in a way different from men, from women workers, and from housewives, even though the latter, too, worked "at home." For women, a room of one's own was inherently transgressive and entrepreneurial in that it denied that women's business was to live and make a home for others. These women entrepreneurs' rooms of their own lined the margin between public and private. Their homes and shops often were, as was Baldwin's, the same. Their private life and status were inseparable from their professional standing. The constant onset of eviction proceedings revealed how fragile was the autonomy of these women's spaces. Men's shops may have been little more stable, but men had other spaces—saloons and clubs, for example—and their relation to the home and the streets differed from that of women.

The status, economic and social, which petty entrepreneurship provided for upwardly mobile women was precarious and individual. Businesswomen carved out a unique place for themselves in the city's geographic, economic, and gender structure, as ostensibly autonomous, enterprising, visible women, but that place—as they conceived and lived it—neither gave them security nor challenged the larger framework limiting their aspirations.

5

Learning to Talk More Like a Man

Women's Class-Bridging Organizations

In 1908, Louise Bosworth and her supervisor in the living-wage study went to lunch on Beacon Hill's Chestnut Street, in the "beautiful old house" of WEIU president Mrs. Mary Morton Kehew. Bosworth found the lunch sumptuous, "though just an ordinary business-day one to her," Bosworth wrote her mother, "for we ate in hats and hurried straight back to the Union, Mrs. K. too, when it was over." She continued,

> Mrs. Kehew is a wonderful woman—never at a loss, and always entertaining but never loses dignity. I am not sure that I like her face—she is something—very often called a snob, and I can believe it, though I have never seen it, and have heard of so many *nice* things she has done very quietly that I am inclined to soften my instinctive feeling toward her. Her sister Miss Kimball [who was also important in women's organizing in Boston, but behind the scenes], seems a much sweeter woman to me. They are daughters of one of the most exclusive of the old Boston families always much wealth, born on Mount Vernon Street . . . and of high social position—everywhere. The politicians of the State House stand in wholesome awe of Mrs. Mary Morton Kehew—she is a woman who

has her way. During her long illness last fall and winter she of course had to be out of public affairs entirely. About the time of her recovery in the spring some man is reported to have remarked to a legislator "I see Mrs. Mary Morton Kehew is recovering."

"Why yes, said the other, I believe she is. How did you know?"

"Because I noticed them cleaning up the State House" was the quite sufficient reply.[1]

Kehew's "business" that led her guests to eat with their hats on was not individual but collective, not self-supporting, but voluntarist and philanthropic, and unabashedly political. She served as one of the last unpaid presidents of the Women's Educational and Industrial Union. What allowed her to do so, to turn her Chestnut Street home into her launching pad for organized political activism, was in part the reimagining and ordering of domestic space by elite matrons discussed in chapter 2: the domestic-based claims of moral authority and the domestic servants who freed the time of elite and upper middle-class matrons. On the other hand, the constant assertions of overworked wives, New Women, working girls, and businesswomen helped determine Kehew's agenda, as was evident in precisely such WEIU-sponsored studies as Bosworth's on the living wage.

Kehew was hardly alone. Women's organizations were not new in the late nineteenth and early twentieth century, but across the United States they exploded in numbers of organizations and in numbers of members among every class and race. This and the following chapters turn from women's "domestic" spaces and individual daily life to their related organized, institutionalized attempts to intervene in urban governance. This chapter takes three organizations as case studies and focuses on the white, Protestant, middle-class and elite women whose organizations in particular dramatically changed their relation to municipal government.[2] The next chapter focuses on women's labor organizing and the final chapter on women's postsuffrage forays into municipal politics as candidates and party organizers.

In the decades surrounding the turn of the century, many of the elite Yankees of the Back Bay and Beacon Hill watched with dismay the rising political power of the Irish, the growing immigration from southern and eastern Europe, and increasing labor unrest. Attempting to fend off these newcomers as they had the commercial district, the elite mustered their forces in the centers of power on Beacon Hill—the State House and city hall. And they used their relatively uncontested power in the statehouse to try to manage the shifting ethnic balance of power in the city. Over the long run, the trends were clear: the breakdown of Yankee and Irish cooperation, the growth of state power over the city, the centralization of urban executive power, and the Irish assumption of Boston's political power. In the short run, however, between 1880 and 1920, Boston survived shifting coalitions, several activist city administrations, two major government reform movements, and two major city charter revisions.[3] It was this uncertain world that the three women's organizations negotiated.

When they founded the organizations, white, native-born, middle-class and elite women leaders had shared a group of oppositional values, now conventionally labeled "woman's culture." The culture that had emerged in the nineteenth century as family became increasingly a private entity (not a social metaphor, reflected in the structure of government) and as individual self-interest and large-scale industrial capitalism increasingly dominated the economy and society.[4] As electoral politics came to embody and represent competing interests, the adherents of this woman's culture sought to provide unity and community to hold the fragmented nation together and prevent the permanent cleavages seen in Europe. They posed the cooperative, nurturing values of home as an alternative to the competitive, individualist values of the marketplace and formal politics. They called on the supposed universal domestic experience of women to cement ties across economic, ethnic, and even racial differences.

But something happened to this vision as organized middle-class and elite women expanded their public roles. By 1920, most historians would agree that the older vision had been largely though not totally replaced by a heterosocial politics reinforced by the bestowal of woman suffrage.

Historians' understanding of organized women's transformations from 1870 to 1940 has benefited from a burgeoning literature on women, reform, and the state.[5] Some historians have referred to the changes of the era as the "domestication of politics," seeing organized reform women's triumphal progress into the public realm under the banner of civic maternalism, trailing their newly created, unaltered institutions behind them.[6] These historians conclude that the women's public conquest made a separate women's politics irrelevant. Others have taken a dimmer view and seen in heterosocial politics the destruction, not triumph, of women's separate vision and often of the women's organizations themselves as they slipped into the mire of co-optation.[7] The three Boston organizations discussed here provide some evidence for both views, but more importantly, they point to the range of choices and the middle ground that Protestant, white, middle-class and elite-dominated women's organizations negotiated for themselves. As they entered the changing but still male-dominated urban milieu, women like Mary Morton Kehew gained new powers and sources of authority and lost some old ones. Where they chose to enter the public arena, they did not do so unchanged. Indeed, these women's triumphal parade took its very shape from the interaction of their reform ideas with the political and social realities of their environment. In short, middle-class and elite white women's class-bridging organizations and their strategies emerged not in an autonomous female realm, but within a complex network of power relations.[8] The three very different class-bridging organizations examined here reveal much about how women achieved power in a male-dominated local political arena, even before women had the vote.

The Fragment Society, founded in 1812; the Women's Educational and Industrial Union (WEIU), established in 1877; and Denison House, a women's college settlement house begun in 1892, all evoked the universalist ideal of woman's culture. They all participated in what the Fragment Society called "the great social reform which every society like ours is trying to push onward" to fend off "by philanthropic" activity European-style "class hatred."[9]

To us, the conservative Fragment Society may look like a completely different beast from the WEIU or Denison House, but to the women of the late nineteenth and early twentieth centuries, they were variations of an attempt to bridge class differences and arrive at social harmony. All of these organizations believed that women of all classes had more in common with each other than had men and that knowing their shared needs allowed women better than men to bridge social cleavages. But even the most radical of them rarely if ever set out to eradicate class difference or fully to incorporate members of all classes on equal terms.[10] While we should make distinctions among women's organizations, we also need to recognize similarities that were important to the women at the time. These similarities help explain, for example, how the same individuals could not only belong to but serve as officers in two such seemingly ideologically antagonistic organizations as the Fragment Society and the WEIU.[11]

The organizations differed markedly in their strategies and ideologies. They ranged from conservative to radical in their thinking about gender and class and reform in general. By looking at organizations across this spectrum within a single political, social, and economic arena, there emerges the complex relation between changes in the politics of women, urban life, and organizations.

Fragment Society

Founded to relieve the poor, by 1870 the Fragment Society had rejected the dominant ideology of mid- to late-nineteenth century reform. Its members referred to themselves as social reformers trying to bridge the chasm between rich and poor, but they remained convinced that the poor existed to test the virtue of the rich in displaying their common humanity and compassion. From the vantage point of Beacon Hill and the Back Bay, Boston's two most elite neighborhoods, they fondly quoted their founding constitution, that it had been "wisely ordained that the poor 'we shall always have with us' " so that the rich could emulate Jesus by gathering up their fragments and, "anxious to relieve the wants of the destitute," as they put it, "cast our mite on the altar of Benevolence." Their benevolence, which usually took the form of bestowing garments, particularly baby sets called layettes, proved them worthy of what they called their "trust," meaning their wealth. It affirmed the rightness of their social and economic position and class distinctions.[12]

The members built their society and their discourse on distinctly familistic rather than overtly class lines, however. Proud of memberships passed from mother to daughter and of cousin and sibling relations among members, they built their organization on the kinship society of Boston's elite neighborhoods well into the twentieth century.[13] The language of kinship allowed them to ignore the structural realities of class increasingly visible around them.

It would be easy to caricature the group and their increasing distance from reality. By the 1870s, their sewing circles had become elegant full-dress dinners after which the ladies sat around in their ball gowns and sewed diapers, euphemistically called "art squares." Such practices could be read as emphasizing class differences rather than fostering class harmony and subjected them to the ridicule of an occasional newspaper article less friendly than the society columns of the *Boston Transcript*, which covered their annual meetings. When they finally abandoned the practice of full-dress dinners, it was due to wartime rationing in the 1940s, to patriotism and not to embarrassment at social inequity.[14] They were unrepentantly a class-ridden society.

Their familistic stance, however, also carried the roots of resistance to certain aspects of a more gender-neutral twentieth-century reform behavior. It carried a dislike of impersonal bureaucracy and a determination to retain the Fragment Society's autonomy. In 1865 they had claimed that "the tiny brook which steals almost unseen through the green meadows [is] as really powerful for good, as where, with broader course and sudden plunge, it sets in motion the busy mill." These women conceived, constructed, and perceived of power in terms of the efficacy of personal relations. The almost invisible, natural, nurturing stream (women in their parlors and visiting the poor) claimed transformative power for humans equal to that by which industry (male controlled) transformed raw materials into finished products by machine. In 1905, the women still perceived themselves a "vital power" in Boston by use of their traditional methods.[15]

Well into the twentieth century, these methods included an insistance on personal knowledge of each recipient not simply for purposes of determining worthiness, though this became an increasing concern with the ascendance of "scientific charity" during and after the Civil War, but to exercise the redemptive power of human love and caring across class lines.[16] The Fragment Society resisted the centralizing, rationalizing pull of scientific charity. They had refused to surrender their autonomy to the Associated Charities in 1879. Led by Robert Treat Paine but directed behind the scenes by Annie Fields, the Associated Charities' motto was "not alms but a friend"; it gave no money but advice, and eventually it took over Boston's social welfare.[17] The Fragment Society insisted, on the contrary, that sometimes quick decisive aid could not be refused and that "there is this heavenly quality even in a deed of misplaced charity, that it makes the heart of the doer sit lightly in his bosom." They admitted the justice of Annie Fields' premises, that "[t]o give education to the children, and lucrative employment to the parents is undoubtedly the best way to administer charity." But, they countered, "to the sick, the aged, and young children, it is impossible often to refuse direct aid, to meet the wants which those who labor among the poor encounter at every step."[18]

This "efficiency" versus "sympathy" debate reflected a dispute over the appropriate manifestation of women's benevolent impulse in public. It contrasted nineteenth-century woman's culture with the ascendant business values; it pitted family against corporation as the key metaphor.[19] In 1870 the society had insisted that "the poor do not require merely to have alms flung at them, as we fling food to a starving animal. They have other needs besides those of the body"; money and goods should be given certainly, but "the manner of giving charity" was crucial to the Fragment Society, the pleasant word and smile, "which shall make a poor person recognize that you consider him as of the same flesh and blood with yourself; not born an inferior, not to be regarded as the off-scouring of the earth, but one of God's children, one for whom, equally with yourself, Christ died." Nearly seventy years later, the society reported that "Times have changed . . . and now the City helps these poor unfortunates, but not in such a personal way."[20] Unlike more modern philanthropic societies that aimed for rapid turnover in clientele, the Fragment Society continued affectionately to mention from year to year those it termed its "pensioners."[21] They retained, in short, their personalist, familistic vision of urban life and retained a place for that vision in the city by their continued participation in quasi-public welfare.

The Fragment Society was not changeless. In the twentieth century, its members no longer found their recipients on their doorstep or among their casual acquaintances. The geography of the city had changed, creating greater spatial as well as social distance between classes and ethnic groups. Increasingly the Fragment Society relied on urban institutions instead of personal knowledge to locate the targets of the beneficence, but they resisted the meaning of that geographical change, insisting, even when working through an institution, on individual knowledge of the person aided, denying their own isolation.[22]

Such a personalist vision had limits for grappling with a transformed city, however. The Fragment Society women were frustrated by the difference in scale between their own efforts and the magnitude of urban problems, particularly the 1890s machine politics they saw "degrading" not only the "respectable foreign population, but also . . . the native born American citizen."[23] Recognizing the necessity of social reform, but convinced that true social reform could come only through individual salvation, the society greeted each new reform epoch with concern, and the occasional warning that "the attempt to alter the form of an old established order generally results in its active decline and destruction." Unlike the other two societies discussed here, they did not celebrate the new century. As the century turned, women from Denison House and the WEIU joined a torchlit parade to the Massachusetts State House to celebrate the dawning of a new age, while the women of the Fragment Society remained in their parlors.[24] As part of a class who witnessed its centralized authority and power in municipal finance and politics waning, they feared not only the future but a government over which they had no control. They saw the danger as structural, but given their fears, they could muster only an individual remedy.[25]

Emblematic of its acquiescence in if not contentment with the status quo, the Fragment Society challenged no spatial boundaries. It met originally in women's parlors, definitively women's space—the private home's interface with the public world. When they escaped these parlors in the 1880s, it was only to move to already dedicated, proven safe space for their class and sex, to Back Bay hotel residences. Then in the 1920s the Fragment Society began occasionally to meet in the buildings erected by Back Bay women's clubs to which some of its members belonged.[26] The Fragment Society never created its own space. It operated ideologically and practically within the confines of its members' world.

It is significant that this, the "reform" organization least interested in effecting any change beyond the personal and individual, remained the most thoroughly in women's hands, retaining female control of its treasury, for example, longer than either of the other organizations and remaining unaffiliated with male-dominated umbrella organizations.[27] These women were determined to remain in their own sphere and to keep men's hands off it. They remained on the margins of the charitable structure of the city, resisted the temptation to expand, and feared reform; they challenged neither class nor sexual inequities. They did not make their own spaces, but they did keep the ones they had, and in them they were able, against the tide, to maintain an alternative: an organization not bureaucratic but personal, informal, and familistic.

Women's Educational and Industrial Union

In the 1940s, the Fragment Society began to meet in the private lunchrooms of the WEIU, to which some of its members belonged. Despite the common membership, the groups had little in common ideologically. Founded in an Emersonian glow of transcendentalist unity in 1877, the WEIU determined to aid all women in gaining more economic and intellectual self-reliance. The Fragment Society was full of women with publicly distinguished husbands; the WEIU was full of women known in their own right, women who had already broken bounds by joining the professions or having a public writing and speaking career, as did Julia Ward Howe. Of eight original members, three, including the founder Harriet Clisby, were practicing physicians.[28]

From the first, the WEIU confronted the very urban phenomena the Fragment Society found so alarming: the increasing distance that separated racial, ethnic, and class groups in the city and women from one another. Harriet Clisby confessed that she "had seen the loneliness, the poverty, the dreadful *apartness* caused by class feeling." Her dream, as she put it, was "an Institution wherein the needs of *all classes* of women would be met, and which should be held together by the bonds of a love whose effects would be shown in *mutual service* and healthy co-operative activities." Unlike the Fragment Society, the WEIU opened not just its purse but its membership to all women.[29]

While Clisby reached out in particular to women who worked, she tried to bridge the gulf between "the better born" and other classes rather than close it. Like the Fragment Society, some members of the WEIU used a language of family to elide realities of class. The WEIU's second president, author Abby Morton Diaz, explained to Robert Treat

Paine that the WEIU aimed for "a social intercourse which ignores the boundaries of sect and caste." Yet she hastened to add, "I do not mean by this that equality is possible. It is not found even in families. Kinship is."[30]

But the WEIU's membership—open to all on an equal basis—demonstrated its belief that inequality outside the organization need not impede unity and equality within it. Though they shared the language of family with the Fragment Society, their definition of family seemed different. The WEIU actively tried to recruit the city's diverse constituency, albeit with mixed success. The largest number of members came from the Back Bay, but Mrs. Louis Brandeis, Josephine Ruffin, and Mary Kenney O'Sullivan (a Jewish woman, a black woman, and a female Irish-Catholic labor organizer) all served not simply as members but as officers in the organization. Moreover, Diaz insisted that the WEIU consisted of not rich women helping the poor, "but [of] all women having needs."[31]

The WEIU had not rejected the vision of city as community, neighborhood, or family; it used new means consonant with the changing physical reality of the city to realize the vision. Immediately, the WEIU created its own space. It rented rooms. This meeting ground for women, Clisby hoped, would break the barriers isolating working women in the city. In the 1880s, the WEIU went a step further. It purchased rooms and buildings downtown and opened lunchrooms staffed by member volunteers to provide safe space and an inexpensive meal to women in the city's center.[32]

Historians are now accustomed to think of urban parks and even streets as contested space—ground contested for its uses and meaning by men and women, middle and working classes. The city center, including legislative halls, was also a space where different groups struggled for position and negotiated status and definitions of place.[33] The WEIU's building added to this sense of the downtown as a "contested space," for the women did not pick the spot for their building randomly, but placed it in the heart of the male-dominated central city.

They wanted to create public space where middle-class and elite women could appear without being declassed and working women could appear in public without having their virtue questioned by being "on the streets." And they were expansionist in their aims. The WEIU bought second and third buildings and opened lunchrooms, employment offices, clinics, and pure milk stations. By the turn of the century, such women's organizations had turned Boylston Street in downtown Boston into virtually a woman's mile. It was not accidental that such proximity to the corridors of power, the state legislature and city hall, coincided with these women's groups' increased lobbying efforts to change the city and their own condition in other ways.

The strategy of welcoming all women to a safe space worked. In the first year alone, the WEIU grew from 8 to 400 members. Ten years later, it had 1,200 members. As planned, they worked together to transform themselves and the city. They experimented with a host of services: employment offices for domestic servants, handicapped women (often meaning women whose only employment handicap was race or age), and college women; vocational advising; a handicraft workshop; a shop selling women's work on consignment; several lunchrooms; kitchens selling nutritional food; school lunches; social investigations; evening classes; milk distribution; lecture series; and Sunday services. When the WEIU eventually persuaded the city to subsidize and then to adopt several of these ventures, the organization itself became part of the government. By altering the relation between the state and public welfare as well as the definition of public welfare, the WEIU succeeded in effecting some of the changes it sought in the nature of thc city to aid women's self-reliance.

Originally an alliance with government had not been part of the plan. This shift in strategy indicated a new WEIU vision of its purpose and of the muncipal government. The WEIU recognized institutionally, as it had spatially, the efficacy of new structures for older ends. The members learned to speak the politicians' and businessmen's language.

The WEIU's creation of its own space in the 1880s had brought men into the WEIU for the first time. Men seem to have been necessary for credit. While the WEIU ultimately had the same size of permanent fund as the Fragment Society, its operating costs were several times as large because of its desire to expand and experiment, and women had little access to the sorts of assets that made them good credit risks for banks.[34] This desire to expand, to conquer new realms of urban space, in turn, warred with the desire for self-reliance, given the economic structure of the city. It required the WEIU to find what historians of imperialism have called indigenous collaborators—in this case elite men—whom they believed they could turn to their own uses.

Yankee male political reformers, in particular, would cooperate because they saw such organizations as benefiting themselves. Looking for ways to outflank ethnic political machines, they might naturally turn to already functioning institutions, to women's organizations. Indeed, women's reform groups tended to sound more like machine politicians than like efficient civil service reformers. Like the machines, they spoke of their desire to humanize the city and their extensive social welfare networks provided jobs, food, coal, child care, and nursing. Women had, in this sense, created their own machine, and their behavior reflected their knowledge of what potential power this machine gave them (as WEIU and Denison House activities showed).[35]

In the 1880s, elite male reform sentiment in Boston coalesced around the issue of civil service reform, and it enjoyed early success. The same year that Boston elected its first Irish Democratic mayor, 1884, reformers and their allies in the state legislature transferred control over Boston's increasingly Irish police from the city to a commission appointed by the governor. The following year, the same forces amended Boston's city charter to shelter budget decisions from the influence of ward-based machine pressures, choosing to centralize authority in the mayor's office as the lesser of two evils.[36]

Women's formal politics simultaneously became enmeshed in a nativist frenzy. Having received the right to vote for Boston School Committee members in 1879, in the 1880s many Protestant women participated in the effort to purge the school board of Catholic influence. The WEIU had members on all sides of the issue, nativists and antinativists, suffragists (who tried to distance themselves from the nativists) and antisuffrage leaders.[37] The WEIU could contain such diversity because it did not look to electoral politics for public influence. With the redesigned city government and their new male allies the WEIU had other options.

By 1891, the mayoralty was back in patrician hands. Nathan Matthews—tall, thin, and with a pince nez—brought reform to city hall. A Harvard graduate, real estate lawyer, trust administrator, and civil service reformer, his profile was identical to the men the WEIU invited in as trustees and treasurers. Like Matthews, they had graduated from Harvard, favored civil service reform, practiced law with corporate connections, belonged to the same exclusive clubs, and appeared in the Social Register. Matthews and his cohort brought tightened and centralized budget keeping to city government at the same time they expanded its realm with urban planning, city parks, and the first U.S. subway. They saw urban problems as those of inefficiency rather than corruption, and they strove to make the city adhere to what they called businesslike methods. Politics, they insisted, had no place in municipal government.[38] In the 1890s, under Matthews and more particularly under his successor, Josiah Quincy, the city government began to take an active hand in civic and social reform.

The WEIU responded to this new opportunity. By the 1890s Darwinian language had displaced the ubiquitous quotes from Emerson in the annual reports.[39] "Survival" and "efficiency" replaced "unity" and "self-reliance" as the hallmarks of the organization. At the same time, professionals and college-educated women began to replace the generation of middle-class and elite transcendentalist volunteers. The new generation of women leaders had attended colleges that taught a male curriculum and read books on political economy and society that predisposed them to arguments of efficiency and respect for a professionalism in which they could now participate. The professionalism of a Clisby or WEIU member Dr. Arvilla Haynes in the 1870s was not the self-conscious professional culture emerging in the 1890s.[40] The Twenty-Ninth *Annual Report* in 1908 displayed the change. Instead of an institution governed by women's greatest needs and love, the report boldly pronounced, in the face of a deficit of $9,500, "The test of the Union's right to ask for support is the test of *efficiency*. *Has the community got its 'money's worth' of results?*"[41] With more than a thousand social service organizations in Boston, only the fittest would survive, WEIU reports warned. One after another, departments were put on a "business" basis. But the shift had come even earlier. In 1900 the union had considered hiring a full-time, paid president. And in the labor-restless 1890s, it had changed the name of the assembly room from "Women's Union Hall," which some now found objectionable, to "Perkins Hall" in memory of a male donor.[42]

As professional workers (who came in before the professional president) occupied committee space and took over planning, donors and members became more distant; they found the WEIU less an outlet for their desire to participate in shaping their world. Turnover increased, and the WEIU worried about the decline in the participation of volunteers. The organization looked more and more like a corporation. It had over a hundred employees by the early twentieth century and an employees' organization.[43] The need to survive had not dictated these changes. The Fragment Society survived without them. It was the WEIU's drive for change and desire to play a role in the transformation of the city that required its new strategies.

In a world increasingly riven by labor strife, including Boston's 500 strikes in the mid-1880s, the younger generation of the WEIU found its elders' ideas of unity and transcendental reality bewildering, quaint, and irrelevant. They conveyed that sense in their reports of attendance at the lectures of or about aging transcendentalists.[44] Yet male transcendentalists and social reformers had valued women and fostered heterosocial organizations because they also valued attributes connected with prevailing notions of womanhood: spirituality, intuition, and compassion.[45] When they favored woman suffrage, they did so not because they saw women and men as alike, but because they thought government would benefit from women's special abilities. With increasing tribute paid instead to efficiency and system, women lost this special intellectual allure. If women now wanted to gain respect and power in realms men dominated, they would have to learn to speak another language, or perhaps men and women would have to learn to speak each other's language.

The older union members did not succumb easily. The women of the Protective Department—a forerunner of legal aid where women volunteers investigated and settled women's cases (usually claims for wages or payment of services) if they could and took them to lawyers if they could not—resisted tampering with their sense of their purpose. Indeed, they would only surrender the organization when the city's official legal aid bureau finally hired a female lawyer in 1920/21.[46] But the initial challenge came much earlier. In 1880 one of the male lawyers on whom they relied came to try to convince them to take a small percentage from what they recovered for claimants:

> He said he did not look upon the question from the money to be gained, but the good resulting to the women themselves, that in

> most of the cases the women would gladly give a Lawyer half of what he could recover, but that most of them were so small that the Lawyer would [not] take them except as a charity. That he did not believe in charity to those who did not need it. That charity in the sense of alms (or time) giving is at best dangerous and requires great care and should only exist in cases of absolute necessity and that in most of the Cases of the Union the women, when money was collected for them could, and often would prefer to pay something, perhaps not the regular rate, but something is always gained by cooperation. He thought the best thing in its favor was that the women would feel that they were helping others, and therefore feel more independent. He believed in helping others to help themselves.

When he had finished, the women of the Protective Department politely thanked him for taking the time, feared that the poor women would think that the union was making a profit from them, and agreed with the lawyer on helping others to help themselves; they tabled the motion for further discussion. Later, meeting without the lawyer, the women stood by an earlier decision that the issue was not charity but justice; the women clients had been wrongfully denied money or services. Justice demanded full restitution, and they continued as before.[47] Two years later, they resisted another lawyer's suggestion that they take the cases contingent on settling them as they thought best. They decided instead that the clients had to be left free to consult someone else if they wanted. Despite its maternalist name, the Protective Department stood firm on rights, not control. But finally, in 1898, even the Protective Department adopted two modifications to make it more "efficient," including charging a commission of 5 percent on all moneys collected, which put this department, too, in their language, on a "business" basis.[48]

The WEIU's use of "efficiency" and "survival of the fittest" did not signify a new attitude toward the poor, but indicated a new standard for judging the success of philanthropic and reform organizations. Persisting in much of its original agenda and continuing to broaden the scope of efforts at municipal reform, the WEIU made the city a better place for women to live as well as equipping women better to live in the city through its vocational guidance, employment bureaus, consignment sales of handicrafts, and so on. But the choice of where to place major efforts and which methods to use was no longer governed only by the members' sense of the greatest need. Efficiency, in this usage, meant concentrating on those projects with results most likely to ensure—or at least not jeopardize—continued support for the organization, support from those who held political and financial power in the city. When Josiah Quincy became mayor, the WEIU reaped some early benefits of this strategy. Quincy was a pro–woman suffrage mayor in the wake of a resounding defeat for the 1895 Massachusetts woman suffrage referendum. He was also a brilliant coalition builder. Along with machine politicians and Boston Brahmins, he brought into his administration WEIU and other women.[49]

A decade later, in 1907, the WEIU inaugurated a school lunch program in Boston, and contrary to its usual policy, it fended off attempts to take it over. It continued to expend its energies on providing lunches and administering the program with the city's funding because the financial scale of the program and the number of its employees gave the WEIU not only patronage and funds, but, according to its officers, legitimacy and stature in the eyes of the businessmen and politicians it needed as allies in its reform agenda. The 1908/9 *Annual Report* celebrated "the added weight which the higher volume of business gives the Union in its study and endeavor to cooperate with employers in allied trades. Every step that carries the Union forward toward the ranks of the major business enterprises," the report continued, "puts it in possession of just so much more power to study business conditions and influence to command a hearing when it speaks."[50] Shifts in language and behavior were driven not simply by socialization and generational shifts, but by the desire for male cooperation and for legitimacy in the eyes of male economic and political collaborators.

In 1909 came another major city charter revision, the culmination of two years' work by the Financial Commission, and the WEIU again responded. The new charter altered Boston's political structure, eliminating ward-based elections, strengthening the mayor, drastically reducing the size of the city council, and imposing two state-appointed watchdog commissions on city finances and appointments. Between 1900 and 1914, WEIU male treasurers and trustees were also members of the Good Government Association, which dominated the charter-revision process and won a majority of City Council seats in 1910.[51] Amidst this activity, the WEIU centralized its own political efforts, taking city and state politics, and not just expansionist city administrators, more seriously. In the *Annual Report* for 1908/9 it commented that all social problems they investigated in the industrial world led to the State House, the city hall, or the police station. It stepped up its lobbying activities, from 1908 to 1918 uniting all the lobbying efforts of the various branches of the union under one department.

Their increasing involvement with the state (in the form of municipal and state government) replaced the sense of the organization as providing an alternative space and vision of the city. The new vision was more aggressively integrationist. This political activity provided a presuffrage training ground for future women politicans (such as Mary Dewson and Ethel Johnson), who would then become part of the appointive political structure. The union hired such women as professionals or college interns for lobbying efforts or investigations of the conditions of working women, often at the behest of municipal, state, or federal government departments. In this way, the WEIU socialized them into the world of politics and the back room.[52]

By 1911, when the WEIU got its first professional president, it would have been hard to find the Emersonian women's group of 1877. The shape of the organization had changed. Professional workers had replaced the volunteers in policy making, and businessmen now sat on the organization's advisory boards. No longer seeking primarily to provide an agency for women's cross-class unity, in 1903/4 the union had even begun admitting men as associate members. By 1927, so changed was the organization that the author of its fifty-year history distorted founder Clisby's words; she quoted Clisby out of context in order to claim that all along the ideal had been an association of "men and women acting together" within the WEIU.[53]

Had success spoiled the WEIU? By the 1920s, the WEIU had approximately 5000 members and 350 paid workers. The choice of Eva Whiting White, head of the Elizabeth Peabody Settlement House and the first recipient of a college degree in social work (Simmons College, 1907), as the new head of the WEIU in 1929 was telling. White was a professional; her political style was strictly that of pragmatic insider and not female identified. She had succeeded in working with the settlement house's ward bosses by refusing to criticize the system of ward politics that survived despite centralized elections, and although she had campaigned for Herbert Hoover, she enjoyed appointments to federal commissions by both Republican and Democratic presidents. She explicitly rejected the label of "reformer" for that of "educator," which she found less inhibiting politically because it allowed politicians, as one reporter put it, to "love and respect her, because . . . she never assumed the role of a 'do-gooder.' "[54]

By the end of the 1940s, the WEIU was still in women's control and focused on women's issues. But in the course of pursuing its goals, which had gradually shifted from cross-class sociability and mutual aid to municipal reform, its methods, language, and ideology had shifted dramatically. The shift had generational roots, as each generation experienced a different socialization process, and also owed something to the aggressive experimentation of the WEIU, present from the beginning. But most fundamentally, in contrast to the Fragment Society, it was driven by the WEIU's desire to change the city and not just individual women.[55] To change the city, women had to create a new source of power, which they achieved through the organization of women and institutionalization of that organization. Then, armed with their collective might, they entered the larger political arena, found collaborators, and altered the political equation.[56]

Denison House

Like the WEIU, Denison House, in Boston's South End, began as a group of professional women with careers in various realms from English literature to economics. Unlike the WEIU, Denison House plunked its middle-class residents not downtown, but in a working-class neighborhood in 1892 on the eve of a major depression. It marked a middle-class Yankee female incursion into a working-class immigrant neighborhood defined as off-limits to middle-class women. Imbued with an ideology of common humanity similar to that of the two other organizations, the settlement house was also a concession to the reality of the class and ethnic differences and geography that called it into being. The increasingly rigid frontier between working and middle class, foreign and native born, turned settlement house residents into brave pioneers.

Like settlement house residents elsewhere, the Wellesley professors of economics, Emily Greene Balch and Katherine Coman, and of English literature, Vida Scudder, who lived at Denison House struggled to define a place for themselves in the neighborhood.[57] Appalled by the standards of cleanliness and lack of gentility around them, they yet determined foremost to be "neighbors." Like the WEIU, they saw themselves providing literally common ground, a physical meeting place for different classes. They did not, in these early years, dictate to the neighbors, but facilitated for them, and they opened their living room to the local people. On their visits in the community, the traditional female method of neighborhood formation, they invited all to return their calls.[58]

Like the WEIU, they tried a host of experiments, from organizing women's labor unions to offering courses on Shakespeare and Dante. They did their best to meet the neighborhood's demands for child care, which to their dismay they found more persistent than interest in poetry. They also tried to compete with the local political machine by mimicking its structure with their own boys' clubs, men's clubs, and reading rooms where men were allowed to smoke.[59]

Their early experience with organized labor gained them rapid, unwelcome press notoriety, and organizing labor unions ceased as settlement work. Unions continued to meet on the premises, however, and Denison House residents continued to be members. They seem to have refused to take the advice of Robert Woods, who ran a nearby men's settlement house, to be neutral in their attitude toward the labor movement; they never seem to have invited or provided equivalent hospitality to corporate leaders and employers, as the *Nation* advised. Indeed, a male treasurer resigned in 1904 because Denison House identified itself too strongly with trade unions. As a result, the board began to pressure the settlement workers to be more discreet, but since under the terms of the College Settlement Association over half the board members had to be college women, and it was these college women who were the radicals, the pressure was relatively mild, at least before World War I.[60]

At the WEIU, a college-educated and college-socialized staff and professional women had contributed to the WEIU's shift in strategy.

Yet Denison House retained an outsider position in the city's politics for a longer time. Both its radical politics, epitomized in a head resident with pacifist and socialist tendencies, and its physical position on the fringes of Boston ensured its marginality. In addition, as a settlement house, Denison House remained committed to a belief in the neighborhood as the essential urban unit, whereas the WEIU focused on the downtown.

In its sphere, Denison House, like the WEIU, inaugurated programs that the city then subsidized and occasionally took over.[61] In this way it, too, became a vehicle for the expansion of municipal government, but on a different scale. When the Denison House women went to lobby the mayor to purchase their gymnasium in the early twentieth century, they came away defeated and overwhelmed by the number of calls on the mayor's purse. As neighborhoods became less powerful in the city's structure, the settlement house paid the price, and its leaders found the requisite shift in strategy trying. Accustomed to raising their own money from other women in bits and pieces usually of less than fifty dollars, they were unprepared for the scale of the city budget and unrehearsed in the language of municipal financial politics.

At the same time, they were not like the Fragment Society, content with their limited resources. Like the WEIU, they dreamed of expanding their geographical reach and influence, of engaging the city in the neighborhood, making the city provide a branch library, a gym, baths, and a community center building, recasting the nature of government and the role of government in the neighborhood.[62] And like the WEIU, they dreamed these dreams in the context of an increasingly professionalized staff. In the end, however, Denison House took a different route.

Denison House's first building—and its second and third—were purchased by a woman, Cornelia Warren, who remained a force in the house until after World War I. There was no need to bring men into the organization. By 1910, however, the women of Denison House wanted more. In desperation to raise funds to build a new building and determined to achieve more influence in the city, Denison House in 1910 decided to organize a men's auxiliary of influential and wealthy Bostonians. Physically marginal, and without the numbers of wealthy and influential women who graced the WEIU, they hoped an auxiliary of prominent men would give them access to the centers of financial as well as political power in the city. They successfully used the fallacious argument that they had previously concentrated their efforts on the women and girls of the community. In fact, they had always attended to the men and boys as citizens and future citizens with greater power to shape the polity, but now they claimed that they wanted to expand their work with boys, so that a men's auxiliary had a sound rationale and incentive.[63]

The balance of the new committee differed from that of their older male advisory board. In 1903/4, their advisory board had consisted of a prominent surgeon, a well-known labor leader, and a Harvard-educated Brahmin doctor. Their 1910/11 committee did include Robert Woods and still had two doctors, but among the other nine members, the majority were well-connected lawyers, an architect who became president of the Boston Chamber of Commerce, and a banker who had helped organize the Good Government Association and the Boston City Club. It had no labor representative.[64]

The ensuing dynamics served as a measure of the disparity of access to political and economic power in Boston by sex. After several meetings of women officers at the settlement house failed to produce promising schemes for fund-raising for the building, the women went to see a representative of their new men's auxiliary. He took responsibility, created a list for soliciting, and within months had the sum they had despaired of raising for years. Similarly, after another failed lobbying attempt, the women approached their new collaborators, who comfortingly promised to see the mayor about the issue personally.[65]

The relation of the settlement house to the neighborhood was also changing. The increasingly professional staff had begun to demand their own private living room in 1903, a place to retreat from the "neighbors," a way to erect a barrier between their professional and private lives. In 1915/16 the board of Denison House calmly separated the settlement workers' residences from the activities center. Such an action turned on its head the original concept of a settlement house whose residents would live and work in the community as the surrounding people did. And the settlement residents were conscious of the shift. In 1912, they baldly reported that the family aspect of the settlement had been outgrown, and it was now a large institution demanding expert workers and adequate salaries.[66] Gone was the original vision of women settling among the poor as true neighbors.

Moreover, the new men's auxiliary, which had seemed so safely compartmentalized, came with its own price. Adept at raising money, the businessmen simply could not understand what Denison House was trying to achieve when its residents remained outspoken pacifists and socialists in the midst of World War I and then a red scare in 1919. One after another, the men declared that if "the workers could not be restrained from talking in public in a radical manner on questions of the day," the men could not help raise money for the house. Some of the women board members, too, spoke of resigning, and the offending parties also offered to resign. Determined not to sacrifice free speech or academic freedom, even after finding out that the federal government had contemplated an investigation of the house, the women board members tried and failed to draft a position paper for the house and finally decided to ask the men to wait and see how the house worked, meanwhile releasing them from their obligation to raise money. After additional negative publicity in the *Boston American*, the board asked the head worker to take "a rest."[67]

This step marked only the beginning of a decline of autonomy of the house and an end to its position as a female settlement house, offering a homosocial refuge for activist women.[68] While the next head worker appointed by the board was a woman, she had to divide her time between Denison House and another social-work center (over the opposition of Denison House residents), and the head worker who followed her in the 1930s was a man. Moreover, in the depressed 1930s, Denison House also joined the Community Federation of Boston, a fund-raising organization that required the house to promise to begin no new line of work without its advice and consideration.[69] Denison House was now thoroughly incorporated into the city's structure, but though the board still had a female president, the women had lost control of the organization as well as their sense of it as a distinctively women's institution.

Learning to Play Politics

Assessing the struggle between Boston's Brahmins and the Irish politicans in this period, Jack Tager concluded, "successful urban government was predicated upon the realities of political accommodation, not upon 'scientific' concepts of efficiency or paternalistic notions of self-improvement." The city's most activist mayors had accommodated both reformers and bosses.[70] The women of these organizations discovered that maternalists, too, had to play the politics of accommodation. They refined and redefined their strategies as the city changed.

None of the three organizations could have redefined their strategies with such a relatively free hand had their claims for cross-class unity been realized in their structure, had any of them really attempted equality in governance. The Fragment Society members would have blanched at the notion of working-class women joining their venerable ivy-laden ranks; they even preferred to help people more like themselves, only fallen on hard times, women to whom a handkerchief or a slip, given at the right moment, made the difference between self-respect and dissolution.[71] And the WEIU, though it invited labor organizers and black women onto its committees and governing body, had its committee and executive board meetings at hours when working-class working women could not possibly have attended. The WEIU welcomed the involvement of wage-earning women but tended to set up separate organizations for them, affiliated with the WEIU but not accommodated on its board.[72] And while Denison House did, ultimately, create "a democratic corporation" in 1919, which included local people as voting members if they had contributed to the settlement house in any amount, it did not create a democratic governing board. Its board boasted instead of a majority of college professors and middle-class or elite volunteers and donors.[73] Moreover, many of the most crucial facets of these organizations shut down entirely during the summer, their schedules governed by the summer vacations of the middle-class and elite women who ran them rather than the perennial needs of the working-class women whose allies they purported to be. Individual members of the WEIU and residents of Denison House did seek the collaboration of the labor movement by joining labor unions, federal unions, and even leading the Boston Women's Trade Union League, but Denison House and the WEIU as institutions ultimately sought the bulk of their collaborators closer to the center of power in the city.[74]

These organizations had a choice along a spectrum from oppositional to integrationist politics. The choice, however, lay within a larger political structure in which they had little power. When they chose integration, the choice changed them. Ultimately, the integration worked both ways. Intent on effecting political, social, or economic change, Denison House and the WEIU became closely connected with men who could provide them with access to power, and at the same time they distanced themselves from the original vision of cross-class, gender-based unity and threatened the female members' control of their own organizations. The Fragment Society remained aloof, retaining female autonomy, but only within a larger system of limits. It was the conservatism of the Fragment Society that made possible its persistently separate woman's culture. The price the Fragment Society paid was continued marginalization. Its impact on the city remained that of a tiny brook in a city at flood tide.

The shift among activist women to political collaboration with men that Denison House and the WEIU demonstrate was not total but fragmented and strategic. It occurred early in the Progressive Era not solely as a response to the failure of suasion, Freudian challenges, or a suffrage they did not yet have nor simply as a "domestication" of politics.[75] It was also a response to new opportunities. It bespoke an ironic socialization of women's groups—who sought greater power to transform society—into patterns, language, and aims more acceptable to the men who held power at the city's center and whose own mode of political behavior was also changing.[76]

The result was more complex than co-optation of women or domestication of men for women did succeed in transforming, somewhat at least not only themselves and the public roles of women, but the city and its government in their own image. Within the middle-class world of gender, the city had learned to behave, because of these women, if not more like a sister and neighbor (the original vision), then more like a mother. The city now provided milk and school lunches, health clinics, vocational guidance, and kindergartens. Certainly Denison House and the WEIU's vision in 1927 differed drastically from the one with which they had started, but so, too, was the city a different place. It may be that the very nature of the welfare city that emerged from this era was shaped by the choices and compromises, the Realpolitik, that these activist women confronted when trying to shape the city to their ends. This maternalist result had not inevitably arisen from women generalizing their experience of motherhood in "civic maternalism" or "municipal housekeeping." Rather it was a statement about power relations (between men and women as well as between women), negotiations, and restricted choices.

6

"We Are Going to Stand by One Another"

Shifting Alliances in Women's Labor Organizing

In December 1891, a future Denison House resident received a letter from Jane Addams, founder of Chicago's Hull House. Hull House had just hosted a meeting of shirtwaist makers who had formed a union. "We find ourselves almost forced into the trades unions," Addams confessed, "there are very few for women in Chicago and we hope to help form them on a conservative basis."[1]

When Denison House opened a year later, it did not rush to follow suit. It took the advice of WEIU president Mrs. Mary Morton Kehew. Running into head resident Helen Cheever on a wintry day in early January, Kehew had "hoped we would commit ourselves to nothing, & would undertake nothing at present—'Do not organize.' "[2] But in November 1893, events and the demands of their constituents overtook them. Like Addams, the women of Denison House found themselves drawn into the union movement by the working women among whom they lived.

The previous chapter focused on how middle-class and elite women made their way into the corridors of urban power. This chapter focuses on the alliances and maneuvers necessary for wage-earning working-class women to reach those corridors and be recognized outside the neighborhood.

Convenient Marriages

The creation of an alliance between Denison House and their wage-earning women neighbors took the form of an intricate dance, each party wary of the other's attempt to lead. They danced around issues of labor conditions, ethnic rivalries, gender tensions, and workers' control. At the end of the night, they went home with new partners.

Beginning on September 6, 1893, when Denison House residents went to visit a local tailor shop, they found themselves running into labor issues, particularly garment workers' issues, at every turn. They had found the foreman pleasant, but that evening Mrs. Quinn, who had showed them round the shop, called at the house. They had a "very interesting talk" with her about abuses in tailor shops. Quinn wanted the facts written up and promised to bring more workers some Saturday evening. She wasted no time. Five days later she appeared with Mrs. O'Dowd and other tailoresses.

The abuses they discussed were not those of wages and hours. In the context of the dire 1890s depression, increasing competition from New York sweatshops, and rising Jewish immigration spurred by increasing violence against Jews in Russia, they discussed instead the "exclusion of the girls from the shops in favor of the Jews."[3]

While Boston's Irish Americans were successfully challenging Yankee Boston's political power in the 1890s, Irish immigrant workers remained predominantly in the lowest-paid occupations. In 1890, 65 percent of Boston Irish male workers were unskilled laborers and fewer than 5 percent held skilled positions.[4] Irish women fared no better. They and their Irish American daughters dominated the clothing trade in Boston. Now they faced increasing numbers of equally desperate new immigrants.

Over the next few days, as individual garment workers continued to visit Denison House, organized labor made an appearance in the shape of Jack O'Sullivan, a labor journalist who came to dinner on September 16. He talked, according to house records, in an "interesting" way about trades unions. Five days later he returned, bringing a Mr. McCreith of the Typographical Union, one of the earliest unions to admit women, and Mr. Jacques of the United Garment Workers. It was, according to the daybooks, an "interesting afternoon. Discussion of women wage-earners, and the possibility of organizing them into Trades-Unions."[5]

The next day Denison House resident Helena Dudley returned to the tailor shop at 40 Kneeland Street and invited the workers to the house. Meanwhile, Mrs. Quinn continued to be an assiduous visitor and, the day after Dudley's visit to Kneeland Street, came to dinner and took two of the residents with her to vespers at St. James.[6]

All this activity had made sufficient impact that, though they did not "organize," they did "study." When the first meeting of the house's new Social Science Club convened, drawing reformers from across Boston, the group decided to study the organization of labor. They took the long view. The first paper covered labor under feudalism.[7] Neighbors had clearly "interested" the residents in the labor issue, but the interest seemed to be rather academic.

In the following days, a veritable united nations of garment workers, one by one, trooped through the house. The day after the Social Science Club meeting, a Mrs. Comiski called and gave an "interesting" account of a strike she had led years ago. Comiski now lived with her sister on Joy Street, across town from Denison House, and it is not clear what prompted her call.[8] The following Monday, came a "young Russian hebrew—most interesting. Secretary of Shirt Makers Union. Told story of strike, etc." The residents responded by asking her to tea on Sunday. On Wednesday, October 11, came Maggie Welsh, of South Boston, a worker in the tailor shop at 40 Kneeland Street. She had made $2.50 in the last week, and only $1.75 the previous week, and wanted extra sewing. The residents sent her to Kehew's organization, the WEIU. The same day, a Miss A. Tracey, also at the tailor shop, called wanting a position to do housework. Denison House sent her, too, to the WEIU and to cooking classes.[9]

On November 6, four days after Balch reported to the Social Science Club on the transformation of the guilds, a turning point came in the form of Miss Dam, a "young Jewess." Dam told "story of wretched conditions in stamping department at Whitney's. Basement steam pipes overhead—incandescent lights—gas stove—naptha—windows closed after 8:30 A.M. Fourteen girls."[10] Dam succeeded in prompting the first action by the house; she mobilized this group to use their connections to elite women.

House resident Vida Scudder wrote to ask Mrs. Ames, one of the state's official female factory inspectors—the one from the ranks of middle-class/elite reformers rather than her coinspector from the ranks of labor—"to inspect the place."[11] When Dam called again three days later, the house found her "excited because Mrs. Ames has inspected the workshop at Whitney's and troubled because of Mr. Whitney's indignation and threats. Fears the girls may be turned off." Ames called the next day "about Miss Dam and Whitneys—the place condemned in toto. 'No sweating-den in Boston worse.' Mr. Whitney very discourteous: says the girls have lost their job."[12]

Disturbed, one of the residents asked Dam to call that evening. "Miss Dam comes after dinner, completely delighted"; it seems Mr. Whitney, his bluff called, had retreated. Dam reported, "The girls are to have a good upstairs work-room and all are radiant—except Mr. Whitney!"[13] Now considered part of the family, Dam found herself being taken to a lecture by Denison House residents three days later, along with garment workers Misses Lifschitz and Levy.[14]

It became increasingly difficult for Denison House residents to separate mediating workplace conditions from their usual attempts to assist neighbors.[15] The 1890s depression had rendered the Denison House women ripe for organizing. On one typical day that winter, five unemployed men and one woman came to the house seeking work. The residents "devised something by which [they] earned meal tickets" and "called on usual people and found all in greater or less hard straights." By July, overwhelmed by the desperation of even their most "respectable" neighbors, Denison House residents simply recorded in their journals, "Men—men—men—for work and food!"[16] Everywhere they went, they found long lines of job seekers. Even the perennial fallback of domestic service failed them. One philanthropic employment office with a "long line of girls waiting," had "five to every mistress seeking help."[17] Neighborliness was clearly inadequate. The need of guaranteed steady employment had become clear, and unions began to seem a possible way to give workers more leverage.[18]

Denison House residents met respectable union men and women everywhere they went. Helen Cheever visited a Mrs. Crowley and met Mr. Crowley, who belonged to the typographical union. The same day, a Mr. Haley, who seemed a nice, fair-minded man, told the house about the roofer's union; later Mrs. Comiski, Mrs. Quinn, and Mrs. Gilson came by, and Mrs. Comiski told again the story of her successful strike twenty years earlier. Talk ran, the daybooks record, on "the wrongs of the women."[19]

In this atmosphere, Comiski's determination to make available her twenty-year-old memories of labor organizing fell on fertile ears. That determination, together with the neighborhood women's knowledge of Comiski that brought her to Denison House, demonstrates, despite all the transience of their lives, a historical memory of labor activism (and the importance of that memory) among women workers that rarely appears in the historical record.[20]

Indeed, some of the problems union organizers would face stemmed precisely from the all too clear memory of prospective members. According to historian Eileen Boris, just three years before, in May 1891, male unionists had been instrumental in getting the Massachusetts legislature to pass an "Act to Prevent the Manufacture and Sale of Clothing Made in Unhealthy Places," the first law in the United States to regulate clothing manufacture in tenements. It prohibited garment making by unrelated people in the home. The unionists hoped to destroy tenement workshops, where most women were employed, in favor of factory shops. Their law would protect a higher male wage and yet preserve home finishing by their family members. But the Brahmins who took over this labor-launched reform movement were just as eager to eradicate home finishing as sweatshops. At a time when an estimated five thousand women in Boston did home finishing, an 1892 amendment to the law required costly licenses for family workshops to guard against contamination of clothing.[21] The movements had a legacy. The Boston *Globe* would later report, "A strong feeling has heretofore existed between the men and women, the latter making bitter complaints that the men were driving them out of the business."[22]

Employers further encouraged distrust between female workers and male unionists. George Ellis, a Boston print shop owner, warned women at a National Association of Working Girls Clubs Convention against trusting unions to work for gender equity. He claimed that in a recent Typographical Union campaign to enlist women and increase their piece rates, employers had threatened to dismiss the women workers, at which point, according to Ellis, a unionist had blurted out, "That is what we are after."[23]

So when in November 1893 Mrs. Quinn came again to Denison House, "much excited . . . as to Knights of Labor in shop, forcing women to pay twenty-five cents each and join," her alarm was not surprising. Scudder and another resident went to the United Garment Workers (UGW) for further information and found out that the union was indeed trying to organize the women at 40 Kneeland Street. In an attempt to quiet the qualms of the tailoresses, the UGW had made certain concessions: "The women are to have separate meetings," Scudder reported, "a chapter of the United Garment Workers, their own officers, etc. As soon as they are organized, the fees will be handed back to them, and in the future they can determine the amount of their own monthly dues." The clerk insisted "they shall stand for equal pay on piece-work for men and women, and that the U.G.W. will help the women when in distress."[24]

Even these UGW promises regarding the local's autonomy were not enough to assuage the working women's fears. That evening, Mr. O'Sullivan and Miss E. F. Pitts, a member of the Typographical Union and general organizer of women in Boston, arrived at Denison House soon followed by nine girls from the shop. O'Sullivan, Pitts, and some residents explained the advantages and necessity of labor unions and advised a separate organization of women cloak makers. "Finally," recorded the house day book, "the women withdrew to the dining room, and with Miss Pitts as go-between, said they wished to have nothing to do with the union, did not feel competent to organize by themselves or appoint a committee to see girls in other shops, but would like to do both if the ladies of the house would help them."[25]

It speaks volumes for both the paucity of available autonomous space for working-class women to gather and for the suspicion with which the women workers viewed the male-dominated unions that this meeting occurred at the settlement house. The women workers were not naive enough to believe that the settlement house "ladies" viewed them as equals or that they shared all their aims. But in choosing between potential allies, each having demonstrated a disposition to dominate, they chose the ones they had, thus far, better succeeded in manipulating. And they chose them as allies not simply in future struggles with employers, but in dealings with the male-dominated unions.

Ignorant of much of the history, Denison House women seemed baffled by the working women's resistance to the UGW. House residents asked the shop girls to come the next Monday night, bringing as many of their friends as they could, with a view to organizing.[26] But that day, the Denison House residents again found "the women suspicious and reluctant to form. Women from Mrs. Quinn's shop willing to do so, if one of the ladies of the house would be president."[27]

Apparently undecided, Scudder, Dudley, and a Miss Woods went visiting sweatshops, under the guidance of O'Sullivan and a Mr. Wilshinski. In the West End they found a shop supposed to conform to the conditions of the law "but whose hall-ways and working rooms were extremely dusty and dirty. Machines close together. Five girls employed. One, 16 years old, by hemming bottoms of trousers and sewing buttons could earn three dollars a week, paid at the rate of $.15 a doz. Fact elicited that the contracter's profit was $.025 a doz—used gas iron. A hot stove for irons close behind the girls. Five windows in the room which were open for more air, but not much light. The walls damp."[28]

The visit was enough. On December 4, Woods and Scudder met with the tailoresses at America Hall, 724 Washington Street, a frequent venue for trade union meetings. They termed the twenty women present "ignorant" and virtually forced them to organize a union and select officers. The workers did so with "some interest, no enthusiasm." The male-dominated union continued to provide a major stumbling block: "Mr. Willshinski [*sic*] and other Hebrew and Mrs. Avery present. Men eager for women to accept financial secretary from general union. Women reluctant. Officers pro tem finally appointed. Miss Pitts, President, Mrs. Quinn vice-president, Miss Annie Ryan, secretary, Miss Scudder, Treasurer, Clara Wohlgemuth, Sergeant at Arms." The Denison House residents had themselves been organized and found themselves officers in a new union—which, they were informed, inherited nearly $100 from its precursor.[29]

Both Denison House activists and the male union leaders saw themselves as forces of enlightenment, aiding ignorant working women. Working women, in turn, saw the risk of finding themselves under the thumb of male unionists or shepherded by their new allies among middle-class and elite women into the potentially disastrous waters of failed strikes, short-term gains, disappearing dues, and unemployment.[30] They knew that their life situations, like their work situations, differed, and that their interests also did. Little better illustrates the difference in situation than the fact that both the residents of Denison House and skilled male unionists in Boston could afford to and did hire working women for general housework, the very job of last resort for desperate tailoresses or other women workers.[31] To compound the difficulty, the tailoresses were still largely Irish, and the UGW men heavily Russian and Polish Jews, from the same families the Irish women saw threatening their jobs.

Denison House proved more eager. In its first annual report to the College Settlement Association in 1893, the head worker announced that the house's leading interests would be university extension and the organization of labor. Rather than credit the neighborhood's working women for the choice, the headworker credited Andover House, through whom they had made acquaintance with several labor leaders. It is telling that Denison House residents saw themselves as learning from the male labor leaders and not the women workers.[32]

The new union local met every second week, from 6:30 to 7:30 in the evening in the Denison House parlor.[33] The house also continued to recruit new members to the union, including at a meeting where socialist Carpenters' Union leader Harry Lloyd talked on the advantages of organizing to a large audience of women who "seemed interested; once initiated."[34] They also drew tailoresses for social events and clubs; indeed, often more tailoresses attended these latter events than the union meetings, possibly because they still distrusted the union.[35] Denison House continued to inform itself on the union movement, and sometimes the events converged; George S. McNeil, a Boston labor union leader, spoke at the Social Science Club on "Women and the Labor Movement" and informally afterward gave "very interesting" reminiscences of his youth in a factory. "Quite a delegation from Tailoress' Club," as well as Mr. and Mrs. Kehew were there.[36]

Continuing in their role as mediators between the tailoresses and the male union movement, Miss Pitts and Helena Dudley became the delegates from their local (no. 37) to the Boston Central Labor Union (BCLU). For those other Denison House members interested in union matters, O'Sullivan organized a federal local (affiliated directly with the AFL), with McNeil the president pro tem, and residents Dudley, vice president; Emily Green Balch, financial secretary; and Mrs. Prince, treasurer.[37]

The house residents found themselves further and further enmeshed in the world of organized labor, joining union leader Lloyd and his wife on their eighteenth wedding anniversary, for example, along with the McNeils. By April 1894, even the Social Science Club had moved from an academic interest to a statement, after a paper on the ethics of trades unions that McNeil applauded, that "some strikes could not be justified on ethical grounds but were some times necessary as war may be."[38] When the house hosted ten to fifteen of the city's leading working men, some of whom brought their wives, for an evening of music, conversation, and speeches on the role of the settlement in organizing labor and "the necessity of a common meeting ground for the working men and people of leisure," they demonstrated the extent of their own integration into organized labor in Boston. They also demonstrated the efficacy of the working women's strategy and their assumption that these women would more nearly be able to meet with male unionists on a level ground.[39]

In some ways, the women of Denison House, rather than the women workers they helped organize, had become the consorts of the male union leaders. This tendency was symbolized by the attendance of Denison House residents, escorted by Mr. O'Sullivan and cordially received, at the Carpenters' Ball (local 33) held at Mechanics Hall.[40] House residents could lose sight of working-class working women altogether in the flurry of federal labor union meetings, Social Science Clubs, and even BCLU meetings. When the public meetings of the federal labor union dwindled, the members decided to focus on the Social Science Club and recruit trade unionists to it. Apparently they meant only male trade unionists since they recruited from the ranks of the same male trade union leadership they regularly met. Similarly, they did their best to get these men, but no union women, into the reformist Twentieth Century Club, though the club accepted both male and female members. They also still actively organized and increasingly spoke at labor rallies, but as the Denison House women delegates witnessed enthusiastically their friends' performances at the BCLU and provided their own venue for such performances, in a sense they positioned themselves like the three muses they admired in Boston's 1894 Labor Day parade, "arbitration, conciliation, and cooperation."[41]

Marginalizing the Ladies

On August 31, 1894, Denison House's Helena Dudley reported "[c]onstant succession of visitors—'classes and masses' " swirling around garment workers' unrest. Miss Kenney went to interview a shirt manufacturer on a cut in the women's wages. The women, Dudley reported, had joined the union and struck.[42]

The arrival of Miss Kenney earlier in the year began to shift the balance of power in working women's organizing away from both their middle-class female allies and male union would-be mentors toward the working women themselves.

Within the next two years, Boston witnessed not only the increasing direct public assertion but the increasing public acceptance of organized wage-earning women. The garment workers were already unlike most women in Boston's other unions—small groups within heavily male-dominated unions—who seldom if ever held offices or even attended meetings. They had their own women's union, however distrustful they remained of it. Mary Kenney (who by October would be married to the *Globe*'s labor editor, general American Federation of Labor [AFL] organizer, BCLU activist, and Denison House ally John [Jack] O'Sullivan) was the national AFL's first official organizer of women. Under her tutelage, the garment workers would take hold of their organization, expand it on a citywide basis, and successfully demand greater recognition from the male unionists and their employers.[43]

Female reform as well as labor connections brought Kenney to Boston. Years earlier, Jane Addams had arranged for Kenney to stay with Helena Dudley, head worker of a Philadelphia settlement house and future head worker of Denison House, and Vida Scudder.[44] Through Addams also Kenney came to the attention of Mary Morton Kehew. When word had reached Boston that working women in Chicago were organizing into unions at Hull House, Kehew's sister, Miss Hannah Parker Kimball, went to investigate. Kehew then asked Kenney to come to Boston, which Kenney did with AFL leader Samuel Gompers's approval.[45] Once in Boston, Kenney lived at Denison House and worked out of the WEIU.[46] This trajectory demonstrates the crucial role of a national reform network of relatively elite women interested in organizing women workers.

Kenney's status as an national trade union official, however, was just as crucial. It gave her credibility with Boston labor leaders. In 1894, Kenney was the only woman participant mentioned in the *Globe*'s coverage of the Labor Day parade. It was both labor and female reform networks that allowed Kenney to succeed in Boston.[47]

Yet Kenney stood apart from all her sponsors in her estimate of women workers. On September 2, 1894, two days after the women garment workers struck, the *Globe* ran a forum, "Labor as Educator."[48] Among the contributors were Kimball, listed as "of Commonwealth Avenue," an elite Back Bay residential street; Mary Kenney, the "only woman ever appointed labor commissioner in the United States"; and Emily Green Balch, "of Denison House," as well as a handful of prominent men. The differences in their views carried crucial implications for how they envisioned their own role in the labor movement, the role of unions vis-à-vis the state and workers, and the role of the workers themselves.

All the writers saw trade unions as of great educational benefit, but they differed in who learned what from whom. To Kimball, trade unions provided an opportunity for untutored workers collectively to seek expert advice from "specialists," such as the professors occasionally invited to address the BCLU, who would supplement the workmen's views with those from "outside." Such "outside" views would broaden workers' perspective on economic issues. She added, "When women once grasp the idea of organization and realize the educational value of discussion of the great industrial questions, interwoven with their very lives as workers, they will doubtless assimilate quickly. . . . Meantime they stay behind; content, even for the same work, to undersell the men." To Kimball, trade unions provided workers a chance to be educated by the putatively detached new middle-class experts. Women, in her view, faced no barriers to organization from labor ("the lists are now freely opened, yet she lingers far behind the men") and no structural reasons for low wages. The impediment was in their heads.

Balch was even more certain that workers required education. She argued that physical laborers with little leisure or education were likely to "fail lamentably both in intelligence and in public spirit," but when they joined unions to improve their conditions, the process of debating and voting quickened their wits and made them less prey to demagogues. Clearly unimpressed with the average day laborer of her acquaintance, Balch's acquaintaince with labor leaders had convinced her that trade unions made good citizens. She pointed out, "It is not to the students of social science, but to the labor leaders that we owe our bureaus of labor statistics and their invaluable reports."

If Balch demanded less middle-class tutelage of labor than did Kimball but still doubted the intelligence of ordinary workmen, Kenney manifested no such doubts. To Kenney, workers, not middle-class experts, were the appropriate educators of other workers. "In the trade unions of our land," she declared, "discussions on the broadest questions are encouraged, and men who, owing to lack of opportunity to get a school education are not supposed to know a great deal, can be found in their unions discussing, from a practical standpoint, questions that have puzzled political economists for all time." Like Balch, she reversed the direction of tutelage that Kimball set up, but did it even more strongly. "No thinking man or woman would dream of proposing a new idea affecting the whole people without first consulting the trade unionist to get his views. . . . This shows," she concluded, "that not only has the labor movement been of educational value to the worker, but it has also been of value to thinking people outside the movement."

In Kenney's depiction, workers educated each other in trade unions, not just about broad economic issues but about political rights: "Women and men who thus associate themselves for industrial improvement get to understand their rights and the rights of others, learn how to obtain these rights without infringing upon the prerogatives of others." They would not simply inform those more powerful or lobby for bureaus of labor statistics, hoping an enlightened nonlaboring public would take appropriate protective measures. They would assert their rights directly.

The message came through clearest in Kenney's description of what women had to gain: "more respect as a woman worker in consequence of her power and intelligence through her membership in her trade union." "Respect as a woman" was a common goal among working-class, middle-class, and elite women, but "power and intelligence" as a vehicle to gain that respect—rather than sexual purity, domesticity, and deference—marked a departure. It smacked of the independent middle-class New Woman and the assertive, autonomous working girl.

Yet Kenney, too, saw the working woman as benefiting from "consulting authorities upon questions she has heard discussed in her union" and as inexplicably "satisfied to accept twenty per cent less wages for her work" than men received. She also noted that union demands must be reasonable and claimed that more often than not subordinates in a factory were responsible for their own grievances, concluding "the tone of the whole labor movement is moralizing to a degree not well understood by those who are not a part of the movement." This last may have simply been a sop to elite readers at a time of violent labor repression, but given Kenney's complaints about immoral women in her neighborhood and rental properties, it may also have represented her sense of a labor force that needed to discipline itself. Believing in the independent intelligence of labor but also in its need for discipline and "authorities," Kenney set out to wean the women garment workers' union from its middle-class sponsors, yet continued relying on her own alliances with those same sponsors.

The Globe forum appeared at a moment of intense labor unrest, where the limits of legitimate independent workers' actions were hotly contested. By autumn 1894, the depression had made Boston's workers desperate.[49] Waves of strikes, mass demonstrations, and political ferment buffeted the city. The garment industry was among the worst hit, with 37 percent of union members unemployed.[50] When Denison House residents tried to attend a State House meeting of the Commission on Unemployed, they could not get through the massed protestors. Instead they saw a parade of militia, a show of orderly state force juxtaposed to the crowd of workers and meant to assert control of the streets.[51]

Workers debated socialism, anarchism, and communism, building on the city's 1880s ferment when the Knights of Labor had claimed 10,000 workers in greater Boston, making it their banner city, and an additional 15,000 workers had joined independent unions or those affiliated with the newer AFL.[52] Their activism bore legislative fruit. In 1892, the legislature had revised downward the 1874 limit of a sixty-hour work week for women and children to fifty-eight hours. The state also established an arbitration board, a weekly payment law, new and more effective factory inspection laws, a union incorporation law, a union label law, new sweatshop regulations, and laws protecting the rights of union members and organizers. By the 1890s, Massachusetts enjoyed a reputation as a model of progressive labor relations.[53]

But the Knights of Labor were not the only force at work, and splits in the ranks of the BCLU and the Knights had helped cause a decline in membership toward the end of the 1880s. By that time, immigrant Jewish socialists, a tiny minority in the heavily Irish-and English-heritage BCLU, had started building their own clubs and societies.[54] In 1893, as Mrs. Quinn had found, these Jewish activists were reaching out to join forces with Irish women who distrusted them and saw them as rivals.[55]

Ethnic divisions joined marital status further to separate women garment workers—*Mrs.* Quinn and *Mrs.* Dowd, in distinction to *Miss* Dam and *Miss* Lifschitz.[56] Denison House took them on separate excursions.[57] To organize across these lines, the center of organizing had to move away from Jewish meeting places and enclaves—or any strictly ethnic or neighborhood base. The advent of Kenney, an Irish American herself and dedicated to union organizing, and the creation of new relatively neutral female spaces was essential. It allowed garment workers to identify themselves and their interests as women garment workers, rather than as Irish or Jewish workers with a worker consciousness built exclusively on their membership in ethnic enclaves or families or frequently hostile male-dominated unions.[58]

But working women had another kind of space to conquer. In the press and so the public eye, "labor" was male. The *Globe*'s reporting repeatedly drove home that working men were actors, women objects of their gaze.[59] On the same page that reported "All May Go Out . . . Garment Workers of Boston Ready to Strike," but made no mention of women workers, an advertisement boasted that "100 PRETTY GIRLS" would be seen in a new burlesque show at the Old Howard theater featuring twenty-five acts with 100 "Beautiful Blushing Beauties" in exquisite poses, continuously from 1 P.M. to 11 P.M. at prices ranging from ten to twenty-five cents.[60]

In the course of the strike, however, working women would begin to join working men on the stage of the *Globe*'s labor pages as workers and activists and not just as "beauties." At first, women appeared in the columns only indirectly, without their own voice, as in need of protection or as troublesome. On September 14, 1894, the *Globe* reported that several delegates to the clothing trades' district council complained that factories were violating the legal maximum of a fifty-eight-hour week for women and children.[61] Three days later, the *Globe* reported the efforts of an exasperated (male) grievance committee member of the BCLU who had tried to settle the shirtmakers union's complaints against the Middlesex shirt company: "He had arrived at what he considered a satisfactory settlement of the troubles, but the sewing girls, who comprise the membership of the union, would not accept the settlement." They instead wanted, "as one young lady said, 'the 'scabs' discharged.' "[62] That night, according to the *Globe*, women attended the mass meeting that declared "war" on the sweating system.[63]

On September 20, when the garment workers launched a general strike of the industry, the *Globe* quoted a woman worker directly for the first time. It found her at strike headquarters, reporting her shop out. She handled the books for an employer who could not read English, and she proved to be well informed on the economics of the trade. She gave a self-portrait typical of the Mrs. Dowds and Mrs. Quinns in the industry: "Working at my best I was only able to earn $4 per week in the busy season, and had to take work home to do after working hours to realize that amount. . . . In the dull season I do not work at all. I simply go to the shop mornings to see if there is an order to be made up, and then finding none, I try to get work scrubbing or anything else that I can do. . . . I have three small children who I am trying to support and educate, and the struggle has been desperate for me sometimes. There are many like me in this trade and we simply will not try to get another job in a coat shop until we feel sure that wages are to be raised."[64]

Over the next week, women workers assumed a more and more prominent role in the coverage and in the minds of the male labor leaders, who were "astonished as the committees from the various shops appeared at headquarters at 116 Eliot Street . . . and reported all hands out." Over 5,000 women and men joined the strike.[65] On September 21, the *Globe* included women workers in one of its four illustrations of the strike, albeit not on the first page.[66]

Women who belonged to no union, even in shops without men, had

KEEPING THE SIDEWALK CLEAR.

WOMEN IN THE FIGHT.

In these illustrations of the 1894 garment workers strike, note the difference between the "lady" with purse in the first illustration and the "women in the fight" in the second. *Boston Globe*, September 21, 1894.

joined the strike. A week later, none were back at work. Their presence, in connection with an organized local of women, promised to transform the garment workers union, finally making the women visible and vocal to the union men as to the press. When local 37 complained that the union had formulated its demands without consulting the women (and so covered women only where they worked the same jobs as men), the officers of the district council promised to have "the women represented hereafter on the executive board of the union."[67]

With the aid of their Denison House allies, local 37 called a mass meeting of women workers at Wells Memorial on September 28, to organize the remaining women into the union. The meeting lasted four hours.[68] By the strike's victorious end, only ten days after it had begun, the *Globe* could report, "for the first time in the history of the union the women in the trade in large numbers are now active members."[69]

By early October 1894, local 37 boasted 700 to 800 members, out of approximately 4,000 GWU members in the city. They worked nine hours instead of ten to twelve a day, and some workers, such as basters, had doubled their wages, from $5.50 per week to $10.00.[70]

Their experience dealing with a male-dominated union as well as male employers had heightened their sense of women's rights, as well as "the wrongs" of women that Mrs. Quinn had discussed with Denison House residents. In 1895, the year of the Massachusetts referendum on woman suffrage, Henry Blackwell (an officer in the Boston wing of the woman suffrage movement) canvassed 150 labor organizations on the issue. Thirty-four supported woman suffrage, 5 opposed it, and 111 ignored him. Only the new women's Garment Workers Union of Boston unequivocally and publicly supported woman suffrage and voting yes on the 1895 referendum.[71]

The women's GWU continued to flourish after the 1894 strike and gradually dispensed with its middle-class aides. Within six months, it elected its own officers. "Real material" according to Kenney O'Sullivan, "was discovered in the ranks." By the end of the year, the women were managing their own books. In December, at a meeting with fifty members, they agreed to an exchange of services—their financial for the men's organizing—with another local (no. 25, pressmen). This exchange not only argued a new assurance in their financial abilities, but manifested their replacement of a close alliance with the Denison House women for one with men in their own union.[72]

All was not sweetness and light, however. The women garment workers continued to have grievances regarding their male co-unionists and continued to use Denison House to deal with them. In January 1895, for example, local 37 sent a committee to meet with Lloyd and O'Sullivan at Denison House to present a statement about their treatment "from the men of the Union," which Lloyd was to report at the BCLU.[73]

Still, the garment workers had been only the vanguard of a new public presence among Boston's working women.[74] In early April, the BCLU admitted "many female delegates," not only from the garment workers union, but from the rubber workers (makers of rain gear) at Hyde Park, horsenail sorters, and others. Female unionists evinced a new sense of solidarity. The female compositors, the *Globe* reported, were "much interested" in the Hyde Park strike "on account of the large number of women involved in the ranks of the strikers." Now women had their own substantial voice, as women workers, at the heart of Boston's labor movement.[75]

When August 1895 arrived, the time to negotiate a new garment workers contract, local 37 had achieved a far stronger position than in the previous year. It produced its own price list a full two weeks in advance of any reported strike sentiment in the industry. When the strike came, the *Globe*, with a somewhat jaundiced eye, labeled it "the annual attack upon the manufacturers in the ready-made clothing trade," but also repeatedly noted, "The fight will vary from last year slightly, for there is a strong union of the women in the trade now, which condition did not prevail last year." The union would present the women's demands first.[76]

Boston's police chose the day after the announcement of the strike to launch a major raid on West End brothels, sending prostitutes from eight houses of prostitution onto the streets in one of the major garment districts.[77] The garment workers were unfazed. After all, the same day's paper reported the presence of no less than nine women (half from Denison House-affiliated unions) on the still heavily male-dominated BCLU's committees.[78] On the other hand, the rank-and-file women seem to have avoided the street tactics Hyde Park's female rubber strikers used earlier in the year to challenge those still working. When the garment strike commenced, experienced women workers lent their assistance to union officers at headquarters, but rank-and-file women, 40 percent of the strikers, met separately from men, and not on the street. While the men gathered at Wells Memorial on Washington Street, the women gathered at 75 Tyler Street, in the South End, away from the brothel raids.

The *Globe* reported on both the men's and the women's strike headquarters, but did so differently. It focused on the plethora of languages among the men: "Groups of men with foreign types of features gathered together and discussed the situation in the English, German, Hebrew, Polish, Italian, Portuguese and Swedish languages." By contrast, the paper focused on the gentility, balanced with business acumen, of the women: "The meetings of the women are particularly interesting, as the officers of the women's union show commendable business judgement and tact. . . . while the men are not invited to attend the women's gatherings, . . . they are treated with a dignified courtesy."[79] Eastern European names prevailed among the male garment worker leaders, and eastern European Jewish immigrant women belonged to local 37. Irish names, however, continued to dominate the women's leadership positions in all these women's unions, as they did in the BCLU as a whole. The relatively homogenous leadership allowed the *Globe* to put first what must have seemed most remarkable to it—their character as respectable women.

The garment workers won the strike in less than a week. Despite the local's increasing autonomy from its middle-class and elite allies, according to Kenney O'Sullivan, it could not have won without them. Denison House not only lent space and gentility, its head resident's friends provided the money to make up for the lack of a strike fund.[80]

After the strike, Denison House, with Kenney O'Sullivan and Mary Morton Kehew, continued to foster the creation of working women's associations and unions and to provide space for their meetings.[81] By 1896, bindery girls, store clerks, and waitresses had organized at Denison House.[82]

At the end of the 1890s depression, women workers seemed poised to take on an ever more central position in the public world of Boston's labor movement. Having moved from a position of uneasy dependence on middle-class and elite allies in their dealings with male unionists, they now served as delegates in their own right of their own union locals, which they officered themselves. Still finding their middle-class and elite female allies of great use, particularly in providing safe meeting space and the resources to originate organizing efforts, they had nonetheless seemed successfully to marginalize their influence. In the public arena of the press and the BCLU, they seemed able to stand alone. When the allies retreated, however, the working women found their position in the labor movement more fragile than it might have seemed.

Retreat and Regroup, 1897–1907

Success and a backlash among donors may have made the middle-class and elite women allies nervous. Not only Denison House but the Massachusetts Association of Working Girls Clubs' sponsors and others retreated from active labor organizing at the depression's end. Denison House did not adopt the neutrality that Robert Woods, head of neighboring South End House, advised, but it did decide, according to its head worker's report in 1897, the fourth and final year of the depression, that "It seemed wiser for certain reasons connected with political and industrial disturbances, not to attempt so much in public lectures" on labor issues. It continued to facilitate the organization of women's unions and to host their meetings along with those of the federal labor union, but the house no longer provided a strong public voice in the unions' support.[83]

Meanwhile, as garment workers organized and pressed for the enforcement of inspection laws, garment shops fled. Boston workers insisted their shops were more sanitary than New York's, where "unfortunate persecuted people" were exploited. They argued for labels indicating not simply union or nonunion workers but the city of manufacture.[84]

They found their middle-class and elite allies only too eager to pick up on the label movement, seeing the consumerist route as less confrontational and risky than organizing labor. Boston Working Girls Club sponsors Edith Howes and O. M. E. Rowes, for example, helped found the Massachusetts Consumers' League (MCL) in 1898. The MCL advocated using publicity and cooperation with employers (rather than primarily with workers—whom they described as "unorganized and helpless") to secure better conditions. Goods manufactured under conditions meeting their standards would receive the Consumers' League label.[85]

The allies of the 1890s wage-earning women's organizing movement seemed to fall into line. The head of Denison House took active interest in the formation of the MCL, securing information from Howes at the WEIU.[86] By 1900 the MCL had a 1,400-member network. To many trade unionists, the new organization seemed to have appropriated a union strategy aimed at a working-class consumer and signifying that conditions were acceptable to workers and to have replaced it with one aimed at middle-class consumers, signifying conditions met with the approval of the consumer.[87]

In 1904, a month after a male Denison House advisory board member had sent in the money he raised and resigned because of the House's continuing if muted identification with trade unions, Mrs. Kenney O'Sullivan (hostile to the Consumers' League line) called an organizing meeting for a Boston Branch of the International *Union* Label League.[88] Denison House activists Vida Scudder and Emily Balch went to Kenney O'Sullivan's meeting. Scudder became the league's president; Dudley, vice president; and O'Sullivan, secretary; and the group began to hold its meetings at Denison House.[89] Despite its obvious connections, Denison House's head worker was careful to report that the league was "not in any sense an enterprise of Denison House."[90]

It was a time of crisis for Boston's parlor socialists. As early as the 1880s, "proper Bostonians," including some members of the Brahmin set (influenced by Edward Bellamy's utopian novel *Looking Backward*, which was set in Boston), had founded the Nationalist Movement, advocating public ownership of production, services, and sales. Also a fan of Bellamy's, but feeling out of place among the Brahmins, Jewish cigar maker David Goldstein founded the Socialist Labor Party. Together with the Nationalists, it launched campaigns for municipal ownership with enough popular support that in 1891 Boston's mayor declared the city had a right to undertake "all functions of a public character now commonly entrusted to private enterprise." In 1893, the year Denison House founded its first trade unions, the *Boston Record* predicted that socialism would become more formally a part of Massachusetts laws within five years than anywhere else in the United States.[91]

But as the Socialist Labor Party grew, so did its factions, mirroring those of the party at the national level. Boston harbored some of the most prosperous sections, who nonetheless dissipated their energy in feuds, at one point seeking to expel the entire Jewish section, among the largest in the state.[92] By 1903, defectors appeared on all sides. The Catholic Church in Boston launched a counteroffensive against the growing if fractious socialist movement, and its organ, the *Pilot*, switched from ambivalence to hostility.[93] Martha Moore Avery, an influential Boston socialist leader, returned to the Catholic Church of her youth, and Goldstein, whose name had long been linked with hers, converted to Catholicism two years later. As of 1904, even the erstwhile socialist carpenters' union leader and Denison House ally Harry Lloyd had become an antisocialist.[94]

In 1906, Boston Socialists sponsored a fund-raising play about the "unjust fate of a lady whose lover was 'beneath her class.' " The leftist *Worker* sneered, "Boston is always radical, radical in religion, radical in politics and ideals, and radically divided into small, autonomous groups. In normal times these professional radicals are hard to find, but on gala occasions they appear as if by magic and applaud and cheer radical utterances and then disappear until the scenery is set to suit their fads."[95] Many of the erstwhile female allies seemed to fit this pattern, as they not only switched from supporting union labels to supporting Consumers' League ones, but switched from fostering women's trade unions to fostering girls' trade schools. This strategy, too, required more cooperation with employers than with workers, and it turned a blind eye to the anti-union origins of trade schools for boys. These women succeeded in establishing the Boston Trade School for Girls in 1904 and the School For Salesmanship, an effort in which Mrs. Lucinda Prince, formerly of Denison House, collaborated with the new Simmons College.[96]

At the same moment Denison House and other allies withdrew officially from active union organizing among women, Mary Morton Kehew, though she worked with Prince on trade schools, picked up the slack.[97] She had Mary Kenney O'Sullivan on her board at the WEIU. Kehew and her sister opened their own homes and their purses to union meetings and needs.[98] And Kehew became the first president of the National Women's Trade Union League (WTUL).

The WTUL, a group that would do more than any other before World War I to organize women into unions, grew logically from the foundation laid by Denison House and Kehew's earlier work. The British version had existed since 1874, and William English Walling, a wealthy Hull House associate, had gone to study it in 1900. When the AFL convention met in Boston in 1903, Walling attended. Together, he, Kehew, Kenney O'Sullivan, Jane Addams, and others founded the American WTUL. It was at Kenney O'Sullivan's urging that Kehew became the president.[99] This organization institutionalized the sort of patronage Denison House (and Hull House in Chicago) had provided for women's unions, demarcating the boundaries of middle-class and elite "allies" (as the group named the elite associates) in union governance and mandating a fifty/fifty split between women workers and "allies" on the group's governing board.[100]

The Boston branch (BWTUL) replaced Denison House as an essential alternative to relying on the male-dominated union movement. Despite the gains of the mid-1890s, Boston's union movement had remained male dominated and fundamentally unsympathetic to wage-earning women. At the depression's end in 1897, Edward O'Dennell, an official of the BCLU, wrote "Women as Breadwinners: The Error of the Age," for the AFL's *American Federationist*. In it he called "the demand for female labor . . . an insidious assault upon the home . . . the knife of the assassin, aimed at the family circle."[101]

While the working men of Boston rebuilt their organization after the 1890s' depression, the working women continued relatively unaffiliated with any type of organization. By 1908, the Massachusetts Federation of Labor boasted over 1,300 locals and 160,000 members. In contrast, to indicate extreme rarity, a WEIU investigator claimed that membership of working women in social and other clubs was "scarcely more common than in trade unions." The organizations working women did join, she continued, "usually combine mutual benefit or insurance features with the social motive." Security in the broadest sense, rather than simply at the workplace, continued to provide a major motivation for overworked working-class, wage-earning women to take time for groups.[102]

The Changing Geography of Working-Class Women's Work, Training, and Aspirations, 1900–1910

The opening of the Boston Trade School for Girls in July 1904 in Boston's South End, may have resulted from a women's reform group opting if not to undermine then to sidestep trade unions, but it also marked the first public acknowledgement that girls as well as boys had working lives, aspired to something beyond domestic service, and would benefit from training. Its aim was to reach girls who needed to begin wage work young and had limited time for training. It would train them for nondomestic service trades under workshop conditions so they could start work at higher wages.[103]

The idea caught on. In 1906, the more centrally located WEIU opened two trade-school shops, including store work. In 1907, the North End's North Bennet Street Industrial School made room for 140 girls in a half-day class. The Women's Municipal League and other groups lobbied for state aid, and in 1909, the Boston School Committee took over the Boston Trade School for Girls as the first state-aided industrial school for their sex.[104] It shifted the ground of women's trade education from home or workplace to school.

In its aim to make women "self-supporting and self-respecting" rather than dependent and thrifty family members, the adoption of the Boston Trade School marked a radical shift in female public education.[105] It came both as a response to the demands of working-girls and as a sign of the gradual and increasing willingness of middle-class and elite reformers to abandon, at least in part, their dreams of turning working-girls into perfect domestic servants.

Even as the trade schools grew, not all working girls had equal access. Trade school girls were largely of Irish stock.[106] Few immigrant girls could afford to delay their entry into the workforce, and southern black migrants rarely benefited because few southern locations made it possible for black children to complete the requisite grammar school.[107] Still, the 86 black girls of 961 total students in the Boston Trade School for Girls by 1909 represented approximately four times their proportion in the population. Like the white population, they split between the older trades of dressmaking and millinery, which promised ultimate independence through entrepreneurship, and the newer trades of stenography and bookkeeping, which offered steady, clean work at good pay. In both the trade school and the WEIU, an investigation reported no friction created by this racial integration but successful placement only of the nonbusiness course black girls.[108]

Others continued to learn on the job. In 1910, over 80 percent of shop girls in the clothing industry learned their trade on the shop floor, usually from the friend who had gotten them the job.[109] These women created career ladders and training programs by constant movement. A twenty-year-old Russian immigrant woman in the West End who lived with her family had been working for wages since she was fourteen. After a year as a bundle girl in a garment factory at $2.00 per week, she switched to the confectionery industry, in which she had six employers (Lowney's, Schrafft, Downes, Robert's, Aldrich and Smith, Fish and Greene's) in six years, steadily increasing her wages from $3.00 to $4.00 to $5.00 to $6.50 to $7.00, and finally to $7.50 per week as a dipper. In her last position she received overtime on Saturday, which raised her wages to $10.20 per week, and annual bonuses of over $20.00.[110]

Trade schools steered youths into factory work when their family poverty made high school impossible. High schools instead focused on the new office trades. In the 1880s, the Boston Girls High School had already taught double-entry bookkeeping for almost fifteen years. In the 1890s, the public high schools added shorthand and stenography, and by the decade's end offered what amounted to a business major.[111] The difference between trade and high school helped sharpen and fix distinctions among wage-earning women. They widened the gulf between second-generation Irish women and immigrant Italian and Russian Jewish ones.[112]

Trade school girls and the factory women they often became worked in Boston's neighborhoods. Clerical workers—for both store and office—worked downtown. By the 1910s, in Boston and elsewhere, jobs downtown held higher status to many women workers.[113] Downtown jobs required more high school or a business course. They also required knowledge of consumer culture, fashion, and the accentless English of those born in the United States or arriving as young children.[114]

Most of the downtown workers came from better-off families. According to Carole Srole, women's office work in Boston had begun as an occupation for upper and middle-class women, often fatherless but relatively well-educated. The field drew from the same pool as teaching: young women who had grown up with a piano in the parlor, lace curtains, financial stability, music concerts, and a mother at home. Teaching and clerical work were both relatively steady, clean, and required education.[115]

By the 1910s, the disjunction between opportunities offered high and trade school girls led to a kind of crisis. Frustrated by their lack of access to new commercial courses, girls in trade schools still rejected a future as a domestic servant ("the school girl would rather starve" noted one report) and also began rejecting factory work. In the school curriculum (and often out of it), that left only dressmaking. In 1913, William C. Ewing of Wells Memorial Institute reported that it was not unusual for seventy women to seek admission to a single dressmaking class with one teacher and an assistant at Wells. Unfortunately for these girls, opportunities in dressmaking had fallen by 50 percent in the previous ten years, as ready-made clothing had achieved an ever wider market and styles had simplified.[116]

Those trade school and other girls wanting to go into the advanced custom needle trades had good reason, despite the oversupply. Dressmaking and millinery work in this period remained well-paying occupations. In 1913, head dressmakers made from twenty-five dollars to thirty-five dollars per week, and design paid far more, from forty to fifty dollars per week.[117] By contrast, in a Boston garment factory in 1911, even a forewoman ("or forelady as some insist upon calling her," noted a WEIU investigation, betraying precisely the class consciousness that helped push working girls toward custom needlework) earned only twenty dollars per week, and her workers made less than half of that.[118] As Wendy Gamber has pointed out, these fields might offer exploitative shop conditions for apprentices, but they also ultimately offered not only relatively high wages but control over production and chances for advancement and social position seldom available elsewhere for, as May Allinson put it in 1916, "the woman of limited education."[119]

While store work seemed to offer similar possibilities—moving up from lowly cash girl to buyer—and held infinite allure to working-class girls, middle-class studies were skeptical. According to a 1906 study, "few cash girls rose to a higher position of clerk, because of lack of education and ability." The WEIU embraced store work as offering a new set of opportunities for women, but other women reformers deplored the tendency of girls to "drift into the large department stores, simply because they do not know how to get any better or more promising position."[120]

Those pushing factory work faced a losing battle. Girls whose parents could afford apprenticeship or school chose the greater gamble of dressmaking and store work. After describing the advantages reported to them by store workers of short hours, vacation privileges, relatively steady work in healthful conditions, opportunity for promotion and "definite business relations with the employer," a WEIU study concluded, "their sum-total of satisfaction . . . is apparently greater" than in other occupations.[121]

The realities of difference in physical labor could not be denied. Miss Goozey, a shoe factory worker in Jamaica Plain, came home "flushed with fatigue." Her low factory wages led her to wait table at the lodging house where she boarded in exchange for her meals. She arrived there already tired from a factory where the air was so heavy that she emerged each night with her shirtwaist wringing wet and her hair soaked with perspiration. Not surprisingly, the living wage investigator found her "evidently in miserable health." She was not alone. Rubber factories were even worse. All but a few women there handled lead compounds; none of the twelve factories surveyed had lunchrooms, and not all factories had washing facilities to allow the women to get the chemicals off their hands before they ate; one had a single cold water faucet for fifty women. Many worked through the noon lunch hour to make their quota, and in 1905 commonly suffered from anemia, headaches, and nausea.[122]

With these alternatives, as demand for women clerical workers rose, more working-class women entered the field. Even the daughters of unskilled laborers might stay in school long enough to qualify for such jobs if they had older brothers already earning. For these families, daughters in clerical work, rather than implying the father could not provide, demonstrated access to education, fine clothes, and prestige.[123]

Black women from any families in Boston found it difficult to get training for these more prestigious jobs and almost impossible to get hired. Telephone exchanges maintained a policy of not hiring blacks (or

Jews) in New England until the 1940s. Offices denied them jobs. Department stores rarely hired them. Smaller stores and shops in Boston had a few black salespeople by the turn of the century, and at least one black person worked as a buyer in a large establishment, but most employers refused to hire them, claiming the other workers or the patrons would resist.[124]

Black women graduated from the best high schools in the Boston area, passed the civil service exams, and were routinely refused jobs. In 1915, one such candidate, after complaining to the state government, got a job as a clerical hospital worker; she insisted on eating in the regular dining room and was fired. Such treatment was not unexpected in Boston's hospitals, whose pattern of segregation was strong enough to generate several attempts to create a black hospital. For years the New England Hospital Training School for Nurses took one black woman in each class, but despite the efforts of the Urban League, refused to hire her.[125]

The carefully managed whiteness and performative gentility of these more prestigious workplaces and their personnel became increasingly coercive. Employees faced more rules in the first decade of the new century than previously regarding dress, cleanliness, and language, particularly in store and telephone work. Adopting a familistic language, when not a paternalistic one, the managers blurred the edges between welfare work and training, as Susan Porter Benson pointed out in relation to Filene's Department Store, where employees were to call the store manager "Dad" and the counselor "Mother" in the 1910s and 1920s. In these workplaces, where, she argues, "social interaction replaced production as the essence of the work process," controlling workers' manners and appearance were the equivalent of controlling chatter on the shop floor. The telephone company similarly introduced matrons to supervise the workers even during their breaks, calling them "mothers"; the workers saw them as "police officers."[126]

In similar ways as men had, women developed a sort of aristocracy of labor, set apart by skill, education, and racial/ethnic identity; reinforced by the structure of hiring and training and the claims to gentility demanded of, as well as by, these workers; and rewarded with better benefits than the ones available to those workers who found factory and domestic work their only options.[127] Such distinctions were codified in space as well. The stark difference between working in another's home, one's own home, or a workplace apart from both remained, still laden with diversely intepreted implications for measures of virtue, status, and dependency. Added to these were distinctions between downtown and neighborhood and between trade school and high school. This shifting relation of woman worker to neighborhood to worksite to coworker overlay the shifting relations between neighborhoods and work sites as the city was spatially reorganized with the advent of large-scale mercantile enterprises downtown. It would generate different consciousness among the different groups of women workers and different results.[128]

At the same time, the meaning of downtown space had changed by the workers' presence. While men downtown still dominated, in the sense that they had more power (as employers and politicians) and resources, the tens of thousands of women store and office workers meant that downtown was no longer uncontested male space. Women spilled onto city streets not only at the end of the day, but at lunch. Most women factory workers ate lunches, brought from home, at their machines.[129] Downtown workers used their lunch time to enjoy the commercial streets.

Worrying over just what they found on those streets and in those cheap restaurants had led the nineteenth-century WEIU to open a lunchroom on Providence Street "to provide a quiet, pleasant room, and hearty food at low prices for wage earning women." By 1910, however, the WEIU had shifted to what it called "preventive" measures, closing the lunchroom and attempting to make employers pay enough for workers to buy lunch at a commercial establishment. No longer, apparently, were they worried about the vulnerability of women on men's streets.[130]

Women, Difference, and the Public Terrain: Labor Organizing, 1910–1915

In the spring of 1913, thousands of Boston's female garment workers and telephone operators voted to strike. Both votes emerged from the transformations of the preceding decade. Both groups relied heavily on the Boston Women's Trade Union League. Yet the differences were equally salient, revealing the different possibilities and constraints for immigrant and Irish American women workers and their allies.

Despite its centrality to these events, it is not easy to get at the history of Boston's WTUL. There are two seemingly incompatible narratives: one of a WTUL that is riddled with class conflict and dysfunctional, perpetually splitting or losing the most effective or most proletarian members, and the other of a fairly steady stream of women's strikes and mobilized elite women who worked on a variety of fronts, simultaneously supporting labor legislation and strikes, even when they involved the radical Industrial Workers of the World (IWW). This problem in the history echoes problems contemporary allies had reaching for the history of the women they helped organize. Sue Ainslee Clark, president of BWTUL in 1911, wrote, "one finds great difficulty in getting any consecutive history of women's trade unions, and still greater difficulty in getting adequate statistics about them."[131]

The competing narratives—in particular the one that middle-class women never really understood the interests and needs of working-class women and so the organization was always falling apart—reflect both the continual rise and fall of women's unions built on low-paying, unsteady employment and the continual struggle to work across class lines. Certainly the sorts of rifts that plagued Boston occurred in other WTUL branches, perhaps the most notorious being New York's. Yet despite the apocalyptic claims that follow each resignation, the BWTUL kept organizing, sometimes reaching new heights just after such putative disasters. The jagged narratives testify to the fragile resources that accompanied women's organizing—who would have kept the history of the garment workers between 1895 and 1913? But they also testify to a coalition whose diverse constituents enjoyed a wide variety of motives, aims, and stages of action and a complex interweaving of competing class and gender agendas.

The decade surrounding the two great 1913 strikes witnessed a labor upswing in Massachusetts. In 1913, the 350 AFL locals affiliated with the Boston Central Labor Union claimed 96,621 members.[132] One-quarter of the adult male labor force in the state belonged to unions.[133] The Democrats, traditional allies of labor, returned to power. In 1910 they won the governorship with Eugene Foss, and in 1913 they elected the first Catholic governor of the state, David Walsh.[134]

Women joined the workforce in enormous numbers. By 1910, not only did most women in their late teens and early twenties earn an income, but nearly all of the 32 percent of women aged twenty-five to forty-five in Boston who were single worked for wages. Boston's women workers were almost evenly split between clerking (store or office) (28 percent) and factory work (24 percent), with both still outnumbered by domestic and personal service workers (38 percent). The professions lagged far behind; teachers comprised 4 percent of women workers and nurses only 2 percent.[135]

Distinctions among women's occupations had become even stronger. A WEIU study had already noted that "the nationality of houseworkers [that is, domestics] is in striking contrast to that of other groups. Among them there are no American born." Immigrant women continued to dominate factory work, as well.[136] But the nationalities had shifted. In the garment factories, few workers were Irish. Russian immigrant Dora Bayrock found English speakers scarce in the Boston shirtwaist factory where she worked in 1912.[137] In 1913, when Mamie Garvin Fields, a black migrant from the Carolinas, worked at a garment factory in Boston, she found "the other girls spoke either Italian or Polish and very little English. I think Myrtle and I were the only Americans there at the time." They talked mainly by "sign language," but "those immigrant girls took us in and made us feel at home, in America, in a foreign-speaking place."[138]

If the garment factories had become quintessentially foreign turf, the telephone exchange signified Americanness, schooled and unaccented. In 1912, when no more than 12 percent of urban children finished high school, telephone operators averaged two years of high school, and in 1913 a majority were high school graduates. Moreover, at the same moment that schools for trade, salesmanship, and social work had been opening in Boston, the telephone company established a training school, headed by the former chief operator of Boston's Main Exchange, Mary E. Harrington.

Harrington applied rigorous standards, rejecting girls whose dress she judged "slovenly" as "careless" and maintaining that "exaggerated dress" was "evidence of poor surroundings, and indicates a person of too light a mind to apply herself well." By 1910, the company had stopped advertising for workers, as, according to Harrington, advertising attracted "foreigners, illiterate and untidy." Harrington preferred word of mouth, the personal referrals of school officials, or, even better, of clergy, usually Catholic priests.

Under Harrington, the company never hired black and only inadvertantly hired two or three Jewish women. Almost the entire workforce was Catholic Irish American. Harrington's promotion of Irish Americans as "Americans," in distinction to "foreigners," stood in marked contrast to Carroll Wright's official usage thirty years earlier; he excluded Irish American working girls, even when their parents had been born in the United States, from his category of "the purely American girl."[139]

Regarding other regions of the United States, scholars have claimed that such exclusions demarcated "white"—meaning those privileged to belong as full members of the polity—from the nonwhite, citing evidence ranging from cartoons to editorials to laws and debates to show, for example, that Irish men were not considered "white" by antebellum Yankees. The Irish men achieved a greater degree of inclusion by their own organized strategems, aided by shifts in the economy and demography. To date, this literature has focused virtually exclusively on Irish men. It is possible that this shift demonstrated at the telephone company in Boston was the Irish female's version of becoming "white," even though the language of "whiteness" is not in evidence. Since, despite Fields's usage, black women were usually not included in the category "American" in studies of working women (see the WEIU study on domestic workers cited above, which excluded the substantial minority of black domestic workers from the category of "American born"), the line between becoming "American" and becoming "white" was a fine one.[140] Shifting the boundary between "American" and "foreigner" further hardened distinctions within the female working class, between not only domestic servants and other workers, but between factory workers and their clerical, pink-, and white-collar peers, and it effected the kind of claims on the public they could make.

There had been sporadic outbreaks of organizing and labor unrest between 1903 and 1911, each revival followed by disintegration.[141] These difficult years left their mark on the WTUL. The depression of 1907/8, in particular, seemed to crystalize two factions within the executive board and polarize the membership. One faction saw the organization's function as primarily educational—to investigate industrial conditions and sponsor legislation to correct them and to acquaint the general public with the working woman's life. The other advocated radical action during strikes and demanded an increased emphasis on organizing new groups of workers and developing leadership qualities among wage-earning members.

In the heat of the controversy, apparently, the BWTUL secretary resigned. While the leadership termed her "incompetent," others saw her problem as "a lack of tact." Emily Green Balch—a Wellesley economist, former Denison House resident, and Boston Central Labor Union member now presiding over the BWTUL—approached Louise Bosworth, a WEIU Wellesley intern, to offer her the secretaryship of the BWTUL. Bosworth was "surprised" at the offer, she confessed, "for I don't even belong to the League and have come in slight contact with it."[142] She refused. Bosworth's distance from labor organizing is telling. It was clearly the Wellesley connection she shared with Balch and her identity as an incipient investigative reformer, rather than any interest in labor organizing, that led to the offer.

The friction reached another peak a year later, when the secretary/treasurer, Eleanor Wood and the leading organizer, Josephine Casey, both members of the more radical faction, resigned. The allies, or middle-class and elite members of the BWTUL, condemned Casey for a "hysterical and exaggerated manner of talking and lack of refinement." Other members less militant than Casey complained that she "tied us up with every labor crook in the business."[143]

In many respects, it is amazing the allies and the workers ever succeeded in collaborating. As Stephen Norwood points out, even beyond the obvious class gulf that separated women with backgrounds well off enough to afford a college education from those for whom a few years of high school seemed a significant stretch, the allies tended to be a generation older and steeped in a homosocial culture of women's colleges, women's clubs, or settlement houses. The younger women workers had often experienced the heterosocial world of coeducational high school and participated in the flippant, iconoclastic working-class youth culture of the turn of the century. Moreover, the allies tended to be Protestant, old Bostonians and the workers, Irish Catholic or Russian Jewish.

Yet the two sides had much to offer each other. The allies gained some sense of control over or guidance of the direction of the labor movement, as Jane Addams had hoped in the 1890s, and some supervision of the streets and the halls where workers met during strikes. They continued a kind of middle-class or elite female surveillance of working-class women in the name of nurturance and bolstered their own public authority in so doing. The workers gained access to financial resources, training in organizational dynamics, and support in relation to the male-dominated trade union movement and the public. While one historian claims that the 1909 resignations left the Boston branch without a "legitimate" labor organizer, another claims that from 1909, despite the resignations, working women had a majority on the BWTUL executive board.[144] And, indeed, BWTUL organizing heated up over the next four years.[145]

Given the various ties between the WTUL and the WEIU, and despite those who see investigating and organizing as mutually exclusive, it is not surprising that a WEIU investigation into conditions in the clothing industry in 1910/11 preceded a renewed organizing drive. In the most significant ways—the prevalence of piecework, dirty surroundings, and unsteadiness of employment—little had changed since the 1890s.[146] Despite the reputation for piecework as divisive, however, the garment workers often pulled together. One girl's shopmates made up her pay when she lost her envelope. Another shop collected Christmas money for a Mrs. B, who had been ill the previous month, and they all hated unjustly partial foreladies who gave their pets the best-paying work and kept them employed in dull times. As they had in the 1890s, without waiting for formal organization, garment workers in individual shops went on strike when conditions warranted it.[147]

While the WEIU investigation exposed potentially useful militance, it also revealed challenges organizers would face similar to those they had faced twenty years earlier. The investigator described one girl as "an earnest, very ambitious and refined little Socialist," but found most workers at best ambivalent about the union. One worker insisted, "it's easier to get a new job than to try to make trouble"; another had lost ten weeks to a strike called by the male operatives (probably in 1907) and refused to attend union meetings, "for the Union is full of men and it's not pleasant at the meetings."[148] The male-dominated unions, the male spaces in which they met, and their indifference to the women they hoped to organize again posed a stumbling block to organizing.

In 1911, at the conclusion of the WEIU investigation, the BWTUL claimed eleven union affiliates and 425 members, including 275 trade unionists and 150 "allies." It hired a new organizer, Helen Pasoff, former president of the English-speaking branch of Boston's shirtwaist makers union. With Pasoff, they launched an organizing campaign among garment workers that, despite the obstacles, took off quickly once given female organizers and female space.[149] Newly reorganized women garment workers told a visiting WEIU member that trade unionism was "perfectly glorious."[150]

Meanwhile, things were heating up in the textile mills of nearby Lawrence, Massachusetts. There, when the AFL refused to organize unskilled workers, the mass of workers headed for the radical IWW.[151] Robert Woods, still directing South End House and a supporter of the BWTUL, criticized the Lawrence workers for joining the IWW. As in the 1890s, Denison House residents proved more sympathetic. They found it impossible to remain loyal to the AFL. When Wellesley professor Vida Scudder went to Lawrence to speak with the Italians, she made it into the Boston press, which accused her of spreading radicalism, and she was asked not to return to the house.

The BWTUL, with several Denison House residents as active members, found itself divided. In 1910, the BWTUL had organized 680 protesting Roxbury carpet weavers, led by Sarah McLoughlin Conboy, into a United Textile Workers' Union (UTW) local and had scored a victory that regained their wage scale and gave them union recognition. Wealthy Elizabeth Gardiner Glendower Evans, in her capacity as a WTUL officer, declared that like the uprising of 20,000 garment workers in New York City earlier that year, it signaled a new era for women in industry and increasing attention from male trade unionists. As a result of that strike, Mabel Gillespie—a Denison House resident, 1905 graduate of the Simmons College School of Social Work, and secretary of BWTUL from 1906 until her death in 1923—represented the BWTUL in its first seat as a fraternal delegate at the Massachusetts State Federation of Labor. Sarah Conboy joined the staff of the National WTUL as an organizer.[152]

Now, in 1912, that same UTW refused to aid the striking women workers in Lawrence and forbade the WTUL to do so. One group in the BWTUL under Mary Kenney O'Sullivan sided with the IWW over the UTW, accusing the latter of indifference to the plight of the workers. Other troubled supporters, such as Elizabeth Evans found the IWW itself dangerous but valuable. She thought the AFL had only itself to blame for the IWW's ascendance. O'Sullivan, the most prominent and among the most successful female union activists in Boston, disheartened by the AFL's behavior and by the halfhearted response of the BWTUL, resigned.[153]

Lawrence and the AFL's behavior and even O'Sullivan's resignation does not seem to have led to a BWTUL collapse any more than the 1909 resignations did.[154] Instead there followed a wave of strikes among women in Boston in which the BWTUL played a vital role. At a single meeting in July 1912, the BWTUL discussed work with garment workers, women at the Grueby Pottery, Leather Novelty Workers, and male members of the Core Makers' Union who wanted BWTUL action "about the foreign women employed at the iron foundries."[155] Although the appearance of the male unionists seems more like an attempt to mobilize the language of respectability to eliminate women from the workplace—they complained, "The work is tremendously heavy and because of the intense heat the women are forced to wear the least possible clothing"—the other initiatives demonstrate widespread organizing. Moreover, organizing along different lines seemed still possible in the BWTUL. The same year in which the BWTUL had hired a new garment workers organizer, Elizabeth Evans reported on her minimum wage commission.[156] Evans commandeered her house as office space, a colleague recalled, vacating the dining table just long enough for "her cook, the . . . president of the union of domestic servants, to serve everyone luncheon" of cold corned beef and kidney beans.[157] To women like Evans, union organizing and legislative measures worked in tandem, not in competition.

In fact, two years later, on a sleety, bitterly cold February 3, 1913, Elizabeth Evans was at the headquarters of the United Garment Workers (UGW) helping the 1,100 women who, along with 4,000 men, had gone on strike in the men's clothing trades.[158] Unlike those in 1895, these women were ready to take to the streets. They volunteered for picket duty, and the men of the UGW called on Evans, Gillespie, and other WTUL allies to prepare them to picket within the law.[159]

These workers were not the ladies' garment workers organizing with the BWTUL for the past year. Those 12,000 workers, largely women, would go on strike a few weeks later. But they shared a common background. They were mostly immigrants, largely from southern and eastern Europe. And they enjoyed the same dichotomous representation in the press—as timid waifs or self-possessed Amazons—depending on the sympathies of the paper. The more conservative *Herald* found, "for the most part, the main strikers were young girls not yet out of their teens. Many could not understand a word of English, and timidly remained in the background, obediently awaiting orders from the interpreters assisting the strike leaders." The *Globe*, however, saw them as more assertive and older. It found "a great many women" as well as young girls in the throng of assembling strikers; "All have a prosperous look and seem very intelligent, and to be determined to win their demands . . . and they gave one to understand that they have been prudent with their earnings and saved a tidy sum, so as to be able to make the fight."[160] They blanketed the 180 men's clothing workshops with flaming red flyers in Yiddish, Italian, and English proclaiming the strike and gathered up workers in a grand procession to strike headquarters at 724 Washington Street.[161]

For a week, the strike remained among "the most peaceful and quietest affairs" in memory. Then, on February 11, nearly a thousand strikers and sympathizers, including an endless chain of picketers, clashed with the workers who had voted not to join the union or the strike at the Macullar Parker shop just down the street from strike headquarters. Benjamin Weinberg, at seventy-five a twenty-five-year veteran of the company, roughly jostled by the crowd, slipped and hurt his head while striker Catherine Sopinski, known as the "Polish Joan of Arc," fared the worse in an exchange of blows with Sara J. Kelley, a woman worker of mature years who knocked Sopinski out. Only Sopinski was arrested, followed by a mob to the police station. The presiding judge denied the company's requested injunction against the union, but the police took an ever more active stand against the strikers, charging into the crowds of picketers, braving volleys of mud, sleet, and snow, and more arrests followed.[162]

The clashes became more than workplace battles. They became struggles over neighborhoods. Those arrested tended to have eastern European names, such as Sopinski, Epstein, Steinberg, and Wynaski. When the police and the press identified a victim at all, rather than "assault against persons unknown," the victims often had, like Kelley and the police officers, Irish names.[163] In some ways this division repeated the tensions of the 1890s strikes, when Irish women had feared displacement by Russian Jews, but in the 1890s the Irish women had led the union. Now they remained at work. In East Boston, where Italian and Russian Jewish immigrants had recently moved in next to older Irish residents, strike protests erupted into full-scale violence on February 20. As 800 strikers, singing the Marseillaise, marched in from Boston, 1,000 East Boston gang members and sympathizers ambushed them to avenge alleged insults against sixteen nonstriking girls working in a local shop. When the police finally appeared, both sides joined forces against them.[164]

Yet community defense was also a tradition the Jewish women and men strikers brought to the streets. Kosher meat boycotts had periodically brought crowds of "men, women and boys" or just of "women and boys," depending on the time of day, into violent conflict in Boston's Jewish neighborhoods when meat prices rose. They pelted shops with decaying vegetables, wrenched the meat out of customers' hands, and stomped it into the ground. Women, as the dominant customer base, took the lead. Like the garment workers later, they braved police harassment. In 1902, the *Globe* reported, "Many of the women taking part in the demonstration against the buyers of meat last night were young and remarkably handsome, so that the task of the policemen in driving them away was not altogether an agreeable one, but they did it." A day later, the glow was gone. The *Globe* changed its characterization to "shrieking women" and declared of a crowd of four or five hundred men and women, "the women the most disorderly of all."[165] Another meat strike occurred just the summer before the garment strike.[166]

When the ILGWU workers struck on February 28, little changed in this pattern of a mobilized, aggressive community. Nine thousand walked out the first day. Endless picket lines of women marched before each open shop, and crowds of male supporters joined the union women on the streets at closing time.[167] Four thousand female pickets trudged through the snow and cold wind and "braved arrest and injury in their zeal to reach the side of well-guarded strikebreakers."[168] And each day police bundled women "who appeared to be mere children" to the *Herald*, but were usually between the ages of nineteen and twenty-four, into patrol wagons and down to the station, along with a few male supporters.[169]

But these women, unlike the UGW strikers, reaped the benefit of a full alliance with the WTUL. Not only did the WTUL's Gillespie post bail, but ally Mrs. Davis R. Dewey, wife of a prominent Massachusetts Institute of Technology professor, witnessed the arrests on the street and the booking at the station. Backed by her lawyer and physician, Dewey used her access to the press and told the *Herald*, "These girls were arrested with absolutely no provocation." "Girls" jostled by the crowd, according to Dewey, were accused of assault.

Like the *Herald*, Dewey never spoke of the strikers as "women." She focused on the moral outrage of having innocent "girls" manhandled by sadistic and possibly lascivious policemen:

> One little girl was led away by two officers—imagine a little girl weighing only about 100 or 115 pounds being taken in charge by two great men! One of them, she said, was a gentlemen; but the other pinched her arm so cruelly that she begged him to stop. . . . The thing that made me most furious . . . was the way young girls were examined by a male official at the police station, before a roomful of men! It would make your blood boil. The girls were frightened to death—nice girls, who had never seen the inside of a police station before.

The police had searched the women for weapons, including running their hands over their stockings, as other police and their prisoners watched. "These girls are not criminals," Dewey's lawyer insisted, "and it was unnecessary to torture them with such a performance."[170]

In light of the simultaneous police insults to marching suffragists in Washington, DC, widely covered in the Boston press due to the heavy participation of Boston suffragists, such claims of police abuse reached sympathetic ears among prominent Boston women. Suffrage workers rallied to the cause.[171] The involvement of these powerful women helped

Note the mix of women, men, and children in this kosher meat market riot of 1902. *Boston Globe*, May 21, 1902.

ensure that public opinion favored the strikers. In March, the WEIU (which still shared board members with the WTUL and included leaders with impeccable Brahmin credentials) used its bulletin to tell its hundreds of middle-class and elite members the rather alarming news that 4,000 women and girl garment workers were justifiably "engaged in labor war against their employers."[172]

Unlike their elite allies, strikers and union women did not always sustain a rhetoric of helpless girlhood that made them seem harmless and needy. At a Faneuil Hall rally sponsored by the BWTUL where the strikers and their allies appealed to the public for sympathy and support, Gertrude Barnum, daughter of a Chicago judge, condemned "society" for being "ineffective in protecting girls in industries, so that the girls have been compelled at last in desperation to take matters into their

Left to Right—Miss Mabel Gillespie, Mrs. William Z. Ripley, Miss Mary Anderson of Chicago.

Boston Strike Picketers, Left to Right— Sarah Turok, Rosa Aissen. Jennie Gitter.

Although often described by their allies (shown here, above) as "helpless victims," these striking garment workers instead defined themselves as fighters. *Boston Herald*, February 10, 1913.

own hands and fight in the streets for a living wage.'' She called the ''girls'' ''naturally peaceable'' but insulted beyond endurance. Rose Schneiderman, New York garment worker and leader, however, looked not to ''society'' but to the ''2,000,000 of organized workers back of them to protect them. Organized labor will insure,'' she insisted, ''that they are not defeated. This is war, absolutely. We cannot always choose the tactics in war, and we cannot always be ladylike when the question of bread is in dispute.'' And Lillian Coblatz, Boston garment worker on strike, looked to her fellow strikers, without mentioning protection at all. ''We are going to stand by one another and we are going to win,'' she declared.[173]

But in the realities of Boston, protection had its uses. Elite pressure had already put an end to male police searches, and pressure increased on the manufacturers to reach a settlement.[174] Meanwhile, the BWTUL formed a committee to patrol the streets in the strike zone to prevent the harassment of peaceful picketers, to supply bail for arrested strikers, and to publicize grievances and picket-line heroics. Another committee guarded meeting halls to prevent disruption, and other members worked at headquarters, arranging picket schedules and providing lunches.[175]

By their actions, these more elite BWTUL allies (almost entirely Protestant and native born), never in danger from Boston's patrolmen, policed the city's public space for women, supervising the strike and male industrialists and their minions in terms of their performance on the streets. The BWTUL women, in effect, claimed the right to become themselves the police, keeping their version of order when, by their lights, the male police and their employers had failed.

On the other hand, protection had its costs. However assertive the women strikers were on the streets, it was more elite women who represented them to the larger public, and it was male union leaders who represented them at the bargaining table. The seeming harmony of these alliances masked more troubling dynamics. The male union leaders negotiated a protocol covering 3,000 workers on March 15, 1913. What they and the women allies hailed as a victory, many of the women strikers accepted only reluctantly. They had reason. Within little more than a year, most Boston shops employed nonunion labor and few workers got the protocol's minimum wage. Disillusioned, the women stopped paying their union dues.[176]

By mid-March, the relatively elite telephone workers, like the suffragists, had rallied behind the garment workers. In their infant union, the operators voted to forgo their Easter finery, devoting the money instead to the garment workers' strike fund, and side by side with social workers took statements from arrested women to use in court.[177] Their own turn came just over two weeks after the garment workers agreed to the protocol. The telephone operators' union, 2,200 strong, meeting at the BWTUL, voted to strike.[178]

Women had worked as telephone operators in Boston since 1878, two-and-a-half years after the invention of the phone.[179] But it was only in the twentieth century that workplace conditions and autonomy deteriorated. Workers found the enhanced and intimate supervision not only irksome and nerve-wracking, but infantalizing. In the aftermath of the 1907/8 depression, they also faced low wages and increasing prices. The workers found the new "split trick," introduced in 1910, the last straw.

The company had responded to Massachusetts' lowered maximum hours laws by reducing the number of shifts for which it hired workers from three to two, and giving each worker two work tours per day, with several hours off (during periods of low telephone usage) between them. It also extended the hours of the night shift at no extra pay. Convenient for the company and exhausting for the workers, the split trick substantially lengthened the work day of operators since the carfare required to go home between shifts would eat up too much of their wages. While technically they worked only nine and a quarter hours, functionally their work day started at 7 A.M. and did not finish until 10 P.M., fifteen hours later.[180] This new regime had sent a relatively small core of twenty infuriated workers in search of a union in March of 1912.

After work, the operators had wandered up Boylston Street and saw the sign for the WEIU, with its distinctive swan and the word "Union" in the title. They went in. The WEIU referred them to the WTUL, nearby at 7 Warrenton Street.[181] There the BWTUL secretary, Mabel Gillespie, talked them out of an immediate strike (that night) and into organizing a union, which could present carefully formulated demands to the company. It was a long talk, and after it was over, the WTUL sent for help from the International Brotherhood of Electrical Workers (IBEW), as the logical allied union. IBEW's general organizer, Peter

Linehan, codirected the campaign with Gillespie, fellow settlement workers Annie Withington (also of Denison House) and Susan Grimes, and the successful carpet workers' organizer and WTUL rising star (she would be a Boston branch vice president in 1913), Sarah Conboy.[182]

The story of the twenty young women wandering off in search of a union is revealing. They did not know where the union was or which union to seek. Although many telephone workers had union men in their families—among them the striking longshoremen and motormen and conductors from the Elevated Company, all largely Irish American—the telephone workers did not go to their male relatives for help in organizing.[183] It may have been that their fathers' and brothers' activities made them think of organizing or sympathetic to organizing, but it did not make them think that familial channels or male unions were their logical allies any more than it had the workers in the 1890s.

Despite management intimidation, including dismissals for union activity, a year later virtually the entire telephone operating force of Boston had joined the union. Even for the first meeting, Linehan had to find a bigger hall, and two weeks later the meeting had over six hundred operators.[184]

Ironically, the split trick at work, in conjunction with the reorganized urban geography of women's work, facilitated the workers' organizing. Working downtown, without neighborhoods in common, it would have been more difficult for telephone workers than for garment workers to organize, to find a supportive community or even create one of their own. Heavily supervised and steadily at work, unlike store clerks, they could not develop such comradery at work. As historian Stephen Norwood points out, the split trick forced the telephone workers out on the city streets for hours at a time and not only allowed but facilitated their congregating "in small groups around the city," where "the operators could fraternize and exchange ideas away from company supervision."[185]

In mid-April 1912, the operators' conference committee had first presented demands to the company. When their immediate superior rejected the demands, they appealed to the company president, who asked time to investigate.[186] The union continued to organize, reaching over a thousand members by May. Inverting the trajectory of the garment workers twenty years earlier, the women then turned to organizing the men. Meeting at Wells Memorial, a neutral space, a committee of twelve operators' union activists described their organization and its growth as over four hundred men in the audience cheered and applied for a charter from the IBEW.[187]

Some concessions from the company forestalled a strike in 1912, but a new president, Philip L. Spalding, who had a reputation for strike-breaking, refused to honor the concessions, and in March 1913 the union again presented its demands. With the aid of Gillespie and Elizabeth Evans, they secured the services of the erstwhile garment manufacturers' lawyer, Louis Brandeis.[188]

When Spalding declared he would never recognize the union, the union women were ready to put Brandeis and other mediaries aside. They demanded a meeting between Spalding and the nine-woman union arbitration committee and appealed to the BCLU (on which they were represented), the WTUL, the Chamber of Commerce, and the mayor to pressure the company into negotiating. They also voted to strike in April by a nine-to-one margin.[189]

Despite the three male IBEW locals voting (at the BWTUL headquarters) to go on a sympathy strike and the unanimous endorsement of the BCLU, Spalding treated the threat as a joke. While the company sent managers in taxis to try to recruit former employees at their homes (without much success) and laid plans to import strikebreakers from across the country, business leaders, with bad memories of the disruptive streetcar strike the previous year, appealed to the mayor to conciliate.[190] The State Board of Arbitration, having met separately with the IBEW vice president, who opposed a strike, and the company attorney, succeeded in persuading the union to delay forty-eight hours.[191]

The city overwhelmingly supported the operators. In some ways, the women reaped the benefit of company policy when the public insisted on seeing them in much the way that Mary Harrington, head of the company's operator training, had posed them. The *Boston Globe*, reporting on the strike vote, commented on the operators' "elegance," their "furs, hats of chic design, and smart-looking and expensive-looking shoes," which could have been read as a stab at their claims of low wages, but instead marked them as respectable, orderly women.[192]

If, unlike the "foreign" garment workers, the telephone workers could be recognized as respectable denizens of downtown by their dress, they also benefited from the literal as well as figurative centrality of their work. The conservative *Herald* warned of business disruption. Unlike the garment workers' strike, the impact would not be localized in neighborhoods. These workers, like streetcar workers, created the web that allowed the city to function as a whole and affected every corner of it, both as centralized corporately and technologically and decentralized by exchanges.

The almost entirely Irish American telephone operators enjoyed centrality in yet another way. They stood at the hub of a network of alliances. They had alliances not only with key women's organizations, but as importantly, with their coethnics who ran Boston's labor organizations, police, and politics. They had representatives on the Irish-dominated BCLU and the Massachusetts Federation of Labor. They had fans among Boston's Irish politicians, who dominated the mayoralty and the Democratic party delegation to the state legislature. In November of 1912, four months before the strike and at the start of the Brahmin social season, the new telephone operators union had given a "grand ball" attended by 2,000 people, including the Massachusetts governor, the Boston mayor, members of the Boston City Council, and several state senators.[193] With this wealth of allies, the workers depended less on their middle-class and elite female connections to police the streets, negotiate the settlements, and win their demands than had the garment workers.

In the State House, Irish politicians attacked the New England Telephone Company, in part as a Yankee Brahmin bastion of arrogance. It was not only that the Irish were now "American," but that America (at least Boston), in some sense, was now Irish. No police would come to rough up *their* picket lines.[194] While Yankee middle-class and elite organized women could identify with the workers' elegance and unaccented English, Irish Boston identified with their roots.

Meanwhile, the company used the forty-eight-hour delay to deploy its national geography to combat the local geography of support for the operators. Within two days it had imported more than a thousand strikebreakers in chaperoned railroad cars from New York, Jersey City, and Phildelphia; gave them magazines, candy, fruit baskets, and a $25 bonus; housed them in twelve Boston hotels; and announced its willingness to spend $800,000 to maintain service.

OUT-OF-TOWN OPERATORS MARCHING FROM BACK BAY STATION TO THE COPLEY-PLAZA HOTEL

Group of Girls Coming to Man Boston Telephone Boards in Case of a Strike.

Monitor Guarding Newly Arrived Telephone Operators.

DEMOCRATS BEGIN FIGHT

THOUSANDS IN DUTIES LOST BY PASS SYSTEM

Pier Privileges Used by Smugglers to Affix Labels to Trunks.

NEW PHASE OF SCHEME

Testimony to show that the government was defrauded of thousands of dollars in customs duties through the abuse of "courtesies" extended visitors to the ocean steamship piers at Charlestown and East Boston was brought out, it is understood, during the first day of the federal grand jury's investigation of the alleged smuggling conspiracy.

By reason of the "courtesies" extend-

The telephone company made certain the young women it imported to substitute for strikers spent only limited and carefully monitored time on the streets. *Boston Herald*, April 9, 1913.

As Stephen Norwood has pointed out, it transported these young working women not just across state lines, but across social ones. It placed women who lived in stuffy $3 a week rooms with a shared bath down the hall, into the brand-new Copley Hotel, where they luxuriated in Jacobean bedrooms with deep velvet curtains, mirrored doorways, and extravagant baths. In the lobby, they rubbed shoulders with Brahmin socialites attending a costume ball, and en route from the train station they enjoyed the admiring glances of MIT men who gathered from their building across the square to watch the procession of women the *Boston*

Post claimed "looked more like chorus girls from some high-class theatrical show than they did telephone operators."[195]

Unlike the neighborhood boys in Malden, who stoned company vehicles coming to recruit former workers, the MIT men downtown did not attack. Positioned as corporate allies by agreeing to scab, the women found themselves physically positioned, suddenly, as social peers of other corporate allies, placed in the ballrooms and playgrounds of the elite not as servants but as consumers. Just as the employee lounges of the telephone company and department stores promoted worker loyalty by providing access to consumer luxury, the telephone company rewarded its strikebreakers with socially specific consumer signifiers.

They were not chorus girls, but it was indeed a kind of theater, and at first the strikebreakers reveled in their role, bantering with the college men, "Be good, you, and maybe we'll invite you to the dance in the gilt ballroom tonight." They also understood, however, the temporary nature of the transgression, explaining to the unionists in Boston, "Oh yes we were told you were talking of striking, but most of us do not intend to stay more than a week. We just came for a good time" and the promise of promotion.[196]

Male labor officials, on the other hand, deployed the ubiquitous language of white slavery and the recent Mann Act to position the company as a pimp, working the "girl traffic," transporting women across state lines for immoral purposes.[197] Other unions pledged their support. The telegraph women and men did so, and both locals of the Boston Hotel Workers' Union voted to strike rather than serve the strikebreakers.

The Chamber of Commerce, increasingly anxious, offered to mediate. The ensuing meeting highlighted the opposing forces in the strike. Heading the corporate side was Chamber of Commerce president James J. Storrow, a Brahmin reformer who had long advised Bell financially and had run in 1910 as the Good Government Association's candidate for mayor against the North End Irish Democrat John F. "Honey Fitz" Fitzgerald, the current occupant of that position (a race Storrow lost by only 1,402 of more than 90,000 votes cast). On the operators' side was union president Annie Molloy, who would later work for the consummate Irish American machine politician, James Michael Curley.[198]

As they squared off at Young's Hotel in the heart of the business

Note the dress and assertive pose of these telephone union officers, with Annie Malloy at their center. *Boston Herald*, April 12, 1913.

district on April 8, it was the male Boston Brahmins against the upstart Irish American women workers. Molloy's teammates included other officers and union members, Mary Meagher (vice president), Mary Mahoney (secretary), Melena Godair (treasurer), Mary F. McCarthy, Bessie S. Shilladay, Alice M. Keating, Mary F. Murray, and Julia S. O'Connor (future BWTUL president).[199]

In some ways, this pairing of the union girls versus Storrow was a replay of his failed election bid, but in the Irish role this time it was women, not men; the economic, not the political sphere. And this time, not being an election, there would be compromise. Not only did the workers win some of their demands, but Molloy must have impressed Storrow. Later in 1913, after the settlement, his wife, Mrs. Helen Osborne Storrow, also an urban reformer, invited Annie Molloy to join the Woman's City Club (WCC), a group dominated by relatively conservative movers and shakers of which Mrs. Storrow was founder and president.[200]

It was an extraordinarily successful staking of a direct claim by these working-class women to Boston's public sphere. The potential strike-breakers were positioned as Brahmin consorts, like idealized Brahmin women (unlike actual ones), confined to domesticlike spaces of hotels and to consumption. The potential strikers—sitting at the bargaining table opposite, and not with, Brahmin men—were positioned as autonomous public actors, yet not masculinized nor seen as disorderly or as immoral in the process.

It is not accidental that it was the Irish American and not the Russian Jewish or Italian immigrant women workers who made this transition to direct self-representation despite the handicaps of sex and class. In the theater of the public, alliances and particular political cultures deeply affected what happened on the streets. As nonvoting recent immigrants, Russian Jewish and Italian workers were socialized into an oppositional politics—a heterosocial world of radical movements, meat boycotts, and mutual aid associations.[201]

Irish American women, by contrast, were socialized into a world of boisterous political street rituals and rallies and party political loyalties that merged neighborhood with ethnic and religious identities in both school board elections (open to Boston women since the previous century) and other city contests. The recent triumph of this ethnic political culture in Boston (witness Storrow's close defeat) was central to the operators' success. The culture of electoral politics permeated their organizing. While other women's unions seldom mentioned their elections, the telephone operators boasted that their annual elections were the most important event in Boston's labor circles, and when armed with full suffrage, Molloy entered the race for city Council in 1922.[202]

In this context, the issue of "whiteness" becomes central to understanding the difference between the garment workers' and the telephone workers' treatment. The telling passage David Roediger has brought to light from W. E. B. DuBois is worth quoting at length. Though DuBois wrote it referring to the South during Reconstruction, it seems tailor-made for Boston in 1913. Regarding the privileges of "whiteness" that compensated even low-wage white workers, DuBois wrote, "They were given public deference . . . because they were white. They were admitted freely, with all classes of white people, to public functions [and] public parks . . . the police were drawn from their ranks and the courts, dependent on their votes, treated them with leniency. . . . Their votes selected public officials and while this had some effect upon the economic situation, it had great effect upon their personal treatment."[203] It was at least in part the claims of whiteness Mary Harrington and the Irish politicians had laid for the telephone workers that made them, in distinction to the garment workers, safe on the streets and gave them access to the negotiating table.

Yet these working women emerged neither precisely like the Irish male labor leaders who dominated the BCLU nor precisely like the Irish politicians who dominated the Democratic Party. Had those been obviously accessible routes for them, they never would have wound up at BWTUL headquarters. They added to the mix what they learned from the cross-class women's reform organizations that had sponsored them, from the urban politics of middle-class and elite women socialized into nonelectoral, often antiparty, appointive and reform pressure groups. Unsatisfied with their subordinate position in the union, and with a clearer sex segregation of labor than the garment workers had, the operators launched an equal-rights campaign in the union, gaining full voting rights and autonomy in 1918. Theirs would become the first national trade union "controlled and officered by women."[204] Their WTUL experience was critical in how they understood equal rights as involving sex at all.

In 1913, after the meeting at Young's Hotel, the union membership rejected a company attempt to settle for far less than they demanded, voting in three shifts at the WTUL (union headquarters) and Wells Memorial. With the aid of their unlikely allies in the Chamber of Commerce, they forced the company back to the bargaining table (unlike the women garment workers) until the union had won virtually all its demands, without ever walking out.[205]

With their victory, the telephone operators became the key component in the BWTUL. Members of the local became the first working-class women presidents of the BWTUL, with Julia O'Connor serving from 1915 to 1918 and Rose Sullivan following her from 1918 to 1919. Two other members of the local joined them on the BWTUL executive board.

Now their union, as much as the BWTUL or other middle-class and elite women's organizations, bridged the gap between women workers and the Boston labor movement, and between classes of women in Boston. They participated in these movements as major players in their own right. By 1914, their membership reached 3,000, all but 5 percent of the company workforce, and it kept growing, reaching 4,000 in 1919. People stood in line for two to three hours to vote for officers, executive board members, adjustment board representatives, and delegates to the BCLU and the Massachusetts State Federation of Labor. Thanks largely to this union, women reached new heights, albeit relatively small ones, of influence in the state's labor movement, rising to as much as 13 percent of the delegates at state conventions.[206]

If the operators had learned from the BWTUL, the organization also learned from them. With operators on their board and their presidency, the BWTUL detailed operators to organize other trades. In 1913/14 they launched organizing drives among candy and newsstand workers and office building cleaners.

Witnessing this mobilization, the AFL insisted on taking control of the candy workers organizing and assigned a male organizer. Not pleased but cooperative, the BWTUL handed over their list of members and contacts. Just as the AFL rejected the BWTUL's female leadership and the IBEW tried to fend off the operators' full participation, the male cigar worker assigned to organize the candy workers rejected the creation of an autonomous female space within Boston's union movement. He refused to hold meetings in the WTUL building.

In all the organizing drives of women workers, the ability to hold meetings in space recognized as female-dominated had been essential. The drive failed miserably. In 1915, fed up with the AFL's mishandling of the candy workers, the BWTUL denounced the AFL as undependable and condescending. According to an infuriated Mabel Gillespie, BWTUL secretary, the AFL had drawn a different conclusion. "It is no use," they said, "we cannot organize women."[207]

Aftermath

As it did elsewhere in the country, the outbreak of war in Europe led to massive economic disruption in Boston. Workers first experienced high levels of unemployment and then a boom leading to the state's lowest level of unemployment in many years, coupled with inflation that doubled price levels between 1914 and 1919.[208]

The unemployment remobilized and redirected the same coterie of social reformers who had organized labor in the 1890s. Helena Dudley of Denison House, Robert Woods of South End House, Louis Brandeis the labor attorney, and Henry Abrahams of the cigar workers joined government committees. Their old concern with the irregularity of work became more general, and this time did not disappear with the return of prosperity.[209] The Boston Chamber of Commerce, confronted with 150 jobless men asking to use their building as a dorm, took up the issue. Increasingly, bolstered by such support and the fear of rising Democratic strength, Republican state legislators voted in favor of labor legislation.[210]

The return of prosperity found Boston in 1915 with nearly three-quarters of a million inhabitants, still a leading financial and commercial center.[211] Recovery, however, failed to still the stirrings of unrest. Workers feared renewed layoffs. Their wages failed to keep pace with inflation. Poverty shadowed them everywhere. They watched bitterly the extravagance of their employers.[212] To this layer of society, U.S. entry into the war in 1917 brought little relief. Indeed, the head worker at Denison House reported, "The winter of 1917/18 was unforgettable—one of those black letter years when greater forces outside our own control all seemed to conspire with the stars in their courses to make life so difficult that every day became a test of faith and character." The coal shortage led to frozen pipes, and the resulting lack of water to unsanitary conditions and illness. The influenza epidemic arrived in Boston that winter, and when Denison House started a Woman's Clinic that fall under Dr. Maude Furniss, they found themselves deluged by babies with flu.[213] Over four thousand Bostonians died in the epidemic of 1918.[214]

Recently elected mayor, James Michael Curley responded to wartime trouble by expanding the city's payrolls, and in its work relief program the Massachusetts Committee on Unemployment paid union wages for unionized occupations. The committee also pushed for unemployment insurance and secured the backing of the Massachusetts Federation of Labor, the Associated Charities, and many business figures. Even the

Chamber of Commerce advocated exploring the issue, as did the Republican Party. In January 1916, the committee introduced the first unemployment insurance bill in the United States to the Massachusetts legislature, only to have the commission created to investigate the matter decide the time was not ripe.[215] The only social insurance remained mothers' aid, enacted in 1913.[216]

Organized workers took matters into their own hands. In October 1915, nearly a thousand railway workers met at Faneuil Hall to secure the eight-hour day. They mobilized their powerful women's auxiliaries and deployed their male members in Democratic politics, building a national political machine.[217] The next year, Boston garment workers struck demanding restoration of their former wages from the wartime national board that oversaw labor standards for army clothing. The board forced the quartermaster to stop putting out contracts with anyone who had work done in tenements, but it neither restored former wages nor addressed the needs of homeworkers.[218] Moreover, the garment workers striking in 1916 were beaten by police, the same as they had been in 1913.[219]

In other sectors, labor organization boomed in the context of virtually full employment. By the war's end, the BCLU, still Irish dominated, was larger and stronger than ever. By 1919 it represented over a hundred thousand members.[220] That year, those members swelled the national strike wave.

Boston's railroad workers joined the strike for nationalization after the war, having generally experienced wartime federal control of the roads, under progressive William McAdoo, as an improvement. The telephone workers also struck, but not for nationalization. Their wartime experience of nationalization differed drastically from the railroad workers'. They struggled under Postmaster General Albert Burleson, for fourteen years a U.S. representative from Texas and the wealthiest man in the cabinet. Julia O'Connor, involved in the Boston union from its inception and president in 1919, declared, "never was the oppressive, anti-union policy of the telephone company so freely and fearlessly exercised as during this period." Unlike the national railroad administration, Burleson's Post Office Department demonstrated concern over neither wages nor conditions and suspended the right to bargain collectively even where it had been recognized before the war.[221] Hit like their fellow workers with inflation, the workers in Boston and elsewhere went on strike.

The 1919 telephone workers' strike repeated many of the lessons of the 1913 action. In February of 1919, two months and a commission after the agreement under which operators had worked expired, 95 percent of operators favored a strike. After acceding to repeated IBEW requests, as in 1913, to delay action, by April Boston's 4,000 operators had run out of patience. At a mass meeting at Fanueil Hall, the operators voted to strike. O'Connor issued the orders to launch the walk out at 7 A.M. on April 15, 1919. As union members and nonmembers walked out, Massachusetts, Rhode Island, New Hampshire, Maine, and Vermont lost all telephone service. The last vestiges of male authority over the telephone operators' union were falling.[222]

As in 1913, the vast majority of Boston's citizens rallied behind the strikers. Almost every Boston paper supported them, even the conservative Boston *Evening Transcript*, which denounced Burleson as a "bumptious bureaucrat."[223] The strikers began each day with mass strike meetings, singing and dancing the shimmie to ragtime tunes. The youthful ebullience, aggressive "modernity," and sexual expressiveness of the young women was again at the fore. Again, the press commented on their attire—the high heels and tight skirts that made keeping up on picket lines difficult, the silk stockings and "up-to-the-minute dressed crowd of girls." Even if the *Evening Transcript* admonished that "fewer fur coats and quieter styles in headgear would have been more appropriate," no one questioned their morality or argued that the protest unsexed the protesters, even when the local's secretary, May Matthews, held a mock wrestling exhibition with another operator before an "uproarious" audience. On the strike's second morning, the operators further imprinted their triumphal claim to public, commercial, and civil space by an impromptu parade through the central business district, more than a thousand of them marching to the Boston Common, where groups of soldiers cheered them. They picketed around the clock. The streets were theirs, at any time of day or night.[224]

Once again the importation of strikebreakers merely cemented sympathy for the strikers, and cab drivers and hotel workers refused to serve the scabs. Firemen, janitors, elevator operators, railroad workers, women doctors, and merchants, particularly in Chinatown, the location of a major telephone exchange, all made their allegiance clear.

Only the most conservative members of elite Boston opposed them, including society matrons who belonged to the Massachusetts Anti-Suffrage Association and many college men and women who acted as strike breakers, sometimes seriously injured by male strike sympathizers. An MIT student, not merely watching female strikebreakers, as his fellows had in 1913, but working for the company lost several teeth at the Main Boston exchange. But the *Harvard Crimson* disavowed the strikebreakers on campus. When Burleson threatened to replace the phone workers with soldiers, the strikers had 100 veterans in uniforms, their brothers and boyfriends, join them in a parade behind the service flag of the union, which had six stars representing members of the union serving with the American Expeditionary Force in France.[225]

Soldiers also came to the aid of the strikers on the fourth day of the strike at the main exchange, where a crowd of 3,000, including many in uniform, beat male strikebreakers. In this incident and in the parade above, the soldiers were framed as chivalric, the women as in need of protection, much as more conservative forces and allies had presented the women garment workers in 1913. May Matthews, who had staged the mock wrestling match, told her fellow unionists, "The soldiers told them they went across to fight for democracy, but they didn't expect to come home and fight against women." And a Boston IBEW official referred in the *Journal of Electrical Workers and Operators* to "Uncle Sam's soldiers and sailors, who are always ready and willing to aid beauty in distress." Moreover, when men joined the strike, on the third day, they assumed responsibility for night picketing.

While the soldiers attacked the strikebreaking college men physically, the operators called the collegians "Lizzies," and taunted them for being wealthy men working at women's jobs as operators. Pursuing one such college student to a movie theater, the strike responded to his invitation to enter by replying they would "when you're a man and grown up." These interactions called into service dominant gender roles and relations, defining appropriate men's and women's work, men's and women's times of day on the street, constructing differences between men (protectors) and women (operators) and punishing transgressions.[226]

Yet the operators had shown little sign of needing protection. Indeed, Matthews reported to the National WTUL (not to the male-dominated union press) on strikers who registered as guests at the hotels where the imported strikebreakers stayed: "We have some very good-looking telephone operators in Boston, and we got the big, stately ones and had them parade through the lobby of the Lenox Hotel. We were sure they could not tell whether they were guests or pickets. The strikebreakers would start down to breakfast. . . . Immediately those fine-looking guests would go in and surround the strikebreakers," inform them of the strike, follow them into elevators, and surround their cars with union cars.[227] Women as well as men could directly intimidate, patrol streets, and block strikebreakers. It was perhaps precisely because these women seemed so self-sufficient that the soldiers and the union men reinforced gender codes.

Once again, their liminal class position and central ethnic position worked in the operators' favor. When eighteen-year-old Anna Weinstock, future president of the BWTUL (1919/20), shouted across the street to another picketer during a neckwear strike of over two hundred women in 1917, she was arrested. In 1919, not a single telephone operator suffered the same fate. Instead the police got picketers lunches and lent them raincoats.[228]

Burleson folded after five days. The 8,000 union telephone operators had won.[229]

The 1919 strike clarified the contingent nature of the space white working-class women had won in Boston. For Irish American women, their soldier consorts helped legitimate their claim as "Americans," the Boston surrogate term for "white." Only the same Brahmin segment, or their female counterparts, who continued to wage a losing battle against Irish American rule in the city, contested the strikers' rights to organize effectively and take over the streets and other public places, including the telephone exchange, itself a quasi-public place, particularly when under federal control.

Irish American men, in the shape of policemen, soldiers, or service workers, would not contest that public dominion by their female counterparts as long as they could continue publicly to play the role of physical protector in relation to those women, more violent than the women, stronger, and morally unendangered at night. Like the working-class men almost a century earlier, whom Carolyn Strange has described as battling with elites over the virtue of a working woman, these men could define themselves as men in the public theater of the streets, in relation not only to the female strikers but to the presumably elite college men. By besting the latter physically in the name of protecting the former, they joined their class and gender positions and, for soldiers, reasserted their masculinity in the domestic arena.

But not all working women were deemed worthy of such protection. An Irish American dominated police force might not arrest an Irish American dominated group of women strikers, but it would not hesitate to arrest less "American" female strikers, such as the largely immigrant women Anna Weinstock led. No more than the middle-class and elite women reformers had the telephone operators won an empowered place in public for all women, nor had they intended to do so. Nonetheless, by inserting and asserting themselves in Boston's public life, as a kind of female labor aristocracy, they had stretched the legitimized public sphere. And like their more elite counterparts, they had not stopped making demands on it.[230]

7

"A Debut or a Fight?"

Class, Race, and Party in Boston Women's Politics, 1920–1940

What a big thing Votes for Women really is. . . . If it just meant votes it would hardly be worth working for, neither would it require much work, for . . . progressive men . . . would accept it as readily as other progressive ideas.

Florence Luscomb

In March 1913, at the same time the garment workers and telephone operators took to the streets, the *Boston Herald* reported yet another successful female invasion: "Woman suffragists came away from the State House yesterday afternoon victorious in the first manoeuvre of their campaign to obtain the submission of a constitutional amendment permitting women to vote."[1]

Nothing more clearly signifies the "public" arena than electoral and party politics. Though the suffragists eventually lost the battle for the 1913 Massachusetts amendment, they won the vote with the federal amendment in 1920. As the 1920s dawned, they stood poised to launch themselves into the fray. They and the other new "women politicians," as the *Boston Globe* called them in 1921, had their training not only in woman suffrage groups, but in trade unions, political families, women's civic lobbying groups, state and municipal appointive offices, and even in antisuffrage groups.

Women's partisan activities in the decades following the granting of suffrage have only begun to be studied. We have some excellent work on women in the New Deal, a handful of state-level studies, and a few studies at the municipal level.[2] Almost universally, those studies focus on activist, relatively elite, white women.[3] They have primarily concerned the continuing involvement of women in the creation of the welfare state and the continuing relative absence of women in electoral offices. Except regarding the 1920s Equal Rights Amendment debates, the studies have largely if not entirely ignored shifting class alliances and conflicts among women over who would represent whom. Yet the failure of suffrage movement leaders to hold together a universalized "woman" after 1920 was not only because of contests among elite white women. It was at least as much because other women could now, and did, speak for themselves.

Women entered the partisan fray through appointive as well as elective office. The structure of their appointive politics emerged from the presuffrage groundwork laid by a wide range of women's civic organizations, including suffrage, class-bridging, and antisuffrage groups. For elite women in particular, their assumptions, plans, and behavior after suffrage continued to rely on an earlier set of paradigms about women's public place and merged uncomfortably with the increasing intrusion of partisanship into their welfare bailiwicks. It is crucial to examine that domain of appointive politics to understand the electoral contests that, even when simultaneous with appointive battles, tended to take their shape instead from the new context of the late 1910s and 1920s, with their different assumptions about women's place, different opportunities and rules for women, and different organizational possibilities. Women politicians negotiated this complicated landscape of potential alliances often by making and remaking themselves; different identities ("woman," party, "labor," "race") offered new opportunities or salience, and old alliances lost their allure. As patterns of protégéeship gave way to contested elections, elite and working-class women politicians followed starkly different municipal political trajectories.

Protégées, Politics, and Class, 1909–1931

The tensions should have been obvious to the suffrage leaders from the start. After all, Boston women had served a long apprenticeship for full suffrage. No sooner had Boston women, by careful precinct-level organization, won the right to vote for Boston School Committee candidates in 1879, than they found themselves at the center of one of Boston's most heated battles between evangelical Protestants and Irish Catholics.[4] Though the conflict, ostensibly over textbook choices, occurred at a peak moment in Boston's nativist tradition, shortly after the induction of its first Catholic mayor, many Bostonians blamed women for fanning the flames. And, indeed, women led the attacks, launching new organizations and splitting old ones.[5]

Even after things calmed down with the defeat of Hugh O'Brien for mayoral reelection and the victory of the radical Protestant slate (endorsed by the Republicans) for the School Committee, the legacy of the conflict lived on. Boston women never comprised more than 20 percent of the School Committee, and in 1895 Boston male voters rejected their bid for full municipal suffrage, two to one.[6] Moreover, women continued to participate prominently in recurrent outbreaks of Protestant Yankee versus Irish Catholic friction.[7] After one such outbreak, the Yankee Republican-dominated state legislature in 1905 limited the Boston School Committee to five members in the name of efficiency.[8] Only three women served on the School Committee for the next forty-five years, one at a time, all of them Protestant Republicans.[9]

While the actual experience of electoral politics had widened the breach between Yankee elite and Irish Catholic women, the suffrage movement tried to build bridges across it. Between 1909 and 1919, the woman suffrage movement in Boston, as elsewhere, reached out with new vigor to working-class white and to black women. As home to Lucy Stone and the headquarters of her American Woman Suffrage Association and its *Woman's Journal*, Boston had been a center of suffrage activity since soon after the Civil War.[10] By the 1890s, members not only of the WEIU but of the black Woman's Era Club affiliated with Stone's suffrage organization. Nineteenth-century bazaars in public halls and early twentieth-century outdoor pageants increased the movement's visibility.[11]

But the success had been limited. Some working-girls' clubs and women's unions came out for suffrage, but their organizations were short-lived, and the members tended not to join general suffrage organizations.[12] In 1909, Boston's suffrage organizations launched a two-pronged campaign to broaden their reach. They changed venues, taking to the streets with motorcades and open-air speeches across the state to reach a working-class audience who would not come to their halls and parlors. And they hired women, including labor union women whom suffrage leaders had met in the course of their other activist work in the WTUL, specifically for the job.[13] The suffragists, like the striking telephone workers a few years later, were staking a new kind of claim to Boston's streets. That fall Boston's first suffrage parade marched from the railroad depot at South Station to the suffrage headquarters at Boylston Street.[14]

It was these women speakers, whether working-class, managerial middle-class, or elite, who became early candidates for public office. They had learned to speak to "arrogant clubwomen, imperious state legislators, devout churchgoers," and hostile street crowds.[15] Susan Walker Fitzgerald, future member of the Massachusetts House of Representatives (elected 1922), daughter of an admiral, wife of a wealthy, Harvard-trained lawyer, and herself a political science major from Bryn Mawr (class of 1893) and veteran of a New York settlement house, led the motorcade. Florence Luscomb, candidate for Boston City Council in 1922, MIT graduate and architect, went along.

Luscomb recalled they would "reach a town, take possession of the busiest spot," and send Fitzgerald to get the police permit. Having borrowed a box from "the obliging drug clerk" where they had left their luggage and bought sodas, Fitzgerald, Luscomb, or one of their cohort would mount the box and start "talking to the air, three assorted dogs, six kids, and the two loafers in front of the grocery store just over the way." Often people came just "to see this strange thing," Luscomb noted, "women speaking outdoors in public." Within ten minutes the crowd would reach 500.[16]

Margaret Foley, a native of Irish Dorchester and Roxbury who had joined the hat trimmers union and then the Boston board of the WTUL, was among the group's most effective speakers. At five feet eight inches and 140 pounds, she was a striking figure with, according to

Alice Stone Blackwell, a voice like a trumpet.[17] In contrast to the elite women she accompanied, she seemed a fearless warrior. At the end of 1909, Margaret Foley together with another suffagist invaded the floor of the Boston Stock Exchange and the Chamber of Commerce to distribute leaflets publicizing the visit of a prominent British suffragist. And it was Foley and her group who started heckling politicians at public rallies for their antisuffrage views.[18]

The spatial boundaries Foley was breaking differed from those of Luscomb, whose mother had a comfortable independent income, and Fitzgerald. Foley had grown up not in the city's genteel spaces but in its working-class neighborhoods. Although she was among the minority of working-class girls to graduate from Girls' High School, when Luscomb and Fitzgerald were attending college, she was working in the hat factory.[19] Press accounts and the private correspondence of suffrage leaders constantly commented on her loudness, size, and assertiveness, attributes they associated with the working class. Boston's society paper, the *Transcript*, in 1909 contrasted her with the slim, delicate (albeit aggressive and confident) Luscomb. Foley "can easily manage seven feet, turn her brown hair to flame, descend like a mountain of bricks and extend her mellifluous accent to megaphonics."[20] Foley transgressed barriers more when entering the elite parlors of the suffrage leaders than when she spoke from street corners.

Foley's induction into the suffrage movement and her subsequent long apprenticeship there typified women's cross-class political relations on the eve of suffrage. She became a crucial part of the movement's outreach, working as paid staff along with Luscomb for both the city's Boston Equal Suffrage Association for Good Government (BESAGG) and the state's Massachusetts Woman Suffrage Association (MWSA).[21] Foley went to black Baptist churches, temples, and Catholic churches; to the Boston Central Labor Union and Women's Trade Union League; and to factories to reach workers in candy, cigar, carpet, rubber, and shoe trades, while also speaking at the Women's City Club and the South Boston Yacht Club.[22] In 1918, she served as a delegate to the MWSA's annual convention. Her work bore fruit, and by 1919, BESAGG's letterhead showed Miss Anna Weinstock, neckwear worker and WTUL president, as one of seven directors.[23]

Despite Foley's dedication and successes, there were signs that BE-

SAGG remained not only heavily dominated by elite women, but class biased. It no longer explained to reluctant suffrage supporters as it did in 1910, that the vote for women "increase the proportion of the educated and native born vote more rapidly than anything that could be done." It was still, however, prone to call special meetings at 3 P.M. on workdays.[24] Moreover, in the MWSA annual bazaars, held at the safely elite Copley Plaza, the members found creative ways to enact their class status and notions of gendered gentility. In 1914, when the slogan had been "Women are PEOPLE" and the logo depicted three women, one a college graduate, one a matron with baby, and the other indeterminate, BESAGG's booth, planned by Mrs. Richard Washburn Child, featured a "display of useful articles . . . including maids' aprons, which will be sold among the crowd by Mrs. Enid Kinder Norcross and Mrs. C. A. LaRue of Mansfield, dressed as maids." The spectacle of Brahmin women dressed, not as local "Bridgets" but as "chic little French maids," could only have been possible in an organization where no actual maids were highly visible in either the membership or the potential "crowd."[25]

For such women, reported BESAGG of the first effort at ward level organization,

> [i]t took some sense of duty, some devotion to our cause, to push us up the dim . . . staircase, to knock at any one of several non-committal doors on the first shabby landing. Probably the woman who answered knew no English, and stared uncomprehendingly. . . . [T]he children, who have learned English, helped; the Yiddish and Italian flyers helped; and best of all the women, as soon as they knew what it was all about, proved so kindly, so approachable, so open-minded and responsive . . . that whatever the future may hold . . . the pilgrimage through ward 8 proved of the deepest interest and meaning.[26]

By 1915, just as the battle for a Massachusetts referendum on woman suffrage reached a peak, however, the thrill of the canvassing "pilgrimage" seemed to have faded for the elite. BESAGG noted, "Most women have neither the time nor the desire"; the organization instead hired canvassers at two dollars a day.[27]

Such class dynamics could be trying for women like Foley. Though in her correspondence with suffragists, she framed herself again and again as a "working woman" and a "trade unionist," Foley had severed her ties with the union movement and cast her lot with the suffragists. She found them inconstant providers of matronage.

There were moments of heady inclusions among the suffrage elite, as when in 1914 a New York friend relayed that in discussions of a major suffrage event, along with Alice Stone Blackwell, Mrs. Park, and Mrs. Page—all leaders of the Massachusetts suffrage movement—the planners had agreed, "of course Miss Foley had to be included among the celebrities."[28] James Michael Curley (by then a suffrage supporter) sent her an invitation to his 1916 gubernatorial inaugural ceremonies.[29] At the other end of the spectrum, Emma Goldman's sometime lover, radical Chicago doctor Ben Reitman, flirted outrageously with Foley, writing that he dreamed of taking a long walk with her, talking about life and work, going home where he "could put my head on your beautiful breast and weep for joy." "Write me. Love me. Want me," he begged. Such connections meant a lot to the hat trimmer from Roxbury.[30]

Just as Amelia Baldwin found her design work for the suffrage bazaars gave her access to Boston's elite, Foley and others like her—working-class women engaged by the movement during its phase of outreach across class—saw in these connections a route to a different world with different jobs, not simply different society but a different kind of relationship to the city's power structure.

Elite feminists were not ideal bosses, however. Foley was not alone in finding perpetually delayed paychecks and disputes over meeting expenses; others found themselves expected not only to organize but to raise their own salaries.[31] The leaders were often clueless about the realities of self-supporting women. Anna Tillinghast wrote to Foley in 1919 that since the organization's money had dried up, she hoped Foley would complete her work for less than the original arranged salary, doing it by the job instead of the week, as though the difference in pay were not salient.[32] Some suffrage workers made up the difference by shifting from organizational wages to personal patronage. Foley resisted that track.[33]

At the same time, movement leaders expected total devotion. Foley found herself, like a contract player, moved around from Boston to state to national suffrage organizations according to where the leaders thought she could serve best and often with little consideration as to her preferences or even her financial needs.[34] Foley's friend Caroline Reilly, working for New York suffragist Alva Belmont, confided to her that even for Belmont, "I won't tie myself down in the way of a contract, because they are all alike,—they think they own you, body and soul, if you leave yourself no loophole to escape."[35]

With the U.S. entry into World War I, Boston's suffrage leaders made choices that threw into sharp relief their attitudes about class and ethnicity. BESAGG's strategy was "organized suffragists will do their part," doing it *as* suffragists.[36] Members involved themselves in many aspects of the war effort, but the organization threw itself most wholeheartedly into Americanization work. Similarly, working with the Bureau of Immigration, the MWSA offered classes that taught women to teach citizenship to foreigners with the aim of safeguarding industries where immigrants worked, speeding up production, and decreasing strikes.[37] This was a different kind of cross-class outreach. Suffrage work would continue, but behind the scenes.

By this time, Foley had bounced around among suffrage organizations across the country for three years.[38] In 1918, she needed work. But Luscomb and Fitzgerald had become more acceptable on the hustings than Foley had in the parlors, despite the high school education that had facilitated her rise within the suffrage movement and the WTUL.[39] Foley found that even her admirer, Alice Stone Blackwell, was unencouraging. The trumpetlike voice was deemed unsuited to the current phase of suffrage work: "In your own line, I think you are unrivalled as a speaker. . . . But in the quiet preliminary work of organizing and getting signatures to petitions, and nosing about under the surface to find out how candidates stand, and to use 'indirect influence' for our friends and against our enemies, I do not suppose you would find your most effective field."[40]

When the contingencies of the elite suffrage leaders' interest in her became clear, and the costs of her own choice to throw in her lot with a group whose commitment to working across class lines now seemed painfully limited, Foley struggled against her exile. Like a machine politician, she reminded Mrs. Anna C. Bird, MWSA head, of past favors when Foley claimed to have shifted the sentiment of a MWSA convention in Bird's favor and secured Bird's election. She accused others of being "jealous of my splendid record as a suffragist and trade unionist." Moreover, she reminded Bird, "I am a well known Catholic in the largest Catholic City in the United States—Boston. . . . Many Catholics joined the suffrage movement because of my activities," and were asking why she was not active now.[41]

Bird, in her kindest tone, responded by advising Foley to remake herself. She tried to tell Foley what the suffrage leaders thought of her, to make her feel she had "something to overcome" and that she could overcome it.[42] In short, what had been Foley's asset—her working-class, Irish Catholic status—when the suffrage movement strove to expand its constituency, became a liability as it readied for the vote.

Resentfully or not, Foley did make a bid for redefinition. She took a course in employment management at Harvard and one in Americanization at the State House.[43] Her attempt to shift from worker to managerial status, however, met with limited success. Her elite connections secured interviews but no jobs.[44] She recast her union experience in terms of "the handling of working people," but it is likely that her worker-centered view of the manager's task was unappealing to prospective employers.[45] The remake incomplete, she met with no success as a personnel manager.

She fared better as an Americanizer. She made her pitch to the MWSA in July 1918, playing again on her ethnic and union background as fitting her uniquely for the job: "The surest and best way to reach the alien is through the churches. Most of the aliens are Catholics and if I could interview the priests . . . you would get the largest attendance and best attention. Of course this would have to be done by a Catholic in order to get the best results."[46]

By 1919, Foley was working for the MWSA organizing Catholic women into the Margaret Brent Suffrage Guild.[47] She threw herself into the work, but quickly found herself at odds with the leadership, who seemed to want to use her identity but not her expertise. In September she complained to the executive board that she had been asked to organize Catholic women under impossible terms—as Catholics but not through the church—and was insulted by the board's lack of respect for her expertise: "Being a trade unionist and an expert in my own line . . . I tried in vain to point out the impossibility of gathering together in a separate group the Catholic women leaders of organized labor." Trade unions were pointedly nonsectarian. But the Yankee Protestants of the MWSA resisted organizing in Catholic churches. When, in addition, Mrs. Minnie T. Wright, a prominent African American Bostonian suffragist, revolted at plans to treat black Catholics separately, the work, essentially, collapsed.[48]

The collapse left Foley's future far from assured. Her patrons suggested appointive office, but her low civil service exam grades, they felt, left them powerless.[49] As a suffrage worker, Foley had eschewed partisan affiliation; now she applied for jobs from both the Women's Republican Committee (the Republican State Committee had hired her the previous season), and the Democrats' speakers bureau. On behalf of the former, Anna Tillinghast rejected her services; Catholics, it seemed, were not "naturally" Republicans, and she and Mrs. Bird had agreed to forgo work among them. "Inasmuch as we must build our organization from the ground," she explained, "we think it will be much better for us to first mobilize the women whose affiliations are naturally with the Republican Party." The Democrats explained that they only used volunteers.[50]

The end of 1920 found Foley picking up money for lectures in parliamentary law and at Catholic women's clubs.[51] Her suffrage movement ties having failed her, she abandoned all pretext of nonpartisanship. Finally, in November of 1920, she received an appointment as deputy commissioner of institutions for the city. Among the letters of congratulations was one from an Alice E. Cram, "I am glad you have been appointed at last, to a job with a decent salary and I am glad you got it from the Democrats."[52]

Margaret Foley's story epitomized the possibilities and limits organized elite women's patronage held for working-class women in the decade surrounding women's suffrage victory. For Foley, party, not gender politics, ultimately secured her future. Mary Meehan, like Foley with ties to the labor movement and its Democratic allies, carries the appointive political story a decade further, where the lines of appointive and electoral politics began to blur. Never a woman's movement protégée, in 1931 Meehan ended up triumphing over Ethel Johnson, a protégée more successful at winning the hearts of the elite Republican woman suffragists than Foley had been.

Meehan, president of the Bindery Women's Union, along with May Matthews, secretary of the Telephone Operators Union, prominent in the 1913 strike and veteran of the National WTUL six-woman suffrage committee, had made labor women's first electoral challenge—their first attempt at electoral self-representation in Boston—in 1918.[53] They ran for School Committee in a field including one other woman, a Brahmin with few feminist credentials, Frances G. Curtis. The only woman on the committee, Curtis had first won election in 1913, backed by the Brahmin reform Public School Association (PSA).[54]

Both Meehan and Matthews campaigned on a labor-centered platform: better conditions and equal pay for men and women teachers, and better general education for students headed for trade schools. Curtis, on the other hand, did not support equal pay and advocated different types of school for differently gifted children. Only Curtis had the backing of Boston's elite reform machinery. Curtis won, but for Meehan, at least, her political career was far from over.[55]

In 1918, Meehan not only presided over one of the largest women's unions in the country, she enjoyed a gubernatorial appointment as the only woman to serve on the Massachusetts War Emergency Commission.[56] In 1924, Meehan was the only unmarried and the only labor union woman to win a slot on the Massachusetts slate for the Democratic National Convention.[57] She ran again for School Committee in 1925. The powerful PSA endorsed Mrs. Jennie Loitman Barron, a prominent lawyer and civic activist and a Republican. Meehan did not receive organized labor's endorsement, either, which went to Henry Wise, lawyer for the telephone operators' union. Barron won; Meehan lost.[58] Labor as well as suffrage could prove an unsteady patron.

The Democrats were more consistent. In 1931, Meehan was the only woman the party nominated for an important position in Massachusetts. The party put her forward for assistant commissioner of the state's Department of Labor. By this time, Meehan had served sixteen years in the International Brotherhood of Bookbinders and fourteen years as vice president of the Allied Printing Trades Crafts of Greater Boston.[59]

The rival candidate for the job was the incumbent, Ethel Johnson, born in 1882, and supported by organized reform women. A normal school graduate and former teacher, Johnson had come to Boston to attend Simmons College's library course, from which she graduated in

1910. She worked her way through as a salesgirl in the food shop of the WEIU, and on her graduation took over the WEIU's library on Women in Industry, running it for eight years. Johnson organized a legislative reference section for the WEIU and the MWSA and served as the WEIU's Legislative Committee secretary, representing the organization at legislative hearings. As other female reform protégées, she entered politics by the back door.

In 1918, after some friction at the WEIU partly due to her parody of antisuffragists, among whom numbered several influential WEIU members, she left the WEIU for the MWSA, serving as Congressional Committee secretary for the MWSA in the summer of 1918, the year she graduated with a bachelor of letters degree from the Boston University College of Liberal Arts (the same year Foley found her services no longer required).[60] From there, Johnson resigned to become the executive secretary of the Massachusetts Minimum Wage Commission at a salary of $2,000 a year, a move in which her WEIU connections proved extremely useful, and then, when the functions of the office moved to the Department of Labor and Industries at the end of 1919, she moved with it, becoming assistant commissioner of the Massachusetts Department of Labor and Industries, at a salary of $3,000 a year.[61]

In later years, Johnson credited the WEIU with getting her hooked on lobbying. And certainly by 1929 her character as a politician was clear to those who knew her best. Her sister plaintively wrote her "Why O Why does my beautiful sister neglect me so—*POLITICS* that's the skeleton in our family closet and ye fair Ethel doth continually rattle its ugly bones to the great dismay of Maid Marion! . . . Heartless Oh so heartless! My sister loveth me not—Instead she loveth the tariff, strange oaths and much legislation. Oh woe is me that I was born the sister of a politician who hankereth to dwell among stinkpots, smoking men, lousy corruption, bare office seekers."[62]

Despite her sister's contention that she longed to dwell among office seekers and lousy corruption, by 1929 Johnson had grown adept at conveying a different view of politics. "There is opportunity for women," she wrote, "to help in making the higher concept of politics the effective one." They could do so not by running for office, but by working within political parties, for "only through the party can they secure effective political expression."[63]

Though it came initially from Republican Governor Calvin Coolidge, Johnson's appointment to the Department of Labor had ostensibly been as a female and not a Republican. A coalition of women's organizations, uniting women across party lines, had won a dedicated woman's slot among the assistant commissioners in 1921, despite bitter opposition.[64] Johnson had then helped construct the Advisory Council on Women and Children in Industry, whose 1928 membership read like a who's who of the suffrage movement (now often listed with their party affiliations), supplemented by leaders of the WEIU and the WTUL and a handful of others.[65]

Within a month of Democratic Governor Ely's proposed appointment of Meehan in 1931, the hearing rooms of the State House were packed with women ready to debate her qualifications for the job. More than 300 women crowded into the chamber, forcing a transfer to a larger room, and thousands of women went on record supporting or opposing Meehan. Meehan's appointment became part of an ongoing debate among organized women on the nature of politics and its relation to women.[66]

While the headlines blared "Women Republicans Opposed Miss Meehan," women Republicans insisted that the issue, instead, was nonpartisanship.[67] Meehan's was not the only patronage case being disputed after a decade of Republican hegemony so strong that the party's members had forgotten it was a party and not a nonpartisan organization. The women (and the fewer men) involved in the dispute deployed the language of expertise, political hackery, and gender to make their case. Meehan's supporters spoke, in addition, the language of class and party.

Johnson's supporters were enraged that what they thought of as their position to control ("matronage"?) should become simply another political plum.[68] Mrs. Esther Andrews went on record as "opposed to establishing the precedent of driving present incumbents from office merely to make room for political reward." Going to the heart of the matter—true women's nonpartisan nature—"Being the only woman member of the Governor's Council," she concluded, "I owed it to my constituents who had elected me to safeguard this group."[69]

Other Johnson supporters mobilized the language of expertise. Dr. Alice Hamilton, a pioneer in industrial medicine at the Harvard Medical School, maintained that the post required a young, vigorous woman, well educated and able to handle statistics.[70] And wool merchants' representatives complained that the framers of the statute providing for a woman commissioner had intended the post to be held by someone representing the "public." The law gave labor and employers each a representative. Meehan, in their view, represented neither "women" nor the "public" but "labor." The avowedly Republican Johnson, on the other hand, to these representatives was nonpartisan and impartial.[71]

Yet part of what Johnson and her supporters faced was precisely the politicization of social work. As social workers became part of a state bureaucracy of appointive positions and Democrats became more successful at the state level, social service appointees became more transparently tied to patronage networks. But trained social experts rising through the ranks in nonprofit organizations, such as Hamilton, Johnson, and her supporters, had been socialized to think of themselves as transcending narrow party interest as part of a new women's politics based on the common welfare over personal advancement and cronyism.[72] They could not see their own advocacy as partisan, as narrow or interested, or, even less, as cronyism—appointing colleagues, protégées, and friends—since only speaking for a "public" that encompassed all parties, classes, and constituents justified their leadership.

The sharp contrast between Meehan's supporters—Democrats, labor union men, and organized Catholic women—and Johnson's—Republican, managerial or employer-based individuals and groups, and Protestant—undermined such holistic claims.[73] Meehan's supporters directly engaged the opposition on its own terms, with Governor Ely critiquing their definition of "expert" in light of Meehan's seventeen years of labor leadership.[74] And former Mayor Fitzgerald claimed for Meehan older virtues of womanhood: citing her "willingness to serve . . . is consecrated in Miss Meehan as in few women," he referred to Meehan as representing "the highest types of womanhood."[75]

Tellingly, the sorts of conflict that emerged in regard to Meehan's appointment had occurred already within the department during Johnson's tenure. Women with laboring connections or experience had continually harassed Johnson since 1919, resenting her appointment. Indeed, the governor initially claimed to be removing Johnson to restore harmony to the department.[76] As opposed to her 1918 and 1925 School Committee races, Meehan now enjoyed the public endorsements of Boston's and national unions and labor leaders. Here, labor could place her in a "woman's" slot. Their coalition with Democrat and Catholic groups enabled Meehan, from the workers' ranks, to prevail over the women's reform protégée.

Meehan's victory signified not only alternative coalitions available to ambitious women politicians and the lack of a credible "woman bloc," but the contingent nature both of women's reform patronage—dependent on class background and view—and of labor and party patronage. More acceptable than Foley in her background, affect, and views, Ethel Johnson had retained the sponsorship of Boston's female reform establishment. It had done well by her for over a decade. But in the increasingly contentious partisan world of the 1930s, its ability to sustain its claims to nonpartisanship severely eroded. The powerful female reform machinery created over the previous forty years began to lose its grip on appointive office long before it lost its turn-of-the-century vision of itself as above political, class, or ethnic strife. To the Meehans, Foleys, and the staff in Johnson's department, that vision had perhaps always been an illusion, but the coalitions that would allow them to dispense with elite women's patronage were just as fragile and contingent, enabling Meehan to take office in 1931, safely in a woman's slot, but not to succeed in 1918 or 1925, running against men for an open slot.

A New Decade: The 1920s

By the late 1910s, the Victorian context that had helped to create a strong women's reform machinery and its power over appointive offices had begun to shift. While women's appointive politics continued to be structured by that older set of assumptions, women's postsuffrage electoral politics took its shape against a different backdrop of assumptions about urban women's place and possibilities.

The successful telephone strike in 1919 had simply cemented the degree to which white women were now accepted as respectable denizens of the streets, the degree to which women, like men, lived in public. Women's clothes became less cumbersome. Skirts were shorter, allowing for greater mobility.[77] Hats were simpler, and if not always precisely helmetlike, always smaller than the towering confections of gauze, feathers, and sometimes entire birds that in previous decades had led Boston theaters to institute rules requiring women to remove their hats.[78] Horse-drawn carriages had given way not only to the crowded streetcars where working women jostled with other passengers, but to the more intimate and private automobiles and taxis. And women at all levels, particularly single women, worked for pay.[79]

The increased presence of women workers did not, however, signal the dawn of a working-class paradise. As a flood of demobilized veterans hit the city, and a disastrous police strike in 1919 followed, Governor Coolidge called in the troops and labeled the strike a "crime against humanity." Under the influence of the postwar red scare, working-girls' clubs focused solely on recreation, the BWTUL shifted from organizing to educating, and labor unions purged their leftist members and even the leftist preambles to their constitutions.[80]

The sharp economic downturn in 1921, during which one unorthodox agitator held "slave auctions" of the unemployed on the Boston Common, together with the shift in Boston from an industrial to a retail base further destabilized workers' organizations.[81] Victories by garment workers proved hollow as factories fled to the suburbs and elsewhere.[82] Men and women continued to suffer intermittent unemployment and poor working conditions, and the declining availability of homework forced working mothers out of the home without offering provisions for child care.[83] Meanwhile, telephone workers' organizational gains faltered under the company's repudiation of independent collective bargaining in late 1920 and the pressure of a new company union in 1923.[84]

When the Boston Telephone Operators' Union launched a strike in 1923, its membership divided, and lacking the press support of earlier years, they no longer ruled the streets. The police who had supported them in 1919 had been replaced in the aftermath of the police strike. On the telephone strike's third afternoon, the new police charged the picket line, clubbing strikers to the ground and arresting eleven operators on charges of "inciting to riot."[85]

If the streets were unsafe for union women strikers, however, they seemed safer for white women individuals. The Women's Municipal League may have hoped to introduce "street matrons" to police the manners of men toward women in the parks and out of them, but

"Stories of Girls," a regular feature in the *Boston Post* by Margaret Orr, former investigator for the state Department of Public Welfare, displayed little anxiety. Where 1890s newspaper columns had spilled copious ink in debates over the safety and propriety of women's urban bicycling and the male cyclists they met, in the 1920s "Maizie," a hardworking office girl, could with impunity mouth slang and prowl "for some King of the Golden Isles to trail across her vision and offer her a real evening—a night that cost at least $2. For, like all her chums, she knew the scale ran like this: 0 to 50¢ equals fun: 50¢ to $1 equals amusement: $1 and over equals RECREATION."[86]

In one particular story, Maizie spots her "happy stranger," a "tall and thick," loudly dressed man who "looked as though he had shaved that morning with a broken beer bottle while standing on a carload of rollicking potatoes." But he has the all important "fistful of yellow backs" which he flashes, asking "Maizie if she knew them by name. And if she didn't have a date that night, would she steer him round to a wild evening?" Instead of hearing alarm bells, Maizie "promised to get most of his bank roll and to meet him that night in the lobby of the St. Bernard." Their evening consisted of a dinner (in which "the flashy, crude, good-hearted Eastern breeze" overordered and overtipped; Maize scooped up the tip "for a pair of stockings" and "stuffed a few olives" for the kids at home, in the stockings she wore), a movie, a play, a poolroom, a ballroom, more dinner, and dancing. When "Bill" totaled up the evening's expenses, "Maizie asked him to copy it off carelesslike on a menu and sign it 'Affectionately Bill.' She wanted to frame it for the family and her girl friends. So Bill doubled the cost everywhere, and did it with a flourish." Finally, "he hired a cream-colored private taxi to take Maizie home."

In another decade the story of Bill and Maizie would have been a sordid tale of seduction of either Bill (the innocent hick) or Maizie (the overworked, overstimulated, overenticed girl) and ruin, particularly given its author's credentials. In the 1920s, women, almost universally poorly paid, still depended on men for a good time, but no longer was the autonomous, dating, prowling, working woman seen as nearly fallen or even evilly greedy and predatory. Rather, in knowing and meeting her own desires, she benefited all parties.[87] According to Brahmin Fanny

Curtis, the former School Committee member, "the independent girl in her own apartment, working hard at her chosen job, is said to be answerable only to her push-button and calling-tube."[88]

While over a quarter of Boston's working women were clerical workers by the end of the decade, women like Maizie could also aspire to new jobs.[89] Sixty women industrial "executives," as they called themselves, gathered regularly in the Boston Forewomen's Council. Personnel managers, industrial nurses, line forewomen, and other female managerial staff from Schrafft candy, Gillette Razor, Carter's Ink, Winchester Laundry, several rubber companies, and over a dozen other businesses, sometimes subsidized by their employers, discussed new management techniques, opportunities, and generally promoted their own increasing importance in the corporate world and their increasing assimilation to it. "The last few years," they noted, "have marked the passing of the forelady. Her displacement by the forewoman indicates more than a mere change of name. It indicates a new attitude toward the job."[90]

Settlement houses expanded their staffs, employing, in Boston's twenty-one settlements, 151 part-time women. Women college graduates went overwhelmingly into teaching, but many also entered business, research, medicine, and—like Jennie Loitman Barron, a successful School Committee candidate—law. They formed professional associations and joined civic ones.[91] Their professional identity was stronger than that of the women doctors and writers who formed the WEIU, and their numbers were greater, if still small compared to those of the men. And, like Barron, they were more often married. Barron credited the possibility of her political career to her husband's willingness to cooperate in child care and other arrangements.[92]

The 1920s were full of mixed messages for women. Curtis saw the newly independent women as free to choose their own "mode of life" but making "no fundamental overturns in living."[93] Harvard and other medical schools imposed a quota of 5 percent on admissions of women. With the Vatican campaign against immoral literature, Boston's Catholic hierarchy joined forces with the Protestant Watch and Ward Society and city officials in banning Theodore Dreiser's *Sister Carrie* and works by Ernest Hemingway, Eugene O'Neill, Upton Sinclair, John Dos Passos, and Carl Van Vechten.[94]

Newspapers worried over marriages in which wives earned more than husbands or in which busy women and men neglected each other. Club women continued to meet, their clubs reaching peak memberships in this decade, and continued to hold "parlor meetings" rather than occupy public space.[95] "Women's Pages" revived in local papers, but broadened beyond recipes and babies.[96] Massachusetts remained one of the few states in which women could not sit on juries.[97] And when Boston hired policewomen, it used them largely, as the Women's Municipal League had proposed, to police morals and "save women and children from some of the annoyances that exist in places of amusement and on the street."[98] Organized women soon complained that the department denied qualified policewomen promotions.[99]

Policewomen were not the only victims of an early and extremely low glass ceiling. The *Boston Daily Advertiser* printed a series of cartoons, "Girls vs. Boys," tracing the fate of office workers who pleased the boss; "But when there's a position higher up, who gets it? All too often," the paper admitted, "the boy is promoted, not the girl, though she may be just as capable as he." The paper blamed "some employers" for believing that while a man went into business "for keeps" to go "as far as his ambition can see," a "girl" might be distracted by thoughts of marriage. The paper did not endorse this view and concluded rather optimistically, "Fortunately, it needn't be fatal, for each individual girl can demonstrate her own single-hearted wish to get ahead."[100]

If white Boston women received mixed messages, the messages white Boston sent to black women were clearer. In the 1920s, black Boston society, increasingly centered in the South End and neighboring sections of Roxbury, was full of club meetings and elegant entertainments, usually at the homes (few respectable public spaces were available to African Americans) of prominent black club women.[101] "Smart sets" of younger people tried to outdo each other in their social clubs and included a small intelligentsia of professional social workers and writers. Eugene Gordon, radical black staff member of the *Boston Post*, edited Boston's black literary magazine, *Saturday Evening Quill*, which boasted among its contributors the playwright and Boston teacher Alvira Hazzard (who also published in the *Post*); Gertrude Schalk, one of the few black Bostonians able to make her living by her fiction (also frequently appearing in the *Post*); Josephine St. Pierre Ruffin's daughter, Florida Ruffin Ridley, a former Boston school teacher and contributor to *Opportunity* and *Our*

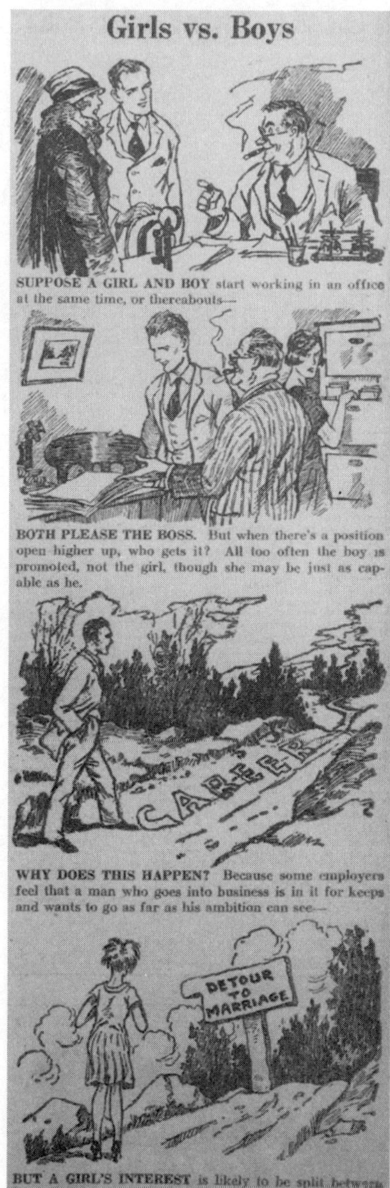

Girls vs. Boys

SUPPOSE A GIRL AND BOY start working in an office at the same time, or thereabouts—

BOTH PLEASE THE BOSS. But when there's a position open higher up, who gets it? All too often the boy is promoted, not the girl, though she may be just as capable as he.

WHY DOES THIS HAPPEN? Because some employers feel that a man who goes into business is in it for keeps and wants to go as far as his ambition can see—

BUT A GIRL'S INTEREST is likely to be split between the job and possible matrimony, so it is thought. This is unjust to many earnest and industrious young women. Fortunately, it needn't be fatal, for each individual girl can demonstrate her own single-hearted wish to get ahead.

Women in the 1920s workforce hit a definite and quite low glass ceiling. *Boston Daily Advertiser*, November 5, 1927.

Boston, staff member at Robert Gould Shaw House, and editor of *Social Service News* (the organ of Boston's social agencies); attorney Joseph Mitchell, graduate of Talladega and Boston University; Marion G. Conover, graduate of Simmons College School of Social Work and Portia Law School and on the staff of the Family Welfare Society of Boston; and Dorothy West, a former Bostonian who had left for New York's Harlem Renaissance.[102]

Migrants from the South and the West Indies, while not as numerous in Boston as in many other northern cities during the decade, formed state and island clubs such as the Bermuda Overseas Club, Inc., and established branches of Garvey's United Negro Improvement Association.[103] The decade's relative prosperity allowed not only for a new stability in the South End, but for new ventures, such as the first private bank to emerge from black Boston, a syndicate of four men including two physicians.[104]

Like Jennie Loitman Barron, black career women in dual-career marriages credited cooperative husbands. "From the beginning of our marriage," speaker and later early childhood specialist Lucy Miller Mitchell recalled, "there had been developed a pattern of shared household responsibilities and of the care of the children." According to Mitchell, most members of the Boston's graduate AKA chapter, a black sorority, were "women who were carrying on careers as well as families."[105]

Most black women in Boston, however, found the city in the 1920s a place that denied them at least as much as it offered them. In 1926, civil rights activist Arthur H. Morse declared in the *Transcript*, "Boston, in spite of its traditions, has lagged behind," generally excluding black workers from even unskilled and semiskilled jobs. One black woman had qualified thirty-five times for a civil service appointment, only to be rejected on account of color each time. "Boston continues to be a leader in supporting the great industrial schools of the South," he warned. "It cannot afford to overlook the problem at its own door."[106] While a few black women did hold clerical jobs, including novelist and essayist Pauline Hopkins at MIT, black women were overwhelmingly confined to domestic service. The Urban League made a special effort to place women with grammar school training in factory and department stores, but had little success. Saleswork became more heterogeneous in the 1920s, employing Catholics and even immigrant Jews, but not blacks.[107]

Black women often could not even gain access to training. The NAACP and Urban League did battle with cooking schools, physical education schools, business colleges, and hospital training programs for nurses. They had little to show for their effort, though at the decade's end they had opened more than a dozen new industrial occupations to African Americans. Finally in 1929, after the threat of opening a black hospital, they succeeded, with the aid of a new youth Interrace Committee at the YWCA, in getting two women accepted to the Nurses Training Course at Boston City Hospital. That December the two became the first black nurses ever appointed there.[108]

Black women had numbered among Boston's suffragists, and elite black women continued to work in organizations with their white counterparts. They, too, were poised for action when suffrage came. At least five of them numbered among the mixed-race group enrolled in Margaret Foley's Parliamentary Law Class in 1918. Four were active suffragists and prominent club women; the fifth was a business woman who would later become active in city and neighborhood politics.[109]

It was these career women who would run for public office and party positions in the 1920s. Black or white, elite, managerial, or working class, their paths to electoral politics would reflect their different experience of this new decade.

Contested Elections, or "The Women Politicians" 1920–1937

There was no "woman's slot" on the Boston City Council. Nor was the council a partially feminized preserve, as was the School Committee. Women had long watched from the gallery and lobbied on behalf of their constituents, but the floor was distinctly masculine. Nonetheless, Boston's electoral system was unusually open. There were no primaries. Candidates needed only sufficient signatures on their petitions. Women threw themselves into the contest as soon as the ratification of the Nineteenth Amendment made it possible. Their presence helped define the 1920s as a new world.

Historians and social theorists have seen the 1920s as a period of declining political participation. As political parties perfected and professionalized their machinery and as interest groups (including angry farmers and feminists) became increasingly effective lobbyists, according to one sociologist, "the formal equality of white male citizens seemed increasingly irrelevant." Those with the vote but without organized, funded influence were not "equal" players.[110] But at the urban level, the formal equality was not irrelevant, much to the lasting frustration of the Brahmins who struggled to wrest control permanently from the predominantly Irish-heritage, Catholic population. They controlled the state, but they continued to be unable to work their will in Boston, with its rising immigrant vote. Urban machines continued to rely on mobilizing popular voters, bucking the trend in national politics.[111]

When a mayoral candidate like James Michael Curley cast his election in terms of fighting the determined power of wealthy Yankees to keep the Irish worker down, his speeches resonated deeply with his audiences. No one with Irish blood ever held any important office in Boston's Chamber of Commerce during the decade; few Irish names surfaced in the Boston Council of Social Agencies. Law firms excluded the largely Irish graduates of Suffolk Law School, a night school regularly deplored by the Massachusetts Bar Association.[112]

On the other hand, Irish heritage workers continued to dominate the leadership of Boston's labor unions. Omitting clothing workers, only 12 percent of Boston's elected labor union offices went to Jews, Italians, French Canadians, or African Americans.[113]

As with the School Committee, and as in other Progressive Era cities, when the Irish had threatened lasting dominance of city government, the Yankees mobilized their forces at the state level to change the structure of Boston's government. Their attempts led to charter revision in 1909. Nonpartisan, citywide elections replaced the old ward-based, partisan ones, and as a result, seven of nine City Council seats in 1910 went to candidates endorsed by the Good Government Association's Citizens' Municipal League.[114] But by the early 1920s, Yankee Republicans' hold on the city had weakened.[115] They could not control the mayoralty. After the war, even their hold on the council proved tenuous, with the majority always in doubt.[116]

When the BESAGG became the Boston League of Women Voters (BLWV) in the fall of 1919, they threw their weight into the contest. Direct heirs of the Victorian women's organizations, their constitution stipulated, "As an organization, the League of Women Voters shall be strictly non-partisan in its policy and work."[117] They had just the previous year witnessed the electoral power of nonpartisanship when a suffragist coalition defeated a senatorial incumbent described as "a thorough going conservative and a bitter anti-suffragist."[118] With this experience, the women of the BLWV saw themselves marching into the electoral realm armed with effective machinery, precinct-level organization, mobilizing and speaking tactics, and the righteous conviction that part of their power came from their ability to represent not even merely "woman" but the best interests of the people, transcending, as they had in the 1918 senatorial race, party for the public welfare.

They had some grounds for their belief. The leadership of the BLWV was relatively homogenous, largely Back Bay and Beacon Hill elite women, often liberal, often also members of the WTUL and other civic organizations, including a few Democrats and many Republicans. But the rank-and-file membership of the BLWV was broad, encompassing working-class and elite women, white and black women, Irish and Yankee.[119]

The *Globe* called the national chairman of the LWV "a new type of political leader," and she, in turn, predicted the "Last Days of [the] Political Boss." Male politicans accused them of being un-American by undermining the two-party system.[120] The Massachusetts LWV dismissed their objections: "men have always disapproved of the things women have done in groups."[121]

Looking increasingly like a political party with everything but a candidate, using the language of "plank" and "platform," and demanding a partylike loyalty from members, in 1921, the BLWV took the next step.[122] They made political endorsements. Boston elections being nonpartisan, they decided they could do so without violating their charter. They elected a Democrat and a Republican delegate from each ward and a representative at large from each political party in Massachusetts to investigate candidates. To ensure neither party dominated, endorsement required a two-thirds vote.[123]

The delegates had a large field from which to select. In addition to a mayoral race pitting James Michael Curley against the reform choice, John Murphy, and three other candidates, eleven largely unknown candidates sought council seats. Six of the eleven had Irish names and a slim majority had experience in office. The eleven included three Democrats, two Republicans, two attorneys, two veterans, three union men, and five members of the petty bourgeoisie (two of whom were in law school). They also included one woman, Mrs. Grace D. Chipman, the only woman, the *Herald* reported "ever to be nominated as candidate for the City Council."

Chipman, fifty, a former school teacher, resident of Boston for ten years, and wife of a politico, took as her slogan, "Fair and consistent recognition of the right of women to participate in the affairs of government." She told the *Globe*, "There are many women tax payers and property owners in Boston and surely they should have a representative on the Council." Beyond claiming to be a woman's representative, Chipman deployed a number of other common suffragist arguments, including that the council, as a municipal governance, needed a woman's touch: "There are many things that come up in the governing of a city's affairs that need the mind of a woman to see clearly what should be done."[124]

Chipman secured the backing of a "Committee of 100," including both men and women. But despite her pledge to work for "the moral and economic welfare of all concerned" and "honest and conscientious service," she failed to secure the backing of the BLWV. The BLWV instead supported two other candidates. It gave no reason for ignoring Chipman, though her standing completely outside its networks cannot have helped her candidacy. The Good Government Association also rejected Chipman, finding her "without any experience in public service and having hitherto shown no active interest in civic affairs."[125] To Chipman, civic affairs meant not investigations, lobbying, and appointive office, but electoral politics. How, Chipman rejoined, would women get experience without the opportunity to acquire it? "Certainly not," she answered with a dig at those who had not endorsed her, "by forever perusing pamphlets or evolving theories."[126]

Having rejected the one woman candidate, the league threw itself most enthusiastically into the race for mayor. Their flyer endorsing Murphy read, "HE BELIEVES IN THE THINGS WOMEN WANT," to wit, careful spending, better health protection, better garbage handling, the finest school system, "clean dance-halls and other amusements," and "equal pay and opportunity for women."[127] They organized in twenty-six wards and went about the campaign with religious fervor, determined to fend off "the return of the spoilsmen." They held an "all women's" rally in the Back Bay, advertised by the BLWV as "for and by women," with Murphy the only male in attendance.

According to one attendee, "it didn't seem the least bit like a political rally . . . it seemed like a Methodist class meeting." BLWV staff member and former suffrage stump speaker Florence Luscomb insisted, "It is not a political game we are interested in. . . . It is far too serious and important for us to regard it in a spirit of levity or play. We're going down to the polls next Tuesday casting a vote for safety and protection to little babies." Another speaker claimed, "In the heart of every woman is the love of straight thinking, fine living, and square dealing. It is older than religion itself."[128]

The *Globe* reported the meeting as encompassing speakers of various "civic, racial and social groups," and indeed elite women of every color and ethnic group crowded into the hall.[129] But getting the vote, as Meehan's challenge in 1918 should have shown, meant that they no longer could speak for "every woman." By 1921, as the BLWV mobilized for John Murphy, they watched former suffragists disperse themselves among the mayoral candidates. In a special feature, the *Globe* pondered, "Boston Women Making Their Political Bow—Is It a Debut or a Fight?"[130] Irish women, former suffragists, telephone operators, and women with political campaign experience featured prominently among the women they interviewed at various candidates' headquarters. While Florence Luscomb stumped for Murphy, her former suffrage ally, telephone operators' union leader Annie Molloy, who had in 1913 given a speech at a woman suffrage mass meeting in Fanueil Hall entitled, "Why the Wage Earning Woman Wants the Vote," now campaigned for her fellow Irish Democrat, James Michael Curley. With her was Mrs. Irving Gross, who had gone to jail for suffrage in Washington, DC, and kept her jail tin cup and plate on her desk. And Mrs. Carrie F. Sheehan, former member of the executive committee of the BLWV and member of the Republican State Committee, chaired the Curley Club of Charlestown. Other activists supported the other three mayoral candidates. Women neighbors hustled door to door for rival candidates. The women "are giving and talking like veterans—are hurling charges and countercharges like old-timers." "Those who are active workers," the *Globe* concluded,

"—that is, we might say, the women politicians—are split up five ways regardless of their party affiliations."[131]

Despite foul weather, women voted heavily in 1921, though the number of registered women voters still trailed far behind those of men.[132] Women school teachers hurried to get to the polls before work, making them often the earliest voters. Mothers showed up with baby carriages. Husbands accompanied wives and often tried to instruct women, who defiantly maintained " 'a poker face' during the whole act." The *Globe* reported, "Mistress and Maid Vote Together" and "In the North and South Ends women in shawls rubbed elbows with women in furs and jewels. One daughter of a well-known Boston millionaire on Beacon Hill voted immediately after her colored maid."[133]

But the vote favored neither the BLWV nor Mrs. Chipman. The latter came in second to last, and Curley beat Murphy in what the conservative *Herald* labeled the "greatest political upset."[134] Women had voted together, but they had not voted alike. While political analysts of the age may have concluded that "in every city in the country and in every state woman suffrage has increased the power of the political machine and political bosses," by lining up the relatives of organization men and granting favors and jobs, women like Molloy, who had sat opposite Storrow at the bargaining table while Curley came to the operators' ball, may have had a different analysis of their political interests.[135]

Curley had provoked laughter by satirizing the BLWV leaders' purportedly intimate involvement in Boston's affairs. The *Globe* reported part of one such speech to a local Boston audience: " 'Perhaps some of you may know them. Here is Evelyn Peterly Coe [a BLWV officer]. Anybody here know Evie?' (Silence) 'What?' in apparent amazement, 'nobody here know Evie? O, yes, I see that Evie lives out to Brookline. Of course you wouldn't know her.' "[136] By endowing each leader with a nickname, including Florence Luscomb as "Flossie," Curley both dug at the pretensions of the BLWV and asserted that politics was a club of regulars, a neighborhood of sorts, where legitimate participants would be known by ordinary people and as ordinary people. Even when women predominated, the *Globe* reported, this act went over "big."[137]

Despite the failure of their crusade in 1921, the BLWV decided to try again in 1922, this time running their own candidate for City Council. Sounding much like Grace Chipman, among the reasons they put

Boston Women Making Their Po
They Are Finding the Boston Mayoralty Fight a
Veterans—Are Hurling Charges and Counte
Campaign Headquarters Revolutionized-
CURLEY
FOR MAYO
VOTE FOR
CHARLES S.
BAXTER

Bow—Is It a Debut or a Fight?

fair, in Which They Are Giving and Taking Like
e Old-Timers—Women's League a Target—
bout the Leaders in the Opposing Camps

As early as 1921, women seemed full if factionalized participants in urban politics. Telephone operators' union leader Annie Molloy, who would be a candidate for City Council in 1922, is pictured second from left. *Boston Globe*, December 4, 1921.

to their membership was, "All government, particularly city government (which is 'municipal housekeeping'), needs the woman's point of view." But not any "woman's point of view" would do; it was precisely because they worried what sorts of women might run that they entered the race themselves: "There will undoubtedly be women candidates next fall, and unless women of a fine type can be assured of the organized support of those having at heart the best interests of the city, undesirable women are very likely to be elected."[138]

And, indeed, it was Annie Molloy, candidate for City Council in 1922, against whom the BLWV would run its own Florence Luscomb. The Storrows may have been comfortable enough with Molloy to invite her to join the Women's City Club, but the leaders of the suffrage movement and the WTUL never had been, and even the Storrows would not vote for her. When they held a parlor meeting during the election campaign, it was for Florence Luscomb.[139]

From the start, BWTUL and suffrage leaders had chosen not Molloy but telephone operators' union activist Julia O'Connor to groom for leadership. When Ethel Johnson created her advisory board in the Department of Labor, it included O'Connor, not Molloy. The leaders saw O'Connor as refined, a natural aristocrat, and she became the first working-woman president of Boston's WTUL in 1915, passing over more prominent union leaders like Molloy. Molloy was selected for the U.S. delegation to the International Congress of Women at The Hague in 1915, but never held an office in the WTUL. Her fellow 1915 delegate Balch saw her as one of a faction in the telephone operators' union opposed to the WTUL. The union's lawyer, who would later secure the labor endorsement for School Committee over Meehan, called Molloy a "rough neck," a " 'wildcat' who often 'cursed' and 'spit.' "[140]

O'Connor and Molloy had engaged in a prolonged and bitter battle for the union's leadership, beginning in 1919, going strong during the 1922 City Council campaign, and climaxing in the disastrous strike and split union in 1923.[141] Anathema to the BLWV and WTUL leaders (often one and the same), Molloy found her base further eroded by the splits in the union rank and file that BLWV and WTUL's patronage of O'Connor had helped engender.

With nineteen candidates in 1922, Molloy and Luscomb entered the largest field since the amended charter.[142] A veteran not only of the suffrage campaign but of the BLWV 1921 campaign, Luscomb had experience with press notices, avenues of access, and funding from the BLWV and its allies, enabling her (unlike Molloy) to be among the high spenders in the campaign.[143] She received far greater press coverage than did Molloy. The reporters all knew her, as did the councillors. The *Boston Globe* painted a flattering picture of her as a feisty contender, who had "tossed her tasseled tam-o-shanter into the dusty arena" with "the promise of fight in her brown eyes." As the BLWV's delegate to the City Council for the past two years, Luscomb also had the advantages and disadvantages of being a familiar figure at City Hall. Curley called her the tenth member of the council.[144] According to the *Globe*, since "she has seldom missed through two years a weekly session of that assembly," she had won "for herself there the deferential title of 'the gallery goddess.' "[145]

The contest almost immediately became imbued with class and ethnic connotations. Luscomb, besides calling for more civic interest in healthy water, pure food and milk, and so forth, called for a more "dignified conduct" of City Council meetings and "careful and conscientious" budget management.[146] Her backers urged support "to arouse the community to the vital importance of clean city government." Brahmins signed public letters en masse, and the GGA endorsed her along with two male candidates.[147] U.S. representative Martin Hays, of Luscomb's own neighborhood endorsed her, "for I believe she is of the type the City Council and the city need. She is descended from that thrifty old Scotch stock that settled in New England in the 1700's and which has played a large part in the history of Massachusetts and of Boston."[148]

By contrast, hostile councillors accused Luscomb of only masquerading as a Bostonian, given her suburban backing.[149] The *Telegram* took on the entire GGA machinery, calling its operators "the self-appointed guardians of public morals and welfare." Of Luscomb, the paper objected that they did not doubt her training "but she is associated with the Boston League of Women Voters, an organization that betrays none too much sympathy for the common people." The *Telegram* instead supported Molloy, as a representative of working women: "We cannot conceive how the ordinary women, who work, can vote for Florence H. Luscomb, when Annie E. Malloy [*sic*] is in the field against her. The Goo Goos [GGA] do not believe Miss Malloy is one of the three best qualified candidates, but the people of Boston when they vote may decide differently. Miss Malloy's experience as a leader of the union telephone girls fits her to serve all the people; Miss Luscomb's experience with a little group of high-brows does not." Appropriating the language of transcending narrow interests, the *Telegram* sought candidates "bigger and better and broader than those the Good Government Association suggests."[150]

Luscomb's campaign venues demonstrated the reach and the limits of the postsuffrage BLWV coalition. The group had never been as narrowly entrenched in the old white Brahmin set as had the antisuffragists.[151] Now Luscomb campaigned at the homes not only of the Storrows and the Murphys in the Back Bay, but at those of African American Republicans Dr. and Mrs. John B. Hall and attorney and Mrs. Butler R. Wilson, at the Meyer Bloomfields' in West Roxbury, and with the WTUL secretary Miss Mabel Gillespie, among others.[152] These were not, however, the *Telegram*'s "ordinary women." They were wives of professionals; they served as club women and were active in civic service, but did not work for wages; or they were professionals in social service. There was a WTUL official, but no women's union official.

Luscomb had her own "dream" about government. It revealed the degree to which, despite her various memberships and sympathies, she adhered to a particular frame of reference that privileged the participation of elite women in city governance: "My dream would be to see a representative group of women, a few from each women's club, attending the City Council where the various municipal problems come up for solution, particularly that of the budget."[153]

On this platform, Luscomb lost, but not by much. She came in fifth. In the Republican ward where the BLWV was particularly strong and women predominated, Luscomb ran ahead of the other GGA candidates. Luscomb outdistanced Molloy in fifteen wards; Molloy ran ahead of Luscomb in the other eleven, including her own. Predictably, Molloy's wards were more heavily working class, Luscomb's upper middle class and elite.[154] Women had shown themselves credible candidates. As the *Herald* put it, "Miss Luscomb made a far better showing than even many of her friends had expected, while Miss Molloy, the president of the Telephone Operators' Union, running eighth in the field of 19, also surprised some of the mossback anti-suffragists."[155]

But there were other results. Luscomb and Molloy's combined total placed them well ahead of the lowest winning candidate. Inasmuch as there might have been a "woman's" vote, the two had split it, to the detriment of each.[156] In deciding that Molloy did not constitute the right kind of woman candidate, the BLWV itself had undermined its contention that "the heart of every woman" would lead her in the same direction.

What is more, endorsing and then running their own candidate had alienated some of the BLWV's members, particularly those active in partisan organizations, who resigned. But even those who remained seemed, like their counterpart LWV members across the nation, to read the experiment as a failure never to be repeated. Only one GGA candidate was among the three winners. Curley had triumphed, achieving a majority of five to four over the GGA in the Council. The BLWV seemed in accord with a female commentator who, despite the unmentioned fact that Susan Fitzgerald (no longer a BLWV member) had been elected to the state legislature as a Democrat only a month earlier, concluded, "Once more in our proud old city of Boston it has been demonstrated that women will not vote for women and that comparatively few men will vote for good women against popular cheap men unless under compulsion." She castigated "the professionally good men and women of Boston," for their inaction. "If Miss Annie Molloy had been elected," she speculated, "she would have been, I believe, a credit to the city and to the organized women whom she represents." "Miss Luscomb did better," she continued, but her prominence in the BLWV "which is a sideline of the Good Government Association," was of little help.[157] Not only did the BLWV not put forth another candidate, no woman from their circles ran for City Council in the succeeding twenty years.

Nor were male politicians anxious to repeat the experiment. Luscomb had run behind (though just) the other two candidates endorsed by the GGA. Yankee Republican men, which would have encompassed virtually all the members of the association, had already demonstrated their diffidence regarding women politicians when they comprised forty-eight of the fifty-two votes in the state legislature against ratification of the Nineteenth Amendment. Three of the remaining four had been Boston Democrats.[158]

The city councillors, once the contest had ended and Luscomb was restored to her proper place in the gallery, were inclined to be conciliatory. One called her "the watch lady of the Council" and advised her to get busy with the books and help shed a "little more light on the question of where the taxpayers' money is being spent."[159] They courted women's votes, speaking at women's clubs and parlors, but they had little interest and few incentives to seek new allies who would disturb the current political relations between women and men.[160]

If 1922 marked a turning point for the BLWV, it also did for the GGA. Since the new charter's adoption in 1909, and including the two victors in 1922, only six of twenty-seven men in the City Council had won without the GGA's endorsement. In 1922 the GGA lost its majority on the council. In 1923, the city's Democrats determined fully to take over the city, seeing the GGA "as a sort of masked edition of the Republican City Committee" and accusing it of having "nothing in common with the plain people," caring for them only during political campaigns. The 1923 election showed even further GGA losses. Curley got only one-third of his choices, but the anti-GGA forces on the nine-member council now outnumbered the GGA forces by two to one.[161] In 1924, in a final blow to GGA influence, the city voted to return to ward-based elections, albeit nonpartisan ones.[162] While Republican conservatives cemented their control at the national and state levels, the city in the 1920s witnessed a resurgence of Democratic power and popular politics.

Luscomb and Molloy may not have succeeded in altering the sexual geography of city hall, but women's votes had altered the geography of urban politics in other ways. The Women's Republican and the Women's Democratic Clubs established themselves on Beacon Hill, just down the street from the city's government buildings.[163] While women's reform organizations had long sought proximity to the corridors of power, these were the first women's partisan organizations to do so.

Such an independent base led to immediate controversy similar to that over the BLWV. The club women, unlike the women in the party divisions and committees, tended to be irregular rather than regular party members. They could and did formulate their own policies and oppose those of the party hierarchy. Their loyalty remained suspect in Massachusetts as in other states. Regular party women tended to despise them. Mrs. Elizabeth Lowell Putnam, a Brahmin antisuffrage activist and delegate to the Republican National Convention in 1924, wrote a friend in 1925, "The Women's Republican Club certainly does goat-like things and I regard it as one of the worst menaces to the Republican party that there is and have always refused to join it."[164]

On a more intimate level of voting booths and party headquarters, the political geography also changed. In 1921, polling places shifted from time-honored ward rooms (the province of cigar-smoking, spitting, machine politicians), schools, and much less savory spots to churches. Lucy Stone had blamed the location of polling places, in part, for low turnouts in nineteenth-century school elections. Now the *Globe* credited the change for 1921's heavy vote by Boston women.[165]

If voting had become sanctified by the switch, changes at party headquarters give new meaning to the phrase "domestication of politics." Women turned homes into campaign headquarters and campaign headquarters into homes. "Our city politics has entered a marvelous era of overstuffed furniture, of huge comfy divans, of beautiful rugs and dainty curtained windows," reported the *Globe* in 1921. "When men fought these battles by themselves, a desk, a few folding chairs, borrowed from a friendly undertaker, and a couple of spittoons completed the headquarters. Alas! for the campaign treasury: these grand ol' days are gone. Now the candidate has got to move half his household furniture down to his political office or hire a suite at a hotel for the convenience of the women workers." But, the reporter was careful to add, the changes did not mark "vain display . . . the women are working and working hard." While the purported message was clear—party politics was no longer the province of squalid, smoky, masculine back rooms, but had moved to female space in the sunlit parlor (a message dear to many suffragists' hearts)—many of the candidates seemed to provide women workers with separate space, an enclave at headquarters, or even a separate headquarters.[166] Space had been rearranged, but the merger, or conquest, was far from complete.

Despite the redecorating of candidates' offices, there was a sense among Boston's elite after Luscomb's defeat, and in the absence of Yankee female candidates for City Council over the next decades, that nice women (also known by some as "real" women) did not run for city office. Running for office at all could smack of self-seeking, even to former suffragists, and could definitely put one in with the wrong crowd. After a decade of watching the political scene, appointive office veteran Ethel Johnson wrote, "I've never seen anything to indicate that politicians in either party were particularly eager about women in public office. And as for the kind of women the politicians would select if they felt they had to offer a sop—from all such, Good Lord deliver us."[167]

City politicians were even more suspect than others. So few women sought Boston city office in the 1920s (approximately three after Luscomb and Molloy), that while longtime School Committee member Fanny Curtis acknowledged in 1930 that Boston women "have always taken an active, if private, part in public affairs," she concluded, "[i]t seems as though the interest of Boston women in municipal government is purely academic and that the practical politics which belong to municipal elections and city management have deterred or, at least, not interested them."[168]

It may have been that former antisuffragist Elizabeth Lowell Putnam had merely been prescient when in 1922 she argued, "the best women are not afraid of the votes of their friends, their neighbors, or of the body politic," but that later, "when women politicians have grown more virulent and offensive the best women may hesitate."[169] But many women, otherwise proponents of democracy, faltered in the perceived face of Boston's electorate. They had not, as had many of Putnam's antisuffrage cohort, resisted woman suffrage on the grounds that it would enfranchise their maids, enhance the power of machines, and decrease their own influence, which did not require the vote. But they participated in a more general decline in the faith of mass democracy, particularly as they watched the GGA falter. Peace activist and suffragist Lucia True Ames Mead in 1922 confessed, "I have the highest respect for many men in public office and feel that our governors, elected by the whole state, are to be trusted by the people"; but she felt entirely differently "with the Boston electorate becoming what it is."[170]

First Murphy's defeat, and then Luscomb's, provided evidence to these women of the electorate's inability to gauge its own collective interests. Such skepticism ultimately infected attitudes toward the state, as well. After Johnson's departure, Massachusetts Consumer's League executive secretary Margaret Wiesman rejected the notion of cooperating with the state's Department of Labor. Not mincing words, she declared flatly, "Our labor department is completely rotten, I wouldn't trust them with any money. . . . We musn't get into dirty state politics, which unfortunately even though we dabble in we can't control; we are just not slimey [*sic*] enough."[171]

If nice women did not run for office, they could still, as in the Consumers' League, prod those who did—and now with enhanced prods, their votes. Historian Nancy Cott has argued that neither voluntarist nor partisan activity was inherently feminist, that voluntarist efforts had met with great success, and that those experienced in voluntarist politics found partisan ones not only seamier but more divisive for women's organizations.[172] While still in Massachusetts in 1912, Mary Dewson may have been exasperated with "the little puttering efforts of women's leagues and societies to influence our city bosses," and so, like many other social workers, turned increasingly to woman suffrage as a solution, but Dewson herself chose prodding over running. She remained on the political appointive track and by that route became a force in national Democratic Party politics in the 1930s.[173]

Successful women office seekers found themselves portrayed, or worked to portray themselves, not as the experienced party politicians they usually were, but as primarily family women and, at most, club women. The 1927 headlines blared, "Home Comes First for Mrs. Andrews," at the appointment of the first woman to the Governor's Council—a position for which Esther Andrews had run and come in second, only to have the winner die. A successful businesswoman who had taken over her husband's firm when he fell ill, a proponent of equal pay for women and men, a leading club woman, and a beneficiary or numerous public appointments including to the advisory board of the Bureau of Prisons, within minutes after learning of her appointment, Esther Andrews declared, "No married woman has any right to go into politics, public service or the professions, if it means giving up her home."[174]

Gone were the feisty women depicted in 1921, hurling charges like veteran politicians. Successful female office seekers later in 1920s Boston promoted their own gentility and, in contrast to the first years after suffrage, hewed to an image of a female politician as an oxymoron. While Mrs. Andrews "confesses, upon being asked," the *Post* reported, that she finds women still being discriminated against in both private business and public life in pay and recognition, "she doesn't mention it unless she is asked."[175] Their legitimacy as public actors continued to

Boston papers tended to portray women politicians (here, Mrs. Esther Andrews of the governor's executive council) first and foremost as housewives. *Boston Daily Advertiser*, November 4, 1927.

rest on their moral authority as homemakers. "Although it's not a necessary qualification," the *Boston Daily Advertiser* captioned its picture of Andrews, Andrews was "a good cook."[176] "But," the *Post* gushed, "for all her activities, she has been first a homemaker" whose "charming home . . . reveals the intimate touch of the perfect housekeeper."

This trend in depiction had increased rather than decreased over the decade. In 1925, Jennie Loitman Barron, albeit shown in the paper with her two children and described as the first mother to sit on the School Committee since Mrs. Julia Duff retired in 1905, had emphasized her dual career marriage and announced, "I am sure the day of the household drudge is over. This means a tremendous social revolution, a great advance in civilization. The cooperation of the men makes it possible." Having worked her way through college and law school and in the WEIU's legal aid department, Barron was full of schemes by which less wealthy women who might have cooperative husbands, but not maids, could join in neighborhood groups to hire a maid to watch the children once a week. "It's fine for the women and fine for the children," she insisted. The same *Globe* that two years later noted that Andrews did "not look a militant woman," unabashedly described Barron as "[n]ot only an efficient and indulgent mother, but a successful lawyer—and a feminist leader, a popular public speaker and an active worker in innumerable philanthropic enterprises to boot."[177]

By 1929, the press erased all traces of a logical trajectory to candidacy. When Mrs. Fred (Elizabeth) Pigeon was elected to the school board, there was no mention of her service as a delegate to the Republican State Committee since 1920.[178] The *Herald*, a Republican paper, did mention, in explanation of her running 25,000 votes ahead of the nearest of eleven other candidates, her active ward organizations and strong Republican support, as well as her history of party activity. But the *Globe* and the *Post* portrayed her as a modest family woman, a "home life adherent," and pictured her with her oldest son and husband (a successful spar maker). "The idea of ever being on the Boston School Committee had never occurred to me," she insisted, "until no woman would go into the field." The press mentioned her involvement in club work, her background in teaching, her settlement house experience, and her current positions on the legislative committee of the State Federation of Women's Clubs and as associate manager of the Home and School Association, but it did not mention her party involvement. Moreover, the descriptions of her extrahousehold involvement came only after a lengthly examination of her relationship with her four sons and her intention to cook Thanksgiving dinner for seventeen herself. Indeed, so thoroughly domestic was the portrait of Pigeon that the person who would have been called a "maid" in Barron's story became "the woman who has helped Mrs. Pigeon."[179]

Both Pigeon and Barron, the only two women to win positions on the committee after Curtis during these two decades, enjoyed endorsement by the Public School Association (PSA). While the GGA had lost control of the City Council, its counterpart, the PSA, retained a firm hold on the School Committee. Those endorsed generally won.[180] In contrast to Mary Meehan, Barron's opponent in 1925 who did not receive the PSA endorsement and was not portrayed as domestic but rather as "one of the best known women in the labor movement," Barron and Pigeon were both active Republicans. Beyond protecting their status as amateurs in the political arena, erasing their party activities allowed the PSA to protect its nonpartisan credentials.

That Barron and Andrews, both safely Republican, had received Yankee backing despite their activities as Jewish women followed in a tradition of some decades that had left professional, assimilated, second-generation Jewish Bostonians well integrated in reform circles. Women's reform organizations had long called on the counsel of progressive rabbis and Jewish labor leaders; the Brandeises went everywhere (even, by this time, the Supreme Court); and the School Committee had had a rabbi as a member in 1882. At the same time, in Boston as elsewhere in the nation, anti-Semitism was enjoying a resurgence. The Harvard Board of Overseers discussed imposing a quota on Jewish students when enrollment reached 20 percent. And when Barron suggested that the committee appoint an attendance officer who understood Yiddish, she was soundly defeated.[181]

Women like Molloy, without Yankee reform backing, had difficulty not only winning, but getting press. In the same year Andrews's appointment garnered so much attention, Mrs. Carrie Sheehan's bid for City Council went virtually unremarked. The *Boston Daily Advertiser* gave an entire page to the election of officers in women's clubs and a column on the loss of the first women to run for mayor in New Hampshire—and not a word to Sheehan.[182] Women candidates for the council were no longer a novelty, though none had yet been elected. Like other women politicians, Sheehan had built a political career over the preceding decade. She had served as a delegate to MWSA annual conventions and as an officer of the BLWV. A loyal Democrat, she had resigned from the BLWV over its endorsement of Murphy. Such loyalty had won her a post as an assistant election commissioner from Curley, but when Curley lost in 1925 to Malcolm Nichols, the last Republican mayor, she lost her job. Running for city council afterward, she found that loyal Democrat though she was, male Democratic council candidates, including the incumbent, would come first in party largesse.[183]

The early 1930s saw little change in this pattern, except that women, though running in greater numbers, were not even winning seats on the School Committee.[184] School Committee contestants received more coverage, however, than many of the women running for City Council. It helped that the School Committee races, still at large, were smaller. City Council elections drew upwards of a hundred contestants. But women candidates were rarely among the dozens profiled. In 1933, other than listing their names with their vote totals, the *Globe* gave absolutely no coverage to candidates Leila W. Miller, a lawyer from Ward 1, or Catherine A. Robbins of Ward 9.[185]

What was new in the 1930s was the candidacy of women for City Council from Irish political families. Previous women candidates had had connections to the labor movement or to women's political and philanthropic groups. These new women, while candidates in their own right, had kinship connections to male-dominated machines. It at least got them more press attention, and ultimately it would bring victory.

In 1931 Mrs. Eleanor C. L'Ecuyer of Dorchester was the first woman to run for City Council since Sheehan in 1927. Born in South Boston, she had graduated from Girls Latin School, studied at Portia Law School, married, and worked as an associate in her father's law office. She had two children and belonged to the BLWV. An effective speaker, according to the press, "she claims that municipal government is simply 'municipal housekeeping' and that the City Government needs the judgment of women in its Council," hardly novel thoughts. None of these attributes distinguished her much from earlier candidates.[186]

Her family, however, did. Her uncle was the late Judge Michael J. Creed and all five of her brothers had served two terms in the Massachusetts House of Representatives. In addition, she was the former vice president of Post 60 American Legion Auxiliary, a group with a different constituency from that of the BLWV. Despite the Luscomb-Molloy campaign and L'Ecuyer's youth (at twenty-four she was the youngest woman to seek office), the *Globe* designated L'Ecuyer as "the first woman who ever made a serious effort to be elected to the City Council."[187]

Even with her organization mimicking that of machine politicians and her political connections, she finished a distant third to the anti-Curley candidate who won and the Curley candidate who lost.[188] It was not until women linked political family status with an inherited council position that they won. In early 1937, by special election, Mildred Gleason Harris, described by the *Globe* as having "brilliant blue eyes," "thick bobbed black hair," and a "ready smile on her small mouth," won the special election to take over the South End/Roxbury City Council seat of her brother, who had died in office. By doing so she became the first woman on the Boston City Council.[189]

Harris was no newcomer to politics. "I've been going to school in politics for fifteen years," she told the *Globe*, "under my brother Dick, who was City Councillor for ten years until his death, and my brother John who was State Representative from Ward 9." When the latter brother had died the previous fall, she had run unsuccessfully against his widow for his vacant legislative seat. Now she had her sister-in-law's support.

Family mattered, but only the political family. While she mentioned her natal family frequently, unlike other women candidates she did not mention her husband, a steamfitter with whom she moved four times from 1935 to 1938, finally settling in the same small apartment building as rival candidate John Craven, and she only mentioned her children to acknowledge that her daughters did most of the housework.[190]

Harris emphasized instead the endless errands, even in the late stages of pregnancy, she had run for her brothers on behalf of their constituents. "They'll tell you that women aren't wanted in public office," she asserted, "but I say whether you are a man or woman has nothing much to do with it. If you can render service to your constituents, they'll vote you into office."[191]

But despite her own depiction of herself as a consummate politician, scion of a political family, the *Globe* chose to present a more mixed tale. Of its four photos, only one bore any resemblance to a political pose, Harris with a female campaign worker. In the other three, she is with her four children, doing dishes, and making a victory cake. The day of her victory, the *Globe* also carried Dorothy Dix's advice column, headlined, "Wives Who Interfere in Their Husbands Business: No Greater Sin."[192] Harris, whose living room the day after the victory "looked as though a tornado had struck it, the floor strewn with papers and cigarette butts, pictures knocked down, rugs kicked up from the horde of friends and well-wishers," was an uncomfortable model of success.[193]

The record of women candidates in Boston's elections during the first two decades after suffrage was hardly stellar. At the beginning of the 1920s, Boston women outnumbered men by nearly 10,000 people and at the decade's end by nearly 20,000, but they only sent one woman

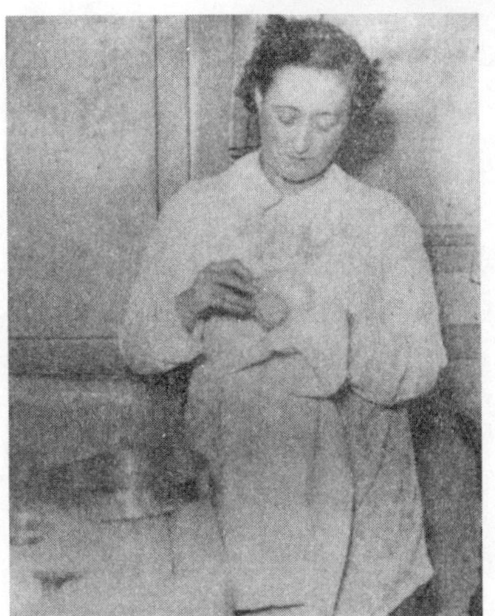

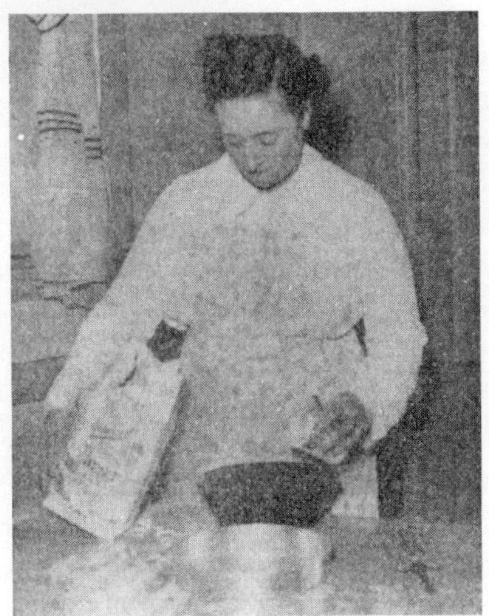

Despite Harris's self-depiction as a machine politician who left her housework to others, the press portrayed her largely in domestic settings. *Boston Globe*, March 31, 1937.

to the City Council and three to the School Committee, none of whom served a second term. More Boston women went to the state legislature than to City Hall. Outside of Boston, Massachusetts women won municipal victories. In Midwestern and Western cities, women won victories.[194] Why, then, not in Boston?

As at the turn of the century, Boston's geography was gendered. A *Boston Post* headline declared in 1929, "Destiny of Three Wards Up to Women." In those three wards, the last Republican strongholds in the city, women predominated heavily even among voters.[195] These wards housed the relatively elite, and the relatively elite women had chosen not to run and not to put women forward for office.[196] They also had refused to back other women who ran. That, too, was an exercise of power.

Elsewhere in the city, the *Post* saw the problem as one of apathy. "Veteran political leaders," it revealed, "feel that the women could dominate the politics of the city if they would take enough interest to register as voters and cast ballots at the polls." Women's registration had come much closer to men's than at the decade's outset, when it was about half. Now female registered voters numbered only about 25,000 fewer than male.[197] But the *Post* had avoided the question of how sincerely those (male) veteran political leaders would have liked women to dominate the city. Certainly, they had learned to court them as voters. In his victorious 1929 mayoral race, Curley inaugurated a series of noontime rallies for women. But there is no evidence that he supported women candidates.

Women's historians have blamed several factors for women's poor showing in elections in the 1920s. The hostility of male politicians, the rising culture of individualism, generational splits among women activists, co-optation by parties, and a continuing diverse array of social causes that drew women more compellingly than electoral politics have formed the chief explanations.[198] But the reason also lay at least as much in class divisions among activist women. The suffragists, never as heavily and exaltedly elite as the antisuffragists, had reached out to working-class women in the last days of the campaign. With the campaign won, however, they dropped their allies like hot potatoes. Few of their working-class allies could qualify in their eyes as true women, as women they would want to represent them or even to represent themselves.

Those women who did run for office developed no new routes to power. They ran as members of political machines—reform or otherwise—or as labor union heroes, or even in one case (Josephine Lally in 1939) as athletes. The machine members, as among the men, fared best.

In some sense, urban politics, even before charter revision in 1925, had reverted to its neighborhood basis. The Back Bay and Beacon Hill had remained neighborhoods tied closely by kinship, reinforced by organizations filled with kinship ties that crossed party and other political lines. The vote had never been essential to the neighborhood women's access to power. They only had to go next door or perhaps just down the hall.

For these women, the 1920s witnessed a decline, not a growth in power. Suburbanization weakened the ability of their male kin to dominate city government as relatives moved beyond the bounds of Boston's electorate. The rise of professional social workers had already challenged their notions of legitimacy in women's leadership, replacing domestic moral authority with scholastic expertise. Woman suffrage further dissipated their power, undermining their claims to speak for "every woman" since they now at times could barely be heard over the clamor of other women's voices, women who entered the political arena directly and with other allies and other neighborhood networks. They remained, as leaders of large and influential voluntary societies and as relatives of powerful men, in positions of power. They could still, at times, control appointments. They could support or withhold support from political campaigns. Their voice was still, in many respects, louder than other women's, but it was no longer the only woman's voice in the arena.

So it was no accident that the first woman elected to City Council hailed not from the Back Bay but the South End, a district particularly hard hit by the Depression and indeed willing to elect a female machine heir rather than risk abandoning the patronage networks altogether.[199] If the postsuffrage decades were not all that nonelite women had hoped, they did see expanded possibilities. Women from Charlestown, East Boston, and the South End could and did run for City Council. Their alliances and modes of organizing differed from those of the women in the Back Bay and Beacon Hill who had led the suffrage movement. And they succeeded despite rather than because of the former leaders of the women's movement.

The Business of [Black] Women—Revisited

In November 1937, Mildred Gleason Harris ran for City Council as the incumbent and as a machine politician. No women's group affiliations appeared in the press, only repeated references to her late brother. As the incumbent and heir of an effective machine, she had the advantage of announcing new public works in ward meetings of her Mildred Gleason Harris Associates. She did so, however, amidst rising racial tensions.

Her ward encompassed the heart of black Boston. In 1935, Harris's brother's election had provoked a race riot between his supporters and those of his African American rival, Ernest D. Cooke, who had tried to quell the violence.[200] Cooke had lost by only 600 votes and demanded a recount, suspecting illegal voting from the camp of the "invincible" Dick Gleason.[201]

At the core of the tension was access to public largesse, from which black Bostonians had benefited disproportionately little.[202] By 1932/33, half the district's people were receiving public welfare. In 1934, over 40 percent lacked jobs. Infant mortality rates skyrocketed until they were the highest in the city. And hundreds of black Bostonians lacked homes, having lost them to the bank after struggling with mortgages for years.[203] Some private Boston schools still refused to educate African Americans, and despite their stated policies, some YWCAs and YMCAs still refused to house them. Offices refused to employ them, and although there were a number of black patrolmen, policemen treated them with increasing violence. In 1934, police shot and killed a black janitor who fled when he saw the motor vehicle police because when previously arrested for a minor traffic violation, police had held him incommunicado for three days.[204]

Police also used brutality to enforce increasingly rigid, sexualized segregation. At a time when southern lynchings appeared in almost every issue of Boston's black press, Boston's police routinely invaded black homes in the South End, particularly if they suspected interracial sex, and they denied protection to black women on the streets or off them. In 1932, as two young black women walked down Tremont Street, two white men assaulted them, first with lewd comments, and then with blows when one of the women, twenty-two-year-old Mrs. Marjorie Trent, made so bold as to resent the insult. Trent's companion rushed to her aid, only to be beaten and kicked by three white men who came from the store to aid her original assailant. The women's screams roused the neighborhood, and the white men fled into a nearby shop and drew their guns. When the police arrived, they refused to arrest the white men. A crowd of black men, manifesting "a sullen rage," remained in the neighborhood along with scores of policemen keeping out whites and dispersing blacks.[205]

The black press called the two women "martyrs for a righteous cause—the right of women to walk the streets unmolested by young ruffians." The paper pointed out that it was the protest by the women, not the insults by the men, that were unusual. "Ordinarily the young women would have borne the insult and carried on," it maintained. "There are many who patiently submit to this treatment in our streets." After the police had arrived, the white men had approached the women, offered them $200 in the presence of the police and told them to "forget it." With one of them bleeding from a blow to the face, the women refused. Offering to pay the women for sexual insult would have reenforced the notion that every black woman's virtue was for sale. White women had finally won almost universal acceptance as public, respectable persons on the street in the 1920s. Even in their own neighborhoods, black women who claimed respectability in the 1930s found their place on the streets as virtuous women contested by whites. In 1938, the black *Chronicle* carried a headline, "Women Say Streets Not Safe Against Mashers And Cops."[206]

Off the streets, they fared little better. After a drunken policeman invaded her home in 1934, antilynching activist Mrs. M. Cravath Simpson declared, "no one's home of color is safe from invasion and trumped up lies though in Massachusetts." Three years later, the paper reported "a respectable couple whose door was ruthlessly kicked in without benefit of a warrant. And all because said officers didn't happen to like the idea of a colored gentleman being married to a white lady." In 1938, the *Chronicle* reported citizens' complaints of renewed police invasions of South End homes without warrants.[207]

As the neighborhood's new white-owned Cotton Club, run on the same basis as that in New York—in the black district but not allowing black patrons—demonstrated, whites saw the heart of the black district, more than ever, as an area of illicit activities, nightclubs, jazz, and gambling, a place they could go for a night's adventure. When a local church led an attempt to oust the Cotton Club, its mortgage was foreclosed.[208] Police enacted this understanding and furthered it, as their attempts at enforcing boundaries and raiding clubs were reported in the white press. To them, all black women on the street, at any time of day or night, were fair game, and all interracial sex was illicit.

Against this backdrop, it was black women, not men, who surged into the Democratic Party. The experience of sexual insult had long had the power to mobilize Boston's black women. It was, after all, Boston's Josephine St. Pierre Ruffin who had launched the National Association of Colored Women in the 1890s to defend black womanhood from just such insults in the national press. Now it led more black women than men out of the Republican and into the Democratic camp.[209]

Already leaders in Boston's antilynching crusades, black women had been aroused en masse against President Hoover's Supreme Court nomination of a man who opposed antilynching legislation and black suffrage, as well as by Hoover's snubbing of black committeewomen at the Republican National Convention and segregating of black women on the postwar voyage of Gold Star mothers (women who had lost sons in the war) to France. They saw little reason for the sort of loyalty that held most of Boston's black men in the Republican camp.[210]

In the early 1930s, black attorney, World War I veteran, 1925 City Council candidate, and Curley supporter Julian Rainey struggled vainly to breathe life into a Colored Democratic League that under Dr. William Worthy had less than a dozen members—all men.[211] Worthy's wife, by contrast, went from success to success at the head of the only incorporated black political organization in the state, the Colored Women's Democratic Club. Mrs. Mabel Worthy's July 1932 meeting of 200 women decided that the lily-white Republicans were more dangerous than the southern Democrats.[212] When an objection was raised to Rainey as delegate at large to the Democratic National Convention because of his position as corporation counsel of Boston, it was Mrs. Worthy (her four children prominently mentioned) who replaced him.[213]

Attorney Matthew Bullock raged that women had gotten the vote too easily in 1920 without understanding the necessity of party loyalty and that "the women in Roxbury were too busy in their political clubs to take an interest in the education and conduct of their girls." But such complaints by Boston's black Republican men were not only a recognition that black women's political interests might differ from those of men, but an attempt to close the barn door after the horse had escaped.[214] Bullock was responding in part to the decline in the political fortunes of black Bostonians. As the 1930s dawned, they had yet to recover from a redistricting in 1895 that had cost them their seat in the Massachusetts House of Representatives and damaged their control over a seat in the City Council. The 1909 charter revision decreasing the size of the City Council had sealed their fate. No black members were elected thereafter.[215]

The decline in direct representation had coincided with a shift in the sympathies of white Boston. Many of the city's leading abolitionists, both white and black, had died in the 1880s. Remaining whites and many blacks viewed the decade's new southern migrants with disdain, finding them, in contrast to earlier migrants, "utterly uneducated and ignorant . . . uncouth . . . crude, dull, and indeed brutish in appearance." The same sorts of white Bostonians who had supported emancipation recoiled as much from the black migrants as from the new European immigrants in the increasingly nativist decades. They found both "ubiquitous." Blacks, according to one 1914 account, "crowded into the cars among white passengers . . . entered restaurants and took seats alongside the white patrons. They even invaded some of the most select Back Bay churches." Some of the whites continued to foster black civil rights efforts in the North, others supported Booker T. Washington's efforts in the South, and some did both. But none restored black Bostonians to their previous positions in political office.[216]

Exasperation with their supposed Republican allies had led one small group of black Bostonians to create the Colored Men's Democratic Club in 1895, the year of redistricting. It netted them minimal advantages. Though Democrats did appoint more blacks to city positions than Republicans did in succeeding years, blacks served on Republican ward committees decades before they would do so on Democratic ones. And the politicians of both parties were far from generous, more liberal with money than with offices.[217]

As a percentage of Boston's total population, even in 1940, blacks comprised only 3.1 percent.[218] But the preceding decades had witnessed the consolidation of Boston's black population, as the West End's black

Yankees joined newer arrivals in the South End and the northern part of Roxbury, particularly in what became Ward 9.[219] Probably viewing them as a potential swing vote in the decade's highly fragmented and contested ward politics, Curley began courting black voters, removing City Hospital privileges from Posse Gymnasium for its avowed policy of admitting no black students in 1923 and publicly criticizing the Ku Klux Klan in 1924.[220] Boston's black Republicans viewed such courtship with deep suspicion. It was only with Hoover's presidency that any significant number of black Bostonians threatened to switch parties permanently.

Many black women continued, as they had for decades, to serve in Boston's Republican ranks. This had its own rewards. While the Colored Democratic Men met at the League of Women for Community Service (LWCS) in the South End, Mrs. Harriet C. Hall, president of the rival Women's Service Club (WSC) a few blocks down, continued her activities at the Women's Republican Club on Beacon Hill, which she had ensured would be integrated when she cofounded it in 1920. Though she had chaired the Boston Anti-Lynching Crusade fund in 1922, she had remained a loyal Republican through Hoover's years. She had been a candidate for the State House of Representatives in 1924, losing by only 224 votes. She toured the United States for the Republicans, often as the only black person in the group.[221]

Like the white women who held party offices, Hall was not necessarily a woman of the people. Married to a Yale and University of Pennsylvania educated physician, she alienated so many black Bostonians when she tried to get the licensing Board to close the largest black-owned South End enterprise, Slade's restaurant, as a public nuisance, that they mounted two rival slates for the Republican Ward Committee.[222] Her organizational connections tended to be relatively elite, both cross-racially and in black organizations. She had long served as an officer of the local NAACP, when it was a bastion of Brahmins, black and white; the WSC, over which Hall presided, tended to be more socially conservative in its membership than the rival LWCS, and then, of course, there was the Women's Republican Club.[223]

With the Depression and continued private and public sector employment discrimination at every level, the index of political leadership rested more than ever on patronage. While Mrs. Worthy ran the Colored Women's Democratic Club and spoke at mixed race political rallies and

Harriet Hall, club woman and doctor's wife, rose in the ranks of the state Republican Party. *Boston Guardian*, July 27, 1940.

Mrs. Hall spoke at mixed rallies and served on Republican state and city committees, the *Guardian* claimed the more plebian Mrs. Edna Black, whose husband and means of livelihood were never mentioned, had done more for the citizens of Roxbury. She had created a strong organization of the rank-and-file members of the ward, controlling the largest single block of votes in her section of Boston; she shepherded federal WPA and welfare relief cases through the government bureaucracy, and she engaged in a constant fight for jobs for loyal black political workers. She had never, however, supported black candidates, and in 1937, she ignored Cooke and backed Harris.[224] Harris won.

Two years later, Harris went up for reelection confident of victory. She did not get it. Sullivan, who had run second to her in 1937, won in what the *Post* termed the upset of the day. Her supporters were stunned. Even the *Guardian* had predicted a smashing victory and claimed Ward 9 needed her with her connections and the respect she received from city and state officials. It had lauded her performance as a mother with six grown children who understood life's problems and received all constituents. "The women of today," it had warned, "demand a place in public life and it's good to see them doing a good job."[225] But it was not a close race. Harris was swamped. Edna Black had taken her group elsewhere, and while their candidate had not won, without her support neither had Harris.

Harris manifested her distance from the black women in the district when, speaking to the Friendship Club, a black women's neighborhood group based at the Robert Gould Shaw (Settlement) House, she "expressed *surprise* and pleasure at finding such a splendid group of women comprising the membership" [emphasis added]. Club members asked for an improved lighting system in the neighborhood. Harris threw the ball back in their court, instructing them to submit the request in writing, and promising that she would then take it to the council.[226] The last straw had been her refusal to name part of a local park after a black war hero. Harris did not deliver for the black residents of the district. Edna Black's actions asserted that if black voters could not control the turf, at least it could not be controlled without them.[227]

Like her white male counterparts and unlike the black female Republican and Democratic party leaders, the unofficial black ward boss was, as the black-run *Boston Guardian* pointed out, not college bred. Edna Black remained skillfully, strategically independent.[228] In both parties, as among whites, the female party leadership tended to come from the elite, from club women of high social standing, light skinned, and often married to professional, Ivy League men. While they led associations of African Americans, they and their husbands usually also had experience in other, white-dominated enterprises. They seemed comfortable working across racial lines, and they formed a coterie of black women whom Boston's elite whites found acceptable in their affect, experience, and attributes.

These party women, too, became experts in patronage, but only by bypassing the city politicians. Mabel Worthy among the Democrats and Mrs. Helen Whiteman among the Republicans both garnered a reputation for getting their constituents jobs, pensions, and raises.[229] They did so despite little interest from the Irish American men who continued to dominate City Council. Few of those men had ties to the New Deal.[230] In contrast, some black politicians, particularly the more elite ones, like Worthy and Whiteman, developed direct links with the federal and state administrations. Indeed, although less so than elite white female politicians, because of their lack of access to power within the city they had always cast their lot as much outside city politics as in it. Now they could find the federal government (for Democrats) and the state (for Republicans) more responsive than the city. Worthy's successes, in particular, stood in stark contrast to the failures of the Urban League's efforts, whose head admitted to being a Democrat only for job-related reasons. While George Goodman repeatedly fumed at his inability to secure black placements on New Deal projects, Mrs. Worthy, through the Honorable Joseph A. Maynard, chairman of the Democratic State Committee, had submitted four young women's names for the clerical list of the National Recovery Administration (NRA). They were all active members of the Massachusetts Colored Women's Democratic Club. All four got jobs.[231] At the turn of the century, female relatives of black politicians had gotten coveted positions as teachers; in the 1930s black women got patronage through their own direct political participation.[232] Unlike the white women in the city's party leadership, however, these relatively elite black women seemed to feel no compunction about recognizing the partisan nature of their efforts.

Not all, even among prominent black women, moved in the direction of the two major parties.[233] The rise of the left had been strongly felt among black Bostonians, to the extent that in 1932, for those in flight from the Republican Party, the Democrats offered themselves as an alternative to the Communists and not the other way around.[234] As Communists in Boston organized on behalf of the Scottsboro defendents, unemployed workers, and black garment workers, Democrat Alvira Hazzard, a columnist for the *Chronicle*, aimed her fire at the Republicans, not the far left. All parties used blacks, she claimed, not just the Communist Party.[235] By 1934, black papers carried news of International Labor Defense (ILD) dances to benefit Scottsboro, annual celebrations of the Young Communists League, and classes under the auspices of the Workers' School.[236] One of the latter, a Negro history class, started with eight people and within three weeks had thirty-five. A successful author, Eugene Gordon, whose departure for Russia was announced the next year with much fanfare, taught the course, but his wife, Mrs. Edythe Mae Gordon, must have provided much of the information. The next year she would receive her master's degree from Boston University for her economics thesis, "The Status of the Negro Woman in the United States from 1619 to 1865." Two months after Eugene Gordon went to Russia, she joined him there, to work on a doctorate at Moscow University covering the status of Negro women from 1865 to the present.[237]

The venue for Gordon's class was the home of Mrs. Mary E. Moore in the South End. She was largely responsible for the increase in attendance.[238] She was also a prominent black businesswoman and would be the Communist Party candidate for secretary of state in 1936.[239] An entrepreneurial black beautician might seem an unlikely candidate for the party, but she was not alone. While the wives of Boston's black lawyers and doctors rose to prominence in mainstream parties, many black businesswomen, like M. Cravath Simpson and Mary E. Moore, moved further left. Indeed, Moore was less unusual than Simpson in some ways. Black businesswomen formed the heart and soul of a number of political movements in the decade. But although Simpson had officered the Woman's Era Club at the turn of the century, until the very end of the 1930s these black businesswomen rarely appeared as officers in the same organizations as black club women like Hall and Worthy. They were not chosen to sit on the board of the NAACP or the WSC or Robert Gould Shaw House. Instead, they spent most of their energies on professional and trade associations and sororal activities.[240] They sought their political outlets, as did Edna Black, elsewhere.

Moore claimed to have opened the first beauty parlor for blacks in New England. She then began manufacturing her own line of toilet articles and traveling the South to create a demand for them. Finally, she launched her own school of beauty culture. Her "Little White Shop" was a bastion of stability among the small businesses of Boston. Her political activism was equally long-lived. Prominent in a demonstration against The *Birth of a Nation*'s being shown in Boston in 1916, in 1933 she was active in organizing the Neighborhood Scottsboro Defense Club that included a fellow entrepreneurial beautician, Estelle Crosby. She also protested Italy's invasion of Ethiopia, and, on a more local level, delays in providing playgrounds in black neighborhoods.[241] It was not Councillor Mildred Gleason Harris, despite her claims, but Moore, along with attorney John S. R. Bourne and others in the Negro Congress, whom the *Chronicle* in 1937 credited with getting money for the rehabilitation of Madison Park.[242]

Black businesswomen were in a unique position for political mobilization. Though much of Moore's custom came from mail order, she maintained a shop in Roxbury that offered hair growing, face powder, bleaching, and the like. In the depths of the Depression, she also opened a dining room in her home, cooking the food herself. Her advertisements, like other black businesswomen's, helped sustain Boston's black press. The dependence was reciprocal. She depended on her neighbors for her livelihood, and she succeeded in becoming central to the community. She won a silver cup as the most popular matron in Boston. As a woman with her own source of income, independent of whites, and with her own semipublic places, she was in a strong position to enter more formal politics, yet she did not have the credentials (college and a professional husband who supported her, for example) that would have given her entree in the mainstream mixed-race party or civil rights organizations.

For Mrs. Hall and Mrs. Worthy, their husbands' identity as physicians was part of their own public identity. For black businesswomen, their husband's identity was a private matter; it was rarely mentioned in press reports. They had their own, independent public identity. But that identity was rarely sufficient to move them into the first circle. Whether that exclusion alone or in tandem with her experiences as a black entrepreneur and her intimacy with her more working-class neighbors helped to radicalize her, Moore, at least, clearly found leftist politics more congenial than mainstream ones.[243]

Not all black businesswomen were devotees of the Communist Party, but many found trade their route to politics. Though black women owned and ran a wide variety of businesses in the 1920s and 1930s—funeral parlors, restaurants, dressmaking shops, music studios, and realty companies—the beauty industry (parlors and schools) clearly predominated.[244] In 1938, Boston's black beauticians organized the Progressive Hairdressers of Massachusetts. The terms in which one of the association's officers, Mrs. Geneva Arrington, described the industry were telling: "There is not another profession outside of the medical profession that has made such rapid progress as hairdressing, recent facts have shown."[245] Medical practitioners stood at the peak of black Boston's

Mrs. Geneva Arrington, a prominent beauty culturist, served as an officer in both the Progressive Hairdressers Association and the Housewives' League. *Boston Guardian*, January 14, 1939.

social hierarchy; black beauticians rarely met them on equal social turf. Professional organizations generally in the United States had been bids for increased stature, respect, and public visibility. This one was no exception.

In the same breath, Arrington, who had run her salon in Boston since 1933 and before that had run one in Philadelphia for ten years, also asserted the "profession's" unique relation to women: "Much of the work of bringing it to this point has been contributed by those who have made it possible for so many of the women of our race to make independent livings through the improvement of the appearances of colored men and women of this country."[246] The contradictions others have pointed out about the black beauty industry applied in Boston as well. Advertisements in the black press depicted white women as models; products promised to "bleach" black women lighter. At the same time, the industry provided unique opportunities for black women *as* black women. It supported a livelihood independent of and not in competition with whites, particularly valuable given the sorts of job opportunities available to most black women in Boston, and a field of enterprise that also did not compete with those of black men.

When black beauticians formed an association as independent, public women, they made a particular kind of claim on the public sphere, but not yet an explicitly political one. In 1939, Mrs. E. Alice Taylor, manager of Boston's Poro [Beauty] College, presided over the Hairdressers of Massachusetts and found herself running a lobbying and educational campaign, including mass meetings and petitions, to protest new state regulations that would damage their business. Taylor engaged Dartmouth and Harvard educated attorney Matthew Bullock, who had enough standing in the Republican Party, from whom he had received several plums, to make him an ideal mediary with the state legislature.[247]

The same year, 1939, Taylor, Arrington, and Crosby founded the Housewives League of Boston. The three were heavily interconnected; Arrington and Taylor were officers of the Progressive Hairdressers Association; Crosby and Arrington were both members of the Wisteria Charity Club and both ran Apex beauty salons. Moreover, Arrington, Crosby, and Taylor all served as officers on the mixed-sex Boston Trade Association, with which the new Housewives League was affiliated.[248]

Why, then, already organized as businesswomen, did they deploy a public identity as housewives? As in Housewives' Leagues across the nation, the first item on their agenda was to increase employment opportunities. In Boston, they launched themselves into an ongoing struggle to force public utilities to hire blacks.[249] Utilities employment seems a bit distant from the direct interests of black beauticians and other businesswomen—the jobs won would go largely to men. But at the time, the unemployment rate among black workers in Boston had reached 50 percent, and it was as wives that the businesswomen had a direct interest, and as community members.[250]

Yet it was as tradespeople, through their affiliation with the Trade Association, that they held their officerships in the Housewives' League. As Mary Moore's activities had shown, black businesswomen had long been central to their communities in more ways than economic exchange. Though the officers were all businesswomen, they hoped to recruit nonbusinesswomen to the club's membership. Certainly their charter membership included prominent members of the WSC and the

Note the classic college caps and gowns in this graduating class picture from the Apex College for beauty culturists; such pictures were a staple in the black press. *Boston Guardian*, July 29, 1940.

LWCS who do not seem to have been leaders in major political party circles. It also included women who do not show up in business organizations or elite black social clubs.[251] In forming a broadly based, unifying organization of women under their own direction, the black businesswomen elevated themselves to and exerted a new kind of formalized leadership in the black community.

Black women were no strangers to community organizing. In 1932, a group comprised largely of black homeowners, including realtor Mrs. E. Z. Roundtree, had stormed the rooms of Boston's Licensing Board to protest granting a license to a poolroom in a residential section of Roxbury.[252] In 1938, as well as demanding better housing, black Roxbury mothers had created a coalition with Polish, Italian, and other neighborhood mothers to demand a Home and School Association from their reluctant headmistress.[253] A busload of South End women invaded the State House the same year to protest a new sales tax.[254] Even before the

GRADUATING CLASS

formation of the Housewives' League, some black businesswomen had been leaders in neighborhood mobilization. In 1938, Mrs. Gladys Howard, a corsetiere who would later serve as the second vice president of the Housewives' League, headed the South End Women's Progressive Club. She offered a resolution demanding model homes for the South End at a mixed-race conference for social legislation in Massachusetts.[255]

Black Bostonians had long faced housing discrimination. They had to pay inflated rates when they tried to buy homes, found limited areas in which they could rent, and few hotels and hostels in which they could stay. With the noticeable rise in population in the 1920s and smaller rise in the 1930s in black Boston, as in other urban black enclaves, conditions worsened.[256] As early as 1933, the head of Robert Gould Shaw House, Julian Steele, had worked out a plan for the Federal Housing Corporation "for the elimination of slums in this neighborhood."[257] Six years later (and a month after Mrs. Howard presented her resolution), Steele presented a plan for a South End housing program to over 400 people. Local leaders, the press reported, saw the meeting as an indicator of the mass pressure they could use to assure the erection of at least one major housing project in the South End.[258] President Roosevelt's decision to spend his way out of the 1937 recession made federal money available.[259] The pilot project Boston had started in 1933 and then halted, in part due to the pressure from large real estate interests, now recommenced.[260]

No sooner was the project won, however, than its unforeseen consequences again mobilized the women. In mid-1939, the Housing Authority took over sites in heart of the black South End by eminent domain. The sites covered the city's worst housing; over a third had no baths, nearly 10 percent had no toilets. Yet consternation greeted the taking. Black tenants, facing eviction, found nowhere they could afford to move.[261] When the South End Women's Progressive League, led by Howard, learned the City Council intended to hold no more ward hearings on the issue, it decided to hold a mass meeting to force the council to consider the needs of the section. In particular, the women demanded additional appropriations. New housing for 300 families, they declared, would only make a small dent in the pressing need for decent homes for black Bostonians. The women pledged to fight until every South End family had a decent home available to them.[262]

None of the black women who organized in the South End achieved all their goals, but they did remap the formal political geography of the district to include their organizations. The *Chronicle* had complained for weeks in 1932 of how politically disorganized Ward 9 was, never having recovered from the gerrymandering of a generation earlier.[263] In 1940, the *Guardian* published a similar lament, but this time it focused on women. Civil rights activist Marie Crawford Boykin, in town on research, urged the women of Ward 9 to unify, regardless of party affiliation, and agree to put one of their own into office.[264] And, indeed, the intervening years had witnessed a series of attempts at coalitions to elect a City Council member with an ever greater representation of women's organizations. Ostensibly nonpartisan and nonpolitical organizations, as the League of Women Voters had in the early 1920s, began to endorse candidates. In 1935, Democrats, Socialists, Republicans, Communists, and Independents met in Ward 9 to try to agree on a candidate, but the only woman mentioned as attending was Mrs. Harriet C. Hall.[265] Two years later, not only Mrs. Worthy's Colored Democratic Club but the Ladies Progressive Hairdressers Association, under president Mrs. E. Alice Taylor, endorsed attorney Roy F. Teixeira for Council.[266] In 1939, a picture of the leading Ward 9 clubs that endorsed John Wyche during a meeting at Estelle's restaurant, which his female relatives co-owned, included two women, Edna Black and a Mrs. Florence Lesueur of the Futurity Club, who would later be the first black woman to head the Boston NAACP.[267] And in 1941, Edna Black announced her intention to run for City Council in the next campaign.[268]

Estelle's Restaurant (where this mixed group of women and men endorsed candidate John Wyche for City Council) provided one of the few autonomous spaces for the black community and so formed a focal point for the network of family, business, and the politics of black women. *Boston Guardian*, September 23, 1939.

Conclusion

It must have seemed to many in Boston that Boston women, veterans of school board elections and appointive office for thirty or forty years, well organized into clubs and associations, would have found elective municipal office a logical and easy step. Instead they found the Boston City Council the hardest nut to crack—the most masculine of political realms, more than the State House and the Senate, more even than the U.S. Congress. Women had achieved appointive office because of the special attributes, in particular their privately funded welfare system, they could bring reformist men battling machines. As independent candidates themselves, they had no special attributes.

In some cities, particularly western ones and smaller ones, women did win elections to main seats of city government, but in 1920s Boston, politics was still a battlefield between Irish and Yankee, elite and working-class. On those lines, the women proved as divided as men, and far less integrated into the wellsprings of money and influence that could win office. White women won their first place on the council only in 1937, and then as part of an Irish political machine. The Yankee-Irish dyad excluded men as well; Boston's large population of Jews only sent its second man to the council in 1933, and Italian men won their first seat only in 1939. Though African Americans had sat in the city government in its earlier incarnation, it would be well after this period that black Boston would again see one of its own in the council.[269]

Both parties and ethnic groups, like their women members, were severely divided. Needing only a petition and not a primary endorsement to run for office, many wards ran more than three candidates for their council seat. The Yankee Brahmins of the Back Bay remained sufficiently united to offer an often uncontested seat to the fortunate candidate (never female), but insufficiently united to manage the same feat on a citywide scale. They often found more than one "nonpartisan" Republican candidate facing a plural number of Democrats in the mayoral contest. The Good Government coalition could not hold together, and the charter reversion to ward-based election was only the final blow on an already weakening hold.

Women made their debut in this roiling political world of perpetual realignment. Some of them, including some of the Women's Trade Union League and suffrage working-class allies, eschewed the rough-and-tumble world of ward politics for protégéeship. The Julia O'Connors, Mary Dewsons, and Ethel Johnsons entered into the appointive political world controlled in part by their elite white mentors as long as Republicans remained in power at the state level. But in the 1930s, when Democrats returned, appointive politics, too, had its rough combat. WEIU protégées like Ethel Johnson began running into trouble.

Working-class women tended to fare poorly as protégées unless they abandoned their trade union roots and adopted elite versions of nonpartisanship. Mary Meehan and Annie Molloy instead seemed tools of machines or organized labor and so Meehan was considered a travesty in the "woman's" slot. The Storrows may have seen Molloy as a fitting member of the eclectic Women's City Club, but even they did not see her as a fitting representative of womanhood in public, that is, on the council.

Other protégées (the Ethel Johnsons, Edith Guerriers, Julia O'Connors, and Margaret Foleys) were often scions of petty bourgeois or farmer families, often class marginal, lower middle-class, or aspiring managerial class. They faced twin dependencies, on more elite women (patron/matrons) and on credentials to oversee the interests of less elite women. They resented as much the elite women who cast them aside at will as they distanced themselves, at times, from factory working-class women.

By the 1930s there were new female players in the patronage game. Mary McLeod Bethune's 1937 visit to Boston jiggled loose promotions for some of the women Mabel Worthy had placed in the NRA and elsewhere. But the gains of black Boston on ward and state committees and patronage jobs favored only the few, the slightly growing black managerial female class of social workers, writers, and professionals. As black Boston struggled to regain its pre-1909 footing, political organizations proliferated, and women found and created new points of entry. Party committees, as among whites, remained the preserve of the relatively elite. Less elite women bypassed the machinery of the major parties and remained aloof from the dominant ward machines. Both offered too little from the inside. Neither did they run for office. But they created their own machines, as Edna Black did. Or they mobilized a base, as the black businesswomen did, and gave it a political voice.

Despite having created the suffrage movement machine, white women entered electoral politics in these decades via men's machines, including the Brahmin women who dominated the suffrage movement and abandoned their working class allies as soon as possible. The former suffragists no longer needed, they thought, to court the working class. Working-class women politicians would no longer be chosen by those more powerful to represent their sex.

But without them, those elite women also lost visibility. They disappeared into party offices or behind the endorsements of male-dominated reform organizations. They could win their way into the semigendered realms of appointive office and the school board, but not into the heart of the machine. They, too, could no longer represent "the sex." Long before they gave up the pretense of doing so, their own strategies and the growing number of other voices crowded them out. After Florence Luscomb, they never even tried.

Eleven women ran for City Council from 1920 to 1940. After 1922, it's not clear that any were Yankees, though many were clearly Irish. Heavily Irish East Boston alone accounted for almost half the candidates, demonstrating that the political culture there crossed gender lines, even if only Susan Donovan in 1939 would come close to winning. Donovan and Harris succeeded not as "women" but as scions of political families, heirs apparent to strong machines.[270]

Yankee women fared better on the School Committee, where all three of the decades' victors were Republicans enjoying the PSA endorsement; two were Yankee and one a Jewish attorney. Of the nine failed candidates, at least seven were Irish. They were not all working class—they numbered three attorneys, three former teachers, a high school athlete, and one labor leader—but they all lost. No Italian names appeared in either list; no Jewish women ran for council, and no black women ran for either office. The women's exclusions precisely mirrored the men's.

One theme of this book has been that women's claims to a legitimate place in the public arena of streets and city councils rested as much on their relation to other women as to men, just as men's claims had always rested on their relation to (dependent) women and other (peer or dependent) men. For both black and white women, class proved a crucial factor in their postsuffrage possibilities. It is not that the decline of an ideology of domesticity created or enhanced divisions, or destroyed a sense of commonality among women, but that the granting of woman suffrage made it increasingly difficult to gloss over the divisions that already existed.[271] The suffrage movement women, after all, had used arguments about the votes of degraded men as well as the women's custodianship of other women in their enlarged (municipal) household. Working-class Irish women did indeed flock to their ward and city machines on getting suffrage. They knew where their interests lay, just as did the elite women who flocked to the Republican standard.

Conclusion

"Woman's Place" differed drastically in 1940 from what it had been in 1870. Women now served not only on the school board but in City Hall. Maizie could pick up her Bill on the street and stay out until all hours of the night without risking her reputation. By the 1930s, no one any longer equated factory or store work with prostitution, and few still hoped to confine either the working girl or her employer within the four walls of her household. The geography of civic virtue had changed.

The increasing ability of women to negotiate the urban terrain on their own terms was not a mere by-product of some relentless process labeled "modernization." It resulted from the determination of individuals and organized groups to redesign the city for their own purposes. More than a backdrop, spatial configurations affected women's abilities to meet their needs and desires. Mrs. Scanlon had to move to survive in 1890s Boston. Mrs. Kehew's Back Bay and Beacon Hill differed dramatically from Mrs. Scanlon's South End, not only in the gracious lines of her home and its servants quarters, but in its proximity to the corridors of power. The centrality of the spatial dimensions of their lives and the relation of place to place showed clearly in women's efforts to alter their physical environments—whether by finding a better tenement closer to work or raising funds for a women's club or organization building.

Entering the public sphere, even if the latter was the space of a newspaper, required women's physical access to other spaces, club buildings, WTUL offices, charity organizations, and the streets par excellence. The power women could wield in their parlors and their tenement kitchens paled before what they could accomplish as legislative lobbyists and streetwise picketers. Women needed organized access to public spaces as their own agents, able to raise their voices, set their agendas, and hold their own. But it was always "women," not "woman," who would gain access, always particular groups, contingent on particular configurations of power and alliances.

The contested meanings of space and place added another dimension to the city's configurations of power, encoded in the landscape—who could walk where unmolested, for example. The meanings with which any given space was endowed, however, were multiple. The city's inhabitants jockeyed for position in a rapidly changing environment. Both neighbors and residents used Denison House to establish their status and to organize in their own interests. No one could completely control the meanings of any given site. Working girls and middle-class and elite reformers had different geographies of danger and morality. But the parties' vastly different access to power meant that elite and middle-class women could, with the right allies, mobilize the state to enforce their meanings, whether through street matrons or through correctional institutions that condemned young women for frequenting certain parts of the city and placed them out, instead, in the kitchens and servants' quarters of elite and middle-class households. Middle-class and elite women had to participate in ordering urban space—labeling, knowing, and defining it, dividing it into "public" and "private," "virtuous" and "immoral"—in order to claim more territory for themselves. The middle-class/elite home became essential, as a concept, to a whole ordering of civic life, to public policies about men's and women's work, about homes, about philanthropies, and about working women's leisure pursuits. In this way, these women entwined the reconstruction of northern domesticity after the Civil War with the postwar reconstruction of the public sphere, demarcating their own zone of public authority while bolstering the purported and unquestionable sanctity of their own homes.

The meaning of traversing the city shifted after the Civil War. Population movements, technology, and the growth of monopoly capitalism transformed urban America. Streetcars, suburbs, new immigrant populations, Irish mayors, and professional police; lodging houses, cafes, and dance halls; bicycles, department stores, and settlement houses characterized the reinvented city, and the contests discussed in this volume—about ordering and reordering that city—helped imbue that new urban landscape with meaning.

The relation between physical and human urban landscapes is intimate and intimately raced and gendered. At the turn of the century, a new streetcar line passed resolutely through the South End, not to serve the workers who lived there, but to serve a middle-class population that could now leapfrog over them to an invented pastorale of suburban America, the invention of which at the same time invented a working-class neighborhood by contrast, not as a village, but as a "slum." The South End, home to African Americans, Chinese immigrants, and young women and men lodgers of every race and virtually every nationality, became a conceptual no-man's land and sexual saturnalia to the middle-class and elite wayfarers, a place to stop on the way home to have a drink, gamble, or visit a prostitute, contaminating neither their downtown work environment nor the sanctity of their suburban homes. In an urban landscape, you know who you are by where you are. At the same time, you understand the nature of the terrain by who lives there. In the 1890s, the South End's wage-earning women organized anew, a new generation of college women ventured forth on their own, and newly invigorated men turned the Republic into an Empire in Cuba, Puerto Rico, and the Philippines. Although the South End's mix of races, classes, and sexes could seem the essence of modernity to a young Louise Bosworth and older labor activist Frank Foster, to the social investigators working for Robert Woods it was America run amok. The new Empire reaffirmed a set of gender and racial hierarchies disrupted by the new developments of the 1890s. Police enforced this vision by breaking into homes of interracial couples, raiding Chinatown, and refusing to protect black women from white men on the street.

As the conflicts in and over the South End demonstrated, the changes in women's public place were neither linear—from private to public space—nor uniform across race, class, and ethnic group. Black women were still unsafe on Boston's streets in the 1940s and could find few respectable public venues for their meetings. Yet as early as 1880, voices warned that women were abandoning the home. Purity reformer and antisuffragist Kate Gannett Wells wrote for the *Atlantic Monthly*: "Women do not care for their home as they did; it is no longer the focus of *all* their endeavors; nor is the mother the involuntary nucleus of the adult children. Daughters must have art studios outside of their home; authoresses must have a study near by; and aspirants to culture must attend classes or readings in some semi-public place. Professional women have found that, however dear the home is, they can exist without it. . . . The simple fact is that women have found that they can have occupation, respectability, and even dignity disconnected from the home."[1] The women Wells worried about deserting the home were white and elite—women whose domestic servants made possible their municipal reform movements, whose money made possible their artist's studios.

While Wells mourned the passing of the selfless, pure, white elite woman who lived for man and family and the centrality of the home, ironically, the home remained central not only to the lives of individual women from 1870 to 1940, but to the ways in which they conceptualized urban space and their own agency. Middle-class and elite matrons loosed the moorings that kept them tied to the kitchen from the 1870s to the 1890s, not by denying the efficacy of the home, but by demanding the labor of others to maintain it. They based their public authority on their ability to maintain virtue in their homes, and they and the New Women of the next generation—seeking homes and making them, but not centered on men—most successfully staked their claims to a public voice when they critiqued the homes of others. Wells may have seen the necessary connection as fading in 1880, but even in the 1920s and 1930s it became apparent that those most public of respectable women, politicians, would still be judged by their relations to the home; they may not have had to defend themselves as Hillary Rodham Clinton did in the 1990s by proving they could bake cookies, but newspapers still found a way to assure their readers that successful female politicians could keep a charming residence and could cook. Their domesticity became a matter of public record. The home had not been destroyed by the modernizing trends after the Civil War. It had, like the nation, been reconstructed.

We are prone to say that immigrant and working-class cultures, black or white, had different notions of domesticity, of public and private, than did the dominant middle-class and elite, but it would be more apt to say that, unlike middle-class and elite black and white women, they simply did not organize their lives around the concepts of "public" and "private." As they jockeyed for status and survival, poor women organized their lives around family and neighborhood obligations, hierarchical confrontations, and sexual pitfalls that did not divide up neatly or could not be organized into private and public. Private and public simply are not the right words, and our allegiance to them has inihibited understanding how working-class women did conceive of and organize themselves spatially, into realms of autonomy and dependence.

When working-class women had to make a living, they also had to make a world—housing, child care, networks, and neighborhoods—all in a city not designed for their needs, as opposed to the middle-class and elite housewife, enshrined in her servanted home, bolstered, sustained, and maintained by the dynamics described in chapter 2. Home finishing did not seem a violation of domesticity to working-class women. The visits of charity workers, however, threatened to turn tenement rooms into not only public but dependent spaces. When they denied charity workers access to their apartments or the right to dictate their job choices, working-class women drew certain boundaries around the elites' "public" sphere.

In Boston, there was a politics of the parlor, the kitchen, the church, and the charity organization, as well as the streets and City Council galleries. It was in all those sites that Boston women, as Elsa Barkley Brown wrote of black Richmonders, "enacted their understandings of democratic political discourse."[2] On an individual basis, in their simultaneous demands for day-care, income, and autonomy, and their incessant visiting; and on a massed basis in their neighborhood protests which united women, men, and children against the unseemly prices of butchers and the labor practices of the garment industry, working-class women asserted their own sense of their rights and their own vision of the city.

It was not only the working-class women who negotiated their identities through their interactions in public. In policing the streets on behalf of striking women, WTUL "allies" defined themselves as public figures capable of protecting the less powerful and fortunate. In much the same way, elite matrons claimed to provide the only safe home to working girls, and elite women proposed a troop of street mothers to patrol the city parks, building their right to a public presence on the foundations of their ability to protect other women from predatory men. They could be defined as virtuous and powerful only in relation both to men and to young and working-class women, and that virtue and power took shape by its enactment in the public theater of the streets and the council hearing rooms. By denying even elite black women the safety of the streets, white Boston denied them the same claims to status, virtue, and power. From the safety of their own parlors, churches, restaurants, and, after World War I, club buildings, black women launched newspapers, held soirees, and joined in uplift activities to represent themselves differently to each other and to the city at large. They, too, created their own stages or arenas of action.

The alliances Bostonians struck, women to women, or women with men, were usually uneasy. Black women who considered themselves respectable were horrified by the behavior of domestic servants tromping, as they did in Pauline Hopkins' novel, on the feet of streetcar passengers. WTUL allies cautioned strikers to tone down their clothing.[3] Wells found the New Women "mannish." Public culture was multiple and not singular. Each group had its own, deeply inscribed and usually spatially specific, rules regarding gender.

And the rules applied differently to different groups of women at different times. Louise Bosworth and other female social investigators could, armed by their expertise and the assumed morality of the middle-class backgrounds, plunge into vice districts that would render working-class women suspect. On the other hand, although no one in Boston intentionally beat up the "allies" in the 1910s strikes, elite women suffragists on parade had been roughly treated in Washington, D.C. Women succeeded in staking a claim on the public terrain only when they managed, as the telephone workers briefly did, their multifarious alliances—across class, racial/ethnic group, and sex boundaries—and when they had learned to read the current map of public culture.

"Women in public" and "women in power" are not synonymous. The Boston prostitutes thrown out on the streets during the 1890s brothel raids were not empowered by being in public. But without a legitimated public presence, it would have been virtually impossible for any of these women to achieve the power to shape their own or other women's lives. Individual women, workers, business women, and working-class and elite matrons, could, by their patterns of daily life, struggle against the confines of the dominant gendered map of the city, but they could not fundamentally change it. Elite women could turn their "homes" into public institutions, foundations of the state. They could deny that label to the homes of others. But that move not only legitimated their labor demands and public forays, it tied them ever closer to the "home."

Like the home, neighborhood was a spatial unit and a concept that refused to disappear and had particular salience for women. While the increasingly centralizing tendencies of the modern city seemed to favor the elite as the decades wore on, the power of the neighborhood reasserted itself in the city's electoral system in the 1920s and 1930s. Working-class matrons, unstable geographically as they were, relied on neighborhood networks they helped create, as did the white immigrant and black shopkeepers in their midst. At the turn of the century, Vida Scudder had pinpointed political platforms as among the few places still excluding women. By the 1930s, women succeeded on the city's hustings, but only as neighborhood machine politicians, not as products of an organized, theoretically unified "womanhood."

Women's conquest of the city streets, like their conquest of electoral politics, is still far from complete. In their campaigns to alter women's place, elite and middle-class women, particularly white women, are still tempted to speak for all others and wounded when the protesting voices of those they purport to represent drowned them out. The alliances that allowed some of the women in these pages to succeed in transforming the city and so their own lives—alliances between men and women in the WEIU, Denison House, and the League of Women for Community Service; among women in all those organizations and in the WTUL, for example—were never eternal. But they were essential. It was when they forgot the need for such alliances—when the elite suffragists dropped their working-class allies, when the male unionists turned their backs on the WTUL—that they courted failure. Skillfully managed and consciously chosen, such alliances allowed striking telephone workers, black club women, white lobbyists, and black businesswomen, to claim a wide range of victories, to expand the spaces in which women successfully could assert themselves, and to redraw the city in their own interests.

NOTES

Introduction

1 Denison House Collection, box 1, vol. 1, Daybook, 1893–94, p. 20, 8/26/93, Schlesinger Library, Radcliffe College, Cambridge, MA (hereafter DH).

2 Sam Bass Warner, *Streetcar Suburbs: The Process of Growth in Boston, 1870–1900* (Cambridge: Harvard University Press, 1962); Stephen Thernstrom, *The Other Bostonians: Poverty and Progress in the American Metropolis, 1880–1970* (Cambridge: Harvard University Press, 1973); Mary Ryan, *Women in Public: Between Banners and Ballots, 1825–1880* (Baltimore: Johns Hopkins University Press, 1990); Valerie Steele, *Paris Fashion: A Cultural History* (New York: Oxford University Press, 1988). On sexuality, see, for example, Kevin T. Mumford, *Interzones: Black/White Sex Districts in Chicago and New York in the Early Twentieth Century* (New York: Columbia University Press, 1997); Mary E. Odem, *Delinquent Daughters: Protecting and Policing Adolescent Female Sexuality in the United States, 1885–1920* (Chapel Hill: University of North Carolina Press, 1995); Ruth Rosen, *The Lost Sisterhood: Prostitution in America, 1900–1918* (Baltimore: Johns Hopkins University Press, 1982); Barbara Meil Hobson, *Uneasy Virtue* (New York: Basic Books, 1987). See also Galen Cranz, "Women in Urban Parks," and Susan Saegert, "Masculine Cities and Feminine Suburbs: Polarized Ideas, Contradictory Realities," in *Women and the American City*, ed. Catharine R. Stimpson (Chicago: University of Chicago Press, 1980), 76–92, 93–108; and Gwendolyn Wright, *Building the American Dream: A Social History of Housing in America* (Cambridge: MIT Press, 1981).

3 Judith Smith, *Family Connections: A History of Italian and Jewish Immigrant Lives in Providence, Rhode Island, 1900–1940* (Albany: State University of New York Press, 1985); Ardis Cameron, *Radicals of the Worst Sort: Laboring Women in Lawrence, Massachusetts, 1860–1912* (Urbana: University of Illinois Press, 1993). See also Ardis Cameron, "Bread and Roses Revisited: Women's Culture and Working-Class Activism in the Lawrence Strike of 1912," in *Women, Work and Protest: A Century of United States Women's Labor History*, ed. Ruth Milkman (Boston: Routledge and Kegan Paul, 1985), 42–61.

4 Kathy Peiss, *Cheap Amusements: Working Women and Leisure in Turn-of-the-Century New York* (Philadelphia: Temple University Press, 1986); and Christine Stansell, *City of Women: Sex and Class in New York, 1789–1860* (New York: Alfred A. Knopf, 1986).

5 See Anne F. Scott, *Natural Allies: Women's Associations in American History* (Urbana: University of Illinois Press, 1991); Dolores Hayden, *The Grand Domestic Revolution: A History of Feminist Designs for American Homes, Neighborhoods, and Cities* (Cambridge: M.I.T. Press, 1981); Suzanne Spencer-Wood, "Domestic Reform and Landscape," in *Case Studies in Landscape Archeology: Method and Meaning*, ed. Rebecca Yamin and Karen Bescherer-Methany (Boca Raton, FL: CRC Press, 1993), and "Diversity and Nineteenth Century Domestic Reform: Class and Ethnicity," in *"Those of Little Note":*

Gender, Cultural Diversity and Invisibility in Historical Archeology, ed. Elizabeth M. Scott (Tucson: University of Arizona Press, 1994); and Gail Lee Dubrow, "Preserving Her Heritage: American Landmarks of Women's History" (Ph.D. diss., Graduate School of Architecture and Urban Planning, University of California, Los Angeles, 1990).

6 See Frederic Cople Jaher, *The Urban Establishment: Upper Strata in Boston, New York, Charleston, Chicago, and Los Angeles* (Urbana: University of Illinois Press, 1982); and Mona Domosh, "Shaping the Commercial City: Retail Districts in Nineteenth Century New York and Boston," *Annals of the Association of American Geographers* 80 (1990): 268–284.

7 Cf. Robin D. G. Kelley, *Race Rebels: Culture, Politics, and the Black Working Class* (New York: Free Press, 1996), 8–9 and 77, quoting James Scott, *Domination and the Arts of Resistance* (New Haven: Yale University Press, 1990).

8 Cf. James J. Connolly, *The Triumph of Ethnic Progressivism: Urban Political Culture in Boston 1900–1925* (Cambridge: Harvard University Press, 1998), 65, on the trajectory from Jewish women's activism in kosher meat riots to a West End Mother's Club organized by settlement workers, which continued the protests and lobbied the state for price regulation.

9 Useful theoretical approaches to space include Henri Lefebvre, *The Production of Space*, trans. Donald Nicholson-Smith (Oxford: Blackwell, 1991); any of several works by Michel Foucault, including the two useful anthologies: *Language, Counter-Memory, Practice: Selected Essays and Interviews*, ed. Donald F. Bouchard, trans. Donald F. Bouchard and Sherry Simon (Ithaca: Cornell University Press, 1977), and *The Foucault Reader*, ed. Paul Rabinow (New York: Pantheon Books, 1984); Michel de Certeau, *The Practice of Everyday Life*, trans. Steven Rendall (Berkeley: University of California Press, 1984). Mary P. Ryan, *Civic Wars: Democracy and Public Life in the American City during the Nineteenth Century* (Berkeley: University of California Press, 1997), 4–16, provides a useful overview of theorists of the public.

10 Cf. Elsa Barkley Brown, "Negotiating and Transforming the Public Sphere: African American Political Life in the Transition from Slavery to Freedom," *Public Culture* 7 (1994): 107–146. Mary P. Ryan, *Women in Public: Between Banners and Ballots, 1825–1880* (Baltimore: Johns Hopkins University Press, 1990), 92.

11 Cf. Patricia Hill Collins, "The Social Construction of Black Feminist Thought," in *Black Women in America: Social Science Perspectives*, ed. Micheline R. Malson et al. (Chicago: University of Chicago Press, 1990), 297–326.

12 P. A. M. Taylor, ed., *More Than Common Powers of Perception: The Diary of Elizabeth Rogers Mason Cabot* (Boston: Beacon Press, 1991), 11; Eva Whiting White Collection, box 1 f. 7, meeting in memory of Francis Rollins Morse (1850–1928), 12/8/28, pp. 4–5, Schlesinger Library, Radcliffe College, Cambridge, MA. Joan C. Tonn, University of Massachusetts, Boston, manuscript on Mary Follett, 283; Frederic Cople Jaher, *The Urban Establishment: Upper Strata in Boston, New York, Charleston, Chicago, and Los Angeles* (Urbana: University of Illinois Press, 1982), 25, 96–97; Geoffrey Blodgett, "Yankee Leadership in a Divided City, 1860–1910," in *Boston 1700–1980: The Evolution of Urban Politics*, ed. Ronald P. Formisano and Constance K. Burns (Westport, CT: Greenwood Press, 1984), 91–92; Walter M. Whitehill, *Boston: A Topographical History*, 2d ed. (Cambridge: Harvard University Press, 1968); Michael P. Conzen and George K. Lewis, *Boston: A Geographical Portrait* (Cambridge, MA: Ballinger Publishing, 1976), 12, 35–37; Stephen Thernstrom, *The Other Bostonians: Poverty and Progress in the American Metropolis, 1880–1970* (Cambridge: Harvard University Press, 1973), 16, 25, 40. On the South End's inhabited wet basements, see Charles D. Underhill, "Public Health," in *The City Wilderness: A Settlement Study*, ed. Robert A. Woods (1898; reprint, New York: Garrett Press, 1970), 59–60.

13 Henry James, *The American Scene* (Bloomington: Indiana University Press, 1968), 231. See also Jaher, *The Urban Establishment*; Alexander Keyssar, "Social Change in Massachusetts in the Gilded

Age," in *Massachusetts in the Gilded Age: Selected Essays*, ed. Jack Tager and John W. Ifkovic (Amherst: University of Massachusetts Press, 1985), 132–147; Thernstrom, *The Other Bostonians*, 25; Blodgett, "Yankee Leadership," 88; Blodgett, *The Gentle Reformers: Massachusetts Democrats in the Cleveland Era* (Cambridge: Harvard University Press, 1966); Blodgett, "Josiah Quincy, Brahmin Democrat," *New England Quarterly* 38 (December 1965): 435–453, notes that there were over seven hundred strikes in Massachusetts in 1886 alone.

14 Frederick A. Bushee, *Ethnic Factors in the Population of Boston* (1903; reprint, New York: Arno Press, 1970), 26; Dwight Porter, *Report Upon a Sanitary Inspection of Certain Tenement-House Districts of Boston* (Boston: Press of Rockwell and Churchill, 1889), 7.

15 William I. Cole, "Law and Order," in *Americans in Process: A Settlement Study* (Boston: Houghton Mifflin, 1903), ed. Robert A. Woods, 218–219. Reed Ueda, *West End House, 1906–1981* (Boston: (West End House, Inc., 1981).

16 Porter, *A Sanitary Inspection*, 70–71. William M. DeMarco, *Ethnics and Enclaves: Boston's Italian North End* (Ann Arbor: University of Michigan Research Press, 1981), 16, 21. The North End had seventy acres of housing and thirty of waterfront. Elizabeth Lunbeck, *The Psychiatric Persuasion: Knowledge, Gender, and Power in Modern America* (Princeton: Princeton University Press, 1994), 15–16. Oscar Handlin, *Boston's Immigrants* (New York: Atheneum, 1976), 98, 101–115; Bushee, *Ethnic Factors*, 26.

17 Jessie Fremont Beale and Anne Withington, "Life's Amenities," in *Americans in Process*, Woods, ed., 225–236; Frank K. Foster, *The Evolution of a Trade Unionist* (n.p., 1901); Lunbeck, *The Psychiatric Persuasion*, 15–16.

18 See, for example, Allen F. Davis, *Spearheads for Reform: The Social Settlements and the Progressive Movement 1890–1914* (New York: Oxford University Press, 1967); Jane Addams, *Twenty Years at Hull House* (1910; reprint, New York: New American Library, 1960); Judith Ann Trolander, *Professionalism and Social Change: From the Settlement House Movement to Neighborhood Centers* (New York: Columbia University Press, 1987); Paul Boyer, *Urban Masses and Moral Order in America, 1820–1920* (Cambridge: Harvard University Press, 1978); Kathryn Kish Sklar, "Hull House in the 1890s: A Community of Women Reformers," *Signs* 10 (Summer, 1985): 658–677; Esther G. Barrows, *Neighbors All: A Settlement Notebook* (Boston: Houghton Mifflin, 1929).

19 Vida D. Scudder, *A Listener in Babel: Being a Series of Imaginary Conversations Held at the Close of the Last Century* (Boston: Houghton, Mifflin, 1903), 88.

20 Walter Muir Whitehill, *Boston: A Topographical History*, 2d ed. (Cambridge: Harvard University Press, 1968), 119–173.

21 See, for example, Robert Woods, "Work and Wages," in *City Wilderness*, ed. Woods, 111–112. Mona Domosh, "Shaping the Commercial City: Retail Districts in Nineteenth Century New York and Boston," *Annals of the Association of American Geographers* 80:2 (1990) : 268–284.

22 Louise Marion Bosworth Papers, carton 1 f. 27, 9/21/07, to her mother, Schlesinger Library, Radcliffe College, Cambridge, MA.

23 See M. Ryan, *Women in Public*, 67–68, on downtown space; on increasingly divided space, see also Boyer, *Urban Masses*; and Gunther Barth, *City People: The Rise of Modern City Culture in Nineteenth-Century America* (New York: Oxford University Press, 1980), particularly "Divided Space," 28–47. Scudder, *A Listener Babel*, 141.

24 See Perry R. Duis, *The Saloon: Public Drinking in Chicago and Boston 1880–1920* (Urbana: University of Illinois Press, 1983), 106–107, 111. See DH Journals, box 1 f. 3–f. 5. In particular, Helen Cheever, 1/31/92, pp. 37–39, and 1/17/93, n.p. See also Roy Rosenzweig, *Eight Hours for What We Will: Workers and Leisure in an Industrial City, 1870–1920* (Cambridge: Cambridge University Press, 1983), particularly 40–48 on kitchen barrooms. On dance halls see Peiss, *Cheap Amusements*, 88–114.

25 Cf. Stansell, *City of Women*; Rosenzweig, *Eight Hours*; and Duis, *The Saloon*, 86.

26 Cf. M. Ryan, *Women in Public*, 62–63, on the cityscape of this era as the creation of men, and 58, on the perception of tourists that women and public were increasingly synonymous particularly in Boston.

27 Peiss, *Cheap Amusements*; Meredith Tax, *The Rising of the Women: Feminist Solidarity and Class Conflict, 1880–1917* (New York: Monthly Review Press, 1980).

28 Scudder, *A Listener in Babel*, 151.

29 Boston City Tax Records, 1887, at Boston Public Library. The reasons are unclear. The owners included widows, single, and married women. Protecting male property from bankruptcy liability does not fully explain the pattern.

30 On female colleges and settlement house connections, see Helen Lefokowitz Horowitz, *Alma Mater: Design and Experience in the Women's Colleges from Their Nineteenth Century Beginnings to the 1930s* (Boston: Beacon Press, 1986), 88–90, and Jill Kathryn Conway, *The First Generation of American Women Graduates* (New York: Garland Publishing, 1987).

31 Bosworth, carton 1 f. 27, 9/18/07, to Eleanora Bosworth (mother). Scudder, *A Listener in Babel*, 47, 50.

32 Scudder, *A Listener in Babel*, 68, 105, 108, 143, 187. And cf. Addams, *Twenty Years at Hull House*. One paralyzing streetcar strike occurred in 1895, for example.

33 Scudder, *A Listener in Babel*, 32.

34 Before the Civil War, women had been instrumental in creating female refuges, such as the Boston Female Asylum in 1800; elite women created such spaces for less fortunate sisters. What was new in this era was women's creation of space for their own use. See Karen J. Blair, *The Clubwoman as Feminist: True Womanhood Redefined, 1868–1914* (New York: Holmes and Meier, 1980); Linda Gordon, *Heroes of Their Own Lives: The Politics and History of Family Violence* (New York: Viking, 1988), 32–33. On the ubiquity and new types of female reform sites, see Suzanne Spencer-Wood, "A Survey of Domestic Reform Movement Sites in Boston and Cambridge, ca. 1865–1905," *Historical Archaeology* 21 (1987): 7–36.

35 Robert Grant (1900, 1904) and Anna Bergengren (1900) quoted in Bernice Kramer Leader, "Anti-Feminism in the Paintings of the Boston School," *Arts Magazine* 56 (January 1982): 114.

36 Julia A. Sprague, *History of the New England Woman's Club from 1868 to 1893* (Boston: Lee and Shepard, Publishers, 1894), and Judith Becker Ranlett, "Sorority and Community: Women's Answer to a Changing Massachusetts, 1865–1895" (Ph.D. diss., Brandeis University, 1974), 169–171.

37 M. Ryan, *Women in Public*, 79. Barth, *City People*, 110–147, on dept. stores; Susan Porter Benson, *Counter Cultures: Saleswomen, Managers, and Customers in American Department Stores, 1890–1940* (Urbana: University of Illinois Press, 1986), 9, 76, 85, 89.

38 See Sarah Deutsch, "Learning to Talk More Like a Man: Boston Women's Class-Bridging Organizations, 1870–1950," *American Historical Review* 97 (April 1992).

39 See DH Journals, box 1 f. 3, C. M. Dresser on Feb. 16 and Cheever on p. 12, re: neighbors refusing to be paid for services; and f. 4 Lucinda W. Prince, their suspicions of any woman who refuses to let them traipse into her home, pp. 100–101. See also Boyer, *Urban Masses*, 134–135, 233–236.

40 DH Journals, box 1 f. 3 Dresser, p. 45, 2/8/93–2/21/93.

41 DH Journals, box 1 ff. 3–5 throughout.

42 Rosenzweig, *Eight Hours*; see earlier references to Denison House.

43 Mary Kenney O'Sullivan Papers, A-085, autobiography, p. 169, Schlesinger Library, Radcliffe College, Cambridge, MA.

44 Kenney O'Sullivan, pp. 117, 137–138.

45 Kenney O'Sullivan, pp. 125, 126. Women's Educational and Industrial Union Papers, Schles-

inger Library, Radcliffe College, Cambridge, MA (hereafter WEIU), series 1 carton 1, *Annual Report* 1882/83, p. 14, presidential address; WEIU, box 1 f. 1, *Annual Report* (January 1910), p. 24.

46 Kenney O'Sullivan, pp. 158–159.

47 Kenney O'Sullivan, p. 155.

48 Kenney O'Sullivan, pp. 165, 180.

49 Kenney O'Sullivan, pp. 196–198; p. 217 on 88 Warrenton. Street; on p. 189, kicks out young woman who has man in room at 7 A.M.

50 WEIU box 1 f. 5, *Bulletin of the Domestic Reform League* 3 (March 1907), on domestic servants' preference for wealthier suburbs on streetcar lines and Catholic preferences. See also *The Hours of Labor in Domestic Service* (Boston: Wright and Potter, 1898), prepared by the Massachusetts Bureau of Statistics of Labor (hereafter MBSL) from information collected by the WEIU, reprinted from *MBSL Bulletin* 8 (October 1898); *Social Conditions in Domestic Service* (Boston: Wright and Potter, 1900) prepared by the MBSL in collaboration with the WEIU, reprinted from *MBSL Bulletin* 13 (February 1900). All these bulletins are in WEIU, box 1 f. 5. Also see "WEIU—Report of the Committee on Domestic Reform—No. 1—The Effort to Attract Workers in Shops and Factories to Domestic Service—April 1898," in WEIU, box 1 f. 5, Domestic Reform League.

51 Bosworth, carton 4 f. 178, 10/17/07. Joanne J. Meyerowitz, *Women Adrift: Independent Wage Earners in Chicago, 1880–1930* (Chicago: University of Chicago Press, 1988), pp. 80–89.

52 Bosworth, carton 1 f. 27, 11/4/07, to mother; and f. 28, 5/5/08, to mother. See also Ranlett, "Sorority and Community," 194–196. Bosworth, carton 1 f. 27, 9/29/07.

53 While some sources (see below) have indicated that the founders were day workers, it is hard to track down that information. According to the *Boston City Directory*, 1905, Prontant Henson, who may have been Henson's husband, was listed at 36 Holyoke. In 1909, there is a Julia O. Henson at another address listed as a dressmaker. Hibernia Waddell, another founder, is listed in the neighborhood, but without an occupation, and the same is true of Annie Young, who in 1905 was boarding in South Boston. According to the 1900 federal manuscript census, Cornelia R. Robinson, a literate Virginian and cofounder, headed her household. Born in 1854, she had no children and worked as a janitress. She lived in the only black household on her block of Pinckney Street. By 1909, the *Directory* lists Robinson as matron at Harriet Tubman House. Albert Boer, *The Development of USES: A Chronology of the United South End Settlements—1891–1966* (Boston: n.p., 1966); *Boston Guardian* 5/2/3; 6/13/03; and 7/26/02; Grace Abbott, "Negro Agencies," report on Harriet Tubman House from 10/19/34 visit, in Edith and Grace Abbott Papers, box 32 f. 15, Special collections, the Joseph Regenstern Library, University of Chicago. *Northeastern News*, February 26, 1976, p. 11.

54 Elizabeth Hafkin Pleck, *Black Migration and Poverty in Boston, 1865–1900* (New York: Academic Press, 1979), xvi, 162, 164, 191, 192.

55 Dorothy West, *The Living Is Easy* (1948; reprint Old Westbury, NY: Feminist Press, 1982), 5.

56 *Woman's Era* 1:6 (September 1894): 8.

57 *Woman's Era* 1:1 (March 24, 1894): 8. See Paula Giddings, *When and Where I Enter: The Impact of Black Women on Race and Sex in America* (New York: Bantam Books, 1984); Cynthia Neverdon-Morton, *Afro-American Women of the South and the Advancement of the Race, 1895–1925* (Knoxville: University of Tennessee Press, 1989); and Evelyn Brooks Higginbotham, *Righteous Discontent: The Women's Movement in the Baptist Church, 1880–1920* (Cambridge: Harvard University Press, 1993), on the theory of "lifting as we climb" and "the politics of respectability" that governed many black women's clubs who saw in their own uplift the uplift of the race in the eyes of whites as well as in their influence on other blacks.

58 *Woman's Era* 1: 1 (March 24, 1894): 4, Mrs. Florida Ridley, secretary of Woman's Era Club.

59 Ibid.; *Woman's Era* 2: 1 (April 1895): 8.

60 *Woman's Era* 1: 1 (March 24, 1894): 15. Cf. Brown, "Negotiating," 118–119, on the importance of newspaper access to African Americans. Andrea Moore Kerr, *Lucy Stone: Speaking Out for Equality* (New Brunswick, NJ: Rutgers University Press, 1995), 130, 142, 145, 147, 152, ff., detailing the struggles over creating the *Woman's Journal* as an alternative to the radical Anthony/Stanton *Revolution*.

61 West, *Living Is Easy*, 168. Dorothy West was born in 1912 in Boston, the daughter of Isaac Christopher West, a prominent black businessman, and Rachel West, a thorough Bostonian. She attended Girls' Latin School and Boston University.

62 Mamie Garvin Fields, with Karen Fields, *Lemon Swamp and Other Places: A Carolina Memoir* (New York: Free Press, 1983), 141–158. See also 153 on her trips to Filene's basement with two friends.

63 Ibid., 150–152.

64 League of Women for Community Service Collection, record books, Schlesinger Library, Radcliffe College, Cambridge, MA, 3 vols., particularly vol. 1, pp. 127, 129, 132, 136, for 3/27/19, 4/2/19, 11/20/19, and 4/17/19; *Boston Chronicle* 6/18/32, 6; *Boston Guardian* 5/6/39; *Boston Globe* 3/20/18 obituary of Mary Wilson; NAACP Collection, Group II-L Addendum 43, annual report of the Boston branch, December 1918, p. 3; and Group I-G f. 88, *Boston Branch Bulletin* 1:1 (May 20, 1920), Library of Congress.

65 Suzanne M. Spencer-Wood, "A Survey of Domestic Reform Movement Sites in Boston and Cambridge, Circa 1865–1905," *Historical Archaeology* 21 (1987): 7–36, has noted the different geography of different types of women's sites in this period. Day nurseries were in working-class neighborhoods and not the Back Bay; women's club buildings were the reverse. See also, de Certeau, *Practice of Everyday Life*.

66 M. Ryan, *Women in Public*, 86–87; Karen Halttunen, *Confidence Men and Painted Women: A Study of Middle-Class Culture in America, 1830–1870* (New Haven: Yale University Press, 1982).

67 See, for example, Steele, *Paris Fashion*.

68 Recent theoretical writing on carnivals, crowds, and parades shows that even this sort of appearance can transform what it purports to represent. Suzanne Desan, "Crowds, Community, and Ritual in the Work of E. P. Thompson and Natalie Davis," in *The New Cultural History*, ed. Lynn Hunt (Berkeley: University of California Press, 1989), 47–71. Jill Kathryn Conway, *The First Generation of American Women Graduates* (New York: Garland Publishing, 1987), 13–15.

69 Scudder, *A Listener in Babel*, 211.

70 M. Ryan, *Women in Public*, 94.

71 Ibid., 92. See also Jurgen Habermas, "Hannah Arendt's Communications Concept of Power," and Hannah Arendt, "Communicative Power," in *Power*, ed. Steven Lukes (New York: New York University Press, 1986), 59–93; also, Pierre Bourdieu, *Outline of a Theory of Practice*, trans. Richard Nice (Cambridge: Cambridge University Press, 1977). See Spencer-Wood, "A Survey of Domestic Reform," 27, on new site types generated by female domestic reformers. Scudder, *A Listener in Babel*, 319.

Chapter 1

1 Mrs. Scanlon also appears as Mrs. Scannell in the records. On January 16, 1895, the last entry regarding the Scanlons records that Charley is seriously ill. DH daybooks, box 1 vol. 1, 8/21/93, 8/26/93, 9/6/93, 9/10/93, 11/1/93, 1/9/94, 3/9/94 (vol. 2), 4/25/94, 1/16/95.

2 On carnival in this sense, see, for example, Clair Wills, "Upsetting the Public: Carnival, Hysteria and Women's Texts," in *Bakhtin and Cultural Theory*, ed. Ken Hirschkop and David Shepherd (Manchester: Manchester University Press, 1989), 130–151. On experience, see Joan Scott,

"The Evidence of Experience," in *The Lesbian and Gay Studies Reader*, ed. Henry Abelove et al. (New York: Routledge, 1993), 397–415.

3 David Montgomery, *The Fall of the House of Labor* (Cambridge: Cambridge University Press, 1987), 140, 147–148. Esther G. Barrows, *Neighbors All: A Settlement Notebook* (Boston: Houghton Mifflin, 1929), 85; Robert Treat Paine II Papers, Josiah Quincy to RTP, 9/3/81, re: the failure of a cooperative store too "far removed from the residences of those we wish particularly to benefit," Massachusetts Historical Society (hereafter MHS).

4 Alexander Keyssar, *Out of Work: The First Century of Unemployment in Massachusetts* (New York: Cambridge University Press, 1986), 45–46.

5 For example, Louise Marion Bosworth Papers, carton 1 f. 28, 3/18/08, to her mother, Schlesinger Library, Radcliffe College, Cambridge, MA.

6 Keyssar, *Out of Work*, throughout, but particularly, 50–59, 100, 103: in the 1890s depression, 51. WEIU, B-8, box 7 f. 54, "The Food of Working Women." Keyssar, *Out of Work*, 145, citing case no. 6, BISU Report, part V, appendix B, pp. 81, 78. And see Roswell F. Phelps, *South End Factory Operatives: Employment and Residence* (Boston: South End House Association, 1903), 32; James R. Green and Hugh Carter Donahue, *Boston's Workers: A Labor History* (Boston: Trustees of the Public Library, 1979), 61–64.

7 WEIU, box 7 f. 49, "Immigrant Women and Children," p. 15. Note that many of the cases recorded in the Denison House Day books included men who made substantially less, $5–7 per week. See also Wigglesworth Family Collection, 1890 *Eleventh Annual Report of the Associated Charities of Boston*, p. 4, MHS. Robert A. Woods, "Work and Wages," in ed. Woods *City Wilderness: A Settlement Story*, 101.

8 Lorinda Perry, *The Millinery Trade in Boston and Philadelphia: A Study of Women in Industry* (Binghamton, NY: Vail-Ballou, 1916), 103–104.

9 Carroll D. Wright, *The Working Girls of Boston* [from the Fifteenth Annual Report of the MBSL, for 1884] (Boston: Wright and Potter, State Printers, 1889), 112–113. WEIU, box 7 f. 49 "Immigrant Women and Girls in Boston" (1906/7). Minot, Lowell, and Willard Street samples, Boston, federal manuscript census, 1880.

10 Leverett Street sample, Boston, federal manuscript census, 1880.

11 The change was not immediate, as a glance at the 1900 federal manuscript census shows. Willard, Minot, and Lowell Street samples, federal manuscript census, 1900, 1910 (thanks to Debbie Birnby). WEIU, B-8, box 7 f. 56, clothing, p. 8.

12 One of these female grocers was married to a mason and took in boarders. Boston federal manuscript census, sample, Willard Street 1910.

13 Frederick A. Bushee, *Ethnic Factors in the Population of Boston* (1903; reprint, New York: Arno Press, 1970), 29; Keyssar, *Out of Work*, 157–158; Dwight Porter, *Report Upon a Sanitary Inspection of Certain Tenement-House Districts of Boston* (Boston: Press of Rockwell and Churchill, 1889), 11, 44. Carole Srole, " 'A Position That God Has Not Particularly Assigned to Men': The Feminization of Clerical Work, Boston 1860–1915" (Ph.D. diss., University of California, Los Angeles, 1984), 496.

14 Bushee, *Ethnic Factors*, 58–59, 68, 70. Srole, "Feminization of Clerical Work," 259, 311 6n. Linda Gordon, *Heroes of Their Own Lives: The Politics and History of Family Violence* (New York: Viking, 1988), 126. Robert A. Woods, "Livelihood," in *Americans in Process: A Settlement Study*, ed. Woods, (Boston: Houghton, Mifflin, 1903), 109. Outside jobs paid better than homework, but created child care problems. A 1913 study found that 48% of Boston widows worked at night, often leaving children unattended or in the care of boarders, lodgers, neighbors, or relatives. See Linda Gordon, "Single Mothers and Child Neglect, 1880–1920," *American Quarterly* 37 (summer 1985): 182–184; and Beverly Stadum, *Poor Women and Their Families: Hard Working Charity Cases, 1900–*

1930 (Albany: State University of New York Press, 1992), throughout. DH Journal, example, Helen Cheever 1/12/93, p. 122. On attitudes toward day nurseries, see Linda Gordon, "Black and White Visions of Welfare: Women's Welfare Activism, 1890–1915," *Journal of American History* 78 (September 1991): 584; Susan S. Walton, *To Preserve the Faith: Catholic Charities in Boston, 1870–1930* (New York: Garland Publishing, 1993); Barbara Miller Solomon, *Pioneers in Service: The History of the Associated Jewish Philanthropies of Boston* (Boston: Court Square Press, 1956); Maureen Fitzgerald, "Charity, Poverty, and Child Welfare," *Harvard Divinity Bulletin* 25 (1996): 12–17; National Urban League Papers, Library of Congress, Washington D.C. Series 13 Box 5, Boston Urban League annual report for 1919/20, 13:5, p. 11; DH, box 1 f. 4; C. M. Dresser; 1/25–2/6/93 f. 3, p. 45, 2/10 Dresser; vol. 2, 7/23/94 pp. 63–64; Lucinda W. Prince 1/24/93, 1/26/93 f. 4; Cheever 1/26/93 and vol. 2, 9/27/94, p. 136; Paul Boyer, *Urban Masses and Moral Order in America, 1820–1920* (Cambridge: Harvard University Press, 1978), 141; Eustache C. E. Dorion, *The Redemption of the South End* (New York: Abingdon Press, 1915), 122. See also Woods, *City Wilderness*, 211, 252 1n, 253; similarly on the North and West Ends, William I. Cole and Rufus E. Miles, "Community of Interest," in *Americans in Process*, ed. Woods, 335–336. Also Paine, Frederic B. Allen to Robert Treat Paine 5/23/81; and Allen to Paine 5/30/85. DH, Prince 1/11/93, p. 127; Dresser 1/11/93, p. 132; and Emily Balch 1/13/93, p. 130. DH, Laura Cate 1/13/93, p. 134. DH, B-27, Box 2 f. 7, vol. 1, Report of Head Worker, 1893, p. 5, 10/18/93, 11/1/93, 11/21/93, 11/24/93, pp. 48, 50, 63. DH, box 1 f. 4, Prince p. 144.

15 In 1910, one-half and one-third of the married black women on Camden Street and Northfield, respectively, had an income. Sixteen on Camden Street were listed with an occupation, and an additional six took in lodgers. Most women who took in lodgers also had another occupation listed. Federal manuscript census samples, 1910. Thanks to Jennifer Mercier. On discrimination see Woods, "Livelihood," 138. According to Elizabeth Hafkin Pleck, *Black Migration and Poverty: Boston 1865–1900* (New York: Academic Press, 1979), 37, the per capita wealth of adult black Bostonians was only 40% of Boston's Irish immigrants; see also 73, on boarding.

16 Green and Donohue, *Boston's Workers*, 57. Srole, "Feminization of Clerical Work," 418; Bushee, *Ethnic Factors*, 57. Jessie Fremont Beale and Anne Withington, "Life's Amenities," in *Americans in Process*, ed. Woods, 245. William M. DeMarco, *Ethnics and Enclaves: Boston's Italian North End* (Ann Arbor: University of Michigan Research Press, 1981), 84–85.

17 Federal manuscript census, vital records, Boston directories, marriage and death records, wills; thanks to Debbie Birnby.

18 See, for example, Solomon, *Pioneers in Service*, 41, on desertion. Dennis P. Ryan, *Beyond the Ballot Box: A Social History of the Boston Irish, 1845–1917* (Amherst: University of Massachusetts Press, 1983), 48, 55 12n, on the high rate of infant mortality among the Irish in Boston. Cf. DH, box 1 f. 4, 1/7/93 Dresser, p. 96. Blacks, as did Irish, suffered disproportionately. In 1880 Boston, of every 1,000 live births, 392 black and only 274 white infants died.

19 DH, B-27, box 1, vol. 2, 9/3/94, p. 119. See also DH Dresser 2/17–/18/93, 2/21/93, and Journals, pp. 44–47, 56–57.

20 Gordon, *Heroes*, 236–239.

21 DH, box 1, f. 3, Dresser 12/30/92, p. 34. Cf. Frances Donovan's 1920s waitresses (*The Woman Who Waits* [Boston: Richard G. Badger, 1920]) refusing marriage as a response to this heritage of struggle.

22 Jonathan Prude speaking at Duke, 2/25/1989.

23 In 1880, 16% of black Boston families were headed by women. In the same year, 27% of Irish families in Boston's South End were headed by women. Gordon, "Single Mothers," 178, using 1885, 1895, and 1905 Massachusetts censuses, which she sees as probably an underestimate.

D. Ryan, *Beyond the Ballot Box*, 55 16n, 50, estimates that 22% of Irish households in 1870 were headed by women. See also, Hasia R. Diner, *Erin's Daughters in America: Irish Immigrant Women in the Nineteenth Century* (Baltimore: Johns Hopkins University Press, 1983), 67–69.

24 Federal manuscript census sample of twenty-five families, 1880, Ward 12, of which nine were households headed by widowed women (seven Irish, two Canadian); thanks for the sample to Keven Owyang. Two of the widows kept boardinghouses, and two worked in factories (one of these also had a child at work); four were supported wholly by their children. According to Srole, "Feminization of Clerical Work," 422, 432, 433, 438, in 1900, fatherlessness was still the greatest factor leading to young Boston women's involvement in the workforce.

25 Mary E. Richmond and Fred S. Hall, *A Study of Nine Hundred and Eighty-Five Widows Known to Certain Charity Organization Societies in 1910* (New York: Russell Sage Foundation, 1913), 30.

26 Carole Srole, " 'Beyond One's Control': Life Course and the Tragedy of Class, Boston, 1800 to 1900," *Journal of Family History* 11 (1986): 43–44, 48, 51, 340: from 1880 to 1900, fathers who worked as laborers died ten years younger than all other fathers.

27 Richmond and Hall, *A Study of Widows*, 9, 15, 20–23, 48. Even among those with young children, the majority worked outside the home (41/60, pp. 22–23). Cf. Stadum, *Poor Women*, 70. See also, Priscilla Murolo, *The Common Ground of Womanhood: Class, Gender, and Working Girls' Clubs, 1884–1928* (Urbana: University of Illinois Press, 1997), 1, quoting the founding statement of the Working Girls' Society of New York City in 1884: "our organization is truly the child of the daughters of labor. Our fathers and *mothers* work." (Emphasis added.)

28 Richmond and Hall, *A Study of Windows*, 20–21. See also Robert Woods, "Metes and Bounds," in *Americans in Process*, Woods, ed., 8; Woods, "Livelihood," 114; Eric C. Schneider, *In the Web of Class: Delinquents and Reformers in Boston, 1810s–1930s* (New York: New York University Press, 1992), 4–5, 11, 73. DH Box, f. 3, Journals, S. W. Peabody, 1/17/93.

29 Richmond and Hall, *A Study of Widows*, 20–21. Schneider, *In the Web of Class*, 4. Stadum, *Poor Women*, throughout.

30 Gordon, "Single Mothers," 174–175; Dawn M. Saunders, "Class, Gender, and Generation: Mothers' Aid in Massachusetts and the Political Economy of Welfare Reform" (Ph.D. diss., University of Massachusetts, Economics, 1994), 34–46; 62–68.

31 DH, box 1 f. 3, Cate 1/11–2/18/93, p. 41.

32 Porter, *A Sanitary Inspection*, 6, 31, 32, 37–39, 46–47.

33 DH, box 1 f. 3, M. Mason 1/10–1/17/93, pp. 107–108.

34 DH, box 1 f. 3, (Associated Charities) (A.C.) Conference, Ward 12, Prince 1/17/93; and f. 4, Prince 1/16/93.

35 Cf. Eileen Boris, *Home to Work: Motherhood and the Politics of Industrial Homework in the United States* (Cambridge: Cambridge University Press, 1994), 49–50, 56.

36 For example, Paine, Annie Fields to Robert Treat Paine 3/10/85. DH, B-27, box 2 f. 7, 1903/04, 1904/05. See also Eric Schneider on the need of private agencies lacking the coercive, *In the Web of Class*.

37 Gordon, *Heroes*, 49.

38 Peter C. Holloran, *Boston's Wayward Children: Social Services for Homeless Children, 1830–1930* (Rutherford: Associated University Press, 1989), 95–96. Cf. Fitzgerald, "Charity"; Walton, *To Preserve the Faith*, 61.

39 Gordon, *Heroes*, 50, 87–89, 107.

40 Gordon, "Single Mothers," 175, 176, 179–80; Schneider, *In the Web of Class*, 2–11, 136–137.

41 Richmond and Hall, *A Study of Widows*, 50–51, 56 no. 55.

42 DH, B-27, box 1 vol. 2, p. 75, Prince 1/17/93, at the Associated Charities Conference of Ward

12. DH, box 1 f. 3–f. 5, 2/7–18/93. Dresser. In a November 1890 symposium in the *Arena*, Edward Hamilton called the Associated Charities a "monopolistic syndicate," quoted in Boyer, *Urban Masses*, 154.

43 For example, DH Journals, Dresser 2/6/93, making calls with Miss Clark, the kindergarten teacher at Tyler Street Day Nursery.

44 DH, box 1 f. 4, 1/10/93, 1/12/93. DH, B-27, vol. 1, 8/23/93; p. 27, 9/6/93. See also DH, box 1, vol. 2, 3/11/95, p. 209, re: Mrs. Annie McFaul.

45 In 1897, for example, reform Rabbi Solomon Schindler, head of the United Hebrew Benevolent Association, held conferences with delegates of the following seven Jewish female charitable organizations to encourage more cooperation: Benoth Israel Sheltering Home, West End Ladies Society, North End Ladies Society, Young Women's Hebrew Association, Roxbury Ladies' Aid and Fuel Society, Austrian Aid Society, Lithuania Society. Solomon, *Pioneers in Service*, 13. See also DH, B-27 box 1, vol. 3, flyer attached to p. 180. Holloran, *Boston's Wayward Children*, 65–66. Walton, *To Preserve the Faith*, 21, points out that Catholic charities took Protestant agencies as adversaries but also as models, starting in 1832 with the Sisters of Charity coming to Boston to run a school for indigent girls. Italians quickly moved to provide for their own. By 1894, a Society for Ameliorating the Condition of Italians and an Italian Protective League offered aid. DH, B-27, box 1, vol. 2, 9/28/94; and 10/11/94.

46 Walton, *To Preserve the Faith*, 22; Solomon, *Pioneers in Service*, 13; Holloran, *Boston's Wayward Children*, 161. In 1893, Mrs. Prescott of 553 Boylston Street and three of her Circle of King's Daughters offered help (financial and material) to Denison House. DH, B-27, vol. 1, p. 62, 11/23/93. Diner, *Erin's Daughters*, 130–131; Walton, *To Preserve the Faith*, 28–30, 426; and Paula Marie Kane, "Boston Catholics and Modern American Culture, 1900–1920" (Ph.D. diss., Yale University, 1987), 54–55. D. Ryan, *Beyond the Ballot Boy*, 27–28. Solomon, *Pioneers in Service*, 65.

47 Walton, *To Preserve the Faith*, 69, finds that such actions drove Germans (1888), Italians (1921), and Poles (1929) to create their own institutions.

48 Solomon, *Pioneers in Service*, 25.

49 D. Ryan, *Beyond the Ballot Box*, 23–30, 37, 39 13n. Mary J. Oates, "Organized Voluntarism: The Catholic Sisters in Massachusetts, 1870–1940," *American Quarterly* 30 (winter 1978): 653. And see Evelyn Brooks Higginbotham, *Righteous Discontent: The Women's Movement in the Black Baptist Church, 1880–1920* (Cambridge: Harvard University Press, 1993).

50 Solomon, *Pioneers in Service*, 49–50. Walton, *To Preserve the Faith*, 61, 75; Saunders, "Mothers' Aids," 57–58; Holloran, *Boston's Wayward Children*, 65–66.

51 Solomon, *Pioneers in Service*, 77–79. Walton, *To Preserve the Faith*, 74. Cf. Schneider, *In the Web of Class*, 128–131, 135.

52 Diner, *Erin's Daughters*, 127; WEIU, box 1 f. 5, "Social Conditions in Domestic Service," *MBSL Bulletin* 13 (February 1900): 8. See also WEIU, box 1 f. 9, Social Statistics of Women Workers, p. 16, based on interviews with twenty women in each of five occupations; nineteen of the twenty houseworkers attended church regularly or occasionally; three-quarters of the houseworkers were Catholics. In addition, nineteen of twenty textile workers, but only twelve shoe workers, fifteen restaurant workers, and six shop workers did so. Cf. Elizabeth Clark-Lewis, in *Living-In/Living-Out: African American Domestics and the Great Migration* (New York: Kodansha International, 1994), 126–128.

53 Walton, *To Preserve the Faith*, 22. Solomon, *Pioneers in Service*, 84–85.

54 Kane, "Boston Catholics," 113–115.

55 Ibid., 98, 109.

56 According to Kane (ibid., 116), these institutions were "often begun by men but run by nuns

and sisters." Of twenty-one Boston Catholic charities in 1907, only two were run by male religious orders. See, for example, Rev. John F. Byrne, *The Glories of Mary in Boston: A Memorial History of the Church of Our Lady of Perpetual Help (Mission Church), Roxbury, Massachusetts, 1871–1921* (Boston: Mission Church Press, 1921), 144–145, 391–393. See also, Diner, *Erin's Daughters*, 132–137; D. Ryan, *Beyond the Ballot Box*, 27–28, on feuds between nuns and male supervisors.

57 Kane, "Boston Catholics," 166.

58 Diner, *Erin's Daughters*, 158.

59 Robert Woods, "Work and Wages," in *City Wilderness*, ed. Woods, 108; *Woman's Journal* 1/16/86, 18, and see 1/23/86, 32; and 2/6/86, p. 48, quoted in Diner, *Erin's Daughters*, 150. See DeMarco, *Ethnics and Enclaves*, 46–51, for comparable relations among Italians.

60 Kane, "Boston Catholics," 113–115.

61 Byrne, *Memorial History*, on the play, 416–422. Cf. Brooks Higginbotham, *Righteous Discontent*, on Baptists. For the nuns, the assertion of authority could be even clearer, as when the mother superior of this school wore the crown of thorns in procession and, at death, in her casket. Women in Roxbury also ran revivals in 1872. Byrne, *Memorial History*, 66, 394.

62 Byrne, *Memorial History*, 458–462.

63 Holloran, *Boston's Wayward Children*, 142–152. See also the Boston Lying-In Hospital's 1908 Annual Report included a photo opposite page 16 of a black parent with twins, recovering from her fifth Caesarian, the first black person I had seen in these pictures, and presented as a kind of technical marvel, while opposite p. 25, the women in the photo of the convalescent ward are all white. And Rutland Corner House Collection, vol. 50, record book, p. 288, 5/4/10 Schlesinger Library, Radcliffe College, Cambridge, MA.

64 John Daniels, *In Freedom's Birthplace* (1914; reprint, New York: Arno Press, 1969), 213.

65 Holloran, *Boston's Wayward Children*, 150; Cole and Miles, "Community of Interest," 336; Pleck, *Black Migration*, 112–113; Daniels, *In Freedom's Birthplace*, 96–97, 196; *Boston Chronicle* 10/8/32, 4; Dorothy B. Porter, "Women Activists, Wives, Intellectuals, Mothers, and Artists," in *Proceedings of a Symposium on Candidates for Rediscovery: The Boston Version*, (Boston: Boston University, Papers of the Afro-American Studies Program, 1957), 80–81.

66 Daniels, *In Freedom's Birthplace*, 190, 193–195.

67 See Jessie Fremont Beale and Anne Withington, "Life's Amenities," in *Americans in Process*, ed. Woods, 247–248; Daniels, *In Freedom's Birthplace*, 262; Pleck, *Black Migration*, 82; and Cole and Miles, "Community of Interest," 332. On white mutual aid associations, see Robert Woods, "Social Recovery," in *City Wilderness*, ed. Woods, 279, among Jews; DH, box 2 f. 7, Reports of the Headworker to the College Settlement Association, 1909/1910 on Italians and Syrians; and see Judith Smith, *Family Connections: A History of Italian and Jewish Immigrant Lives in Providence, Rhode Island, 1900–1940* (Albany: State University of New York Press, 1985), and Lizabeth Cohen, *Making a New Deal: Industrial Workers in Chicago, 1919–1939* (Cambridge: Cambridge University Press).

68 DeMarco, *Ethnics and Enclaves*, 2, 40, 43.

69 Daniels, *In Freedom's Birthplace*, 199–203, 238, 248, 250–261.

70 Clark-Lewis, *Living-In/Living-Out*. Daniels, *In Freedom's Birthplace*, 260–261.

71 Daniels, *In Freedom's Birthplace*, 254, 258–259, 260–261.

72 Ibid., 180–181; cf. book by the African American Bostonian Pauline E. Hopkins, *Contending Forces: A Romance Illustrative of Negro Life North and South* (1900; reprint, New York: Oxford University Press, 1988), 104, on the politics of domestic servants' dress. See also Robin D. G. Kelley, *Race Rebels: Culture, Politics, and the Black Working Class* (New York: Free Press, 1994), 50. One can only imagine, in this context, the feelings of black Red Cross volunteers during World War I, particularly those who had escaped domestic service, who had to be urged, as they were at a

black Soldiers Comfort Unit meeting, to wear their uniforms when they served, including the white apron and cap. League of Women for Community Service Collection, minutes 9/12/18, Schlesinger Library, Radcliffe College, Cambridge, MA.

73 In addition, women spoke from the pulpit in some of these churches; the North Russell Street Church, in 1885 the only branch of Zion AME in Boston, used women readers, including Miss Hattie L. Smith; and a Miss Rosa Saunders gave a speech on behalf of the church and its auxiliaries. *Advocate* (Boston) "South End Notes," 6/27/85, p. 3; 7/4/85, p. 3; 7/18/85, p. 3.

See Elsa Barkley Brown, "Negotiating and Transforming the Public Sphere: African American Political Life in the Transition from Slavery to Freedom," *Public Culture* 7 (1994): 114, 120; Brooks Higginbotham, *Righteous Discontent*, 6–10, 14. On respectability see Brooks Higginbotham, *Righteous Discontent*, 191–194. Cf. Pleck, *Black Migration*, 73, 81. And on relief activities, for example, *Guardian* 11/23/07, 8, Woman's Baptist Mutual Relief Harvest Offering. And see Hopkins, *Contending Forces*, 142, 183, 186, 316, on class dynamics in black Boston churches. James Oliver Horton and Lois E. Horton, *Black Bostonians: Family Life and Community Struggle in the Antebellum North* (New York: Holmes and Meier Publishers, 1979), 37, on meeting places.

74 Pleck, *Black Migration*, 162, 164, 191, 192.

75 Ibid., 66, 67, 73, 75. Daniels, *In Freedom's Birthplace*, 175–177, 180–181.

76 Daniels, *In Freedom's Birthplace*, 180–181.

77 Stadum, *Poor Women*, xiv, xvii, 45, and throughout.

78 Barrows, *Neighbors All*, 13, claimed by around 1910 South End House residents averaged 300 calls per week. DH Journals, example, B-27, box 1, vol. 2, Freeman 7/20/94, pp. 59–60, on jelly; and 12/21/94, on door-to-door visiting up Tyler Street. *Guardian* 7/26/02, 5, City News; and *Advocate*, "South End Notes" 7/4/85, 7/11/85. And see Pleck, *Black Migration*, 198, quoting Alvan Francis Sanborn, *Moody's Lodging House and Other Tenement Sketches* (Boston: n.p., 1895), 116; and Sanborn, "The Anatomy of a Tenement Street," *The Forum* (January 1895): 554–572.

79 See Judith Fryer, "What Goes on in the Ladies Room? Sarah Orne Jewett, Annie Fields, and Their Community of Women," *Massachusetts Review* 30: 4 (winter 1989): 621–623, on the meaning of visiting to more elite women. Gordon, "Black and White," 572; DH, Prince 1/9/93, p. 104. Earl Lewis, *In Their Own Interests: Race, Class, and Power in Twentieth-Century Norfolk, Virginia* (Berkeley: University of California Press, 1991), 101–109.

80 For example, David Montgomery, *The Fall of the House of Labor* (Cambridge: Cambridge University Press, 1987), 140, 147–148.

81 DH, box 1 f. 3, Cheever Nov. and Dec., p. 12. See also DH, box 1 f. 4, Cheever 1/29/93. Bosworth, carton 4 f. 170, interviewed (no. 4).

82 DH Journal, Box 1, f. 4. Dresser 1/5/93, p. 80.

83 DH, box 1 f. 4, Dresser 1/14/93, pp. 41–42; box 1, vol. 2, 7/16/94, p. 52.

84 DH, Box 1, vol. 1 p. 100, 1/7/93. Dudley to Jane Addams in 4/30/02 (Jane Addams Papers, ed., Mary Lynn McCree Bryan, University of Illionis at Chicago, University Microfilms International, 1984) on the false nature of these visits.

85 DH, box 1 f. 3– f. 4, pp. 169–170, with a list of visits; box 1 f. 4, Dresser 1/7/93, p. 95, on Lizzie Smith search; B-27, vol. 2, 10/30/94, p. 152 on NEK; 11/7/94, p. 157; Prince 1/7/93, p. 100; and Cate 1/10/93, p. 107.

86 DH, box 1 f. 4, Cheever 2/9/93.

87 Alexander von Hoffman, *Local Attachments: The Making of an American Urban Neighborhood, 1850–1920* (Baltimore: Johns Hopkins University Press, 1994), xxii, xxiv.

88 Green and Donohue, *Boston's Workers*, 68.

89 DH, box 1 f. 3, Cheever 3/21/93; and B-27, box 2 f. 7, reports of the headworker to CSA, 1913/14.

90 DH Journals, box 1 f. 5, Cheever 2/1/93.

91 DH Journals, box 1 f. 5, Balch 2/5/93; and box 1, vol. 1, 11/12/93, p. 63.

92 Miss Follett's "Report on School Houses as Social Centers," in Elizabeth (Lowell) Putnam Papers, box 4, Women's Municipal League, "An Account of the WML of Boston" 1/20/09 (Boston: Southgate Press, [c. 1909]), Schlesinger Library, Radcliffe College, Cambridge, MA, Cf. Mary Kenney O'Sullivan's autobiography, pp. 165–166.

93 Bosworth, carton 4 f. 178, case no. 341, 9/30/07 Miss Kirby, 59 Worcester Street, South End, and 7 Poplar Street; and 9/17/07.

94 DH, box 1 f. 5 Balch 1/18/93.

95 Bosworth, carton 4 f. 178, case no. 341, Miss Kirby 9/30/07, 59 Worcester Street, South End, and 7 Poplar Street; and 9/17/07.

96 Bosworth, carton 4 f. 178, second visit to Swisky sisters and cousin; Ida Chisholm, 42 Rutland Sq., no. 61; Libby Harrington, 4 Parker Street, JP factory; Miss Jackson, factory, case no. 8; and f. 174, on domestic servants. And see Walton, *To Preserve the Faith*, 93–94, citing a story, "Being a Lady," from the *St. Vincent de Paul Quarterly* 18 (1913): 102.

97 For example, DH, box 1 f. 4, p. 60, Wier 1/2/93: Mrs. Brennan, 141 Tyler Street, husband a janitor at the YMCA on Boylston Street; B-27, vol. 1, 8/26/93, p. 20, "Arabian woman" on Palace Court; 9/9/93, p. 28, Mrs. Chee Chang at 50 Oxford Place; and 10/4/93, the Warners, 94 Tyler Street, "Nice Americans, used to better circumstances." DH Journal, Balch 1/14/93, p. 137, Dr. and Mrs. Frank, 33 Common St., magnetic physician; and Miss Davis, the enthusiastic public school teacher/reformer whom Denison House accepted as one of themselves (box 1 f. 3, 11–12/92 pp. 12, 14, Cheever), had a sister who had "been at our house as a dressmaker." See Brian Gratton, *Urban Elders: Family, Work, and Welfare among Boston's Aged, 1890–1950* (Philadelphia: Temple University Press, 1986), 31; Elizabeth Y. Rutan, "Before the Invasion," in *Americans in Process*, ed. Woods, 36–39.

98 DH, B-27, box 2 f. 7, Report of the head worker to the College Settlement Association, fall 1893; DH Journals, Dresser, 2/7–18/93 and 2/23/93, pp. 49–50 noted "a very comfortable home—piano &c."

99 DH, box 1 f. 4, Balch 1/6/93.

100 William J. Lloyd, "A Social-Literary Geography of Late-Nineteenth-Century Boston," in *Humanistic Geography and Literature: Essays on the Experience of Place*, ed. Douglas C. D. Pocock (Totowa, NJ: Barnes and Noble Books, 1981), 164–165, 170. See also Elizabeth Lunbeck, *The Psychiatric Persuasion: Knowledge, Gender, and Power in Modern America* (Princeton: Princeton University Press, 1994), 15–16; Dorion, *South End*, 22.

101 DH, box 1 f. 4, Prince 1/7/93; f. 3, Cheever 12/27/92, p. 11, and Cheever 2/1/93. See also, DH, box 1 f. 3, Dresser 12/30/92.

On aspiring to middle-class, DH Journals, Mason 2/2/93. And Barrows, *Neighbors All*, 41, 70, on class and "Americanness" (that is, a large buffet and cut glass punch bowl). On crossethnic community ties see Ardis Cameron, *Radicals of the Worst Sort: Laboring Women in Lawrence, Massachusetts, 1860–1912* (Urbana: University of Illinois Press, 1993), 75–116, on Lawrence; Green and Donohue, *Boston's Workers*, on Boston, 69–70.

102 DH, box 1 f. 4, Balch 2/7/93. By playing at poverty, Shea could show she was not actually poor. And see Barrows, *Neighbors All*, 190, at South End House: "Our visitors so often spoke of 'the class among which you live' that we began to wonder just what they meant in a neighborhood where we saw finer social discrimination than ever existed in the Back Bay."

103 DH, box 1, vol. 1, 4/1/94, Mrs. Sterne (who ran a tailor shop with her husband, see sporadic entries 2/6/93–9/94) named Mrs. Prince, and 4/3/94, p. 142, Mrs. von Haugensvoll (who ultimately took a job as a wetnurse, 4/6/94).

104 DH Journals, Cheever 1/23/93.
105 DH Journals; Cate 1/3/93, p. 49.
106 Cf. Perry R. Duis, *The Saloon: Public Drinking in Chicago and Boston, 1880–1920* (Urbana: University of Illinois Press, 1983); DH, box 1 f. 4, Balch 1/31/93. See also, Roy Rosenzweig, *Eight Hours for What We Will: Workers and Leisure in an Industrial City, 1870–1920* (Cambridge: Cambridge University Press, 1983).
107 See, for example, DH Journals, box 1 f. 4, Cheever 1/11/93, p. 119.
108 See Gordon, *Heroes*, throughout; Kathleen Canning, "Feminist History after the Linguistic Turn: Historicizing Discourse and Experience," *Signs* 19 (winter 1994): 384; Elizabeth Ewen, *Immigrant Women in the Land of Dollars: Life and Culture on the Lower East Side, 1890–1925* (New York: Monthly Review Press, 1985), 266. Cf. Kathy Peiss, *Cheap Amusements: Working Women and Leisure in Turn-of-the-Century New York* (Philadelphia: Temple University Press, 1982); Christine Stansell, *City of Women: Sex and Class in New York, 1789–1860* (New York: Alfred A. Knopf, 1986); and Vicki L. Ruiz, " 'Star Struck': Acculturation, Adolescence, and the Mexican American Woman, 1920–1950," in *Building with Our Hands: New Directions in Chicana Studies*, ed. Adela de la Torre and Beatriz M. Pesquera (Berkeley: University of California Press, 1993), 109–129.
109 DH, B-27, vol. 1, p. 56, 11/15/93; and Vida Scudder 11/19/93. DH, B-27, box 2 f. 7, "Reports of Headworkers to College Settlement Association" on small children. Similarly, see WEIU, acc. no. 81-M237, carton 7, Befriending Record Book, Nov. 1906. In 1906/7 Denison House's math and English classes paid particular attention to the needs of young women intending to take civil service exams. DH, also B-27, box 1, vol. 3, flyer attached to p. 181. Supplicants also shaped services by their refusals. See WEIU, Carton 7 befriending record book, Nov. 1906, p. 3; DH, B-27, box 1 vol. 1, example, 8/15/93; 8/17/93; and 8/15/93.
110 Stadum, *Poor Women*, 91, 4; Schneider, *In the Web of Class*, 11.

Chapter 2

1 Roger Lane, *Policing the City: Boston 1822–1885* (Cambridge: Harvard University Press, 1967), 186, on public outrage at abortionists in 1870s Boston, example, *Boston Herald* 10/10/73.
2 Kathy Peiss, *Cheap Amusements: Working Women and Leisure in Turn-of-the-Century New York* (Philadelphia: Temple University Press, 1982); Joanne Meyerowitz, *Women Adrift: Independent Wage Earners in Chicago* (Chicago: University of Chicago Press, 1988), and Meyerowitz, "Sexual Geography and Gender Economy: The Furnished Room Districts of Chicago, 1890–1930," in *Unequal Sisters: A Multicultural Reader in U.S. Women's History*, ed. Vicki L. Ruiz and Ellen Carol DuBois, 2d. ed. (New York: Routledge, 1994), 186–202; Elizabeth Lunbeck, *The Psychiatric Persuasion: Knowledge, Gender, and Power in Modern America* (Princeton: Princeton University Press, 1994); and Christine Stansell, *City of Women: Sex and Class in New York, 1789–1860* (New York: Alfred A. Knopf, 1986).
3 Joan W. Scott, "The Evidence of Experience," in *The Lesbian and Gay Studies Reader*, ed. Henry Abelove et al. (New York: Routledge, 1993), 409, urges us to examine "the operations of the complex and changing discursive processes by which identities are ascribed, resisted, or embraced, and which processes themselves are unremarked and indeed achieve their effect because they are not noticed."
4 Cf. Sonya O. Rose, *Limited Livelihoods: Gender and Class in Nineteenth Century England* (Berkeley: University of California Press, 1992), 8, quoted in Eileen Boris, *Home to Work: Motherhood and the Politics of Industrial Homework in the United States* (Cambridge: Cambridge University Press, 1994), 3n. 4, on cultural production.
5 *Thirty-first Annual Report of the Industrial Aid Society for the Prevention of Pauperism* (1866): 14, quoted in Elizabeth Hafkin Pleck, *Black Migration and Poverty: Boston, 1865–1900* (New York: Academic Press, 1979), 26.

6 WEIU, box 1 f. 5, *Bulletin of the Domestic Reform League* 3:1 (October 1908): 4. Frederick A. Bushee, *Ethnic Factors in the Population of Boston* (1903; reprint, New York: Arno Press, 1970), 63. WEIU, box 7 f. 46, "Percentage of Servants and Waitresses of Different Nationalities to Total Number of Women Wage-Earners in Same Nationality." See WEIU, B-7, f. 49, immigrant women and children, p. 10. Phyllis M. Palmer, *Domesticity and Dirt: Housewives and Domestic Servants in the United States, 1920–1945* (Philadelphia: Temple University Press, 1989), 71. See John Daniels, *In Freedom's Birthplace* (1914; reprint, New York: Arno Press, 1969), 162 on "uppishness," and 320; WEIU, box 1 f. 5, *Bulletin of the Domestic Reform League* 2 (February 1907): 2, and 5 (May 1907): 3; *Boston Herald* 1/3/00, help wanted—female ads, for example, and Barbara M. Brenzel, *Daughters of the State: A Social Portrait of the First Reform School for Girls in North America, 1856–1905* (Cambridge: MIT Press, 1983), 140 on hiring preferences. And cf. Jane Addams, *A New Conscience and an Ancient Evil* (New York: Macmillan, 1913), 169, and Tera W. Hunter, "Domination and Resistance: The Politics of Wage Household Labor in New South Atlanta," *Labor History* 34 (spring–summer, 1993): 211. By 1920, black women in Boston comprised 11% of servants and 29% of laundresses. David M. Katzman, *Seven Days a Week: Women and Domestic Service in Industrializing America* (Urbana: University of Illinois Press, 1978), 293. On Boston population by ethnic/racial group, see Michael P. Conzen and George K. Lewis, *Boston: A Geographical Portrait* (Cambridge, MA: Ballinger Publishing, 1976), 25. See Louise Marion Bosworth Papers, carton 1 f. 29, 7/16/08, to her mother, Schlesinger Library, Radcliffe College, Cambridge, MA, for example. See also, Pleck, *Black Migration*, 30. The proportion of Irish servants in Boston was considerably higher (almost twice) and blacks much lower (about one-fourth) than nationally. WEIU, box 1 f. 5, *Bulletin of the Domestic Reform League* 3:1 (October 1908): 4. For accounts of multiservant households in the 1870s, see P. A. M. Taylor, ed., *More Than Common Powers of Perception: The Diary of Elizabeth Rogers Mason Cabot* (Boston: Beacon Press, 1991), 260–261, 270; Samuel Eliot Morison, *One Boy's Boston, 1887–1901* (Boston: Houghton Mifflin, 1962), 16 ff.

7 In 1880, 44.8% of Boston's women wage earners were domestics; in 1900, 31.9%; in 1920, only 12.9%. Katzman, *Seven Days a Week*, 287. The ratio of servants per family in Boston had also drastically declined, from 2.19 per 10 families in 1880 to 1.67 in 1900 to .79 in 1920. Ibid., 286. WEIU, B-8, box 7 f. 46, from U.S. Census. See WEIU, B-8, box 7 f. 47, research for exhibit on domestic service.

8 Mary Dewson Papers, box 1, biographical information from a letter of 10/20/59 to Barbara Solomon, and 11/21/52 to Dear Hick, Schlesinger Library, Radcliffe College, Cambridge, MA.

9 See, for example, WEIU, box 1 f. 5, *Bulletin of the Domestic Reform League* (January 1907). Also in this folder, see "Efforts to Attract Workers in Shops and Factories to Domestic Service," *Bulletin of the Domestic Reform League* (April 1898): 3; MBSL, *Trained and Supplementary Workers in Domestic Service* (Boston: State Printer, 1906); "Hours of Domestic Service," *MBSL Bulletin* 8 (October 1898); "Social Conditions in Domestic Service," *MBSL Bulletin* 13 (February 1900); "Household Expenses," *MBSL Bulletin* 15; "Social Statistics of Working Women," *MBSL Bulletin* 18 (May 1901). And in WEIU, box 7 f. 48, Mary Smith, *Immigration as a Source of Supply for Domestic Workers (Based upon a Study of Conditions in Boston)* (1905); WEIU, box 1 f. 6, employment committee, "Report of the School of Housekeeping for the year ending April 1900" (chairman: Mrs. Mary Morton Kehew).

10 Edward A. Filene, "The Betterment of the Conditions of Working Women," *Annals* 27 (June 1906), 158–159, quoted in Katzman, *Seven Days a Week*, 14. WEIU, box 7 f. 48, Margaret Francis Secker and Francis Wadsworth Valentine, "Report of an Investigation of 500 Immigrant Women in Boston Conducted by the Research Department of the WEIU," June 1907. Another worker claimed she "would sweep the streets before she would do housework." WEIU, box 4 f. 9, Social Statistics of Working Women, p. 20.

11 See Vice Commission of Chicago, *The Social Evil in Chicago* (Chicago, 1911); Fred Robert Johnson, *The Social Evil in Kansas City* (Kansas City, MO, 1911); Jane Addams, *A New Conscience and an Ancient Evil* (1912); Illinois General Assembly Senate Vice Committee, *Report of the Senate Vice Committee* (1916); and State of Massachusetts, *Report of the [Massachusetts] Commission for the Investigation of the White Slave Traffic, So Called*, House Doc. no. 2281 (Boston: Wright and Potter Printing, 1914). *The Social Evil in Syracuse [NY]: Being the Report of an Investigation of the Moral Condition of the City Conducted by a Committee of Eighteen Citizens* (1913; reprinted in *Prostitution in America: Three Investigations, 1902–1914* [New York: Arno Press, 1976]) alone makes no mention of any former domestic servants among its cases.

12 Carroll D. Wright, *The Working Girls of Boston* [from the Fifteenth Annual Report of the MBSL, for 1884] (Boston: Wright and Potter Printing, 1889), 5. Mary Conyngton, *Report on Condition of Women and Child Wage-earners in the United States*, vol. 15, *Relation Between Occupation and Criminality of Women*, 61st Congress, 2d sess. S. Doc. 645 (Washington, DC: Government Printing Office, 1911).

13 Gertrude L. Marvin, "The Lodging House Problem in Boston," *Wellesley Magazine* 15 (March 1907): 246–253, especially 250; Conyngton, *Occupation and Criminality*, 10. See also, Kathleen Canning, "Feminist History after the Linguistic Turn: Historicizing Discourse and Experience," *Signs* 19:2 (winter 1994): 368–404, about contested notions of the body and regulating the sexuality of women workers.

14 C. Wright, *Working Girls*, 20–21.

15 Ibid., 49.

16 Conyngton, *Occupation and Criminality*, 86. Conyngton reported that figures from refuges matched those of the courts and prisons, revealing that of prostitutes who had formerly been self-supporting women, "far more" came from domestic service than from any other occupation, at a rate nearly three times their proportion of the female labor force—70.3% versus 24.1% (pp. 30, 84). There was a tendency Conyngton noted among her investigative peers to dismiss such findings, claiming that prostitutes would declare themselves domestic servants though their actual downfall had come at a time when they had occupied higher status jobs. Conyngton herself found, however, "that throughout this investigation the whole tendency of the women examined seemed to be the other way. If they had ever held any position implying education or intellectual or social standing they claimed it strenuously" (pp. 41–42). Aware that some wardens of relevant institutions had confessed to just putting down "housework" without careful questioning of the women, Conyngton limited her study to states demanding information and to institutions in those states where "officials carried out the law intelligently and sympathetically" (p. 14). See also Dewson, box 1 f. 3, Mary Dewson, "Conditions that Make Wayward Girls," based on 1909's commitments to the Massachusetts State Industrial School for Girls. Dewson found that 65 of 121 girls committed were charged with prostitution or streetwalking: 44 of the 121 had been in housework; 38 in mill, factory, or store; and 20 attending school. The *Annual Reports* of the New England Moral Reform Society similarly revealed that in 1914 42 of 110 admitted had been in housework (p. 20), and the reports gave similar figures in other years. In 1893, for example, they reported that they received "[M]any from domestic service, some from shops and factories . . . still others from their own homes" (p. 10). According to the U.S. Census reports, in 1880 44.8% of Boston's wage-earning women were domestic servants or laundresses, 31.9% in 1900, and 12.9% in 1920. In Massachusetts as a whole in 1895, 48.55% of women wage workers were in manufacturing and only 27.09% in domestic service. Katzman, *Seven Days a Week*, 287. Cf. Mary E. Odem, *Delinquent Daughters: Protecting and Policing Adolescent Female Sexuality in the United States, 1885–1920* (Chapel Hill: University of North

Carolina Press, 1995), 58–59: of thirty cases of sexual assault in southern California, 17% were attacked in their place of employment, all but one of which was domestic service.

Several people have pointed out to me that domestic servants were not only more vulnerable to sexual predation, but often without homes of their own to which to retreat, and so would have been more likely than women in other occupations to need an institutional house of refuge. Nonetheless, it is striking how investigations and house of refuge matrons turned even this heightened visibility into invisibility.

17 Conyngton, *Occupation and Criminality*, 105–106.

18 Ibid., 106. Cf. Addams, *A New Conscience*, 176.

19 Boston Lying-In Hospital, Case Records, Courtway Library of Medicine, Harvard Medical School, Boston; *Annual Reports* of the Boston Lying-In Hospital (Boston: Boston Lying-In Hospital, Inc., 1875–1917), Widener Library, Harvard University, Cambridge, MA (for example, in 1877, 130 patients were unmarried and 108 married; in 1878, 98 were unmarried and 115 married; and in 1879, 110 were unmarried and 102 married. The year 1887 was the last year in which unmarried women outnumbered married women among the patients, 207 to 181; by 1900, as hospitalization for birth became more generally acceptable, 170 were unmarried and 469 married). Rutland Corner House Collection, box 15, Schlesinger Library, Radcliffe College, Cambridge, MA. New England Moral Reform Society (early title: New England Female Moral Reform Society), *Annual Reports* (some of these are printed in the society's publication, *Friend of Virtue*), 1864, 1866, 1867, 1892–1896, 1899–1918, 1920, Boston Public Library. Boston Municipal Court Docket Book, Non-Payment of Support, January 1860–December 1874 [bound over to Superior Court, Civil], at Massachusetts State Archives (must be ordered in advance as are stored in a rat-infested vault without electricity and whose shelves are collapsing); Massachusetts Superior Court Docket Book, Criminal, January 1881–July 1882, Massachusetts State Archives.

20 New England Moral Reform Society, *Annual Report*, 1893, 10; *Annual Report*, 1911, reported a nineteen-year-old Russian girl employed by a Russian immigrant who led her astray, 12; *Annual Report*, 1912, reported a Nova Scotian girl, alone in the United States at age nineteen, had gone into housework for a private family, where the husband of the family "took advantage" of her, leading to her "ruin," but the mistress was sympathetic to her, called in the family physician, and had the man pay the expenses (pp. 10–11); *Annual Report*, 1917, reported that a Finnish girl had come to the United States at the age of eighteen only to be seduced by the student son of her housework employer, believing his intentions honorable, 10. Many other stories in the annual reports focused instead on sons of neighbors, demented boarders, and friends of the family as culprits in the girls' downfall. In 1900, the society pointed to an increase in the number of very young girls, aged fifteen to sixteen, half of whom were "ruined" by married men three to four times their age, whereas in 1909 they reported that twenty-four of eighty-four fathers were aged fifteen to twenty. Unlike the Boston Lying-In Hospital, with its entirely male board, though ultimately a female coterie of visitors, the New England Moral Reform Society had a female doctor as president in 1893 (Caroline E. Hastings, M.D.) and a female attending physician in 1901 (Julia Morton Plummer, M.D.). Reports are at Rare Book Room, Boston Public Library.

See also WEIU, box 8 f. 62, case records from investigation of dance halls and vice; two of eight extended cases where the initial seduction was known concerned young women seduced by domestic employers (cases 3 and 8).

More cases showed up at the Boston Psychopathic Hospital. See Lunbeck, *The Psychiatric Persuasion*, 192, 197, 206, 214, 275–276, 408 78n. Regarding girls placed out by state institutions, one woman "dismissed her state charge after she overheard her husband suggest they have sex." Another young woman became pregnant by the household's thirty-five-year-old widowed son, after having sex "in the 'hall, pantry or anywhere.' " Many but not all of these domestic servants seem to have been willing, and the hospital cast them, as Conyngton did, as pathologically immoral. Lunbeck, too, sees them as active sexual agents, though not pathological.

21 Faye E. Dudden, *Serving Women: Household Service in Nineteenth Century American* (Middletown, CT: Wesleyan University Press, 1983), 216; Katzman, *Seven Days a Week*, 293. And cf. Paula Giddings, *When and Where I Enter: The Impact of Black Women on Race and Sex in America* (New York: Bantam Books, 1984), 101, on black domestics.

22 Odem, *Delinquent Daughters*, 14, 83 n; 200. n.83 It was thirteen in the late 1880s. WEIU, series 1 carton 1, *Annual Report* 1886/87, p. 43.

23 Barbara Hobson, *Uneasy Virtue: The Politics of Prostitution and the American Reform Tradition* (Chicago: University of Chicago Press, 1990), 68–69. Even in places where seduction laws existed, such as Canada, in the 1880s and 1890s, according to Karen Dubinsky, "civil seduction suits could not be initiated by the woman involved; rather, her father would have to seek damages himself." According to Carolyn Strange, between 1880 and 1930 not one Toronto domestic who laid a complaint of indecent assault or rape against a master saw him punished. Dubinsky, " 'Maidenly Girls' or 'Designing Women'? The Crime of Seduction in Turn-of-the-Century Ontario," 149–187, and Strange, "Wounded Womanhood and Dead Men: Chivalry and the Trials of Clara Ford and Carrie Davies," 149–187, in *Gender Conflicts: New Essays in Women's History*, ed. Franca Iacovetta and Mariana Valverde (Toronto: University of Toronto Press, 1992). And cf. Odem, *Delinquent Daughters*, 78. Lunbeck, *The Psychiatric Persuasion*, 393, n. 20, 214, points out also the "immense skepticism" with which authorities met women's claims of violation in the 1910s.

24 Marybeth Hamilton Arnold, " 'The Life of a Citizen in the Hands of a Woman': Sexual Assault in New York City, 1790–1820," in *Passion and Power: Sexuality in History*, ed. Kathy Peiss and Christina Simmons, with Robert A. Badgug (Philadelphia: Temple University Press, 1989), 35–56. See also Strange, "Wounded Womanhood," the maleness of the courtroom: juries, lawyers, judges, and its tendency in such cases to become a drama of male honor (pp. 153, 168); Strange also points out that if a woman were actually raped, prior virginity was, of course, that much harder to prove. "Vigilantism," she concludes from her study of two acquitted female murderers, "was more effective than litigation as a remedy for sexual violence" (p. 177). Note also that most women appearing in court were prostitutes. Hobson, *Uneasy Virtue*, 68–69 on seduction law in Massachusetts. The situation was even more difficult for black women. Jane Addams, with no whisper of criticism, refers to "the colored girl [in domestic service], who because of her traditions is often treated with so little respect by white men, that she is constantly subjected to insults," and yet that "so universally are colored girls in domestic service suspected of blackmail that the average court is slow to credit their testimony when it is given against white men." Addams, *A New Conscience*, 169, 170.

25 WEIU, series 2 carton 6 f. 106, Protective Committee Minutes, 4/28/79. On Wells, see Polly Welts Kaufman, *Boston Women and City School Politics* (New York: Garland, 1994), 59–60.

26 WEIU, box 1 f. 9, "Social Statistics of Working Women," p. 22.

27 WEIU, box 1 f. 5, *Trained and Supplementary Workers in Domestic Service*, pp. 34–35. Similarly, in WEIU, box 1 f. 5 "Efforts to Attract . . . ," p. 10, "Nearly one-quarter of the factory women spoke of the loss of independence" in domestic service work as a reason to reject it; they considered isolation and long hours a tremendous drawback. And cf. in this vein, Dudden, *Serving Women*, 212, and Ruth Rosen, *The Lost Sisterhood* (Baltimore: Johns Hopkins University Press, 1982), 156, on postbellum working women's sense that middle-class women viewed them

as slaves or dogs "to kick around," the disdain of other working women, and the sense that prostitution was only a single narrow step further down.

28 Joy Parr, *Labouring Children: British Immigrant Apprentices to Canada, 1869–1924* (Montreal: McGill-Queen's University Press, 1980), 82, 114–117. Addams, *A New Conscience*, 168. Lori Rotenberg, "The Wayward Worker: Toronto's Prostitute at the Turn of the Century," 47, and Genevieve Leslie, "Domestic Service in Canada, 1880–1920," 85, in *Women at Work*, ed. Janice Acton, Penny Gold Smith, and Bonnie Shepard (Toronto: Canadian Women's Educational Press, 1974), both agree that many domestic servants were sexually exploited while in service; cited in Deborah Nilsen, "The 'Social Evil': Prostitution in Vancouver, 1900–1920," in *In Her Own Right: Selected Essays on Women's History in British Columbia*, ed. Barbara Latham and Cathy Kess (Victoria, BC: Camosun College, 1980), 205–228, who adds, "A woman may have reasoned that since her sexual services were clearly of value, her present situation differed from prostitution only in being more laborious." As for being "alone," in Boston, in a 1900 study of 181 families, the WEIU found that 101 had one servant, 49 had two, and 14 had three. WEIU, Box 1 f. 5 *Social Conditions in Domestic Service, MBSL Bulletin* 13 (February 1900), p. 4. Moreover, in 1880 40% and by 1900, over 60% of servants in Boston were foreign-born, largely Irish. Katzman, *Seven Days a Week*, 65–66.

29 Such women might not, of course, give seduction or rape as the cause of their becoming prostitutes, choosing rather the proximate cause: better money, better clothes, few options. Rosen, *Lost Sisterhood*, 149; Hobson, *Uneasy Virtue*, 60; W. Peter Ward, *Birth Weight and Economic Growth: Women's Living Standards in the Industrializing West* (Chicago: University of Chicago Press, 1993), 92; Boston Lying-In Hospital, *Annual Report*, 1875, p. 9, report of visiting physicians: "We have almost daily application for admission from women utterly destitute of money and friends, who beg to be allowed to come and work for their board till the time of their confinement. Most of them we have to refuse"; for other parts of the scenario, see *Annual Report*, 1876, pp. 8–11; 1887, p. 9; 1897, p. 19; 1900, p. 11. Hobson, *Uneasy Virtue*, 85–109, discusses the various routes by which women entered and left prostitution. She finds the routes varied according to the women's rural or urban roots, immigrant or American-born status, and age. She also finds that prostitution alternated with legal employment or marriage and could be a way out of a bad marriage as well as out of unsavory employment. It could mark an escape from a violent or simply restrictive family. Unlike most occupations open to women, prostitution offered women sufficient means to survive independent of family. Hobson does find that all the women who became prostitutes tended to have few options and few family resources on which to rely. Prostitutes, she reports, when asked, tended to see themselves as having made a choice, rather than as victims. In listing reasons for entering prostitution, destitution came first, and then inclination.

On the difficulty of getting into temporary homes, see, for example, Rutland Corner House, vol. 50, record book no. 4, 8/7/01, p. 5; 6/4/02, p. 33; and 5/4/04, p. 100. Peter Holloran, *Boston's Wayward Children: Social Services for Homeless Children 1830–1930* (Rutherford: Associated University Press, 1989), 36–37, on the Boston Female Asylum carefully selecting for Yankee girls, refusing Catholics, African Americans, and illegitimate girls.

On the lack of options, see Dudden, *Serving Women*, 214, on Caroline B. White whose servant, Katie Burke, in 1874 left pregnant, and three months later, at the charity home in Boston (Chardine Street House), White reported of her, "She does not know what she will do or where she will go." Jane Addams reported, "A surprising number of suicides occur among girls who have been in domestic service, when they discover that they have been betrayed by their lovers. Perhaps nothing is more astonishing than the attitude of the mistress when the situation of such a forlorn girl is discovered, and it would be interesting to know how far this attitude has influenced these girls either to suicide or to their reckless choice of a disreputable life, which statistics show so many of their number having elected. The mistress almost invariably promptly dismisses such a girl, assuring her that she is disgraced forever and too polluted to remain for another hour in a good home. In full command of the situation, she usually succeeds in convincing the wretched girl that she is irreparably ruined," *A New Conscience*, 172–174.

In contrast, Laura Prince, in the Denison House journal, reported in the context of visiting a young single pregnant woman in her parental home, that many such girls ultimately made good marriages, implicit was the requisite that they be sufficiently maintained with the child in the meantime, DH Journals, box 1, 1/26/93, 1/28/93.

While George J. Kneeland, *Commercialized Prostitution in New York City* (1913; reprint, Montclair, NJ: Patterson Smith, 1969), 107, found many prostitutes over thirty, he also found a drop at age twenty five.

30 Mrs. Edholm, "The Traffic in Girls and Florence Crittenton Missions," in *National Purity Congress: Its Papers, Addresses, Portraits*, ed. Aaron M. Powell (New York: American Purity Alliance, 1896); Hobson, *Uneasy Virtue*, 75; Mark Thomas Connelly, *The Response to Prostitution in the Progressive Era*, (Chapel Hill: University of North Carolina, 1980), 34; Dudden, *Serving Women*, 212–214, 217; Kneeland, *Prostitution* 102 2n, 184–185.

31 Hobson, *Uneasy Virtue*, 55 ff, 70–72, and 97. Hobson claims, as does Katzman, that the trope continues throughout the nineteenth century, but Katzman offers no citations and Hobson's are all from before the Civil War. According to my own research, the annual reports of the New England Moral Reform Society show a hiatus in such accounts from the Civil War to about 1910. They mention, as in 1893, that they received many girls form domestic service, but choose other anecdotes to include in the report; in 1911, 1912, and 1917, on the other hand, they include anecdotes from domestic service, though not many.

32 Barbara Ryan, "Kitchen and Parlor: Defining Domestic Space Before and After Slavery," (paper presented at the annual conference of the American Historical Association, Atlanta, January 1996).

33 On female moral authority, besides those authors already cited here, see, for example, Peggy Pascoe, *Relations of Rescue: The Search for Female Moral Authority in the American West, 1874–1939* (New York: Oxford University Press, 1990); Nancy Cott, *Bonds of Womanhood: Woman's Sphere in New England, 1780–1835* (New Haven: Yale University Press, 1975); Barbara Berg, *The Remembered Gate: Origins of American Feminism: The Woman and the City* (New York: Oxford University Press, 1978); Nancy Hewitt, *Women's Activism and Social Change: Rochester, New York, 1856–1872* (Ithaca: Cornell University Press, 1984); Mary P. Ryan, *Women in Public: Between Banners and Ballots, 1825–1880* (Baltimore: Johns Hopkins University Press, 1990); Stansell, *City of Women*; Lori Ginsberg, *Women and the Work of Benevolence: Morality and Politics in the Northeastern United States, 1820–1885* (New Haven: Yale University Press, 1990); Anne Firor Scott, *Natural Allies: Women's Associations in American History* (Urbana: University of Illinois Press, 1993); Sarah Deutsch, "Learning to Talk More Like a Man: Boston Women's Class-Bridging Organizations, 1870–1950," *American Historical Review* 97 (April 1992): 379–404. Note that, as these works and the other works cited in this essay reveal, male reformers often endorsed middle-class women's moral authority.

34 For example, WEIU, carton 8 f. 130A, "Young Persons Employed in Retail Selling" [c. 1917], 117, 119, 162 implies that one reason for the Massachusetts minimimum wage in retail was to halt immoral conditions that had led "moral" employers, knowing they paid too little to subsist legally, to insist their female employees live at their parental homes; Dennis P. Ryan, *Beyond the Ballot Box: A Social History of the Boston Irish, 1845–1917* (1989), 46; Susan Porter Benson, *Counter*

Cultures: Saleswomen, Managers, and Customers in American Department Stores, 1890–1940 (Urbana: University of Illinois Press, 1986), 134–137; B. O. Flowers, "Some Causes of Present Day Immorality and Suggestions as to Practical Remedies," in *National Purity Congress,* ed. Powell, 313; Conyngton addressed this prevailing mythology regarding saleswomen, and disputed it, 94–96.

35 Cf. Strange, "Wounded Womanhood," 152. Also Albert Benedict Wolfe, *The Lodging House Problem in Boston* (Boston: Houghton, Mifflin, 1906), and Wright, *Working Girls,* throughout; Hon. Elbridge T. Gerry, "Childsaving and Prostitution," in *National Purity Congress,* 336–348 on the factories "looked upon almost, so to speak, as mills from which are ground out the material out of which youthful prostitutes are made." Men participated in this discourse as well as women; ultimately, in reinforcing the institution of the Victorian home, it also reinforced their own authority, as well.

36 WEIU series 1 carton 1, *Annual Report,* 1885–86, Abby Morton Diaz's presidential address, p. 8.

37 Boston YWCA chief clerk quoted in investigation in WEIU box 7 f. 48, "Immigration as a Source of Supply . . ."; leaflet is c. 1900 in box 1 f. 5 see also box 1 f. 6, "Report of the Employment Committee," 1896, p. 40 and 1898, pp. 49–50; and *Trained and Supplementary Workers in Domestic Service,* 10, 11, 30.

38 Contrast records of the WEIU Protective Department (minutes as well as annual reports) with those of the WEIU Domestic Reform League. The protective committee repeatedly complained of the high proportion of its recovery-of-wage cases that consisted of domestic servants trying to obtain wages owed them; see, for example, in 1887/88. WEIU, carton 1 series 1, *Annual Report,* 1887/88, pp. 35–36; and 1879/80 *Annual Report,* 38.

39 WEIU, box 1 f. 5, *Trained and Supplementary Workers,* p. 17 no. 250, p. 19 no. 69, p. 29 no. 76, p. 26 no. 37, p. 27 no. 258. Day work, nonetheless, made steady headway. See WEIU, box 1 f. 5, Bulletin of the *Domestic Reform League* 1 (January 1907). The league filled 580 orders for day workers in 1898, a figure that steadily rose to 3206 in 1906.

40 WEIU, box 1 f. 5, *Trained and Supplementary Workers,* p. 29 no. 78, p. 28 no. 58; see also p. 27 no. 235; and p. 29.

41 Hazel V. Carby, "Policing the Black Woman's Body in an Urban Context," *Critical Inquiry* 18 (summer 1992): 738–755, especially 744. See also Judith R. Walkowitz, "Male Vice and Female Virtue: Feminism and the Politics of Prostitution in Nineteenth-Century Britain," in *Powers of Desire: The Politics of Sexuality,* ed. Ann Snitow, Christine Stansell, and Sharon Thompson (New York: Monthly Review Press, 1983), 419–483, particularly, 427.

42 Katzman, *Seven Days a Week,* 114.

43 WEIU, box 1 f. 5, *Trained and Supplementary Workers,* p. 29 no. 139.

44 WEIU, box 1 f. 5, *Trained and Supplementary Workers,* pp. 34–35. Katzman, *Seven Days a Week,* 61; according to Carole Srole, " 'A Position That God Has Not Particularly Assigned to Men': The Feminization of Clerical Work, Boston 1860–1915" (Ph.D. diss., University of California, Los Angeles, 1984), 337, whereas fewer than 3% of working-class families hired servants in 1880 if they did not have boarders or lodgers, over half of professional or executive headed families did, over one-quarter of small business owners, and one-quarter of clerical and service sector headed families.

45 WEIU, box 1 f. 5, *Trained and Supplementary Workers,* pp. 18, 26–32.

46 Pleck, *Black Migration,* 135. See also WEIU, box 7 f. 49, immigrant women and girls in Boston, 1906–07, pp. 2–3, 16; box 7 f. 48, investigation of 500 immigrant women. See WEIU, box 1 f. 5, social conditions in domestic service, p. 6.

47 Dudden, *Serving Women,* pp. 3–4, 7 81, 229, 234. Louisa May Alcott wrote to Abby May from Concord 2/23/77 (May-Goddard Papers, A-134, box 1 f. 33 Schlesinger Library, Radcliffe

College, Cambridge, MA) that "the Belles of the Kitchen on a strike. I do *so* love to say to em 'go, I can do without you,' when they get rampageous," but then reported her plunge from litteratoes to slops and cinders at one dive. Domestic workers also refused to work outside their usual tasks and threatened to quit without notice at crucial moments in order to better their pay. See WEIU, box 1 f. 5, *Trained and Supplementary Workers*, p. 27 no. 187; WEIU, series 1 carton 1, *Annual Report*, 1899–1900, p. 51, Protective Committee. Cf. Sondra Lauderdale Graham, *House and Street: The Domestic World of Servants and Masters in Nineteenth-Century Rio de Janeiro* (Cambridge: Cambridge University Press, 1988), p. 22: "what counted most was obedience—euphemistically phrased as 'good conduct' or having 'good habits.' "

48 WEIU, box 1 f. 5, *Trained and Supplementary Workers*, p. 18 no. 53, p. 17 no. 103.

49 On the ubiquity, see above concerning lecherous employers, etcetera, and, for example, Margaret Deland to Miss Clarke regarding one reforming unwed mother who was now commuting to work with Deland's husband, Lorin, learning office work and living with a family near Deland. That combination of factors made day work safe, in Deland's view; otherwise, she admitted, "I think the being on the street night and morning is unwise." Margaret Wade Campbell Deland Papers, f. 1,/29/84, Schlesinger Library, Radcliffe College, Cambridge, MA. Cf. relations between white middle-class women and black women in the South after the Civil War in Jacquelyn Dowd Hall, " 'The Mind That Burns in Each Body': Women, Rape, and Racial Violence," in *Powers of Desire*, ed. Snitow, Stansell, and Thomson, 328–349.

50 See, for example, Linda Gordon, *Heroes of Their Own Lives: The Politics and History of Family Violence* (New York: Viking, 1988), 125 ff, who concludes about Boston, "so strong was the ideal of domesticity among the child-savers that they interpreted the gregariousness of the urban poor to mean that these people had no *homes*."

51 Besides those cases mentioned above from the New England Moral Reform Society, see Mary E. Richmond and Fred S. Hall, *A Study of Nine Hundred and Eighty-five Widows Known to General Charity Organization Societies in 1910* (New York: Russell Sage Foundation, 1913), 33–36, 40–41, 45, 51. The relative ease with which child-savers removed children from poor families itself testified to their sense that these were not, in fact, "families." See, in this connection, DH Journals, box 1 f. 5, Emily Balch 2/11/93. Dwight Porter, *Report Upon a Sanitary Inspection of Certain Tenement-House Districts of Boston* (Boston: Press of Rockwell and Churchill, 1889), 28–39. See also, Edward Everett Hale et al., *Workingmen's Homes: Essays and Stories* (Boston: James R. Osgood, 1874), 172; Secker and Valentine, "500 Immigrant Women." WEIU, box 7 f. 49a, *Immigrant Women and Girls in Boston* (1906–7), p. 14, contended that 35 of 141 homes had "bad conditions." Final quotation is from WEIU, box 1 f. 5, *Trained and Supplementary Workers*, pp. 27–29 no. 80. Cf. also Beverly Stadum, *Poor Women and Their Families: Hard Working Charity Cases 1900–1930* (Albany: State University of New York Press, 1992).

52 Hale et al., *Workingmen's Homes*, 77, 81. WEIU, box 7 f. 49, *Immigrant Women and Girls in Boston* (1906–7). And see Bushee, *Ethnic Factors*, 109. Roswell F. Phelps, *South End Factory Operatives: Employment and Residence* (Boston: South End House Association, 1903), 8. Cf. colonial America, where a desire for privacy led to suspicions of immoral intent. David H. Flaherty, *Privacy in Colonial New England* (Charlottesville: University Press of Virginia, 1972—I am grateful to Rosemarie Zagarri for this citation).

53 C. Wright, *Working Girls*, 21; Hale et al., *Woorkingmen's Homes*, 77, 81.

54 WEIU, box 1 f. 5, *Trained and Supplementary Workers*, pp. 18, 26–32.

55 Wolfe, *Lodging House Problem*, 64–65, 139, 141–142; Lunbeck, *Psychiatric Persuasion*, 17; and Addams, *A New Conscience*, 71–72 and Bushee, *Ethnic Factors*, 109 that working-class families afforded some barrier to their daughters becoming prostitutes.

56 Wolfe, *Lodging House Problem*, 64–65, 139, 141–142; see also, Marvin, "Lodging House Problem," 248 who repeatedly called the women "selfish" and "ungenerous"; it was almost as though making housing into commerce was similar to making sex into commerce, turning what were defined as intimate, private, affectionate relations into public, commercial ones. Hon. Elbridge T. Gerry, "Childsaving and Prostitution," in Powell, ed., *National Purity Congress*, 336–348 on the factories "looked upon almost, so to speak, as mills from which are ground out the material out of which youthful prostitutes are made." C. Wright, *Working Girls*, 118, 122–123.

57 Louise Marion Bosworth, *The Living Wage of Women Workers: A Study of Incomes and Expenditures of 450 Women in the City of Boston* (New York: Longmans, Green, 1911), 23. "In two or three instances," she admits, "pathetic little stories came from girls evidently too ignorant to protect themselves or too miserable to care to conceal their plight; but they were not stories that dealt with lodging house life." Wolfe, *Lodging House Problem*, 143; *Report of the [Massachusetts] Commission*, pp. 22–23. Wolfe himself, *Lodging House Problem*, 138, and one of his case studies, who admits, "There was no time I was there that I felt in personal peril," 145–148. Also see Roswell F. Phelps, *South End Factory Operatives: Employment and Residence* (Boston: South End House Association, 1903), 9 in direct contradiction to his assertion above, "In our inspections in this city we observed scarcely any enormities such as appeared in the investigations to which I have just referred, and yet abundant data were obtained as to the existence of extensive and serious overcrowding." And Conyngton, *Occupation and Criminality*, 90, on the "overcrowding" resulting from poverty: "the dangers of such promiscuity are evident. . . . The only matter for astonishment is that these risks produce so few apparent results, and that the girl growing up in such surroundings can, and in the majority of cases does, remain unharmed." Rosen, *Lost Sisterhood*, 143, also reminds us that despite the popular ideas on the subject, most prostitutes were not living alone in boardinghouses before they became prostitutes. Middle-class women's reform groups seemed always on the watch for such incidents and not finding them, cf. WEIU box 7 f. 49 *Immigrant Women and Girls*, p. 7 nos. 20 and 21, pp. 8–9. See also D. Ryan, *Beyond the Ballot Box*, 28, on investigators finding no evidence of procurers haunting the East Boston docks, despite numerous rumors in the 1890s.

58 Gill Valentine, "Images of Danger: Women's Sources of Information about the Spatial Distribution of Male Violence," *Area* 24: 1 (1992): 22–29, and "The Geography of Women's Fear," *Area* 21: 4 (1989): 385–390. Cf. F. M. Lehman and Rev. N. K. Clarkson, *The White Slave Hell, Or With Christ at Midnight in the Slums of Chicago* (Chicago: Christian Witness, 1910), 185, quoted in Meyerowitz, *Women Adrift*, 62, that the U.S. district attorney for Chicago claimed "no girl can safely go to a great city to make her own way who is not under the eye of a trustworthy woman who knows the ways and dangers of city life." Meyerowitz, *Women Adrift*, 27 reports that in a group interview at Almagamated Clothing and Textile Workers' Union Retirement Center in Chicago in 1980, one woman confessed, "If a girl didn't live at home, we thought she was bad."

59 Elizabeth Wilson, *The Sphinx in the City: Urban Life, the Control of Disorder, and Women* (Berkeley: University of California Press, 1992).

60 Gordon, *Heroes*. Cf. Mrs. Mary Livermore in *National Purity Congress*, ed. Powell, 387, that young women were "safe because they are under the protection of the American man. And there is no other man like the American man. Whatever woman may come to in the future her best protection must always be in the heart of man." Contrast to Henry Blackwell, Powell, ed., 426, paraphrasing Thomas Wentworth Higginson, that woman suffrage means "self respect and self protection."

61 Bosworth, *Living Wage*, 23: "Most experiences of an unpleasant nature one learns at third or

fourth hand, seldom directly. However, the existence of such a possibility is an ever-present anxiety to the girl seeking rooms." *Report of the [Massachusetts] Commission*, 22–23, found on investigation that the stories were simply vague rumors or imaginary.

62 In addition to works cited above, see Hale et al., *Workingmen's Homes*, 80; WEIU, box 1, f. 5, *Trained and Supplementary Workers*, pp. 29, 32, on the Household Aid Company of Boston (1903–05); and WEIU, "Immigration as a Source of Supply," pp. 9–10.

63 See Strange, "Wounded Womanhood," 149–187.

64 Besides the works cited above on female moral authority, in this connection see Brenzel, *Daughters of the State: A Social Portrait of the First Reform School for Girls in North America, 1856–1905* (Cambridge: MIT Press, 1983); Estelle B. Freedman, *Their Sisters' Keepers: Women's Prison Reform in America, 1830–1930* (Ann Arbor: University of Michigan Press, 1981), and the annual reports of the WEIU on efforts to get female police matrons for female prisoners.

65 Hobson, *Uneasy Virtue*, 127.

66 Dudden, *Serving Women*, 169. See also Rosen, *Lost Sisterhood*, chap. 4, and the long struggle of the Women's Educational and Industrial Union in Boston first to reform servants and then to reform employers, in WEIU records of the Domestic Reform League, for example, box 1, f. 6, "Report of the Employment Committee," May 1898, pp. 48–49; Holloran, 36–37; WEIU Papers, box 7 f. 48, "Training of Immigrants," on the Boston YWCA School for domestic service. See DH Journals, E. M. Dresser 1/6/93, pp. 92–93, And see Margaret Deland, *Golden Yesterdays* (NY: Harper, 1941), 153–155. WEIU, box 1 f. 5, *Trained and Supplementary Workers*, p. 4. Conyngton, *Occupation and Criminality*, 71n. As late as 1916, the WEIU investigator of "A Study of the Vocational Trend in Massachusetts Schools," p. 35, found one school "of all that I visited, where the prevailing opinion seemed to be that if the girls could be persuaded to go into domestic service, the problem of women in industry would be solved," and so discouraged girls from learning machine work.

67 Brenzel, *Daughters of the State*, 8.

68 Quoted in Lunbeck, *The Psychiatric Persuasion*, 206. And cf. Judith Walkowitz, *Prostitution and Victorian Society: Women, Class and the State* (Cambridge, UK: Cambridge University Press, 1980), 223.

69 See Carol Smart, writing on England, in "Disruptive Bodies and Unruly Sex: The Regulation of Reproduction and Sexuality in the Nineteenth Century," in *Regulating Womanhood: Historical Essays on Marriage, Motherhood and Sexuality*, ed. Carol Smart (London: Routledge, 1992), 29. See also Carroll Smith-Rosenberg, *Disorderly Conduct: Visions of Gender in Victorian America* (New York: Alfred Knopf, 1985). See, for example, Isaac H. Clothier, "Protection for Young Women in Stores, Factories and Other Places of Business," in Powell, ed., *National Purity Congress*, 433. Cf. Carby, "Policing," Michel de Certeau, *Heterologies Discourse on the Others*, trans. Brian Massum (Minneapolis: University of Minnesota Press, 1986), 196.

70 See chap. 3 above on Kneeland Street Home, Immigrant Home, etcetera, and Wright, *Working Girls*, 122; Hobson, *Uneasy Virtue*, 75; and cf. Lucy Bland, "Feminist Vigilantes of Late-Victorian England," in Smart, ed., *Regulating Womanhood*, 47, on "protective surveillance."

71 Phelps, *Factory Operatives*, 37; Hale et al., *Workingmen's Homes*, 3.

72 Quoted from her 1892 report in Michelle Reidel and John Potter, " 'Suppose it Were Your Daughter': Gender, Class and Work as Perceived by Women Factory Inspectors in Gilded Age Massachusetts" (paper presented at Southwestern Labor Studies Conference, U.C. Santa Cruz, 4/29–30/1994), 9 (forthcoming in *Labor History*).

73 Frances Fern Andrews Papers, Schlesinger Library, Radcliffe College, Cambridge, MA, box 15 f. 225, executive committee minutes of BESAGG 1909/10. Mrs. Lucia True Ames Mead, reformer and peace activist, drafted the letter. The Women's Municipal League, with much the same constituency in terms of class, wondered whether better lighting might not do the trick.

See also, Perry R. Duis, *The Saloon: Public Drinking in Chicago and Boston, 1880–1920* (Urbana: University of Illinois Press, 1983), 280, and cf. Odem, *Delinquent Daughters*, 110–111 on early police women's duties in Los Angeles (1910–14).

74 Wolfe on Canadian cousins in lodging houses, *Lodging House Problem*, 82; Meyerowitz, *Women Adrift*, 24; C. Wright, *Working Girls*, 120.

75 Wright, 3.

76 Cf. Meyerowitz, *Women Adrift*, 50 on activities of YWCA.

77 WEIU, box 1 f. 5, *Trained and Supplementary Workers*, p. 14.

78 Wolfe, *Lodging House Problem*, 115, 168. *Report of the [Massachusetts] Commission*, 66, quoted in Mark Thomas Connelly, *The Response to Prostitution in the Progressive Era* (Chapel Hill: University of North Carolina Press, 1980), 30. Katzman, *Seven Days a Week*, 95; WEIU, B-8, box 1 f. 5, *Trained and Supplementary Workers*.

79 Meyerowitz, *Women Adrift*, xxiii; and 39–40. See also Meyerowitz, "Sexual Geography," 187, 195–197. WEIU, box 1 f. 5, "The Effort to Attract" 1898, pp. 8–9.

80 Cf. Meyerowitz, *Women Adrift*, 117–139, 343–368.

81 C. Wright, *Working Girls*, 5, 119, 120. On Conyngton, see Freedman, *Their Sisters' Keepers*, 122.

82 These seemingly competing views could reside in a single report, as in "Immigration as a Source of Supply," where the author wrote, p. 2, "The spirit of democracy, of freedom, is consciously or unconsciously in the heart of the American-born, and to be a servant is to be peculiarly bound to the will of another"; "yet in these new relations [day work] she finds business method, not mere whim or caprice. She is not constantly at the beck and call of her employer, but has absolutely beyond his control more than half the hours and sometimes sixteen and eighteen out of the twenty-four. She is her own mistress and the feeling of 'servant' is gone"; as opposed to a few pages later, p. 8 recommending more Immigrant Homes that give, "The right impression of home life, to show her the advantages of choosing household work for her occupation," and p. 10, "many capable girls found satisfactory work [when placed as domestic servants] who otherwise might have been enticed to hotels, lodging houses and other places treatment would be unjust, temptations great and morals lax." See also WEIU, box 1 f. 5, *Trained and Supplementary Workers*, p. 35. On the shift of WEIU employment concern to middle-class, see WEIU, box 8 f. 67, Appointment Bureau, "Outline of Growth"; WEIU, *Annual Report* for 1911–12, p. 19, on registering more college women at the Appointment Bureau; WEIU, series 2 carton 6 f. 104, "Industrial Committee," c. 1908/09 on the Wellesley fellow's series of articles for *Wellesley Magazine* on business opportunities for women; WEIU, box 10 f. 103, vocational conferences starting by 1915 and culminating in 1919's creation of the Intercollegiate Vocational Guidance Association in Boston. Lunbeck, *The Psychiatric Persuasion*, 19, calls this part of "the break up of the Victorian gender synthesis."

83 For example, Samuel Eliot Morison, *One Boy's Boston*, 13, of his childhood home where the family kept a staff of several servants and a slop closet for the third and fourth floors.

84 My thinking in this respect has been particularly influenced by Clair Wills, "Upsetting the Public: Carnival, Hysteria and Women's Texts," in *Bakhtin and Cultural Theory*, ed. Ken Hirschkop and David Shepherd (Manchester: Manchester University Press, 1989), 130–151; Lunbeck, *The Psychiatric Persuasion*, and Michel Foucault (various texts). In addition, by recognizing the connections between industrial and domestic labor, constructions of domesticity and institutions affecting working-class women's options, I am participating in the project of breaking down the constructed separation between women's and labor history, work and home, domestic and industrial labor, a split Eileen Boris rightly claims "obscures the ways that each realm shapes the other." Eileen Boris, "Beyond Dichotomizing: Recent Books in North American Women's Labor History," *Journal of Women's History* 4 (winter 1993): 162–179, particularly 162.

Chapter 3

1 Louise Marion Bosworth Papers, Schlesinger Library, Radcliffe College, Cambridge, MA, carton 4 f. 178.

2 Bosworth, for example, to her mother, carton 1 f. 27, 11/27/07; f. 28, 1/30/08; f. 29, 7/21/08.

3 Priscilla Murolo, *The Common Ground of Womanhood: Class, Gender, and Working Girls' Clubs, 1884–1928* (Urbana: University of Illinois Press, 1997), 12.

4 Carole Srole, " 'A Position That God Has Not Particularly Assigned to Men': The Feminization of Clerical Work, Boston 1860–1915" (Ph.D. diss., University of California, Los Angeles, 1984), 418; Frederick A. Bushee, *Ethnic Factors in the Population of Boston* (1903; reprint, New York: Arno Press, 1970), 57.

5 WEIU Papers, series 4 carton 8 f. 133, "Exhibit of Industrial Conditions in Relation to Public Health, Safety, and Welfare," Boston, April 7–14 [c. 1906]; Carroll D. Wright, *The Working Girls of Boston* [from the fifteenth Annual Report of the MBSL, for 1884] (Boston: Wright and Potter Printing, 1889), 36–37, 127; WEIU, *Annual Report* 1889–90, series 1 carton 1, p. 7; WEIU, B-8, box 7 f. 56, Boston sample of clothing operators, p. 4; WEIU, series 2 carton 6 f. 104, "Industrial Committee," 1907–8, p. 5; WEIU, B-8, box 7 f. 54, "The Food of Working Women," 1916; Srole, "Feminization of Clerical Work," 418, 420, 433. Paula Marie Kane, *Separatism and Subculture: Boston Catholicism, 1900–1920* (Chapel Hill: University of North Carolina Press, 1994), 245.

6 Wendy Gamber, "The Female Economy: The Millinery and Dressmaking Trades, 1860–1930" (Ph.D. diss., Brandeis University, 1990), 140, 141, 147.

7 Roswell F. Phelps, *South End Factory Operatives: Employment and Residence* (Boston: South End House Association, 1903), 13–14.

8 Susan Porter Benson, *Counter Cultures: Saleswomen, Managers, and Customers in American Department Stores, 1890–1940* (Urbana: University of Illinois Press, 1986), 190–192, 194–196, 201, 203.

9 Gertrude L. Marvin, "The Lodging House Problem in Boston," *Wellesley Magazine* 15 (March 1907): 246–247.

10 Bosworth, Carton 4 f. 178, 10/4/07, case no. 80. And see Bosworth, carton 4 f. 170, case no. 303 and case no. 253. Bosworth, carton no. 4 f. 170, on installment buying. WEIU, box 1 f. 9, "Social Statistics of Working Women," pp. 12–14.

11 One investigation of 97 of Boston's 275 retail milliners, found that the number of employees ranged from 143 to 1429 in any given year, a tenfold difference. Lorinda Perry, *The Millinery Trade in Boston and Philadelphia: A Study of Women in Industry* (Binghamton, NY: Vail-Ballou, 1916), 110. C. Wright, *Working Girls*, 112, 121; Barbara M. Brenzel, *Daughters of the State: A Social Portrait of the First Reform School for Girls in North America. 1856–1905* (Cambridge: MIT Press, 1983), 110.

12 Alexander von Hoffman, *Local Attachments: The Making of an American Urban Neighborhood, 1850–1920* (Baltimore: Johns Hopkins University Press, 1994), 57. Benson, *Counter Cultures*, 34.

13 Bosworth, carton 1 f. 28, 5/20/08, to her mother.

14 WEIU, series 1 carton 1, *Annual Reports*, 1880/81, p. 40; 1881/82, p. 46; 1882/83, p. 47; 1883/84, pp. 43–44.

15 Louis Levine, *The Women's Garment Workers: A History of the ILGWU* (New York: B. W. Huebsch, 1924), 7.

16 WEIU, box 7 f. 56, machine operating women's clothing, 1910–11. Edward Everett Hale, *Workingmen's Homes: Essays and Stories* (Boston: James R. Osgood, 1874), 65. Srole, "Feminization of Clerical Work," 25. Other female manufacturing sectors followed suit. DH, box 1, vol. 2, 2/11/95. WEIU, box 7 f. 58, opportunities for girls in manufacturing—paper boxes.

17 Von Hoffman, *Local Attachments*, 57. WEIU, box 7 f. 60, industrial opportunities for women in

Cambridge, Somerville, 1910–1911, pp. xvi, 4–5. WEIU, box 7 f. 56, clothing, pp. 3, 5–9, 12.

18 Srole, "Feminization of Clerical Work," 24–27. WEIU, box 11 f. 117, chemistry.

19 Perry, *Millinery Trade*, 24. Gamber, "Female Economy," 473. WEIU, box 7 f. 60, Cambridge industry, pp. 51, 54.

20 Benson, *Counter Cultures*, 34. WEIU carton 8 f. 130A "Young Persons Employed in Retailed Selling," (1915/16) 19, 23.

21 WEIU, box 7 f. 60, Cambridge industry, pp. 30, 32–33, 47, 56. See von Hoffman, *Local Attachments*, xx, 24–25. Bosworth, carton 4 f. 178. William M. DeMarco, *Ethnics and Enclaves: Boston's Italian North End* (Ann Arbor: University of Michigan Research Press, 1981), 84–85. C. Wright, *Working Girls*, 71; Phelps, *Factory Operatives*, 15–18.

22 WEIU, box 7 f. 60, Cambridge industry, pp. 30, 32–33, 47, 56.

23 Benson, *Counter Cultures*, 4–5, 197, 233–234.

24 See for examples Roy Rosenzweig and Elizabeth Blackmar, *The Park and the People: A History of Central Park* (Ithaca: Cornell University Press, 1992); Roy Rosenzweig, *Eight Hours for What We Will: Workers and Leisure in an Industrial City, 1870–1920* (Cambridge, UK: Cambridge University Press, 1983); John Kasson, *Amusing the Million: Coney Island at the Turn of the Century* (New York: Hill and Wang, 1978); Kathy Peiss, *Cheap Amusements: Working Women and Leisure in Turn-of-the-Century New York* (Philadelphia: Temple University Press, 1982); and Paul Boyer, *Urban Masses and Moral Order in America, 1820–1920* (Cambridge: Harvard University Press, 1978), 233–236, 242, 244–249, 279. Vida Scudder, *A Listener in Babel: Being a Series of Imaginary Conversations Held at the Close of the Last Century* (Boston: Houghton, Mifflin, 1903), 218–222.

25 Joanne J. Meyerowitz, *Women Adrift: Independent Wage Earners in Chicago, 1880–1930* (Chicago: University of Chicago Press, 1988), 96–115. See also Kathy Peiss, *Cheap Amusements*; Eric C. Schneider, *In the Web of Class: Delinquents and Reformers in Boston, 1810s–1930s* (New York: New York University Press, 1992); Elizabeth Lunbeck, *The Pyschiatric Persuasion: Knowledge, Gender, and Power in Modern America* (Princeton: Princeton University Press, 1994); Christine Stansell, *City of Women: Sex and Class in New York, 1789–1860* (New York: Alfred A. Knopf, 1986); Mary E. Odem, *Delinquent Daughters: Protecting and Policing Adolescent Female Sexuality in the United States, 1885–1920* (Chapel Hill: University of North Carolina Press, 1995).

26 WEIU, box 7 f. 49, immigrant women and children, 1906/7, p. 13. Mary Conyngton, *Report on Condition of Woman and Child Wage-earners in the United States*, vol. 15, *Relation Between Occupation and Criminality of Women* (Washington, DC: Government Printing Office, 1911), 94, 112.

27 Italics mine. Brenzel, *Daughters of the State*, 119–124, 126–128. Bushee, *Ethnic Factors*, 106. Linda Gordon, *Heroes of Their Own Lives: The Politics and History of Family Violence* (New York: Viking, 1988). Peter C. Holloran, *Boston's Wayward Children: Social Services for Homeless Children 1830–1930* (Rutherford, NJ: Associated University Press, 1989), 186–190.

28 Bosworth, carton 4 f. 170, cases 37B and 26B.

29 Bosworth, carton 4 f. 170, cases 37B and 26B.

30 Marvin, "Lodging House Problem," 1907, 251.

31 For example, *Boston Globe* 8/11/95, 29, and 8/18/95, 25, "Everybody's Column" on bloomers; 10/3/94,/8, "New Woman's 1200-Mile Bicycle Trip in Trousers." And *Boston Globe* 4/14/95, 32, reprinted from the *(Chicago) Post*, "Modern Girl's Handicap," in which a mother doubts that praising her daughter's athletic prowess is the best way to find her a husband. *Globe* 9/2/94, 25, "Boston's Girl Athletes." And cf. Ellen Gruber Garvey, "Reframing the Bicycle: Advertising Supported Magazines and Scorching Women," *American Quarterly* 47 (March 1995): 66–101. *Boston Globe* 10/28/94, 29, "Everybody's Column"; 10/14/94. *Globe* 9/2/94, 24, "Everybody's Column," "Story of a Man Whose Wife Spanks Him Soundly." *Boston Globe*/10/14/94,

29, "Everybody's Column," it became apparent that many husbands were whipped by wives. *Boston Globe* 10/14/94 "Everybody's Column," 29; 10/7/94, 29, "Everybody's Column." *Boston Globe* 4/7/95, 29.

32 *Boston Globe* 10/21/94, 29; "Everybody's Column." For a seduction tale, see *Boston Globe* 4/29/95, 7, "Life of Sorrow." Cf. Judith R. Walkowitz, "Going Public: Shopping, Street Harassment, and Streetwalking in Late-Victorian London," *Representations* 63 (spring 1998): 1–30.

33 On the strikes, see chapter 7.

34 *Boston Globe* 9/27/94, 5, "Landladies' Union" and "Women Organize in Defense of the Social Evil." See also *Boston Globe* 10/3/94, 2, "Landladies Ask for Licenses"; 1/18/95, 6, "Big Raid in West End," on eight houses; and 9/28/94, p. 3. And see Perry R. Duis, *The Saloon: Public Drinking in Chicago and Boston, 1880–1920* (Urbana: University of Illinois Press, 1983), 244–250.

35 Rev. [Mrs.] Mary Whitney's "Vigorous Advice to Unfortunate Young Girls," front-page story in the evening *Boston Globe* 8/14/95, 1. Feminist temperance worker Mary Livermore supported her views, but Dr. Salome Merritt opposed such action as vigilantism. The more violently disposed women did not exempt their own sons from such vengeance.

36 On the black women's convention, see *Boston Globe* 8/1/95, 4, "It Was Spirited." Mrs. Agnes Adams, Boston, spoke on Social Purity. *Boston Globe* 9/1/94, evening edition 1, "Anti-Lynching Society."

37 See Duis, *The Saloon*, 88–89, 175, 180, 188–189, 204–229, 234–240. See also William I. Cole, "Introduction"; Frederick A. Bushee, "Population"; Robert A. Woods, "Work and Wages" and "The Total Drift," all in *City Wilderness: A Settlement Study by the Residents and Associates of the South End House*, ed. Woods (New York: Houghton, Mifflin, 1898), 4, 6, 34–35 on the mansions becoming lodging houses; 82 on "no-man's—land"; 85, 309 on the elevated. Von Hoffman, *Local Attachments*, 32, 36. Roger Lane, *Policing the City: Boston, 1822–1885* (Cambridge: Harvard University Press, 1967), 173–175. William I. Cole, "Law and Order," in *Americans in Process: A Settlement Study* ed. Robert A. Woods (Boston: Houghton, Mifflin, 1903), 191, 198, details the process by which police rid the North End of prostitution. William I. Cole, "Criminal Tendencies," in *City Wilderness*, Woods, ed. 155. On race, see also Hazel V. Carby, "Policing the Black Woman's Body in an Urban Context," *Critical Inquiry* 18 (summer 1992): 751–753. See also Joanne Meyerowitz, "Sexual Geography and Gender Economy: The Furnished Room Districts of Chicago, 1890–1930," *Gender and History* 2 (autumn 1990), reprinted in *Unequal Sisters: A Multicultural Reader in U.S. Women's History*, ed. Vicki L. Ruiz and Ellen Carol DuBois, 2d ed. (New York: Routledge, 1994), 186–202; and Kevin J. Mumford, *Interzones: Black/White Sex Districts in Chicago and New York in the Early Twentieth Century* (New York: Columbia University Press, 1997). And see Elizabeth Hafkin Pleck, *Black Migration and Poverty, Boston 1865–1900* (New York: Academic Press, 1979), 79–80.

38 Duis, *The Saloon*, 162–63, 189. DH Journals, box 1 f. 4 1/4/93; Box 1 vol. 2, pp. 35–36; Helen Cheever 1/31/93, pp. 38–39,

39 Duis, *The Saloon*, 27, 32, 250. DH, Box 1 f. 3, Cheever 1/31/93, pp. 37–39.

40 Nichols-Shurtleff Family Papers, Box 8, f. 34, Robert A. Woods to Miss Nichols on the stationery of the Licensing Board for the City of Boston, 7/3/15, enclosing circular no. 1, series 1915, May 1, Schlesinger Library, Radcliffe College, Cambridge, MA. Cole, "Criminal," 159–164.

41 Marvin, "Lodging House Problem," 246. Cole, "Criminal," 159–164.

42 William I. Cole, "Law and Order," in *Americans in Process: A Settlement Study* (Boston: Houghton, Mifflin, 1903), ed. Robert A. Woods, 199–200, 214, 217–218. Frederick A. Bushee, "The Invading Host," in *Americans in Process*, ed. Woods, 55. And see Lunbeck, *The Psychiatric Persuasion*, 204–205.

43 Federal manuscript census, 1880, Ward 9, pp. 21–22, 41. Linda Gordon, "Black and White Visions of Welfare: Women's Welfare Activism, 1890–1945," *Journal of American History* 78 (September 1991): 566.

44 Pleck, *Black Migration*, 114–116. Holloran, *Boston's Wayward Children*, 147. Dennis P. Ryan, *Beyond the Ballot Box: A Social History of the Boston Irish, 1845–1917* (Amherst: University of Massachusetts Press, 1983), 47; Pleck, *Black Migration*, 114–115. Bushee, "The Invading Host," 66, 143–145. But he found interracial marriages rare. James Oliver Horton and Lois E. Horton, *Black Bostonians: Family Life and Community Struggle in the Antebellum North* (New York: Holmes and Meier Publishers, 1979), 23. John Daniels, *In Freedom's Birthplace* (New York: Arno Press, 1969), 474. See Hasia R. Diner, *Erin's Daughters in America: Irish Immigrant Women in the Nineteenth Century* (Baltimore: Johns Hopkins University Press, 1983).

45 *Boston Globe* 8/29/95, 6; K. Scott Wong, " 'The Eagle Seeks a Helpless Quarry': Chinatown, the Police, and the Press. The 1903 Boston Chinatown Raid Revisited," *Ameriasia Journal* 22:3 (1996): 81–103; *Boston Guardian* 3/5/04, 1, 8, "Jap Weds Colored Woman."

46 Holloran, *Boston's Wayward Children*, 150–152.

47 Murolo, *Working Girls' Clubs*, 130–133, 136. On Irish Americans in Boston's working-girls clubs, see DH Journals.

48 DH, box 1 vol. 1, p. 53, 11/11/93; and p. 66, 11/28/93.

49 Cole, "Criminal," 167. Holloran, *Boston's Wayward Children*, 155.

50 Bushee, "Population," 46. Shih-Shan Henry Tsai, *The Chinese Experience in America* (Bloomington: Indiana University Press, 1986), 106.

51 Wong, "Chinatown," 88.

52 *Boston Herald* 10/12/03, p. 8; and 10/27/03, p. 8; *Boston Globe* 10/14/03, p. 3; 10/12/03, pp. 1, 8; and 10/16/03, pp. 1, 8 (the *Globe* seemed a good bit more sympathetic to the Chinese than did the *Herald*); cited in Wong, "Chinatown," 89, 95. On opium/women issue, see *Boston Globe* 11/27/03, pp. 1, 8; *Boston Herald* 11/27/03, 12; and 1/27/04, p. 11; and John Kuo Wei Tchen, "Modernizing White Patriarchy: Re-Viewing D. W. Griffith's *Broken Blossoms*," in *Moving the Image: Independent Asian Pacific American Media Arts*, ed. Russell Leong (Los Angeles: UCLA Asian American Studies Center, 1991), 132–143, cited in Wong, "Chinatown."

53 The protest drew Chinese merchants in American dress, and William Lloyd Garrison, Jr., who warned that next might come attacks on blacks or Jews. *Boston Herald* 10/12/03, 8; and 10/27/03; *Boston Globe* 10/14/03, 3; 10/12/03, 1, 8; and 10/16/03; cited in Wong, "Chinatown," 89–95. See also Bushee, *Ethnic Factors*, 99–100, 115, 145; Wong, "Chinatown," 90–92; Holloran, *Boston's Wayward Children*, 220.

54 On the North End, see Schneider, *In the Web of Class*, 84–86, 128–130, 142–143.

55 Cf. Mumford, *Interzones*, xiii, xv, 112–113, on sex districts as modernity and on the increasing sexual stigma applied to black women. Daniels, *In Freedom's Birthplace*, 202. D. Ryan, *Beyond the Ballot Box*, 134–136.

56 Pauline E. Hopkins, *Contending Forces: A Romance Illustrative of Negro Life North and South* (1900; reprint, New York: Oxford University Press, 1988), 110–111.

57 Cf. Elsa Barkley Brown, "Negotiating and Transforming the Public Sphere: African American Political Life in the Transition from Slavery to Freedom," *Public Culture* 7 (1994): 107–146; Iris Marion Young, "Impartiality and the Civic Public: Some Implications of Feminist Critiques of Moral and Political Theory," in *Feminism as Critique: On the Politics of Gender*, ed. Seyla Benhabib and Drucilla Cornell (Minneapolis: University of Minnesota Press, 1987), 77–95.

58 H. L. Higginson Collection, Baker Library, Harvard Business School, Allston, MA, case XII–13, f. 1912 E-F, William C. Ewing, Superintendent, Wells Memorial Institute, 10/18/12, pp. 985–989; Washington Street, 10/18/12; "The Roots of Political Power," in *City Wilderness*,

ed. Woods, 122; Duis, *The Saloon*, 252, 294–295. And Cole, "Law and Order," 192 on North End dance halls and prostitution. See also WEIU, series 2, carton 6 f. 104, "Industrial Committee 1907–8," pp. 9–10; and box 7 f. 51, 1910/11, p. 11, on student housing. In early 1911, the secretary of the Massachusetts Republican Club introduced a petition that later became a bill in the state legislature to prohibit intermarriage between whites and blacks, Indians, or "mulattos." By March, the bill had been killed. *Boston Guardian* 1/28/11, p. 1; and 3/11/11, p. 2.

59 For example, see DH Journals, C. M. Dresser 2/8/93, p. 54. WEIU, box 1 f. 5, "The Hours of Labor in Domestic Service," *MBSL Bulletin* 8 (October 1898), reprinted by MBSL with WEIU data (Boston: Wright and Potter, 1898), 3–4. See WEIU, box 1 f. 9, "Social Statistics of Working Women," 1901, pp. 11–12. Mary Williams Dewson Papers, box 1 f. 3, "The Eight Hour Day and Rest at Night by Statue" (1920), pp. 1–2, Schlesinger Library, Radcliffe College, Cambridge, MA.

60 Other girls interested in church work included Bosworth, carton 4 f. 178, Miss Rider, 10/17/07. Cf. William I. Thomas and Florian Znaniecki, *The Polish Peasant in Europe and America* (Chicago: University of Chicago Press, 1918–20), on which Oscar Handlin based *The Uprooted* (New York: Grosset and Dunlap, 1951), in contrast to John Bodnar's more recent, *The Transplanted: A History of Immigrants in Urban America* (Bloomington: Indiana University Press, 1985), a study emphasizing continuity and cohesion rather than disruption.

61 Conyngton, *Occupation and Criminality*, 95; see also 76–77.

62 Perry, *Millinery Trade*, 103 in 1911; C. Wright, *Working Girls*, 127. Srole, "Feminization of Clerical Work," 283–284. Gamber, "Female Economy," 128. Meyerowitz, *Women Adrift*, 4, citing the U.S. Bureau of the Census, *Statistics of Women at Work* (Washington, DC: Government Printing Office, 1907), 29. Benson, *Counter Cultures*, 240. On the nature of lodgers see Cole, "Criminal," 167; Bushee, "Population," 49–51; Robert A. Woods, "Livelihood," in *Americans in Process*, ed. Woods, 125, 140; Bushee, "The Invading Host," 56–57.

63 Albert Benedict Wolfe, *The Lodging House Problem in Boston* (Boston: Houghton, Mifflin, 1906), 83, 85.

64 Bosworth, carton 4 f. 178, 10/10/07. DH Journals, S. W. Peabody 2/6/93. David M. Katzman, *Seven Days a Week: Women and Domestic Service in Industrializing America* (Urbana: University of Illinois Press, 1978), 212.

65 DH, box 1 f. 3, chronology; vol. 1, 9/30/93, p. 35. DH, box 2 f. 7, 1905/06 Report of the Headworker to the College Settlement Association.

66 Bosworth, carton 4 f. 178, 10/07; interview no. 341, 9/30/07; 10/9/07; 9/17/07. Robert A. Woods, "Social Recovery," in *City Wilderness*, ed. Woods, 277.

67 Judith Becker Ranlett, "Sorority and Community: Women's Answer to a Changing Massachusetts, 1865–1895" (Ph.D. diss., Brandeis University, 1974), 194–196. *Guardian*, Jan. 28, 1911, 5, "No Color Line at Girls Lodging" re: Franklin Square House. On the YWCA see NAACP Papers, Group II L f. 43, December 1918, Annual Report of the Boston Branch, Library of Congress; NAACP Group I G f. 88, 1/27/26, Loud to Pickens; Sharlene Voogd Cochrane, " 'And the Pressure Never Let Up': Black Women, White Women, and the Boston YWCA, 1918–1948," in *Women in the Civil Rights Movement: Trailblazers and Torchbearers, 1941–1965*, ed. Vicki L. Crawford et al. (Brooklyn: Carlson Publishing, 1990), 260; Edith and Grace Abbott Papers, box 32 f. 15, 10/19/34, date of visit to Harriet Tubman House, Special Collections, Regenstein Library, University of Chicago; executive committee minutes, June 8, 1938, NAACP Group I G f. 90.

68 Hopkins, *Contending Forces*, 85, 102, 104, 106.

69 Frank K. Foster, *The Evolution of a Trade Unionist* (n.p., 1901), 1–2, 37, 97–99.

70 Bosworth, carton 1 f. 27, 11/4/07, to her mother.

71 Bosworth, carton 4 f. 178, 10/17/07.

72 In a 1910 manuscript census sample of Minot Street in the West End, only two of the six female lodgers were without relatives in the household where they lodged. Those two both worked with a female who lived where they lodged. Federal Manuscript Census, 1910. Mary E. Richmond and Fred S. Hall, *A Study of Nine Hundred and Eighty-five Widows Known to Certain Charity Organization Societies in 1910* (New York: Russell Sage Foundation, 1913), 29–30. Similarly, Ardis Cameron, *Radicals of the Worst Sort: Laboring Women in Lawrence, Massachusetts, 1860–1912* (Urbana: University of Illinois Press, 1993), 38. Meyerowitz, *Women Adrift*, 188.

73 Meyerowitz, *Women Adrift*, 8. WEIU, B-8, box 7 f. 56, "Clothing," pp. 6–10. The WEIU, box 7 f. 49, "Immigrant Women and Children," pp. 11, 13–14, 21. Bosworth, carton 4 f. 178 and f. 170. Benson, *Counter Cultures*, 208–209.

Unhappiness could stem from too much rather than too little family. See WEIU, box 7 f. 49, "Immigrant Women and Children," p. 11. Bosworth, carton 4 f. 170.

74 Bosworth, carton 4 f. 178. See also Bosworth, carton 1 f. 27, 9/21/07, to her mother, that three of the girls they visited in Jamaica Plain had men in their rooms; and see carton 4 f. 178, Emma Goozey and group, 336 Center Street, Jamaica Plain factory. See also Bosworth, carton 4 f. 178, Marie Doyle (no. 90), 24 Wyman Street, Jamaica Plain, shoe factory worker; Miss O'Connell (no. 95), also a shoe factory worker in Jamaica Plain, 9/19/07. Marvin, "Lodging House Problem," 250.

75 Bosworth, carton 4 f. 178. On working girls' nutrition, see WEIU, series 4 carton 8 f. 133, *Story of New England Kitchen* (October 1890), 13, 15.

76 Benson, *Counter Cultures*, 208. (See also Bosworth, carton 4 f. 170, the stenographers and secretaries tended to have no roommates, and also to have paid vacations.) WEIU, Box 1 f. 5, "Social Statistics of Working Women," p. 10.

77 Mary Jane (McGrath) Sheldon Papers, autobiography, Schlesinger Library, Radcliffe College, Cambridge, MA. Srole, "Feminization of Clerical Work," 496, 502–503, 527 54n.

78 Bosworth, carton 4 f. 178.

79 See Duis, *The Saloon*, 263, 286, on the "bohemian resorts" catering to college-age people and Revere House, a hotel whose bar was nicknamed "Purgatory" and could seat 300 men and women largely seeking sex. And see Meyerowitz, *Women Adrift*, 77, citing Lucile Eaves, *The Food of Working Women in Boston*, vol. 10 of WEIU Studies in Economic Relations of Women (Boston: Wright and Potter, 1917), 168. Bosworth, carton 4 f. 170, case no. 5; case no. 303. Woods, "Work," 104. And see Esther G. Barrows, *Neighbors All: A Settlement Notebook* (Boston: Houghton Mifflin, 1929), 122–123, on women in bars.

80 Bosworth, carton 1 f. 27, 9/29/07, to her mother. On working-girls clubs, see Murolo, *Working Girls' Clubs*. See also, Robert A. Woods, "Social Recovery," in *City Wilderness*, ed. Woods, 262, on the Shawmut Club.

81 Bosworth, carton 4 f. 178, 10/4/07.

82 The food at the YWCA, on the other hand, she found good and ample and, as at the New Waverly, only 25 cents. The room was half full at 6:15. Bosworth, carton 4 f. 178, "YWCA Warrenton Street October 5 #8."

83 Stephen H. Norwood, *Labor's Flaming Youth: Telephone Operators and Worker Militancy, 1878– 1923* (Urbana: University of Illinois Press, 1990), 244–245. Cf. Mary P. Ryan, *Civic Wars: Democracy and Public Life in the American City during the Nineteenth Century* (Berkeley: University of California Press, 1997), 6, locating public life outside the state in the press, cafés, and clubs.

84 Foster, *Trade Unionist*, throughout, particularly, 7–10; 16 on bicycling; 38 on picnic with 300–

400 female and male printers and on crossing the common; 43–44, on swimming at the picnic where Lizzie swims so far out she is in danger of drowning, only to be rescued (unbowed) by Charles Morton whom she will later marry; 23–24 on late night café.

85 Ibid., 144–145.

86 Ibid., 166.

87 Ibid., 164.

88 Ibid., 3.

89 Ibid., 33. WEIU, box 8 f. 62, 1913 investigation of prostitutes. Lane, *Policing the City*, 168–170.

90 Foster, *Trade Unionist*, 104.

91 Example, Frances Donovan, *The Woman Who Waits* (Boston: Richard G. Badger, 1920).

92 Mary Jane (McGrath) Sheldon, "The Little Print Shop that Grew and Grew and Grew," at Schlesinger Library, Radcliffe College, Cambridge, MA.

93 While this level of approved social autonomy—keeping company alone with a man in a confined space—seems to have been limited to working-class women in Boston, William Dean Howells's 1880s divorce novel, *A Modern Instance*, depicted middle-class women behaving similarly in the New England smaller towns, with a few sentences acknowledging the difference between such customs and those in Boston.

94 Bosworth, carton 4, survey 1907/8.

95 On leisure preferences of working women, see WEIU, box 1 f. 9, p. 17. For other Denison House residents' assessments of South End theater see DH Journals, box 1, f. 4, Laura Cate 1/3/93, pp. 50–51; Irene Weir, p. 58; Mason 1/25/93; and Lucinda W. Prince. 1/27/93. On leisure choices, see also Bosworth, carton 4 f. 170.

96 DH Journals, box 1 f. 4 Weir 12/31/93, pp. 57–58.

97 Twentieth Century Club Papers, MHS, J. Walter Reeves, "Report of Certain Vaudeville and Motion Picture Theaters in Boston," 1912. DH, box 1 f. 4, Emily Green Balch, 2/7/93. There were also the "legitimate" theaters, to which organizations such as Denison House created excursions for their working-class neighbors. Some theaters were enormous. The Grand Opera House, Washington Street, sat 3000. Fred E. Haynes, "Amusements," in *City Wilderness*, ed. Woods, 184.

98 Bosworth, carton 1 f. 28, 1/30/08. F. Haynes, "Amusements," 176–180, 189.

99 WEIU, B-8 box 7 f. 51, "Student Housing" 1910/11, pp. 8, 11, and individual school reports. Norwood, *Flaming Youth*, 106–107. According to Sherri Maxine Broder, "Politics of the Family: Political Culture, Moral Reform, and Family Relations in Gilded Age Philadelphia" (Ph.D. diss., Brown University, 1988), 3, 6–7, the Gilded Age working class made sharp distinctions between "respectable" and "rough" behavior.

100 DH, box 1 f. 4, Prince 1/26/93; 1/28/93; 2/1/93.

101 In some respects, they had to invent professions because extant professions such as medicine and law closed their doors to women. DH, box 1, vol. 2, 8/8/94, p. 96, CLS. On female organizations as employers of female professionals, see, for example, DH, box 1 vol. 2, 11/9/94, p. 159, Dr. Culbertson from a dispensary; DH, box 1, vol. 2, 11/14/94, p. 162, Dr. Sarah E. Palmer, corner of Beacon Street and Dartmouth; and 2/1/93, Dr. Mary Hobart at the New England Dispensary with a private office at 320 Marlboro Street; and see Barbara Miller Solomon, *Pioneers in Service: The History of the Associated Jewish Philanthropies of Boston* (Boston: Court Square Press, 1956), 56–57.

102 Bosworth, carton 1 f. 27, 9/18/07 and 9/21/07, to Eleanora Bosworth (her mother). See Sharon Wood, "Wandering Girls and Leading Women: Sexuality and Urban Public Life in Davenport, Iowa 1880–1910" (Ph.D. diss., University of Iowa, 1997), on the moral reasoning of the older generation of women and their claims on the public; see Meyerowitz, *Women Adrift*,

186, for example, on the increasing public discussions and displays of sexuality in popular magazines, newspapers, and entertainments from 1890 to 1930, on which many of the younger women built their careers as investigators, arbiters, or interpreters. Solomon, *Pioneers in Service*, 90–91.

103 Scudder, *A Listener in Babel*, 297, 313–315, 319. See, also Wood "Wandering Girls."

104 DH, box 1 f. 4, Balch 1/6/93.

105 Polly Welts Kaufman, "Foreword," in *An Independent Woman: The Autobiography of Edith Guerrier*, ed. Molly Matson (Amherst: University of Massachusetts Press, 1992). Kane, *Separatism and Subculture: Boston Catholicism, 1900–1920* (Chapel Hill: University of North Carolina Press, 1994), 244.

106 James J. Keneally, *The History of American Catholic Women* (New York: Crossroad Publishing, 1990), 105.

107 Dawn M. Saunders, "Class, Gender, and Generation: Mother's Aid in Massachusetts and the Political Economy of Welfare Reform" (Ph.D. diss., University of Massachusetts at Amherst, 1994), 70.

108 Bosworth, carton 1 f. 27, 9/29/07.

109 Ibid., carton 1 f. 27, 11/4/07. Phelps, *Factory Operatives*, 35, found Boston's rents higher than other U.S. cities.

110 Bosworth, carton 1 f. 27, 11/4/07.

111 Bosworth, carton 4 f. 160.

112 Ibid., carton 1 f. 27, 11/19/07; 12/15/07; and 4/15/08.

113 Kaufman, "Foreword," xvi, quoting Guerrier, 68, 88.

114 On offering sewing as charity work, see von Hoffman, 157; Robert Treat Paine II Papers, MHS, 5/23/81 Frederick Baylies Allen to Paine. DH Journals, box 1 f. 4, Dresser, 89–90.

115 DH, box 1 f. 2, Marie Gullet to Mrs. Davis 1/29/[c. 12]. DH, box 2 f. 7, Report of the Head Worker to the College Settlement Association, 1896/97. Perry, *Millinery Trade*, 123.

116 Bosworth, carton 1 f. 28, 5/29/08, to mother, Cf. *Boston Globe* 8/11/95, 29, cartoon, "A Twentieth Century Summer Resort When the New Woman Can't Get Away From the City." It showed a house, "The Eveless Eden," with only men—men dancing with men to an orchestra composed of three women in bloomers, and on the ground a letter explaining that some woman could not get away, on the letterhead of Jones Sisters, Attorneys at Law.

117 See, for example, Judith Fryer, "What Goes on in the Ladies Room? Sarah Orne Jewett, Annie Fields, and Their Community of Women,"*Massachusetts Review* 30 (winter 1989): 610–628; Lilian Faderman, *Surpassing the Love of Men: Romantic Friendship and Love Between Women from the Renaissance to the Present* (New York: William Morrow, 1981); Judith Schwarz, "Yellow Clover: Katherine Lee Bates and Katherine Coman," *Frontiers* 14 (spring 1979): 59–67; History Project, comp. *Improper Bostonians: Lesbian and Gay History from the Puritans to Playground* (Boston: Beacon Press, 1998), 70–87.

118 Bosworth, carton 1 f. 28, 2/11/08, to mother.

119 Kaufman, "Foreword," xi–xii, xvii.

120 *Boston Globe* 8/5/95, 5, on the Central Labor Union. See 1900 Manuscript Census and Boston Public Library Personnel Questionaire, 7/28/39 (at Boston Public Library) (thanks to Debbie Birnby).

121 Kaufman, "Foreword," xi–xii, xv, xvii, 136 11n.

122 Ibid., xiii–xv.

123 Cf. Isabel Hyams (MIT 1888) and Frances Stern (Garland Kindergarten School) who taught in Mrs. Hecht's Sunday School. She encouraged them to start their own settlement, and their

experiments in domestic science for girls at the Louisa Alcott Club led ultimately to the Boston Dispensary's Food Clinic. Solomon, *Pioneers in Service*, 52.

124 See *Boston Globe* 9/5/94, 4, "Colored National League," which appointed a committee to go to the Boston School Board "and ascertain why young colored women are refused positions in Boston schools."

125 This was in 1892, for the 1895 state census. She held the job for four years. *Colored American Magazine* 2 (January 1901): 215–219. See also Hopkins, *Contending Forces*, 127–128.

126 "Boston's Smart Set," *Colored American Magazine* 2 (January 1901): 204–207. On Hopkins's interest in uplifting the race, see, for example, *Colored American Magazine* 1 (May 1900): 63–64.

127 *Guardian* 12/9/39, "A Warrior" by Mary E. Moore, profile of Cravath Simpson. See also *Guardian* 4/23/32, p. 1; 6/24/39, p. 5; 7/29/39, p. 1; 12/23/39, p. 1; 2/10/40, 5; 1/11/41; p. 4; and *Chronicle* p. 1; 9/3/32 pp. 1, 4. *Guardian* 12/30/11, Cf. NAACP, Maud Cuney Hare, Group II-L Addendum 43, 3/24/15; and Gordon, *"Black and White,"* 568–569.

128 Cf. Murolo, *Working Girls' Clubs*, 75.

Chapter 4

1 Sarah Elbert, introduction to *Work: A Story of Experience*, by Louisa May Alcott (New York: Schocken Books, 1977), xxxvi.

2 Based on samples from the Boston city directories, percent of women's businesses operated out of their homes or (at most two or three) next door—absolute numbers follow in parentheses

1870	1880	1890	1900	1910
78 (115/147)	70 (80/114)	65 (32/49)	60 (45/75)	45 (39/85)

1920	1930	1940
53 (46/87)	29 (35/130)	4 (2/48)

3 On boarding and lodging houses, see Mark Peel, "On the Margins: Lodgers and Boarders in Boston, 1860–1900," *Journal of American History* 72 (March 1986): 818, 820; by 1900 Boston had 2,703 boarding or lodging houses and hotels, and women headed 53% of the boarding and lodging proprietor households, up from 35% in 1860.

Percentages of shop owners who are definitely women, by various business sectors

	1870	1880	1890	1900	1910	1920
Bakers	4.1	4.5		15.8	13.8	13.1
Confectioners	5.2	14.0	9.9	9.8	5.6	
Secondhand clothes		33.0				
Dry goods	13.2	15.4	18.3	25.3		
Employment office				45.9		
Fancy goods	18.7	27.3		37.0		
Grocers[a]	13.9	21.0	10.7	18.9	19.5	19.7
Liquor[b]			0.8	0.3		
Restaurants	21.1	8.5[c]	8.2[d]	10.0[e]	10.9[f]	
Variety[g]	33.3		44.6	50.0	47.3	26.6

[a]Based on a sample of 222 in 1870, 200 in 1880, 550 in 1890, 450 in 1900, 435 in 1910, and 564 in 1920; a larger sample of approximately 1,080 names in 1910 yielded 21.7% women.
[b]Based on a sample of 600 each in 1890 and 1900.
[c]Based on a sample of 246 names.
[d]Based on a sample of 450 names.
[e]Based on a sample of 500 names in 1900.
[f]Based on a sample of 750 names in 1910.
[g]Represents total number of variety stores: 36 in 1870, 370 in 1900, 455 in 1910, 531 in 1920.

One recent, careful historian calculated roughly 1.7 self-employed women per 1,000 Bostonians in 1880. She admitted the number is an underestimate. Women petty entrepreneurs are more elusive for historians than they were for their contemporaries. Census takers did not indicate whether women were self-employed, and city directories did not always list first names or endow initials with an honorific "Mrs." or "Miss." Nor could it be assumed that initials absent a "Mrs." or "Miss" represented men. For example, in 1880, of forty-three variety-store owners listed only by initials in the directory's business section, the residential section revealed seven to be women. Many petty entrepreneurs—kitchen barroom keepers, for example, but also informal boardinghouse keepers—were not listed at all. Wendy Gamber, "A Precarious Independence: Milliners and Dressmakers in Boston, 1860–1890," *Journal of Women's History* 4: 1 (spring 1992): 60–88, 64, for the estimate. The figures on initials and sex are from tracing in the *Boston City Directory*, 1880. Cf. Lucy Eldersveld Murphy, "Her Own Boss: Businesswomen and Separate Spheres in the Midwest, 1850–1880,"*Illinois Historical Journal* 80 (autumn 1987): 157, 159. Although in Boston, according to the census, businesswomen comprised only about 4% of the female labor force in 1910 (Elizabeth Lunbeck, *The Psychiatric Persuasion: Knowledge, Gender, and Power in Modern America* [Princeton: Princeton University Press, 1994], 316), in Illinois in 1870 they comprised 11.25% of working women over the age of nine. See also Wendy Gamber, *The Female Economy: The Millinery and Dressmaking Trades, 1860–1930* (Urbana: University of Illinois Press, 1997).

4 Gamber, "Precarious Independence" 65; *Boston City Directories*, 1870–1940; for maternity ("lying-in") hospitals, see *Reports of Proceedings of the City Council of Boston for the Year Commencing January 4, 1897, and ending January 1, 1898* (Boston: Municipal Printing Office, 1898), 3, 55–56. As late as 1910/11, the *Reports of Proceedings of the City Council of Boston for the Year Commencing 2/7/10 and Ending 2/4/11* (Boston: City of Boston Printing Department, 1911) included two petitions for lying-in hospitals, one female (approved) in East Boston and one male.

5 WEIU Papers, box 7 f. 48, "Immigration as a Source of Supply" (1905) for domestic workers, p. 15; box 1 f. 5, "Trained and Supplementary Workers" in domestic service, p. 11. See also WEIU, box 7 f. 48, chart on domestic servants in hotels, including a seventeen-year-old chambermaid and a pantry maid who both wanted to learn cooking. John Daniels, *In Freedom's Birthplace* (1914; reprint, New York: Arno Press, 1969), 338.

6 Susan Porter Benson, *Counter Cultures: Saleswomen, Managers, and Customers in American Department Stores, 1890–1910* (Urbana: University of Illinois Press, 1986), 24–25.

7 R. G. Dun records have many examples of shops launched by former workers at R. H. Stearns and Company, such as Miss M. F. Fisk, a glove shop 12 Temple Place, launched in 1884, having spent the past eleven years working for Stearns in charge of their glove department. She had inherited and saved between three and four thousand dollars (5/9/48, 7/21/84 entries); similarly, Mrs. Mary E. Paige, stamping and embroidery business, previously with Jordan Marsh

and Company (8/21/84), Mass. Vol. 89, p. 119 and Mass. Vol. 90, p. 327, R. G. Dun and Co. Collection, Baker Library, Harvard University Graduate School of Business Administration.

8 WEIU, series I carton I, *Annual Report* 1903/04, pp. 33–34.

9 Lorinda Perry, *The Millinery Trade in Boston and Philadelphia: A Study of Women in Industry* (Binghamton, NY: Vail-Ballou, 1916), 106–107. WEIU, series carton I, *Annual Report* 1891/92, p. 40–41. WEIU, *Annual Report* 1890/91, pp. 33, 36. DH Journals, Laura Cate 1/6/93, p. 134, and 1/13/93, p. 86.

10 DH Journals, Box I f. 3, Helen Cheever, Nov. and Dec. 1892, p. 12. Similarly, Carole Srole, " 'A Position That God Has Not Particularly Assigned to Men': The Feminization of Clerical Work, Boston 1860–1915" (Ph.D. diss., University of California, Los Angeles, 1984), 332.

11 WEIU, Box I f. I *Annual Report* 1890/91, p. 36.

12 Gamber, *The Female Economy*, 5.

13 Gamber, "Precarious Independence," 67–68, on dressmakers; Perry, *Millinery Trade* 113–114 on milliners. Mass., Vol. 80, p. 359, R. G. Dun & Co. Collection on wife loaning to husband, Mrs. Harriet S. Hatch, 11/2/85; on husband's support, Mass. vol. 86, p. 60, Mrs. C. W. Randall's millinery business on Washington Street. Randall had worked for a milliner in Worcester, Massachusetts, before her marriage. Her husband worked for the piano company, Chickering and Sons, manufacturing strings for $1,500–1,600 a year; 8/23/83, 7/10/86. Similarly, Mrs. Kate A. Chelins, Mass. vol. 86. p. 83, enjoyed the support of her husband, head twiner for Emerson Piano Company at $1,200 per year, in her millinery business, 9/28/78, though she was not as successful as Mrs. Randall, and Mrs. J. and Mrs. M. Parmelee, Mass. vol. 81, p. 64, sisters-in-law, launched their business with the support of their hack-driver husbands (7/26/83, 1/15/85, 1/22/85, 7/10/86). On friends lending, see, for example, in Mass. vol. 88, p. 103 Misses A. and M. Coleman, infants clothing (9/13/83, 7/21/84, 7/25/85). For other family backing, see Mass. vol. 89, p. 148, Miss L. D. Walker, a milliner at 20 Temple Place, whose brothers and sisters could assist her (3/8/83).

14 DH Journals, box I f. 5, Laura Cate 1/21/93, p. 164.

15 Gamber, "Precarious Independence," 73–74.

16 Gamber, "Precarious Independence," 67, 73. See Chapter 2, above, on Mrs. Brest. R. G. Dun & Co. records are also full of examples. For instance, Mass. vol. 80, pp. 317, 344, Mrs. H. B. Chapman, succeeding her husband in a fancy dry goods shop in 1878 (8/1/78), having formerly assisted him in the store. Occasionally the tables were turned, as when Madame F. Linz's husband, Louis Long, who helped her in her embroideries and laces business, carried on the business after her death (7/22/78, 1/10/79, 6/23/81). Other women opened businesses on becoming widows, using their husbands' insurance policies as seed money, for instance Mrs. H. H. Diver's liquor store, Mass. vol. 86, p. 42, R. G. Dun & Co. Collection. Her husband was a teamster who left her a few thousand dollars in life insurance and about two thousand dollars in real estate (4/6/83). On the lack of capital among immigrant dressmakers, see Elizabeth Ewen, *Immigrant Women in the Land of Dollars: Life and Culture on the Lower East Side 1890–1925* (New York: Monthly Review Press, 1985), 244–245; and WEIU, box 7 f. 49.

17 See table above (note 2) on location of shops. There were, however, differences in the trades. Judging by the city directories, milliners were far more likely to have a separate business address than dressmakers were, probably partly because of their need to keep stock. Gamber, "Precarious Independence," 63–64, 70, on millinery and dressmaking; city directories on the switch to beauty shops. There were still about 900 dressmakers listed in 1920, but only 470 listed in 1930 and 430 in 1940. In 1930 there were about 620 beauty shops listed, and 700 in 1940.

18 *City Directory*, 1920, p. 1909; 1910, p. 2139 listed twenty-one interior decorators, again all male.

19 Baldwin's father was a grocer according to Amelia Muir Baldwin Papers, A-131, box 1 f. 6, Schlesinger Library, Radcliffe College, Cambridge, MA. On her uncle, see box 1 f. 3, 12/30/76, William H. Baldwin to Baldwin's parents, Loammi and Louise. In 1941 (Dec. 2), Robert Baldwin, vice president of the Second National Bank of Boston, addresses her as "Cousin Amelia," and she calls him "Robert," but he seems to have had no earlier part in her enterprise.

20 I'm assuming the undated letters in Baldwin, box 1 f. 8, are from high school, from which Baldwin graduated in 1894.

21 Baldwin, box 2 f. 30, job correspondence 1934/35, 5/14/35 to Dr. Codman: nine years oriental rug shop, Arthur Williams keeping books and writing letters; seven years private secretary, Arthur N. Milliken with short hours so she could take an English class at Radcliffe.

22 According to the biographical note in box 1, Baldwin worked as a saleswoman at A. H. Davenport from 1913 to 1915, where she learned interior decorating and took courses in decorative arts from Huger Elliot at the Massachusetts Fine Arts Museum. Suffrage bazaars are in box 2 f. 21 and oversize; Baldwin also did other nonsuffrage bazaars.

23 WEIU, box 11 f. 128, interior decorating, Martin, 1909–1910.

24 WEIU, box 11 f. 128, interior decorating, Martin, 1909–1910. Cf. Bertha Mahoney (1882–1969), who launched her children's bookstore in 1916 with the support of her connections at the WEIU, where she had worked after graduating from Simmons College in 1903. See entry in Edward T. James et al., eds., *Notable American Women 1607–1950: A Biographical Dictionary*, vol. 2 (Cambridge: Harvard University Press, 1971), 474–476 (thanks to Pamela Phillips), and on Alice Freeman Palmer, vol. 3, 4–8.

25 Baldwin, box 1 f. 6, clipping.

26 Baldwin, box 2 f. 28, Women's City Club, NY—recreation committee.

27 Baldwin, box 2 f. 29, to Magnus Alexander, 5/24/19; nominal salary of $30/week.

28 Baldwin, box 1 f. 15, articles on art and decoration 1916–1927.

29 Baldwin, "The Influence of the Empire Style," *Architectural Forum* (October 1923) in Baldwin, box 1 f. 15.

30 Baldwin, box 2 f. 29, National Industrial Conference Board, statistics department 1919, for example, 8/18/19 memo to Alexander; and 7/14/20, Louise Keller to Baldwin.

31 See Baldwin, box 1, f. 17, articles on housing.

32 Baldwin, box 1, f. 25, Phil A. Foster to Baldwin, 1/13/19.

33 Baldwin, box 1 f. 25, to Foster, 6/22/20.

34 Baldwin, box 1 f. 9, Bourne to Miss Rebecca R. Joslin, 7/6/22, Baldwin says she has spent $2,886.42 on the house of which $541.50, they claimed, the landlord would usually have covered. Joslin credits her with $70; in 1920/21 Baldwin writes she is willing to put up $1,500 of her own money for the renovations, expecting to stay at least ten years, and insisting that people in "our district" demand fireplaces, plumbing, etc.

35 See Joni Seager, " 'Father's Chair': Domestic Reform and Housing Change in the Progressive Era" (Ph.D. diss., Geography, Clark University, 1988); Sarah Elbert's introduction to *Work* by Louisa May Alcott and Virginia Woolf, *A Room of One's Own*.

36 WEIU, B-8, box 11 f. 128, interior decorating, Martin, 1909/10, on the difference between studios and workshops and fitting out the studio to be beautiful.

37 WEIU, B-8, box 11 f. 128, field work, interior decorating, Lucy O'Meara, T. F. Welch and Company, interviews 2/11/22.

38 WEIU, B-8, box 11 f. 128, field work, interior decorating, Lucy O'Meara, T. F. Welch and Company, interviews 2/11/22.

39 Baldwin, box 1 f. 3, monthly budget for 1883.

40 Baldwin, box 1 f. 9, 12/17/21, to Frank Bourne.

41 Baldwin, box 1 f. 9, 12/10/20, 1/4/21, 8/13/21, 8/31/21, to Bourne on the various alterations she suggests; 12/17/21, on her bankruptcy; his to her, 2/5/23, disputing her interpretation of what is owing him; 2/7/23, hers to him in same vein; and hers to him, 2/10/23, using "courteous."

42 Baldwin, box 1 f. 11, 7/10/21.

43 Baldwin, box 1 f. 11, to Billy (lawyer William P. Everts), 9/6/21.

44 Baldwin, box 1 f. 11, 9/6/21.

45 Baldwin, box 1 f. 11, Joslin to Baldwin, 10/20/22.

46 Baldwin, box 1 f. 11, to Joslin, 11/2/22; and 11/4/22.

47 Baldwin, box 1 f. 11, 5/17/33, Joslin to Baldwin.

48 Baldwin, box 1 f. 11, to Joslin, 6/12/33, and 3/29/34.

49 Baldwin, box 3 f. 39.

50 Baldwin, box 3 f. 38, correspondence and bills: bankruptcy 1921–23.

51 Baldwin, box 4 f. 56, Boston Society for Decorative Art, 1902, 1920–21. Baldwin wrote that she "came for the express purpose of smartening up the shop" and had not understood that she had the responsibility of saving the society on $5,000. Baldwin had already proven too expensive for Bigelow Kennard and Company, gold and silver smiths who hired her for a brief stint in 1916, see the biographical note in box 1 and box 2 f. 23 on her relations with this company. On 12/9/15 she wrote to Mr. Bigelow apologizing "not to be able to summarize the items in the order books, so as to render a business-like account of the work." Bigelow decided, similarly to the Society for Decorative Art, to terminate the experiment, and dispose of the interior decorating department.

52 Baldwin, box 3 f. 38, 3/19/32, to Moulton.

53 Baldwin, box 3 f. 39, to Moulton, 5/16/34.

54 Baldwin, box 1 f. 11, to Joslin, 3/29/34.

55 For example, WEIU, *Annual Report*, 1879/80, pp. 34–40, Protective Department, Kate Gannett Wells. See particularly p. 38. WEIU, *Annual Report*, 1881/82, Protective Department, p. 48.

56 Baldwin, box 3 f. 39, correspondence—legal re: bankruptcies, mortgage, 1922–35.

57 Cf. women on welfare's description of the state as "the man." Johnnie Tillmon in *America's Working Women: A Documentary History 1600 to the Present*, ed. Rosalyn Baxandall et al. (New York: Vintage Books, 1976), 355–358.

58 Baldwin, box 3 f. 39, 3/12/30, Walker to Baldwin.

59 Baldwin, box 3 f. 39, 5/16/34, to Moulton.

60 Baldwin, box 2 f. 30, 12/30/41, to Mrs. Edward E. Wise, WPA Regional Office, Park Square Building, Boston.

61 Baldwin, box 3 f. 40.

62 Eviction from Elizabeth Peabody House is in Baldwin, box 3 f. 32, 4/29/54, Thomas B. Gannett to Baldwin.

63 Mortgage information in Baldwin, box 3 f. 39; box 1 f. 11, 5/25/21, to Joslin referring her to Mr. March G. Bennett and William P. Everts, Esq., as having known her for many years. Everts was her legal adviser.

64 LaRue and Dorothy Kircheway Brown (but largely the latter) created these positions for her at the Friends of Framingham. See the biographical note in Baldwin, box 1.

65 Gamber, *The Female Economy*. See, for example, William Dean Howells's *A Woman's Reason* (1883).

66 Gamber, *The Female Economy*.

67 Cf. Murphy, "Her Own Boss," 155–176, especially 157.

68 Mamie Garvin Fields with Karen Fields, *Lemon Swamp and Other Places: A Carolina Memoir* (New York:

Free Press, 1983), 150–151. Partnerships were not unusual, particularly in the needle trades. The city directories are full of jointly named businesses, almost always indicating women partners. Gamber, "Precarious," 65.

69 See, for example, Mrs. Robert H. S. Kelly, grocer, Mass, vol. 77, p. 182, R. G. Dun & Co. Collection who took over her husband's business in 1865 when he died, and though she remarried (an expressman) in 1867, continued to run the business (6/24/64, 1/28/65, 6/8/67). This pattern held for African- as well as European-American women. For example, when businessman P. E. Richardson died in 1924, his two sisters, Misses Margaret and Ida Richardson, took over the store. *Guardian* (at Boston University) 4/7/34, 1. For other examples, of 61 women running dry goods stores listed in the City Directory in 1900, 27 bore the honorific "Mrs." and 5 "Miss"; in 1890 of 33 women, 14 were "Mrs." and 7 "Miss." Of a sample of grocers in 1900, 85 were women, 39 "Mrs." and one shop was owned by a partnership of "Misses." Residential listings from 1890 to 1910 proved most of the "Mrs." to be widows. Those not listed as widows, often lived with male family members, probably sons, who were listed often as clerks. There were exceptions, among blacks as well as whites. While most black women ran millinery, dressmaking, or beauty shops, the *Colored American Magazine* 1 (May 1900); 64, celebrated the first black woman undertaker in New England, a woman who had graduated from a school of embalming. And there were several family partnerships by the late 1930s/early 1940s, for example, Clarence H. Adams ran a funeral home, and Theresa L. Adams served as its director (*Guardian* 3/18/39, 1). Sometimes couples ran complementary businesses, as when Ralph J. Banks ran his real estate business from the same address as Alice C. Banks ran her insurance business. (*Guardian* 11/21/42, 3.) Cf. Gamber, "Precarious," 66.

U.S. Census Office, *Eleventh Census*, 1890, vol. 1, part 2, *Population* (Washington, DC: Government Printing Office, 1897), 638–639. In 1870 (U.S. Census Office, *Ninth Census, 1870*, vol. 1, *Population of the United States and Social Statistics* [Washington, DC: Government Printing Office, 1872], 778), of the 5.2% of "merchants" (excluding boarding and lodging house keepers and women in the needle trades) who were women in 1890, 76.5% were single (35.6% of the whole never-married, widowed, or divorced) and 58.1% were foreign-born, by far the largest part being Irish, who accounted for 33.3% of all merchant women that year. In addition, hotel and boardinghouse keepers included 1,360 women, 44.1% of whom were foreign born, with an additional 21% having foreign parents. Only 28.5% of them were married. Another 19.9% had never been married, and 48.8% were widowed. By contrast, the women in the needle trades in 1890 were about two-thirds native born and more than two-thirds never married.

70 From 1890 to 1900, in a sample of about 550 grocers, of 6 shops that survived which had ever been in women's hands, 1 shifted from male to female ownership within the same family, and 1 from female to male. Among confectionary dealers, the 1 shop owned by a woman (Margaret Murphy) to survive to 1900 was by then run by T. I. Murphy. Among a sample of 180 bakers, 59 survived from 1910 to 1920, including 2 that shifted from male to female ownership and 1 from female to male. Among a sample of about 297 grocers in 1880, 93 survived into 1890 including 3 that switched from male to female, and 1 from female to male. Other widows kept shops going for a surprising length of time. Among the seven variety stores to survive from 1890 to 1910, three had changed hands from husband to wife by 1900, including A. Toole to Mrs. A. Toole, Joseph Sanders to Mrs. Annie Sanders, and H. F. Taylor to Mrs. Clara H. Taylor.

Among both black and white women there were exceptions, women who had successful businesses and brought them to their marriages (see 13, 16, and 69 above) and, for example, Mary Church Terrell's mother in Stephanie J. Shaw, *What a Woman Ought To Be and To Do: Black Professional Women Workers During the Jim Crow Era* (Chicago: University of Chicago Press, 1996), 39.

Advertisements by women in the *Guardian* for 10/11/02, 6, and 1/10/03 show three hairdressers or hairworkers, two dressmakers, one milliner, two music teachers, and an experienced nurse. Three of the nine were "Miss," five "Mrs.," and one without honorific.

71 Gamber, "Precarious Independence," 73, 80.

72 Ibid., 74–76, and see 64, quoting *The Milliner* (1913).

73 See, for example, *Guardian*, 4/1/39, 8; 12/16/39; and 12/4/40, 1, on the Boston Trade Association, and "A Debut or a Fight," below for more on black tradeswomen's affiliations. Black business women in Boston seem to have been more likely than white women to join trade associations, though my evidence is hardly conclusive. As early as 1903 (*Guardian* 6/20/03, 5, "Women's 20th Century Business Club), they had joined in a cross-trades business association.

74 Mass. vol. 77, p. 166, R. G. Dun & Co. Collection.

75 Gamber, "Precarious Independence," 70, 76.

76 The figures for bakers' and milliners' survivals are based on my own tracing of samples in city directories for 1910, 1911, and 1912. The directories are, however, notoriously inaccurate, and a few of the businesses gone in 1912 crop up again in 1920.

Decadal survival rates for total (men and women) and for women in various business sectors, using city directories for Boston—in percentages of those from the first year appearing in the second

	1890–1900	1900–1910	1910–1920	1930–40
Bakers				
Confectioners	27.2/12.5[a]	7.4/0		
Secondhand clothes				
Dry goods	32.8/36.4			
Grocers[b]	20.9/10.2	26.7/9.4		30.8/20[c]
Interior decorators				28.2/33.3
Milliners			25.6	
Restaurants		19.4/7.7[d]		
Variety	14.6/19.0	19.2/17.3	15.4/14.0	21.8/18.6[e]

[a] Sample of 81 dealers in 1890, 8 of whom were women.

[b] Based on a sample of 450 names in 1890 of which 85 were women and on a sample of 435 names in 1900, of which 85 were women.

[c] Based on a sample of 130 in 1930. In a sample of only women, 15/44 in 1940 had been there since 1930.

[d] Based on a sample of 160 names in 1900.

[e] Based on a sample of 294 names in 1930; six variety store owners in 1940 had survived since 1920, including 2 women.

The closer similarities between total and female dry goods and variety stores could be partially explained by the lack of large-scale shops in either sector, so that *small* business women and *small* business men were relatively comparable in their success rates, but that is only one possible explanation.

77 For example, Mass. vol. 77, p. 158, R. G. Dun & Co. Collection, Miss A. Jennie W. Meehan and Miss Lillie A. Brown of Meehan Brown & Co., small wares.

78 Gamber, *The Female Economy*, 47–48; Mass. vol. 77, p. 8, R. G. Dun & Co. Collection.

79 An 1855 Massachusetts law granted married women the right to engage in business independent

of their husbands, and to control completely their own earnings. Gamber, "Precarious Independence," 79.

80 For 1900, Srole, "Feminization of Clerical Work," 261–263 found women immigrants comprised 45.8% of proprietors, and Peel, "Margins," 820 found that 46% of boarding and lodging households had foreign-born heads.

81 Gamber, "Precarious Independence," 68.

82 Cf. Robert A. Slayton, *Back of the Yards: The Making of a Local Democracy* (Chicago: University of Chicago Press, 1980), 77–79.

83 Cf. Micaela di Leonardo, *The Varieties of Ethnic Experience: Kinship, Class, and Gender among California Italian-Americans* (Ithaca: Cornell University Press, 1984), 136, 140.

84 See Chap. 7 below.

85 Much of the story for African American women matches that of white women, including the importance of neighborhood networks in maintaining shops, the variety of entrepreneurial activities including music teaching, and the social origins of female entrepreneurs. At the same time, as "businesswomen" among whites came to mean clerical workers or managers, a Housewives' League formed around housing issues had as officers the same businesswomen who, with men, ran the Board of Trade. See the *Guardian* (which Maude Trotter Stewart edited when her brother, William Munroe Trotter, died) and the *Chronicle*, two black Boston papers, as well as the records of the NAACP and the Urban League in the Library of Congress.

86 For example, Mrs. Geneva L. Smith, a restaurant owner, founded the Haywood Social Club. See her obituary, *Guardian*, 4/25/42, 4. See also Adelaide M. Cromwell, *The Other Brahmins: Boston's Black Upper Class 1750–1950* (Fayetteville: University of Arkansas Press, 1994), 53, on Phoebe Whitehurst Glover. And *Guardian*, 5/25/50, 1, "Hair Style Show Huge Success," with a picture of Mrs. William "Easter" Moore, described as a "charming social leader," wife of a prominent Boston clubman.

87 *Guardian* (BU) 7/3/34, 8, City News.

88 Baldwin, box 2 f. 26, "Report," p. 1.

89 Gamber on women's rights, *The Female Economy*, 138–139.

90 *Boston City Directories*, 1900 and 1910. Of the ninety-one bakers in 1910 who had survived since 1900, twenty-four had moved in the interim, including three of the ten women.

Chapter 5

1 An earlier version of this chapter appeared as "Learning to Talk More Like a Man: Boston Women's Class-Bridging Organizations, 1870–1940," *American Historical Review* 97 (April 1992): 379–404. Louise Marion Bosworth Papers, carton 1 f. 29, 7/5/08, Bosworth to her mother, Schlesinger Library, Radcliffe College, Cambridge, MA.

2 For example, Karen J. Blair, *The Clubwoman as Feminist: True Womanhood Redefined, 1868–1914* (New York: Holmes and Meier, 1980); Paula Giddings, *When and Where I Enter: The Impact of Black Women on Race and Sex in America* (New York: Bantam Books, 1985).

3 Paul Kleppner, "From Party to Factions: The Dissolution of Boston's Majority Party, 1876–1908," 111–132, and Constance K. Burns, "The Irony of Progressive Reform: Boston 1898–1910," 133–164, in *Boston*, ed. Formisano and Burns; Michael P. Conzen and George K. Lewis, *Boston: A Geographical Portrait* (Cambridge: Ballinger Publishing, 1976), 12–13, 31; Richard M. Abrams, *Conservatism in a Progressive Era: Massachusetts Politics, 1900–1912* (Cambridge: Harvard University Press, 1964); Robert A. Silverman, "Nathan Matthews: Politics of Reform in Boston, 1890–1910," *New England Quarterly* 50 (December 1977): 626–643.

4 Barbara J. Berg, *The Remembered Gate: Origins of American Feminism: The Women and the City, 1800–1860* (New York: Oxford University Press, 1978); Nancy Cott, *The Bonds of Womanhood: 'Woman's Sphere'*

in New England, 1780–1835 (New Haven: Yale University Press, 1977); Nancy A. Hewitt, *Women's Activism and Social Change: Rochester, New York, 1822–1872* (Ithaca: Cornell University Press, 1984).

5 For example, Paula Baker, "The Domestication of Politics: Women and American Political Society, 1780–1920," *American Historical Review* 88 (June 1984): 620–647; Linda Gordon, *Heroes of Their Own Lives: The Politics and History of Family Violence* (New York: Viking, 1988); the special issue of the *American Historical Review* 95 (October 1990), particularly Maureen A. Flanagan, "Gender and Urban Political Reform: The City Club and the Woman's City Club of Chicago in the Progressive Era," 1032–1050, and Seth Koven and Sonya Michel, "Womanly Duties: Maternalist Politics and the Origins of Welfare States in France, Germany, Great Britain, and the United States, 1880–1920," 1076–1108; Eileen Boris, "The Power of Motherhood: Black and White Activist Women Redefine the 'Political,' " *Yale Journal of Law and Feminism* 2 (1989): 25–49; Peggy Pascoe, *Relations of Rescue: The Search for Female Moral Authority in the American West, 1874–1939* (New York: Oxford University Press, 1990); Robyn Muncy, *Creating a Female Dominion in American Reform, 1890–1935* (New York: Oxford University Press, 1991); Kathleen D. McCarthy, ed., *Lady Bountiful Revisited: Women, Philanthropy, and Power* (New Brunswick, NJ: Rutgers University Press, 1990); and Linda Gordon, ed., *Women, the State and Welfare* (Madison: University of Wisconsin Press, 1990).

6 See, for example, Baker, "Domestication," and Muncy, *Creating a Female Dominion*. Muncy offers a powerful and essential explanation of how reform ideology was sustained in a conservative era, and an excellent account of the institutionalization of women's reform impulse and the networks that made it effective, but I believe she overstates the degree to which women controlled the socialization of social workers and the female ability to create anything in the public sector unmodified (and not simply limited) by other sources of power.

7 For example, Pascoe's nuanced and sensitive analysis, *Relations of Rescue*, 191.

8 Cf. Koven and Michel, "Womanly Duties" 1080, 1107. I am grateful to Eileen Boris for suggesting the term "class-bridging" to me. I have used "class-bridging" rather than "cross-class" to acknowledge the middle-class dominance of all these organizations. Hewitt, in *Women's Activism*, has convincingly argued that differences in strategies among middle-class women's antebellum organizations (ultraist, reform, and benevolent) stemmed from their socioeconomic backgrounds—as old, secure elite; newly and precariously wealthy; or in decline. My focus is rather on differences in groups' relation to the city's structure.

9 Fragment Society Papers (hereafter FS), Annual Report, 1896, pp. 4–5 Schlesinger Library, Radcliffe, Cambridge, MA.

10 Cf. Nancy Schrom Dye, "Creating a Feminist Alliance: Sisterhood and Class Conflict in the New York Women's Trade Union League, 1903–1914," 225–246, and Robin Miller Jacoby, "The Women's Trade Union League and American Feminism," 203–224, in *Class, Sex, and the Woman Worker*, ed. Milton Cantor and Bruce Laurie (Westport, CT: Greenwood Press, 1971); Elizabeth Payne, *Reform, Labor, and Feminism: Margaret Dreier Robins and the Women's Trade Union League* (Urbana: University of Illinois Press, 1988). Nancy A. Hewitt, "Beyond the Search for Sisterhood: American Women's History in the 1980s," in *Unequal Sisters: A Multicultural Reader in United States Women's History*, ed. Ellen Carol DuBois and Vicki L. Ruiz (New York: Routledge, 1990), 1–14.

11 Mrs. George Warren, Mrs. Thomas Mack, and Mrs. George H. Norman were all active in both organizations in the late nineteenth century. FS, box 1 f. 2, for FS memberships and WEIU, series 4 Carton 8 f. 124, "Officers of the WEIU 1898–99"; and f. 12, vol. 3, "Subscription Members from the Beginning of the Union," May 1877, and Annual Reports of the WEIU 1880s–1890s. Mary Morton Kehew, president of the WEIU, also served as treasurer of Denison House in the late 1890s. DH Papers, box 1, vol. 5 1892–1899, minutes of the executive

committee, 11/3/97 pp. 243–244, 2/9/98 p. 253, 2/23/98 p. 254, Schlesinger Library, Radcliffe College, Cambridge, MA.

12 I am grateful to Anne Firor Scott, who first brought this society to my attention. FS, box 1 f. 1, Marjorie Drake Ross, "A Brief History of the Fragment Society 1812–1962," pp. 1–3; Annual Report 1901, p. 3, Monks. See also Anne Firor Scott, *Natural Allies: Women's Associations in American History* (Urbana: University of Illinois Press, 1993), particularly 25–36.

13 On familial language, see FS, Box 3 f. 14, 12/9/35 minutes, also 4/12/38; box 1 f. 1, Ross, "A Brief History," pp. 4, 7; and Box 1, 1916 Souvenir Yearbook, pp. 24–25, 31, which points out that the list of officers since founding was short. The membership was more or less consistently 130–150 throughout the period. Also, on the same lines, FS, Box 1, Yearbook 1923, f. 4; Box 1, Yearbook 1925, p. 4, "generation after generation following one another mean much in these changing times." On this matter of stability in a rocky world, see also FS, box 3, vol. 13, 10/13/73 and 10/16/81 minutes. And FS, Box 1, Yearbook 1934/35, p. 4, two new members of the board had had mothers on the board of managers for many years. On the other hand, it may be significant that kinship rhetoric increases in the twentieth-century records of the organization.

14 FS, Box 1, Annual Report 1870, H. L. Brown, secretary, 5. And FS, box 2, 1883/84 minutes; Box 1 Yearbook 1941, p. 13; and Ross, "A Brief History," p. 6. Cf. Blair, *Clubwoman*.

15 In that year they gave away 924 garments, 547 pairs of boots, and 45 baby suits, a figure not much changed before or after, for the most part, FS, Box 1 10/9/65. Yearbook 1905, p. 3; and box 3, vol. 13, minutes.

16 FS, Box 1, Yearbook 1916, and similarly, 1936/37, 1939, 1941, 1945, 1949, all in box 1 f. 5. FS, box 4 f. 19, indicates that even in 1971 the FS meeting included a prayer and Bible reading.

17 On scientific methods during the Civil War see Lori D. Ginzberg, *Women and the Work of Benevolence: Morality Politics and Class in the Nineteenth Century United States* (New Haven: Yale University Press, 1980), 133–173. See James T. Fields Papers, Addenda, box 5, draft speeches on charity, Huntington Library, San Marino, CA. Also Robert Treat Paine II Papers, Annie Fields to Paine, 3/28/84, MHS. And Nathan Irvin Huggins, *Protestants, Against Poverty: Boston's Authorities, 1820–1900* (Westport, CT: Greenwood Publishing Co., 1971) 61–62, 173–174.

18 FS box 3, vol. 13, Annual Reports 1870/71, 1877/78, 1885/86.

19 Huggins, *Protestants*, 65–66, 118. See also Paul Boyer, *Urban Masses and Moral Order in America, 1820–1920* (Cambridge: Harvard University Press, 1978), 279; Roy Lubove, *The Professional Altruist: The Emergence of Social Work as a Career, 1880–1930* (Cambridge: Harvard University Press, 1965), 11–49; Thomas L. Haskell, *The Emergence of Professional Social Science: The American Social Science Association and the Nineteenth-Century Crisis of Authority* (Urbana: University of Illinois Press, 1977), 86–87; Ginzberg, *Women*; Ruth Bordin, *Women and Temperance: The Quest for Power and Liberty, 1873–1900* (Philadelphia: Temple University Press, 1981). Cf. Vida D. Scudder, *A Listener in Babel: Being a Series of Imaginary Conversations Held at the Close of the Last Century* (Boston: Houghton, Mifflin, 1903); Boyer, *Urban Masses*, 155–159.

20 FS, Box 1, Annual Report 1870, p. 4; and Yearbook, 1939, annual meeting, p. 6. In the 1880s there was a brief scientific tendency and a shift in language from brotherhood to trying to "make them help themselves" instead of helping the poor to do so, see FS, Annual Report for 1882, p. 7, and 1887, p. 5; an apparent pride in FS "efficiency" in Annual Report for 1880/81 and the minutes of the 10/9/76 and 10/16/81 meetings (recorded by van Brunt), box 3, vol. 13. But the dominant line is the one described in the text, see FS, Annual report 1885/86, box 3; box 3, vol. 13, annual meeting 2, 1879 annual meeting, minutes; and box 2, minutes 1870/71 (heavenly quality in misdeed), and comment on increased suspicion as in-

creased foreign component among those helped. On personal nature of FS service, see Yearbooks 1909, 1923, 1925, 1934/35.

21 FS, Box 1, Annual Report 1870, p. 5; Annual Report 1893, p. 4; and box 2 f. 14, minutes 1926–1938, Feb. 1927: Mrs. Turner took over the protégé of Mrs. Lincoln, the mother of whom was the grandchild of the original protégé.

22 FS, Box 1, Yearbook, 1941, p. 10. FS, Box 1, Annual Report 1887, p. 4; and Yearbook 1949, p. 13. Contrast with 1859, when the FS secretary wrote, "We cannot look from our windows, we cannot take our daily walk, without meeting want and degradation at every step." Quoted in A. F. Scott, *Natural Allies*, 31.

23 FS, Box 1, 1895 Annual Report, on municipal politics; and Annual Report 1896, pp. 4–5.

24 FS, Box 3, vol. 3, Annual Report 1897, Janet Monks 11/1/97; and see uncatalogued, unprocessed collection of the Twentieth Century Club at the Massachusetts Historical Society.

25 See Frederic Cople Jaher, *The Urban Establishment: Upper Strata in Boston, New York, Charleston, and Los Angeles* (Urbana: University of Illinois Press, 1982), particularly 15–158. FS, Yearbook 1906, p. 4; and Yearbook 1916, p. 29.

26 See FS, box 3, vol. 13, minutes of meetings and yearbooks for meeting places. In the 1880s, they began occasionally meeting in the Hotel Vendome; in the 1920s, they met at the Women's Republican Club frequently and occasionally at the Chilton Club, the College Club, the Algonquin Club, and the Women's City Club. See also Joni Seager, "Father's Chair: Domestic Reform and Housing in the Progressive Era" (Ph.D. diss., Clark University, Geography, 1988).

27 On finances, see, for example, FS, Box 1, f. 3, Yearbook 1916, p. 34. On FS's organizational structure, see, for example, FS, Box 3, f. 14, minutes, 12/13/38 minutes.

28 WEIU, B-8, vol. 1, S. Agnes Donham, "History of the WEIU, Boston," 1955, typescript, p. 8. See, for example, Mann, 11, 22; Blair, *Clubwoman*, 77.

29 WEIU, carton 1 series 2 f. 7, addenda, History WEIU, "Organizing of WEIU" extract from Dr. Harriet Clisby's "Some Reminiscences of Australia and America," n.d. (c. 1907), 107–108.

30 Paine, Jan.–Apr. 1883, Abby Morton Diaz to Robert Treat Paine, 1/28/83.

31 Donham quoting Diaz, WEIU, B-8, vol. 1, "History of WEIU," p. 23. According to annual reports, Ruffin served on the domestic reform league committee in 1908, O'Sullivan was a director from 1895 to 1897 at least and served on several committees as well, and Brandeis was on a standing committee from 1897 to 1898 among other years. All of these women were, in some sense, members of an elite. It is less clear whether they were the sole representatives of their racial and ethnic groups. In the Moral and Spiritual Development Committee's efforts at true ecumenicism, they had difficulty finding a rabbi and a priest to participate in their Sunday services.

32 WEIU, *Annual Reports* 1886/87, p. 12, 1887/88, on growth making it necessary to hire some workers for the lunchrooms and provide some food, pp. 41–42 (125–150 were using the six tables daily between 11:00 and 3:00); 1893/94, p. 37; and B-8, vol. 1, Donham, "History of WEIU," p. 29.

33 Kathryn Kish Sklar, "Hull House in the 1890s: A Community of Women Reformers," *Signs* 10 (1985); Elizabeth Blackmar and Roy Rosenzweig, *The Park and the People: A History of Central Park* (Ithaca: Cornell University Press, 1992); Dolores Hayden, The *Grand Domestic Revolution: A History of Feminist Designs for American Homes, Neighborhoods and Cities* (Cambridge: MIT Press, 1981); Mary P. Ryan, *Women in Public: Between Banners and Ballots, 1825–1880* (Baltimore: Johns Hopkins University Press, 1990); Christine Stansell, *Women of the City*, 193–216, for examples and ideas of contested space.

34 WEIU, B-8, vol. 1, Donham, "History of WEIU," pp. 10, 31, 32; WEIU, *Annual Reports* 1889/90, 12–13.

35 See William L. Riordon, recorder, *Plunkitt of Tammany Hall* (New York: E. P. Dutton, 1963), 92–93; Huggins, *Protestants*, 177; Robert K. Merton, "Latent Functions of the Machine," in *American Urban History: An Interpretive Reader with Commentaries*, ed. Alexander B. Callow Jr. (New York: Oxford University Press, 1982), 183; Holli, "Varieties," 210–225. Wiebe, *Search*, 171. See Boyer, *Urban Masses*, 181, and Allen F. Davis, *Spearheads for Reform: The Social Settlements and the Progressive Movement, 1890–1914* (New York: Oxford University Press, 1967), 174–175, on Josiah Quincy III, reform mayor from 1895 to 1899 who delivered gyms, bathhouses, and playgrounds. Thomas H. O'Connor, *Bibles, Brahmins and Bosses: A Short History of Boston*, 2d ed. (Boston: Trustees of the Public Library of the City of Boston, 1984), 133.

36 On male reform politics in general see, for example, Robert H. Wiebe, *Businessmen and Reform: A Study of the Progressive Movement* (Cambridge, MA: Harvard University Press, 1962), 108–109. See also, Holli, "Varieties," 210–214; Boyer, *Urban Masses*, 155–159. Jaher, *Urban Establishment*, 99; Geoffrey Blodgett, *The Gentle Reformers: Massachusetts Democrats in the Cleveland Era* (Cambridge: Harvard University Press, 1966); Kleppner, "From Party to Factions," 117; Geoffrey Blodgett, "Yankee Leadership in a Divided City, 1860–1910" in *Boston*, ed. Formisano and Burns.

37 Lois Bannister Merk, "Boston's Historic Public School Crisis," *New England Quarterly* 31 (1958): 172–199; WEIU, *Annual Report* 1897/98. See also Burns, "Progressive Reform," 140–141.

38 Silverman, "Nathan Matthews," 626–628, 633–636, 643. The WEIU men in the 1890s included Henry H. Sprague, Samuel Wells, and George Wigglesworth. Information on these men was located in *Who's Who in Massachusetts*, 1940–41; *Who Was Who in America*, vol. 1, 1897–1942; *National Cyclopedia of American Biography; Who's Who in New England*, 1909; *Dictionary of American Biography*.

39 For Emerson quotations see, for example, WEIU, B-8, box 1 f. 1, *Annual Reports* 1881/82, pp. 11–19; and 1883/84, p. 13. Ginzberg, *Women*, 133–173, noticed a similar shift during the Civil War in the Sanitary Commission.

40 See, for example, Haskell, *Emergence of Progressional Social Science*; Burton J. Bledstein, *The Culture of Professionalism: The Middle Class and the Development of Higher Education in America* (New York: W. W. Norton, 1976); Lubove, *Professional Altruist*; Jill Kathryn Conway, *The First Generation* of *American Women Graduates* (New York: Garland Publishing, Inc., 1987); and Barbara Miller Solomon, *In the Company of Educated Women: A History of Women and Higher Education in America* (New Haven: Yale University Press, 1985).

41 WEIU, box 1 f. 1 *Annual Reports* 1908, pp. 16–17, emphasis in original; see also series I carton 1, 1891/92, pp. 22, 24; 1896/97 re: Committee on Food; 1897/98, p. 12, the Handwork Department; 1898/99, p. 41, and 1910/11, p. 49, the Industrial Departments; versus 1887/88, p. 26, Industrial Department.

42 WEIU, series I carton 1, *Annual Reports* 1891/92, p. 17; and 1899/1900, p. 8.

43 WEIU, series I carton 1, *Annual Report* 1890/91, p. 9; and 1897/98 on lack of volunteers. WEIU, B-8, vol. 1, Donham, "History of WEIU," pp. 2, 99, 112. In 1905 Kehew replaced a large number of volunteers with professional staff; Blair, *Clubwoman*, 82, gives 120 as the figure.

44 See, for example, Julia A. Sprague, *History of the New England Women's Club from 1868–1893* (Boston: Lee and Shepard Publishers, 1894), 27.

45 See Mrs. John T. Sargent, *Sketches and Reminiscences of the Radical Club of Chestnut Street, Boston* (Boston: James R. Osgood and Company, 1880), 28, 41–46, 383–84. See also, New England Women's Club Papers, box 10 f. 40, Mrs. Ednah Dow Cheney, booklet of memorial meeting, for example, F. B. Sanborn, pp. 6–7, at the Schlesinger Library, Radcliffe College, Cambridge, MA. And see Fields, Addendum, box 41 FI2933, Mary Livermore to Fields, 7/12/73, Huntington Library, Pasadena, CA.

46 WEIU, B-8, vol. 1, Donham, "History of WEIU," p. 154; WEIU series I, carton 1, *Annual Report* 1887/8, p. 37 for WEIU hiring a female attorney.

47 See WEIU, series 2 carton 6 f. 106, Protective Department, Protective Committee minutes 1878–1894: 2/23/80 ff; 3/8/80 by seven to two they voted "that the Protective Dept. shall give its Labor free to working women." See also, WEIU, series I carton 1, *Annual Report* 1878/79, p. 22.

48 WEIU, series 2, carton 6, f. 106, Protective Department minutes, 4/17/82; WEIU, series 1 carton 1, *Annual Report* 1898/99, p. 50.

49 Blodgett, "Yankee Leadership," 98; Silverman, "Nathan Matthews," 640; Marilyn Thornton Williams, "Urban Reform in the Gilded Age: The Public Baths of Boston," in *Massachusetts in the Gilded Age: Selected Essays*, ed. Jack Tager and John W. Ifkovic (Amherst, MA: University of Massachusetts Press, 1985), 210–231. Kehew served on the Bath Commission in 1896, for example; Geoffrey T. Blodgett, "Josiah Quincy, Brahmin Democrat," *New England Quarterly* 38 (December 1965), 440; James J. Kenneally, "Woman Suffrage and the Massachusetts 'Referendum' of 1895," *Historian* 30 (August 1968): 617–633. Burns, "Progressive Reform," 136–150.

50 WEIU, box 1 f. 1, *Annual Report* 1908/9, p. 36: By this time, the Lunch Department receipts were $180,000/year, and it employed 160 workers, feeding 4,500 to 5,000/day, p. 37. On the attempt to take it over, WEIU, *Annual Report* 1910/11, p. 47, and see City Council minutes of that year. See WEIU, box 1 f. 1, *Annual Report* 1907, p. 40. Cf. Pascoe, *Relations of Rescue*, 180–183.

51 Blodgett, "Yankee Leadership," 105–106. WEIU, box 1 f. 1 *Annual Reports* 1900–1914; Burns, "Progressive Reform," 148–158, 163 57n; Davis, *Spearheads*, 179. On the Good Government Association see Abrams, *Conservatism*, 144, and Peter K. Eisinger, "Ethnic Political Transition in Boston, 1884–1933: Some Lessons for Contemporary Cities," *Political Science Quarterly* 93 (summer 1978): 217–239. WEIU men included George Crocker and Edmund Billings, for example. Also see Davis, *Spearheads*, 176–178, and on at-large elections as increasing the power of business forces, see Boyer, *Urban Masses*, 281–282.

52 On lobbying, see, for example, WEIU, box 1 f. 1, *Annual Reports* 1903/4, pp. 36–37; and 1908/9, pp. 18–20, 27–30. And at the Schlesinger Library see the papers of Ethel Johnson, Mary Dewson, and Louise Marion Bosworth, all of whom worked as investigators for the WEIU. See WEIU, B-8, vol. 1, Donham, "History of WEIU," pp. 83–84, 95–97, 107, 115–116, 142–143, 166. Topics included trade schools for girls, industrial conditions of women and children, and employment agencies.

The Women's Municipal League (hereafter WML), launched in 1909 in Boston, also reflected these changes in Boston's politics. See Putnam Papers, box 4 f. 51, WML *Annual Reports* for 1909 (quotation appears on p. 1), 1912, 1914, 1921, Schlesinger Library, Radcliffe College, Cambridge, MA. Cf. Elisabeth S. Clemens, "Organizational Repertoires and Institutional Change: Women's Groups and the Transformation of United States Politics, 1890–1920," *American Journal of Sociology* 98 (January 1993): 784–786, for other states' women's voluntary societies developing lobbying arms.

53 WEIU, box 1 f. 1, *Annual Report* 1903/4, p. 11. For the history, WEIU, Addenda, carton f. 12, Cornelia James Cannon, *The History of the WEIU: A Civic Laboratory, 1877–1927* (Boston: Thomas Todd, Printers, [c. 1927]); and Clisby's own "Reminiscences," 125–126.

54 *Simmons College Review*, n.d., p. 10, Eva Whiting White collection, Schlesinger Library, Radcliffe College, Cambridge, MA.

55 As early as the 1885/86 WEIU *Annual Report*, the president claimed the object was to change existing conditions, p. 7.

56 This understanding of power builds on Hannah Arendt, "Communicative Power," 59–74; Jurgen Habermas, "Hannah Arendt's Communications Concept of Power," 75–93; and Michel Foucault, "Disciplinary Power and Subjection," 229–242, in *Power*, ed. Steven Lukes (New York: New York University Press, 1986).

57 See, for example, Sklar, "Hull House"; Davis, *Spearheads*; Judith Trolander, *Professionalism and Social Change: From the Settlement House Movement to Neighborhood Centers 1886 to the Present* (New York: Columbia University Press, 1987), and Jane Addams, *Twenty Years at Hull House*.

58 Susan Traverso has written a splendid undergraduate thesis on Denison House: "The Road Going to Jericho: The Early History of Denison House, 1887–1912," B.A. honors thesis, Simmons College, May 4, 1983; and see Denison House Papers, particularly box 1, f. 3–5, which contain daily journals kept by the first resident workers.

59 On organizing women see, for example, DH, daybook, box 1 vol. 1, 1893/94, 9/22/93; only with the aid of Denison on p. 59, 11/21/93 and 11/27/93, p. 65, also see 1/9/94, p. 103; and 2/4/94, p. 117; 3/3/94, p. 131. On daycare, see, for example, 8/26/93, p. 20. They also dispute the Associated Charities tactics (8/29/94, pp. 56–57, in the minutes of the executive committee, 1892–99, vol. 5). Denison House was also active in the formation of a Boston Branch of the Union Label League. DH, box 1, vol. 3, daybook, 11/00–2/08. 1/11/04, p. 120.

60 See the *Nation*, 1/3/95 referred to in DH, box 1, vol. 2, 5/7/95; vol. 3, 9/20/04, p. 135; and vol. 6, executive committee minutes, 2/9/04, pp. 79–80, and 3/8/04, p. 85. Traverso, "The Road Going to Jericho," 79. Davis, *Spearheads*, 229, claims that Dudley resigned in 1912 lest her radicalism hurt the house financially.

61 For example, their manual training classes. See DH, box 2, vol. 2, directors' meetings minutes, 3/14/10, p. 140, for example.

62 On involvement with the city: DH, box 2 vol. 7, directors' meeting minutes 9/22/08, 78; 12/7/08, pp. 88–90; 1/18/09, p. 92; 9/30/09, p. 114; 10/25/09, p. 124, each display a greater sense that it is the city's and not Denison House's job to provide such services.

63 DH, box 2, vol. 7, directors' meeting minutes, 1/13/10, p. 132; 3/14/10, pp. 141, 145; 5/9/10, p. 152; box 1 vol. 5, minutes of executive committee meetings, 11/5/95, p. 140; 9/28/05, p. 135; vol. 6, 4/25/05, p. 125.

64 Dr. J. E. Goldthwaite, George Edwin McNeil, and Dr. Edward Osgood Otis were on the first committee; the second included Robert Gardiner, Stanley King, Richard Hale, Joseph Coolidge, and Edmund Billings. DH, directors' meeting minutes, box 2, vol. 7, 1906–1911, 5/8/10, p. 152. Information on these men was located in *Who's Who in Massachusetts*, 1940–41; *Who Was Who in America*, vol. 1, 1897–1942; *National Cyclopedia of American Biography*; *Who's Who in New England*, 1909; *Dictionary of American Biography*.

65 It is telling that by 1931/32 there were fourteen boys' clubs and only four girls' clubs. DH, box 2 f. 8, reports to College Settlement Association. On the building fund see box 2, vol. 7, directors' meeting minutes for September 1910; on 10/9/11, the women for the first time voiced the hope of being more businesslike in the future, p. 199.

66 DH, box 2, executive committee minutes, vol. 6, 1/23/03, p. 43; box 2 f. 8, excerpts from annual reports to CSA, 1915/16; Box 2, vol. 8, directors' meeting minutes, 1/8/12. See also Conway, *The First Generation* and Muncy, *Creating a Female Dominion*, xiv–xvii, 18, 72–77, 80–83.

67 DH, box 3 f. 9, directors' meeting minutes, 2/10/19, 3/15/19, 1/17/19, 4/21/19, 2/16/20, and box 4 f. 29, special committee report, 1919 (typescript), p. 17, on the displeasure of their Syrian neighbors with their stand on suffrage and prohibition.

68 See DH, box 3 f. 9, directors' meeting minutes, 7/15/18; Lillian Faderman, *Surpassing the Love of Men: Romantic Friendship and Love Between Women from the Renaissance to the Present* (New York: William Morrow, 1981); Judith Schwarz, "Yellow Clover: Katharine Bates and Katharine Coman," *Frontiers* 14:1 (spring 1979): 59–67; Scudder, *A Listener in Babel*.

69 DH, box 3, f. 9, directors' meeting minutes, 4/15/20; executive committee, box 3, vol. 9, 11/8/35, and 12/17/35. Cf. Judith Ann Trolander, *Settlement Houses and the Great Depression* (Detroit:

Wayne State Press, 1975), on masculinization of settlement houses and on community funds. Lubove, *Professional Altruist*, 196.

70 Jack Tager, "Reaction and Reform in Boston: the Gilded Age and the Progressive Era," in *Massachusetts*, ed. Tager and Ifkovic, 244.

71 FS, box 1, Yearbook 1914, p. 3; Yearbook 1916, p. 29, quoting 1863 report, also p. 34; Yearbook 1927, p. 3; Yearbook 1933, p. 3; box 3, minutes 11/11/38; and box 2 f. 14 minutes 12/1929.

72 This practice differed from the black League of Women for Community Service, which started as a Soldiers Comfort Unit during World War I and always met in the evenings. Probably the best evidence of the failure of cross-class efforts at the WEIU was the organization's obsession with domestic service, how to get women into it, how to train workers, how to train employers, how to make it work. Their 1897/98 *Annual Report*, p. 16, claimed that domestic service lay at the foundation of social life and threatened its destruction. Other working girls organizations sponsored by the WEIU included a cash girls club, which renamed itself as a Junior Workers' Club (*Annual Report* 1895/96, pp. 49–50) with some success. See League of Women for Community Service Minutes, 1918–21, 1924–38, at the Schlesinger Library, B-L434, microfilm. As a soldier's Comfort Unit, the organization enjoyed government support for its programs (and also investigated claims of racial discrimination at nearby Fort Devens); that support ended abruptly with the war. When the organization decided to continue the unit with a new name, in 1919, they had to seek alternate sources of funding, and when they decided to move from their current quarters and purchase a building, they found black male backers.

73 DH, box 3 f. 9, directors' meeting minutes, 12/15/19.

74 See chapter 6 and Blair, *Clubwoman*, 83. Judith Becker Ranlett, "Sorority and Community: Women's Answer to a Changing Massachusetts, 1865–1895" (Ph.D. diss., Brandeis University, History of American Civilization, 1974), 180–181. See Ranlett, throughout, for such overlapping memberships.

It may well be that Kehew and others like her belonged to organizations with seemingly contradictory constituencies or philosophies precisely because of the different strategies, connections, and alliances each offered. The WEIU *Annual Report* for 1903/4, p. 11, notes that recent steps had been taken significant of a truly democratic policy "essential in its creed," an affiliation with the Union for Industrial Progress, which also had Kehew as its president, with the aim of organizing working women to improve their character and their condition; each organization would henceforth be represented on the board of the other, and, in addition, on p. 12, it noted that they had organized a union of WEIU employees, so that they can "become a real part of the Union for which they work."

75 All of these are common explanations for the shift, see Ginzberg, *Women*; Bordin, *Women and Temperance*; Conway, *First Generation*; and Baker, "Domestication," for examples.

76 Conway, *First Generation*, 112, 321, concludes, "in Boston the ethic of service operated upon both men and women, and the separation of sex roles which was so clear in the mid-west simply could not be discerned."

Chapter 6

1 DH, box 1 f. 2, extracts from letter of Addams to Coman, 12/7/91.

2 DH, box 1 f. 4, Helen Cheever 1/12/93, p. 123; 1/16/93 pp. 156–157. See also, on encounters with garment workers, DH journals, box 1 f. 4, Laura Cate 1/3/93, pp. 46–47; B-27, box 1, vol. 2, 12/28/94, p. 184.

3 DH, vol. 1, 9/6/93; and 9/11/93. In 1873 Boston had 2,500 Jews; c. 1890, it had 20,000; in 1902, 40,000; and in 1907, 60,000. They included Lithuanians (who would form their

own garment workers' local), Ukrainians, Poles, Latvians, Estonians, Romanians, Hungarians, Bulgarians, Galicians, and Russians and did not see themselves as others often did, as all "Russian." Barbara Miller Solomon, *Pioneers in Service: The History of the Associated Jewish Philanthropies of Boston* (Boston: Court Square Press, 1956), 9, 30–36. Carroll D. Wright, *The Working Girls of Boston* [from the Fifteenth Annual Report of the MBSL, for 1884] (Boston: Wright and Potter Printing, 1889), 12–15. WEIU, series 1 carton 1, *Annual Report* for 1889/90, protective committee, p. 44. Denison House recorded a "hot" debate in the Central Labor Union over whether to restrict municipal jobs to citizens (DH, box 1, vol. 1, 2/4/94). Alexander Keyssar, *Out of Work: The First Century of Unemployment in Massachusetts* (New York: Cambridge University Press, 1986), 203, 210. Michael P. Conzen and George K. Lewis, *Boston: A Geographical Portrait* (Cambridge, MA: Ballinger Publishing, 1976), 25–26. The *Boston Globe*, 9/2/94, p. 4, "Looking into the Labor Question."

4 This latter proportion stood in marked contrast to the British (43%), German (48%), Canadian (51%), and Scandinaivan (85%) immigrants, Boston's largest groups before the increasing numbers of southern and eastern immigrants in the ensuing decade. James R. Green and Hugh Carter Donahue, *Boston's Workers: A Labor History* (Boston: Trustees of the Public Library of the City of Boston, 1979), 53–54, using Stephen Thernstrom's figures from *The Other Bostonians: Poverty and Progress in the American Metropolis, 1880–1970* (Cambridge: Harvard University Press, 1973) and Geoffrey Blodgett, *The Gentle Reformers: Massachusetts Democrats in the Cleveland Era* (Cambridge: Harvard University Press, 1966); Conzen and Lewis, *Boston*, 26.

5 DH, box 1, vol. 1, 9/13/93; 9/16/93; and 9/22/93. Ethel Johnson, "Labor Progress in Boston, 1880 to 1930," in *Fifty Years of Boston: A Memorial Volume*, ed. Elisabeth M. Herlihy (Boston: n.p., 1930), 218; Priscilla Murolo, *The Common Ground of Womanhood: Class, Gender, and Working Girls' Clubs, 1884–1928* (Urbana: University of Illinois Press, 1997), 85.

6 DH, box 1, vol. 1, 9/23/93; and 9/24/93.

7 DH, box 1, vol. 1, 10/5/93. See also William Leach, *True Love and Perfect Union: The Feminist Reform of Sex and Society* (New York: Basic Books, 1980), 134, 289, 297.

8 DH, box 1, vol. 1, 10/6/93. The name, as is common in the day books, appears with a variety of spellings.

9 DH, box 1, vol. 1, 10/9/93; and 10/11/93.

10 DH, box 1, vol. 1, 10/25/93; 11/2/93; 11/5/93; and 11/6/93.

11 See John Potter and Michelle Reidel, " 'Suppose it Were Your Daughter': Gender, Class and Work as Perceived by Women Factory Inspectors in Gilded Age Massachusetts" (paper presented at Southwestern Labor Studies Conference, University of California, Santa Cruz, 4/29–30/1994), forthcoming in *Labor History*.

12 DH, box 1, vol. 1, 11/10/93.

13 DH, box 1, vol. 1, 11/10/93.

14 DH, box 1, vol. 1, 11/12/93.

15 For example, DH, box 1, vol. 1, 11/9/93; and 11/12/93.

16 DH, box 1, vol. 1, 12/21/93; Irene Weir 2/21/94, p. 126; see also 2/22/94, p. 127; B-27, vol. 2, 7/25/94, p. 66; and see vol. 1, 7/18/93 or 10/3/93.

17 DH, box 1, vol. 1, Dudley 11/8/93, p. 51. P. A. M. Taylor, ed., *More Than Common Powers of Perception: The Diary of Elizabeth Rogers Mason Cabot* (Boston: Beacon Press, 1991), 289. See Keyssar, *Out of Work*, 254–258, on the unprecedented scale of official and unofficial relief efforts.

18 See the 1897/98 report to the College Settlement House Association (DH, box 2 f. 7), in which the settlement house's head showed signs of exasperation and discouragement.

19 DH, box 1, vol. 1, 11/13/93.

20 Cf. Alice Henry, *The Trade Union Woman* (New York: Burt Franklin, [c. 1915]), 16.

21 Eileen Boris, *Home to Work: Motherhood and the Politics of Industrial Homework in the United States* (New York: Cambridge University Press, 1994), 49–50, 56, 61–62.

22 *Boston Globe* 9/27/94, 12, "Backing Assured."

23 Murolo, *Working Girls' Clubs*, 104–105.

24 DH, box 1, vol. 1, 11/21/93. UGW was an AFL affiliate, though its founders had been Knights of Labor men. Murolo, *Working Girls' Clubs*, 85.

25 DH, box 1, vol. 1, 11/21/93. Murolo, *Working Girls' Clubs*, 104–105.

26 DH, box 1, vol. 1, 11/21/93. Murolo, *Working Girls' Clubs*, 83.

27 DH, box 1, vol. 1, 11/27/93.

28 DH, box 1, vol. 1, 11/28/93.

29 DH, box 1, vol. 1, 12/4/93.

30 See Murolo, *Working Girls' Clubs*, 86, 88.

31 For example, DH, box 1, vol. 1, p. 95, 12/29/93, a Mr. Joseph G. Clinkard, of the Carpenters. Union at 699 Washington Street, Room 20921, wanted a reliable woman for general housework. And see WEIU, series 1, carton 1, *Annual Report* 1889/90, p. 45. WEIU, box 1 f. 5, Domestic Reform League (hereafter DRL) bulletin no. 2, vol. 2, 12/07. Similarly, DRL bulletin no. 4, vol. 2, 11/08, p. 4.

32 DH, B-27, box 2 f. 7, report of the headworker to the College Settlement Association, fall 1893.

33 For examples, see DH, box 1, vol. 1, 12/18/93, p. 84; 12/26/93, p. 92; 1/9/84, p. 103; 3/6/1894, p. 131; and 4/3/94, p. 142.

34 DH, box 1, vol. 1, 2/20/94, p. 126. See Green and Donahue, *Boston's Workers*, 84–85, on Lloyd.

35 DH, box 1, vol. 1, 1/1/94, p. 97; 2/1/94, p. 115.

36 DH, box 1, vol. 1, Wilshinski 1/25/94; p. 112, McNeil 2/1/94, p. 115. See also DH, 1/30/94. Kenneth Fones-Wolf, "Boston Eight Hour Men, New York Marxists and the Emergence of the International Labor Union: Prelude to the AFL," *Historical Journal of Massachusetts* 9 (June 1981), 47–54, and Green and Donahue, 72, 74–75.

37 Miss Pitts also joined. DH, box 1, vol. 1, 2/4/94, p. 117, Dudley and Pitts delegates, and Scudder went along; 3/3/94, p. 131, on the federal union; also 3/12/94 (with five new members, Dudley chairing); 4/10/94; vol. 2, 4/24/94, finally, at an open meeting of the federal union on 5/8/94, the president of the Typographers Union gave a paper on "Organization for Women." The Social Science Club also continued to study the matter, on 3/1/94 hearing a paper on New Trades Unions; 3/15/94, p. 136, McNeil on Knights of Labor (a large meeting); and Mrs. Ames came to the Club, in the audience, for a 5/4/94 meeting where Dean Hodges presented on "What the Church as an Organization can do for the Labor Movement," vol. 2. See also MHS, Boston Central Labor Union (CLU) records, 1890–1894, which in the minutes for 5/7/93 recorded that the "Ladies from Wellesley College" were absent at roll call, and 9/17/93 during which the auditors allowed the Wellesley College ladies to stay.

38 DH, box 1, vol. 1, 4/18/94, p. 145, Dudley taking tea with the Lloyds and McNeils, and 4/19/94, p. 146, on Social Science Club; the paper was Mr. Brent's.

39 DH, box 1, vol. 2, 4/20/94, p. 1. Denison House also continued a close relationship with Mrs. Quinn: DH, box 1 vol. 2, 4/30/94, 10/3/94, 10/28/94, p. 150; 7/27/95, p. 238.

40 DH, B-27, box 1, vol. 2, 11/9/94.

41 DH, box 1, vol. 2, 1/9/95, mentioned a Garment Makers Union meeting with 100 members the day after a meeting at the WEIU with Samuel Gompers on the benefits of organized labor drew an audience of only 50 despite the 600 invitations sent out. DH, B-27, box 1, vol. 2, 1/8/94, on Gompers. The union message seemed ubiquitous in the winter of 1894/95, appearing at the WEIU, Faneuil Hall, Wells Memorial, and the Church of the Disciples in the

speeches of various unionists including Gompers, Lloyd, McNeil, and Dudley. DH, box 1, vol. 2, 1/2/95; 1/8/95; 2/11/95; and 2/12/95. On the other hand, the Federal Union repeatedly could not get a quorum, as in 12/11/94, at its public meetings, despite continuing to initiate new members at its business meetings (1/21/94, it initiated Mrs. Kehew, Miss Coman, Conyngton, Sanford, among others). They continued both to talk and to take action, aiding the Haverhill strikers for example and urging them to unite after the strike was declared "off" (2/11/95; 3/11/95). And it continued to be a site in which reformers could learn about labor issues, as in 5/13/95 when O'Sullivan gave a history of the Hyde Park strike and a discussion of the politics of the Central Labor Union occurred. There is little record of the attendance of any women workers, however. (See other entries, such as 11/11/95; 1/14/96; 2/10/96; 3/9/96; 10/13/96; see 3/26/95, very few working men; 5/21/95; 12/3/95; 1/7/96; 1/28/96; 2/11/96; 2/18/96; 3/3/96; 3/10/96; and vol. 3, 11/17/00, p. 4, on the Anthracite Coal Strike with a large attendance despite the storm.)

DH, box 1, vol. 2, 10/17/94, on Mr. Billings's proposal of a plan by which trade unionists would come into the Twentieth Century Club; well received by those present, and 12/26/94 Dudley and Warren went to the Club to hear Mrs. Hicks of London on women in the Labor Movement, and Lady H. Somerset and Frances Willard and others spoke, and Willard said she would like to join the Federal Labor Union. On 3/13/01 (vol. 3), several residents went to hear Prince Kropotkin on the modern development of socialism at the club, and the house continued to have relations with the club, see 1/9/07 and 4/28/07. DH, box 1, vol. 2, 11/8/94, p. 157, for letting the public meetings of the FLU lapse and having the SSC take its place, inviting more working men and having meetings in the evening, and 11/10/94 the SSC committee decided on a list of "working men" to invite. This strategy seemed to work, in that the meetings of the SSC were well attended. 11/19/94 of forty-five present, eight were trade unionists. These meetings seemed to become increasingly male dominated in its speakers and discussants—male labor leaders and male reformers; see 1/10/94; 1/16/95; 1/29/95; 2/12/95; and 2/26/95. The attendance remained between forty-five and fifty. The notes on CLU meetings never mention women union speakers, see DH, box 1, vol. 2, 7/15/94; 9/2/94; 11/18/94; 1/20/95; 3/3/95; 4/7/95; 7/7/95; 10/19/95; and 10/18/96. On labor day parade, DH, box 1, vol. 2, 9/3/94. Cf. David Montgomery, *The Fall of the House of Labor* (Cambridge, UK: Cambridge University Press, 1987), p. 280 61n.

42 DH, box 1, vol. 2.

43 Murolo, *Working Girls' Clubs*, 86, 92–94, 98, 103. DH box 1 vol. 2. 10/17/94, p. 146. Denison House is giving a supper to Mr. and Mrs. O'Sullivan and toasts to them.

44 Mary Kenney O'Sullivan Papers, A-085, autobiography, pp. 87–88, Schlesinger Library, Radcliffe College, Cambridge, MA.

45 Kenney O'Sullivan, pp. 115–116.

46 DH, box 1, vol. 2, 12/3/94, p. 172.

47 *Boston Globe* 9/4/94, 1, 4.

48 *Boston Globe* 9/2/94, 24.

49 DH, box 1, vol. 2, 8/28/94, p. 115.

50 Green and Donohue, *Boston's Workers*, 75–76, photo on p. 76. See Keyssar, *Out of Work*, 224–230, on Morrison Swift who led every major unemployed demonstration in Boston from 1894 to 1914, including the one the *Boston Globe* called "The Invasion of the State House" on 2/20/94.

51 DH, B-27 box 1, vol. 2, 10/9/94. In late December 1896, the streetcar workers struck, forming the backdrop to Foster's later novel. DH, B-27, box 1 vol. 2, 12/24/96; and 12/26/96.

52 On related Boston politics, see, for example, Robert A. Silverman, "Nathan Matthews: Politics

of Reform in Boston, 1890–1910," *New England Quarterly* 50 (December 1977): 637–638; Green and Donohue, *Boston's Workers*, 39–40. See also, DH, box 1, vol. 2, 8/10/95, p. 242, Wells Memorial meeting debate on communism; David M. Katzman and William M. Tuttle, Jr., eds., *Plain Folk: The Life Stories of Undistinguished Americans* (Urbana: University of Illinois Press, 1982), 132–136, James Williams; Green and Donohue, *Boston's Workers*, 78; Montgomery, *Fall of the House of Labor*, 167–168. See Keyssar, *Out of Work*, 101, on the 1880s depression. Geoffrey T. Blodgett, "Josiah Quincy, Brahmin Democrat," *New England Quarterly* 38 (December 1965): 437. Green and Donohue, *Boston's Workers*, 36–38. See also James Lazerow, " 'The Workingman's Hour': The 1886 Labor Uprising in Boston," *Labor History* 21 (Spring 1980): 215, on Labor Day; Leon Fink, *Workingmen's Democracy: The Knights of Labor and American Politics* (Urbana: University of Illinois Press, 1983), 28. See Lazerow, "Workingman's Hour," 205–206, 210–216, on Knights versus AFL and the BCLU.

53 Blodgett, "Josiah Quincy," 437. See also Dawn M. Saunders, "Class, Gender, and Generation: Mothers' Aid in Massachusetts and the Political Economy of Welfare Reform" (Ph.D. diss., University of Massachusetts, Amherst, Economics, 1994), 51; Green and Donohue, *Boston's Workers*, 39. Lorinda Perry, *The Millinery Trade in Boston and Philadelphia: A Study of Women in Industry* (Binghamton, NY: Vail-Ballou, 1916), 3. Lazerow, "Workingman's Hour," 218–219.

54 Louis Levine, *The Women's Garment Workers: A History of the ILGWU* (New York: B. W. Huebsch, 1924), 21, 29, 47–48, 56. According to Green and Donohue, *Boston's Workers*, 77–78, in the 1890s the Boston Socialist Labor Party split into "English" (German American) and "Hebrew" sections (Russian Jewish). See also, Boris, *Home*, 55, 60; Levine, *ILGWU*, 10; C. Wright, *Working Girls*, 66–69.

55 Alexander von Hoffman, *Local Attachments: The Making of an American Urban Neighborhood, 1850–1920* (Baltimore: Johns Hopkins, 1994), 26. DH, box 1, vol. 1, 11/21/93, p. 59, refers to the clerk of the Garment Makers Union as "(Jew)" rather than by name. DH, box 1 vol. 1, 11/6/93, p. 50, refers to Miss Dam as "young Jewess" and 11/12/93 refers to taking Misses Lifschitz, Dam, and Levy to a lecture, versus 9/11/93, p. 29. On 9/11/93 they take Quinn and others to Wellesley.

See also Susan Glenn, *Daughters of the Shtetl: Life and Labor in the Immigrant Generation* (Ithaca: Cornell University Press, 1990), 189–191, re: Dora Bayrack, who is active in the New York strike in 1909 and had been active in Boston before that (though her story may refer to a 1907/08 strike rather than the 1890s activity).

56 Mrs. O.'Brien was another garment worker within Denison House's ambit. DH box 1, Journals, Cate 1/18/93. And see Murolo, *Working Girls' Clubs*, 102.

57 For example, DH, box 1 vol. 1, 11/9/93; and 11/12/93.

58 Note, too, that not all workers lived in the immediate neighborhood of the shops, and with increasingly irregular employment in hard times, workers in any given shop could be scattered across the city. See also, Green and Donohue, *Boston's Workers*, 78.

59 *Boston Globe* 9/4/94, 1.

60 *Boston Globe* 9/10/94, 3.

61 *Boston Globe* 9/14/94, 3, "Talking Strike."

62 *Boston Globe* 9/17/94, 3, "Central Labor Union."

63 *Boston Globe* 9/18/94, 3, "Ready to Strike."

64 *Boston Globe* 9/20/94, 1, "Over 5000 Out."

65 *Boston Globe* 9/20/94, 1, "Will Quit" and, same page, "Over 5000 Out."

66 *Boston Globe* 9/21/94, 1, 3, "Strike May Be Short." Captioned "Women in the Fight," this drawing depicted three women on the street in quiet conversation, modestly dressed, though

one woman's hat boasted a feather, and, in contrast with the woman in the the first page illustration of male workers on the street ("Keeping the Sidewalk Clear"), without the purses that would apparently have marked them as consumers rather than workers.

67 *Boston Globe* 9/20/94, 1, "Over 5000 Out"; 9/27/94, 12, "Backing Assured."

68 Fifty of the sixty women present joined local 37 on the spot. DH, box 1, vol. 2, 9/26/94, p. 135; and 9/28/94, p. 137. They elected Kenney president and Denison House's Helena Dudley as treasurer.

69 *Boston Globe* 9/30/94, 6, "Will Return to Work Wednesday."

70 *Boston Globe* 10/5/94, 7, "Garment Workers."

71 James T. Kenneally, "Women Suffrage and the Massachusetts 'Referendum' of 1895," *Historian* 30 (August 1968): 626–627, see MWSA directors' meeting, 6/7/95, 37 in the Women's Rights Collection, Schlesinger Library, Radcliffe College, Cambridge, MA, and *Women's Journal*, 10/19/95. The BCLU had endorsed woman suffrage in 1894, see BCLU records, minutes 2/4/94, p. 104, MHS.

72 *Boston Globe* 8/21/95, evening edition, 1, 5, "Piles of Coin," for the four garment workers' locals in Boston—the other two were no. 1, tailors and operatives, and no. 43, Lithuanians. DH, B-27, box 1, vol. 2, 11/5/94, 11/6/94, pp. 154, 156; 11/7/94, 11/28/94, pp. 157, 169, attending GWU; 12/12/94, raising initiation fees.

That month, also, at the 12/19/84 meeting, in contrast to the previous year's dues collection of under $3, $23 in dues were collected, women were initiated, and about 250 members were present. DH, B-27, box 1, vol. 2, 12/19/94, 250 present; 1/9/95, conflict with reading class. Kenney O'Sullivan, pp. 159–160. (Kenney's dates, drawn from memory, at times do not accord with those in the *Globe* and the DH journals, written at the time.)

73 DH, box 1, vol. 2, 1/11/95. See also, DH, box 1, vol. 2, 2/6/95 and Keyssar, *Out of Work*, 188–189. See DH, box 1, vol. 2, 3/8/95 and 5/3/95 on penmanship class, pp. 208, 225; 3/11/95 and 9/16/95 on meetings.

74 *Boston Globe* 10/15/94, evening edition, 1; 4/11/95, 4, "Getting Together," on a convention of shoe workers in which the women delegates were "as active in the debates as any of their male associates." On the Hyde Park rubber workers' strike: DH, box 1, vol. 2, 4/13/95, pp. 219–220; and 5/20/95, 228, re: meeting at WEIU. See also, *Boston Globe* 4/19/95, 6, "Klous is Firm." According to the *Globe*, about three-quarters of the "girls" were out. *Boston Globe* 4/21/95, 1, "Gossamer Girls Parade."

75 *Boston Globe* 4/8/95, 5, "labor news" on delegates; 4/15/95, p. 3, "Labor Notes." In August, the new women's unions would send three delegates, all working women, to the state Federation of Labor convention in Boston. *Boston Globe* 8/5/95, p. 5, "Federation of Labor Convention."

76 *Boston Globe* 8/2/95, 7, "Price List for Clothing Trade"; and 8/17/95 p. 5, "Prepared for a Strike." For other *Globe* mentions of the novelty of the women's organization, see 8/21/95, 1, "Going Out Today"; 8/21/95, evening edition, p. 1, "Piles of Coin."

77 *Boston Globe* 8/18/95, 6, "Big Raid in West End."

78 *Boston Globe* 8/18/95, 7, "For Free Speech." See *Boston Globe* 8/22/95, p. 1, "Partial Victory," for Collins's position.

79 *Boston Globe* 8/21/95, evening edition, 1, "Piles of Coin"; 8/23/95, 7, "Set Rapid Pace"; 8/22/95, 1, "Partial Victory," for meeting place.

80 Kenney O'Sullivan, p. 162. *Boston Globe* 8/22/95, 1, "Partial Victory" on money.

81 DH, box 1, vol. 2, 11/9/96, p. 289; DH, box 1 vol 2, 2/25/96, p. 272; 3/2/96; 3/10/96; 3/18/96; and 11/9/96. Murolo, *Working Girls' Clubs*, 107–108.

82 DH, box 1, vol. 2, 3/6/96, p. 273; and 3/10/96. DH, box 2 f. 7, 1901/02 report of headworker

to College Settlement Association; DH, B-27, box 1, vol. 3, 9/20/04, p. 135. See C. Wright, *Working Girls*, 12–15, 45, on bindery workers' nationality and gender. DH, box 1, vol. 2, 11/17/96, p. 289, on waitresses.

83 DH, box 1, vol. 2, 5/7/95. DH, box 2 f. 7, 1901/02 report of the headworker to CSA; Box 2 f. 7, 1896/97 report of headworker to College Settlement Association, p. 20.

84 Keyssar, *Out of Work*, 207, citing the Board to Investigate the Subject of the Unemployed, hearings in the 1890s, and the quotation is from the Massachusetts AFL Convention Proceedings: eighteenth, 1903, pp. 46–47.

85 Consumers' League of Massachusetts Papers (hereafter CLM), box 1 f. 1, call to first meeting of the Consumers' League of Massachusetts, 1898, Schlesinger Library, Radcliffe College, Cambridge, MA.

86 See the daybooks for 1897 and the reports to the college settlement association. Murolo, *Working Girls' Clubs*, 110.

87 Murolo, *Working Girls' Clubs*, 110. CLM, box 1 f. 2, "The Consumers' League of Massachusetts November 1898 to March 1900," p. 1. Boris, *Home*, 91–92; WEIU, box 7 f. 52, Women's Trade Unions.

88 DH, box 1, vol. 3, 3/21/04, p. 125. On tensions over union support, see also DH, box 2, vol. 6, directors' meeting minutes, 1901–1906, pp. 79–80; and p. 85.

89 DH, box 1, vol. 3, 1/11/04, p. 120; 1/24/04; and 5/16/04, p. 128.

90 DH, box 2 f. 6, excerpts from headworker reports, 1903, p. 34. DH, box 2 f. 7, report of the headworker to College Settlement Association, 1902/03; 1903/04. Just as the seduction of Denison House into the union movement had been a slow and intricate dance, so was the weakening of the tie. DH, box 1, vol. 3, 10/20/02, p. 76; 3/11/03; and box 2 f. 7, report of the headworker to the College Settlement Association, 1901/02.

91 Henry F. Bedford, *Socialism and the Workers in Massachusetts 1886–1912* (Amherst: University of Massachusetts Press, 1966), 11–13, 16–17, 167–168. Green and Donohue, *Boston's Workers*, 75.

92 Bedford, *Socialism*, 1–2, 37, 64, 96. Robert A. Woods, "Social Recovery," in *The City Wilderness: A Settlement Study by the Residents and Associates of the South End House*, ed. Woods (1898; reprint, New York: Garrett Press, 1907), 282–283; and in the same volume by an anonymous author, "The Roots of Political Power," 134. Five years later, William A. Cole and Rufus E. Miles, "Community of Interest," in *Americans in Process: A Settlement Study*, ed. Woods (Boston: Houghton, Mifflin, 1903), 342, noted many socialists among Jews in the North End and a few among Italians.

93 Bedford, *Socialism*, 181–182, 194. Paula M. Kane, *Separatism and Subculture: Boston Catholicism 1900–1970* (Chapel Hill: University of North Carolina Press, 1994), 296. See Rev. John Byrne, *The Glories of Mary in Boston: A Memorial History of the Church of Our Lady of Perpetual Help Mission Church, Roxbury, Massachusetts 1871–1921* (Boston: Mission Church Press, 1921), 404–405.

94 Bedford, *Socialism*, 143–147, 189–191. Montgomery, *Fall of the House of Labor*, 295.

95 Quoted in Bedford, *Socialism*, 231–232. The phrase "parlor Socialists" comes from Franklin Wentworth, on the same page.

96 Murolo, *Working Girls' Clubs*, 100, 111.

97 By 1906/7 the Dension House head worker had clearly shifted from a view of labor organizing as central to the house to a view of workers as "the 'other side.' " DH, Box 2 f. 7 report of headworker to College Settlement Association, 1906/07. See also, DH, box 1 f. 1, Scudder, 1937, "Early Days at Denison House."

98 Kenney O'Sullivan, pp. 117, 125–126, 137–138.

99 Elizabeth Anne Payne, *Reform, Labor, and Feminism: Margaret Dreier Robins and the Women's Trade Union League* (Urbana: University of Illinois Press, 1988), 45–51. Payne dismisses Kehew as "never

more than a titular leader." The standard histories of the WTUL virtually ignore her and the 1890s background.

100 DH, box 1, vol. 3, 4/23/06, pp. 176–77. Denison House residents also supported the WTUL, 4/23/07, p. 177, but the house and its head worker's reports took far less note than of the Label League.

101 Edward O'Dennell, "Women as Breadwinners: The Error of the Age," *American Federationist* 4 (October 1897): 186, quoted in Alice Kessler-Harris, "Where Are the Organized Women Workers?" *Feminist Studies* 3 (fall 1975), reprinted in *Women's America: Refocusing the Past*, ed. Linda Kerber and Jane Sherron De Hart (New York: Oxford University Press, 1995), 248.

102 WEIU, box 1 f. 9, "Social Statistics of Working Women," pp. 16–17. On federation membership, see Keyssar, *Out of Work*, 179–180.

103 WEIU, box 7 f. 55, "Trade School for Girls in Boston." See also, Barbara M. Brenzel, *Daughters of the State: A Social Portrait of the First Reform School for Girls in North America, 1856–1905* (Cambridge: MIT Press, 1983), 147.

104 WEIU, box 7 f. 55, "Trade School for Girls in Boston." By 1909, the Trade School had moved to 620 Massachusetts Avenue. See also Susan Porter Benson, *Counter Cultures: Saleswomen, Managers, and Customers in American Department Stores, 1890–1940* (Urbana: University of Illinois Press, 1986), 150.

105 Elizabeth (Lowell) Putnam Papers, box 4, Women's Municipal League (WML), "An Account of the Women's Municipal League of Boston," as given at the first meeting, 1/20/09, p. 11, Schlesinger Library, Radcliffe College, Cambridge, MA. See Solomon, *Pioneers in Service*, 50–52.

106 Perry, *Millinery Trade*, 97.

107 WEIU, box 7 f. 49, immigrant women and children, 1906–07, p. 12, only 4 of the 500 in the sample were in training school, 1 as a nurse and 3 as domestic servants. John Daniels, *In Freedom's Birthplace* (1914; reprint, New York: Arno Press, 1969), 315.

108 Daniels, *In Freedom's Birthplace*, 379–381. Elizabeth Hafkin Pleck, *Black Migration and Poverty in Boston, 1865–1900* (New York: Academic Press, 1979), 103. And see *Guardian* 11/18/16, 1, "Work for Colored Girls."

109 WEIU, box 7 f. 56, clothing 1910–11, pp. 1–3, 6. Perry, *Millinery Trade*, 99–100, 105–106.

110 Louise Marion Bosworth Papers, carton 4 f. 170, no. 4, Schlesinger Library, Radcliffe College, Cambridge, MA.

111 Carole Srole, " 'A Position That God Has Not Particularly Assigned to Men': The Feminization of Clerical Work, Boston 1860–1915" (Ph.D. diss., University of California, Los Angeles, History, 1984), 58–59, 63–65. WEIU, series 1 carton 1, *Annual Report* 1888/89, pp. 29–31. On college preparatory training for girls, see Judith Becker Ranlett, "Sorority and Community: Women's Answer to a Changing Massachusetts, 1865–1895" (Ph.D. diss., Brandeis University, History of American Civilization, 1974), 154.

112 Murolo, *Working Girls' Clubs*, 20–21.

113 Robert Woods, "Work and Wages," in *City Wilderness*, ed. Woods. Cf. Robert A. Slayton, *Back of the Yards: The Making of a Local Democracy* (Chicago: University of Chicago Press, 1986), 57.

114 Benson, *Counter Cultures*, 8–9, 208–209. WEIU carton 8 f. 130A, "Young Persons Employed in Retail Selling" (1916), pp. 58, 87, 157. Stephen H. Norwood, *Labor's Flaming Youth: Telephone Operators and Worker Militancy, 1878–1923* (Urbana: University of Illinois Press, 1990), 42, citing *Labor News* 7/13/23.

115 Srole, "Feminization of Clerical Work," 542, 545, 547, 552, 555–557. Also 245, 237–238, 301, n31.

116 WEIU, box 11 f. 161, "A Study of the Vocational Trend in the Schools of Massachusetts," pp. 24–25, 28, 30. Henry L. Higginson Collection, case XII-13 f. E, 1913, William C. Ewing to Higginson, 3/15/13, Baker Library, Harvard Business School, Cambridge.

117 Wendy Gamber, "The Female Economy: The Millinery and Dressmaking Trades, 1860–1930" (Ph.D. diss., Brandeis University, History of American Civilization, 1990), 461, 463. See also, Gamber, *The Female Economy: The Millinery and Dressmaking Trades, 1820–1930* (Champaign: University of Illinois Press, 1997), and Perry, *Millinery Trade*, 16–18; WEIU, B-8, box 7 f. 60, Cambridge industry (1910), p. 47.

118 Gamber, "The Female Economy," 483–484. On "forelady," see WEIU, box 7 f. 56, clothing, pp. 5–6, 9, 10.

119 Quoted in Gamber, "The Female Economy," 102, 152–155.

120 WEIU, box 7 f. 60, Cambridge industry, pp. 19–20, citing the report of the Commission on Industrial and Technical Education, 1906. DH, B-27, Box 2 f. 7, 1903/04 report of the head worker to the College Settlement Association. Benson, *Counter Cultures*, 8–9, 266. See also, WEIU, box 7 f. 60, Cambridge industry, p. 32.

121 WEIU, box 1 f. 9, social statistics of women workers, p. 22. WEIU, series 2 carton 6 f. 104, Employees' Benefit Association, c. 1908/09. Cf. C. Wright, 57, 72, 74. Norwood, *Flaming Youth*, 51. See also WEIU, box 1 f. 9, "Social Statistics of Working Women," *MBLS Bulletin* 18 (May 1901): 15. Quoted in Gamber, 129, 131.

122 Bosworth, carton 4 f. 178 no. 78, 10/4/07, 10/9/07. WEIU, box 2 f. 14, pamphlet, "Women's Work in Rubber Factories and its Effect on Health," 1905.

123 Ileen A. DeVault, *Sons and Daughters of Labor: Class and Clerical Work in Turn-of-the-Century Pittsburgh* (Ithaca: Cornell University Press, 1990), 73–118. Srole, 261–263, 267, 271. Srole, "Feminization of Clerical Workers," 230–232, documents the class shift in clerical workers' backgrounds, and see 218, 247, 249, 254, on rising numbers.

124 Daniels, *In Freedom's Birthplace*, 321–322. In her samples of 2,000 women over fifteen in each of the 1880 and 1900 censuses for Boston, Carole Srole found only 1 black clerical worker in 1880 and 6 in 1900. Srole, "Feminization of Clerical Workers," 256, 309 53n, 257. Cf. Pauline E. Hopkins, *Contending Forces: A Romance Illustrative of Negro Life North and South* (1900; reprint, New York: Oxford University Press, 1988), her dialogue about the difficulty of securing clerical work for black women, 127–128.

125 Srole, "Feminization of Clerical Workers," 256, 309 53n, 257, on the hospital worker citing Philip Foner, *Women and the American Labor Movement* (New York: Free Press, 1979–80), 464. On nurses, see Peter C. Holloran, *Boston's Wayward Children: Social Services for Homeless Children 1830–1930* (Rutherford, NJ: Associated University Press, 1989), 155.

126 Norwood, *Flaming Youth*, 12–13, 25, 29–36. Factory women and girls were known for their "bad language"; in both telephone work and store work managers wanted employees to mimic the language of polite gentility their clients used, albeit with a reassuringly subservient inflection severely at odds with the independent peer culture of youth at leisure. See "Pilgrim's Progress in a Telephone Exchange," *Life and Labor*, part I (January, 1921); part 2 (February, 1921), pp. 236–240, reprinted in *America's Working Women: A Documentary History 1670 to the Present*, ed. Baxandall et al. (New York: Vintage Books, 1976), 335–358. WEIU, Befriending Record Book 11/06—, carton 7, 12/27/06, Miss Heming, Roxbury Street., Roxbury, age twenty-four, English, working at Plants Factory, says girls she has to associate with there use "bad language." On language, see also Kathy Peiss, *Cheap Amusements: Working Women and Leisure in Turn-of-the-Century New York* (Philadelphia: Temple University Press, 1982), example, p. 66. See also work by Margery W. Davies, *Women's Place is at the Typewriter: Officework and Office Workers, 1970–1930* (Philadelphia: Temple University Press, 1982); Lisa M. Fine, *The Souls of the Skyscraper: Female Clerical*

Workers in Chicago, 1870–1930 (Philadelphia: Temple University Press, 1990); Angel Kwolek-Folland, "Gender, Self, and Work in the Life Insurance Industry, 1880–1930," in *Work Engendered: Toward a New History of American Labor*, ed. Ava Baron (Ithaca: Cornell University Press, 1991), pp. 168–190; DeVault, *Sons and Daughters*, and Maureen Weiner Greenwald, *Women, War, and Work: The Impact of World War I on Women Workers in the United States* (Ithaca: Cornell University Press, 1980). On salesgirls, see Benson, *Counter Cultures*, 130, 231.

For similar trends in clerical work, see Benson, *Counter Cultures*, 10, 139–143; "Young Persons in Retail," pp. 80–81, 152. Violet Bacon Foster, the Marlborough, to Dear Margaret [Foley], on stationery of the Department of Commerce, 2/24/[16?], Margaret Foley Papers, carton 1 f. 26 Schlesinger Library, Radcliffe College, Cambridge, MA.

127 Norwood, *Flaming Youth*, 42–43. On such distinctions earlier, see DH, box, 1 f. 3, Cate 1/11–2/18/93, p. 42; Higginson, case XII-13 f. D, 1913, Newton to H. L Higginson, 10/3/13.

128 Cf. Lisbeth Haas, "La relacion entre la protesta colectiva y el espacio social del barrio, 1890–1930" in *Culturas Hispanas en los Estados Unidas de America* (Madrid: Ediciones de Cultura Hispana), 229–238. And see, for example, Glenn, *Daughters*, 204–206.

129 For example, Bosworth, carton 4 f. 170 case no. 12B, Feb. 1907. Cf. DeVault, *Sons and Daughters*, 146, on the increasing concentration and centralization of corporate headquarters and business activities in the central business district of Pittsburgh.

130 WEIU, box 7 f. 56, clothing; WEIU, *Annual Report*, Jan. 1910, p. 17.

131 WEIU, box 7, Sue Ainslee Clark, "Women's Trade Unions in the United States," 5/5/11, p. 2, quoted in Norwood, 96.

132 Green, 87.

133 Gamber, The *Female Economy* 180 84n.

134 Saunders, 51, 53, 55. Keyssar, 235, 269–272. Perry R. Duis, *The Saloon: Public Drinking in Chicago and Boston 1880–1920* (Urbana: University of Illinois Press, 1983), 283–284.

135 Mary J. Oates, "Organized Voluntarism: The Catholic Sisters in Massachusetts, 1870–1940," *American Quarterly* 30 (winter 1978): 659.

136 WEIU, box 1 f. 9, "Social Statistics of Working Women," p. 8. Patricia Cooper, *Once a Cigarmaker: Men, Women, and Work Culture in American Cigar Factories, 1900–1919* (Urbana: University of Illinois Press, 1987), 63. Saunders, "Class, Gender," 60–61.

137 Glenn, *Daughters*, 155. Robert A. Woods, "Livelihood," in *Americans in Process: A Settlement Study*, ed. Woods (Boston: Houghton, Mifflin, 1903), 125.

138 Mamie Garvin Fields, *Lemon Swamp and Other Places: A Carolina Memoir* (New York: Free Press, 1983), 149–150.

139 Norwood, *Flaming Youth*, 8, 40–44, citing Mary E. Harrington, "The Training of Operators in Boston," *NETT* (June 1910): 18. Wright, *Working Girls*, 22. And see Mary Kenney O'Sullivan autobiography, p. 123.

140 See David Roediger, *The Wages of Whiteness: Race and the Making of the American Working Class* (London: Verson, 1991), and Noel Ignatiev, *How the Irish Became White* (New York: Routledge, 1995), for examples of this literature.

141 Levine, ILGWU *The Women's Garment Workers*, 117, 127–128, 134.

142 Bosworth carton 1 f. 28, 2/2/08, to her mother.

143 Carolyn Daniel McCreesh, *Women in the Campaign to Organize Garment Workers 1880–1917* (New York: Garland Publishing, 1985), 112, citing NWTUL Papers, Gertrude Barnum, National Organizers Report, Dec., 1905 (1909?), Library of Congress; New York WTUL minutes of the executive board 3/18/09 and *Union Labor Advocate* (March 1909): 25. On Barnum, see Alice Henry, *The Trade Union Woman* (New York: Burt Franklin, [c. 1915]), 77–78.

144 McCreesh, *Campaign to Organize*, 112; Norwood, *Flaming Youth*, 144.

145 Secretary's Report, Boston Women's Trade Union League, "Biennial Convention," NWTUL 1913, p. 8, WTUL smaller collections reel, Schlesinger Library, Radcliffe College, Cambridge, MA (hereafter BWTUL), quoted in Norwood, *Flaming Youth*, 144.

146 WEIU, Box 7 f. 56, clothing, pp. 1, 4–5, 9, 14–15, 21, 23–25. On ties between WEIU and WTUL, see WEIU, vol. 1, S. Agnes Donham, *History of the Women's Educational and Industrial Union* Boston, 1955; Fannie Fern Andrews Papers, box 34 f. 400, 10/24/11, Secretary of the Massachusetts Association for Labor Legislation to F. F. Andrews. Schlesinger Library, Radcliffe College, Cambridge, MA.

147 WEIU, box 7 f. 56, clothing, pp. 4, 7, 8, 12–13, 19.

148 WEIU, box 7 f. 56, clothing, pp. 4, 7, 8, 12–13, 19.

149 McCreesh, *Campaign to Organize*, 170.

150 Green and Donohue, *Boston's Workers*: 87. Norwood, *Flaming Youth*, 97. WEIU, B-8, box 7 f. 52, "Women's Trade Unions in the United States," 5/5/11, by Mrs. Sue Ainslee Clarke.

151 Ardis Cameron, *Radicals of the Worst Sort: Laboring Women in Lawrence, Massachusetts, 1860–1912* (Urbana: University of Illinois Press, 1993), 127.

152 Norwood, *Flaming Youth*, 97, 102, 145. On Gillespie, see *The Social Worker* (August 1945), p. 9, in Eva Whiting White Papers, box 1, Schlesinger Library, Radcliffe College, Cambridge, MA; Johnson, 219, 221–222; and Ethel McLean Johnson Papers, box 1 f. 2, May 1923, giving references, Schlesinger Library, Radcliffe College, Cambridge, MA.

153 Payne, *Reform Labor*, 106; Green and Donohue, *Boston's Workers*, 89, on Woods and Scudder; McCreesh, *Campaign to Organize*, 189, on O'Sullivan with BWTUL against UTW.

154 Green and Donohue, *Boston's Workers*, 90, versus Payne, *Reform Labor*, 106.

155 BWTUL, carton 1 f. 28, executive committee minutes, Foley, 7/12/(12?). On store and office workers, see Benson, *Counter Cultures*, 145; H. L. Higginson case XII-13 f. HE-HZ, 1912, Hickox to Higginson, 3/29/12; WEIU, box 1 f. 3, *Union News Items*, 7/31/12.

156 BWTUL, carton 1 f. 28, executive committee minutes, Foley, 7/12/ (12?) 8 P.M.

157 Mary Williams Dewson Papers, box 1 f. 8, 1/20/38, Dewson to Felix Frankfurter, Schlesinger Library, Radcliffe College, Cambridge, MA.

158 *Boston Globe* 2/3/13, 1, 4 "Strike."

159 *Boston Herald* 2/1/13, 1, "Strike,"; and 2/4/13, 1, "Nearly 5000."

160 *Boston Globe* 2/3/13, 1, "Strike"; *Herald*, 2/4/13, 1, "Nearly 5000." And see Glenn, *Daughters*, 184.

161 *Boston Herald* 3/1/13, 1, "4000 Garment Workers"; 2/2/13, 4; 2/3/13, 1, "Strike."

162 *Boston Herald* 2/9/13, 1, "Big Garment"; 1/12/13, 1, 6, "Woman Picket is Arrested"; 3/13/13, 4, "Garment", and 2/15/13, 14, "State Board." Sopinski was released and the case dismissed when Kelley failed to appear. *Boston Globe*, 2/12/13, 9, "Union Enjoined." *Boston Herald* 2/18/13, 1, "Five Arrests."

163 For example, *Boston Herald* 2/20/13, 2, "Charge Police"; 3/4/13, 1, "Garment Shop"; 3/13/13, 1, "Garment Riots."

164 *Boston Herald* 2/20/13, 2, "Charge Police"; 2/21/13, 1, "Strike Riot"; and 2/22/13, 2, "12,000." For evidence of Eastern European Jews and Italians moving into East Boston, see *Boston City Directory*, 1913.

165 *Boston Globe* 5/22/02, 8, "Big Crowds Out"; 5/22/02, evening edition, 1, 9, "Check Meat Riots"; 5/23/02, 1, 4, "Thousands in Meat Riot."

166 *Boston Herald* 2/11/13, 2.

167 *Boston Herald* 2/28/13, 1, "9000 Workers."

168 *Boston Herald* 3/3/13, 1, "Whirlwind of Snow" and "4000 Pickets"; 3/4/13, p. 1, "Garment Shop District."

169 *Boston Herald* 3/4/13, 1, 3, "Garment Shop District." See also, Levine, *ILGWU*, 228; McCreesh, *Campaign to Organize*, 179–180.
170 *Boston Herald* 3/4/13, 1, 3, "Garment Shop District" and "Social Workers Interfere"; and 3/6/13, 2, "Denounces Police."
171 *Boston Herald* 3/5/13, 1, "Scores Police for Insults to Suffragists"; and 3/13/13, 1, "Garment Riots" and "Suffrage Workers Plan Help."
172 WEIU, box 1 f. 3, *Union News Items* 2:5 (March 1913): 14.
173 *Boston Herald* 3/18/13, 2, "Girls Appeal for Help."
174 Levine, *ILGWU*, 228, on the manufacturers' association. For other treatments of such strikes sensitive to spatial issues see, for example, Meredith Tax, *The Rising of the Women* (New York: Monthly Review Press, 1981), and Cameron, *Worst Sort*.
175 McCreesh, *Campaign to Organize*, 179–180. *Boston Herald* 3/18/13, 2, "Strike Again."
176 Levine, *ILGWU*, 229, 234, 276, 311. *Boston Herald* 3/18/13, 2, "Strike Again," reported that 1,000 of the 6,000 who had settled had walked out because they found nonunion operatives in their shops. Henry Lee Higginson displayed some of the mixed feelings of many Brahmins who, in the end, supported the strikers. H. L. Higginson case XII–13 f. B-BE, Miss Gertrude Barnum BWTUL to HLH, 1913; Meyer Bloomfield to HLH, 3/13/13; f. D, 1913, HLH to Henry P. Davison, Esq., NY; and HLH to Miss Frances Curtis, 12/18/13.
177 *Boston Herald* 3/13/13, 1, "Garment Riots" and "Girls Forfeit Easter Finery"; and 3/14/13, "Effort to End Strike Fails."
178 Norwood, *Flaming Youth*, 107–108.
179 "Women Hold Posts of Power in Realm of Communications," *Christian Science Monitor*, 12/7/31.
180 Norwood, *Flaming Youth*, 47, 98–99. Gamber, 180 84n.
181 Norwood, *Flaming Youth*, 100.
182 Ibid., 100–102. On Conboy, Higginson, case XII–13 f. B-BE, 1913, BWTUL letterhead of letter to Henry Higginson from Gertrude Barnum, June 1913.
183 Norwood, *Flaming Youth*, 97–98, on the male strikes of 1912. On some of the sources of operator militance, see 6–7, 19, 91–93, 94–96, 122.
184 Ibid., 102, citing *Boston Globe* 4/15/12.
185 Ibid., 100. On this strike, see also Greenwald, *Women, War, and Work*, 204–207.
186 Ibid., 103–105.
187 Ibid., 105.
188 Ibid., 105, 107–108. Levine, *ILGWU*, 117, 127–128, 134.
189 Norwood, *Flaming Youth*, 110.
190 Ibid., 108–109.
191 Ibid., 110.
192 Ibid., 110. As early as 1898, Robert A. Woods in "Work and Wages," in *City Wilderness: A Settlement Study*, ed. Woods (1898; reprint, New York: Garrett Press, 1970), 107, noted the well-dressed nature of certain workers. Also on clothing, see Norwood, *Flaming Youth*, 11–12; Bosworth, carton 1 f. 28, 5/5/08, and 5/16/08, to her mother; Benson, *Counter Cultures*, 78; and Fields, *Lemon Swamp*, on Filene's basement, 153.
193 Norwood, *Flaming Youth*, 145. See Greenwald, *Women, War, and Work*, 204–207, on the Boston origin of the Bell system.
194 Norwood, *Flaming Youth*, 7, 15–16, 92. The BCLU met every two weeks and enjoyed extensive press coverage, with a column in the *Globe* and the *Post*; between 1902 and 1923 Irish mayors governed for sixteen of twenty-one years.
195 Ibid., 110–113. The tonier *Boston Herald* 4/6/13 compared them to "boarding-school girls," "young and pretty" and "dressed modishly."

196 Norwood, *Flaming Youth*, 49, 110–113. See Benson, *Counter Cultures*, for department store lounges. The would-be strikebreakers found themselves imprisoned in their roles, not allowed to leave the hotels and under the same sort of constant supervision they faced at the workplace. Those not even compensated by being placed at the best hotels were outraged. *Boston Herald* 4/10/13, 5, "Strict Hotel Guard Disappoints Girls."

197 Norwood, *Flaming Youth*, 113.

198 Ibid., 115–117. Molloy's work for Curley was covered in a feature in the *Boston Globe* 12/4/21, 2, of the features section, "Boston Women Making Their Political Bow—Is It a Debut or a Fight?" See chapter 7. According to James J. Connolly, *The Triumph of Ethnic Progressivism: Urban Political Culture in Boston 1900–1925* (Cambridge, MA: Harvard University Press, 1998), 99–103, Storrow had worked to make the Chamber of Commerce more open, revitalizing "the moribund Yankee enclave," and had mediated ethnic politics on the School Committee. On Storrow, Philip J. Ethington, "Urban Constituencies, Regimes, and Policy Innovation in the Progressive Era: An Analysis of Boston, Chicago, New York City, and San Francisco," *Studies in American Political Development* 7:2 (fall 1993): typescript version 5/20/93, 8, 10.

199 Norwood, *Flaming Youth*, 115–117. On Young's, see Moses King, comp., *King's Handbook of Boston* (Boston, 1889), 66.

200 Norwood, *Flaming Youth*, 223. Polly Welts Kauffman, foreword to *An Independent Woman: The Autobiography of Edith Guerrier*, ed. Molly Matson (Amherst: University of Massachusetts Press, 1992), p. xv, on Mrs. Storrow. On the WCC, see Elizabeth (Lowell) Putnam Papers, box 33 f. 571, Helen Storrow to Haynes and "The Women's City Club of Boston organized June 20, 1913," pp. 4–5 Schlesinger Library, Radcliffe College, Cambridge, MA; Andrews, box 152; and George W. Coleman, "Progressive Movements in Boston," in *Fifty Years*, ed. Herlihy, 638.

201 See Glenn, *Daughters*, Robert A. Woods, "Traffic in Citizenship," in *Americans in Process A Settlement Study*, ed. Woods (Boston: Houghton, Mifflin, 1903), 157, 162. See also Patricia A. Cooper, *Once a Cigar Maker: Men, Women, and Work Culture in American Cigar Factories, 1900–1919* (Urbana: University of Illinois Press, 1987), particularly 6–7.

202 Norwood, *Flaming Youth*, 14, 91–92, 121, 137, 146–147. And see Susan S. Walton, *To Preserve the Faith: Catholic Charities in Boston, 1870–1930* (New York: Garland Publishing, 1993), 55, 126–127, 144–145. On Irish women's exposure to party politics, see, at the Massachusetts Historical Society, Boffin's Bower, *Fourteenth Annual Report* (Boston: Franklin Press, 1881), 7: "In a political campaign they [working girls] are called upon by their brothers to furnish funds to purchase uniforms, torchlights and music." I am indebted to David Zonderman for finding these. And "The Roots of Political Power," in *City Wilderness: A Settlement Study*, ed. Robert A. Woods (New York: Houghton, Mifflin, 1898), 120, on the socials held by young men's political clubs: "About the same class of girls attend all the socials; they go from one club to the other. Almost without exception they are factory girls, and nearly all of them are bold and vulgar."

203 Roediger, *Wages of Whiteness*, 12, quoting W. E. B. DuBois, *Black Reconstruction in the United States, 1860–1880* (1935; reprint, New York, 1997), 700–701.

204 Norwood, *Flaming Youth*, 151, credits the BWTUL with preparing them for an independent national union. On workers' education see 225. For the rest see 2, 4–5, 91, 148–151.

205 Ibid., 117–120, 147.

206 Ibid., 14, 91–92, 121, 137, 146–147; Green and Donohue, *Boston's Workers*, 87.

207 Norwood, *Flaming Youth*, 143. There seemed to be a spillover impact from unionizing. See "Young Persons in Retail," 81.

208 Saunders, "Class, Gender," 49.

209 Keyssar, *Out of Work*, 149, 265–266, 268. DH, box 2 f. 7 report of headworker to college settlement association, 1914/15.

210 Keyssar, *Out of Work*, 235, 269–272.
211 Ibid., 41.
212 DH, box 2 f. 7, report of Headworker to College Settlement Association, 1916/17.
213 DH, box 2 f. 7 report of headworker to College Settlement Association, 1917/18.
214 Solomon, *Pioneers in Service*, 119.
215 Keyssar, *Out of Work*, 272–276.
216 Saunders, "Class, Gender," 80–81, 88.
217 Montgomery, *The Fall of the House of Labor*, 367–369.
218 Boris, *Home to Work*, 135–136, 146.
219 Green and Donohue, *Boston's Workers*, 94, 98.
220 Ibid., 72. See also, Cooper, *Cigar Maker*, 274, 278, 284–285, 289, 296–298, on the anti-radicalism of the BCLU.
221 Norwood, *Flaming Youth*, 1, 158–164.
222 Ibid., 168, 170–181. Greenwald, *Women, War, and Work*, 218–220.
223 Norwood, *Flaming Youth*, 181–182. The *Globe* did not support the strikers.
224 *Boston Evening Transcript*, 4/17/19 and 4/18/19, quoted in Norwood, *Flaming Youth*, 182. Cf. Jacquelyn Dowd Hall, "Gender and Labor Militance in the Appalachian South," *Journal of American History* 73 (1986): 354–382.
225 Norwood, *Flaming Youth*, 184, 189–191; Green and Donohue, *Boston's Workers*, 96; Greenwald, 220–227.
226 Norwood, *Flaming Youth*, 184–185, 188–189, 192–193.
227 Ibid., 183, quoting NWTUL, "Proceedings of the 1919 Convention," p. 115 reel 22.
228 Norwood, *Flaming Youth*, 185–186.
229 Ibid., 1, 193–194.
230 Ibid., 226, 228, 230–231, 242.

Chapter 7

1 *Boston Herald* 3/14/13, 1.
2 Felice Gordon, *After Winning: The Legacy of the New Jersey Suffragists, 1920–1947* (New Brunswick, NJ: Rutgers University Press, 1986); Pamela Tyler, *Silk Stockings and Ballot Boxes: Women and Politics in New Orleans, 1920–1963* (Athens: University of Georgia Press, 1996); Susan Ware, *Beyond Suffrage: Women in the New Deal* (Cambridge: Harvard University Press, 1981); Elisabeth Israels Perry, *Belle Moskowitz: Feminine Politics and the Exercise of Power in the Age of Alfred E. Smith* (New York: Oxford University Press, 1987); Kristie Miller, *Ruth Hanna McCormick: A Life in Politics 1880–1944* (Albuquerque: University of New Mexico Press, 1992); Nancy F. Cott, *The Grounding of Modern Feminism* (New Haven: Yale University Press, 1987).
3 Exceptions would include a few works on women and the welfare state that engage with black women's history, such as Linda Gordon, "Black and White Visions of Welfare: Women's Welfare Activism, 1890–1945," *Journal of American History* 78 (September 1991): 559–590; and Stephanie J. Shaw, *What a Woman Ought to Be and to Do: Black Professional Women Workers During the Jim Crow Era* (Chicago: University of Chicago Press, 1996).
4 Polly Welts Kaufman, *Boston Women and City School Politics, 1872–1905* (New York: Garland Publishing, 1994), xi–xiii, 1, 3, 33–34, 37–38, 47, 124; Lois Bannister Merk, "Boston's Historical Public School Crisis," *New England Quarterly* 31 (1958): 173.
5 Kaufman, *Boston Women*, xi–xiii, 160 ff, 188, 209–210, 217–221. See also Dennis P. Ryan, *Beyond the Ballot Box: A Social History of the Boston Irish, 1845–1917* (Amherst: University of Massachusetts Press, 1983), 60; James J. Connolly, *The Triumph of Ethnic Progressivism: Urban Political Culture in Boston 1900–1925* (Cambridge: Harvard University Press, 1998); Merk, "Public School Crisis,"

176–180, 182–183. See also Stone to Mrs. Upton (c. 1893) on the back of a flyer naming Women Voter's candidates for the School Committee, finding that only some "necessity like this of Catholic interference with the school" would spur women to vote. Alma Lutz Collection, M-105, Schlesinger Library, Radcliffe College, Cambridge, MA. The Boston Woman Suffrage League, an MWSA affiliate, on the other hand, had Dr. Salome Merritt and others speak at an indignation meeting to offset the Protestant extremists. Merk, "Public School Crisis," 185.

6 Kaufman, *Boston Women*, xiii, 269; Merk, "Public School Crisis," 188, 189.

7 Kaufman, *Boston Women*, 306, 309, 323, 332–333, 336, 338, 343 (over half the graduates of the Boston Normal School had Irish surnames in 1901), 349–353; Constance K. Burns, "The Irony of Progressive Reform: Boston 1898–1910," in *Boston 1700–1980: The Evolution of Urban Politics*, ed. Ronald P. Formisano and Constance K. Burns (Westport, CT: Greenwood Press, 1984), 140. See also, Philip J. Ethington, "Recasting Urban Political History: Gender, the Public, the Household, and Political Participation in Boston and San Francisco during the Progressive Era," *Social Science History* 16:2 (summer 1992): 321–323.

8 Kaufman, *Boston Women*, 349–350, 381.

9 Kaufman, *Boston Women*, iv, 384, 393; Ethington, "Recasting," 322–324.

10 Harriet Hanson Robinson, *Massachusetts in the Woman Suffrage Movement: A General, Political, Legal and Legislative History from 1774 to 1881* (Boston: Roberts Brothers, 1881), 59; Andrea Moore Kerr, *Lucy Stone: Speaking Out for Equality* (New Brunswick: Rutgers University Press, 1995), throughout.

11 Kerr, *Lucy Stone*, 158, 160, 225, 234 on bazaars, 245 for a visit of Mrs. Ruffin and Mrs. Sparrow on Stone's deathbed, 191 on the Fenno Tudor reception and its press. See Amelia Muir Baldwin Collection, Schlesinger Library, Radcliffe College, Cambridge, MA, for pageants, which she designed.

12 See Kerr, *Lucy Stone*, 225; chapter 6 on the garment workers; Priscilla Murolo, *The Common Ground of Womanhood: Class, Gender, and Working Girls' Clubs, 1884–1928* (Urbana: University of Illinois Press, 1997), on working-girls' clubs; and Polly Welts Kaufman, foreword to *An Independent Woman: The Autobiography of Edith Guerrier*, ed. Molly Matson (Amherst: University of Massachusetts Press, 1992), xv, on Guerrier's Saturday Evening Girls.

13 Stephen H. Norwood, *Labor's Flaming Youth: Telephone Operators and Worker Militancy, 1878–1923* (Urbana: University of Illinois Press, 1990), 142; Sharon Hartman Strom, "Leadership and Tactics in the American Woman Suffrage Movement: A New Perspective," in *Our American Sisters: Women in American Life and Thought*, 3d ed., ed. Jean E. Friedman and William G. Shade (Lexington, MA: D.C. Heath and Co., 1982), 381.

14 Strom, "Leadership and Tactics," 383.

15 Ellen Cantarow with Susan Gushee O'Malley and Sharon Hartman Strom, *Moving the Mountain: Women Working for Social Change* (Old Westbury, NY: Feminist Press, 1980), 16, quoting Luscomb.

16 Florence Luscomb, "Our Open-Air Campaign," c. 1909, in the Women's Rights Collection, Schlesinger Library, quoted in Strom, 381–382; Florence Luscomb, OH-2, Twentieth Century Women Oral Histories, p. 46, Schlesinger Library, Radcliffe College, Cambridge, MA.

17 Strom, "Leadership and Tactics," 383; Margaret Foley Collection, 81-M58, carton 1, inventory, Schlesinger Library, Radcliffe College, Cambridge, MA; carton 1 f. 7, "B" Christmas cards, Blackwell to Foley, an undated one says Foley's voice is like a trumpet.

18 Strom, "Leadership and Tactics," 384–385. On such tactics gaining press coverage, see Fannie Fern Andrews Collection, A-95, box 15 f. 225, executive board minutes, Boston Equal Suffrage Association for Good Government (hereafter BESAGG), 9/14/10, 1/11/11; and 3/2/11, Schlesinger Library, Radcliffe College, Cambridge, MA; as opposed to clippings in Foley, carton 1 f. 37; *Sunday Globe* paid Foley $10, 1/7/13, for contributing to their editorial symposium on equal suffrage, and Andrews, box 15 f. 228, 11/4/15, Ryan to Andrews.

19 Foley, carton 1, inventory. Foley was born in 1875.

20 Strom, "Leadership and Tactics," 383. And see Foley, carton 1 f. 20, 4/17/20, James A. Mayer, director of Department of Education, State House, Boston; D. Ryan, *Beyond the Ballot Box*, 51–52; and 5/21/20, Edith M. Haynes to Foley, Foley, carton 1 f. 7.

21 Cantarow, *Moving the Mountain*, 26.

22 Foley, carton 1 f. 2, diaries. Strom, "Leadership and Tactics," 376, 378; Andrews, box 15, f. 225, executive board minutes, BESAGG, 12/2/08; and 1/6/09. See Andrews, box 15 f. 225, for other relevant executive committee minutes of BESAGG, particularly, 11/21/08, 12/2/08, 2/3/09, 4/7/09, 5/13/10, 9/14/10, 1/11/11, 2/8/11, and 12/28/08.

23 Andrews, box 15 f. 226, 8/4/19, Pinkham to Andrews; Foley, carton 1 f. 39, delegates to the MWSA annual convention, 1918; and f. 225, 6/13/10. Cf. Ellen Carol DuBois, "Working Women, Class Relations, and Suffrage Militance: Harriot Stanton Blatch and the New York Woman Suffrage Movement, 1894–1909," *Journal of American History* 79 (June 1987) reprinted in *Unequal Sisters: A Multicultural Reader in U.S. Women's History*, 2d ed., ed. Vicki L. Ruiz and Ellen Carol DuBois (New York: Routledge, 1994), 228–246.

24 Andrews, box 15 f. 226, 1/3/10 Ames, BESAGG to Andrews; and 4/16/17, Eleanor O'Brien, sec. of BESAGG, calling the special meeting. And see Aileen S. Kraditor, *The Ideas of the Woman Suffrage Movement, 1890–1920* (New York: W. W. Norton, 1981), 31–32, 39 n54, 158–159.

25 Baldwin, box 2 f. 21.

26 BESAGG, 6th Report, 1910–12, pp. 14–16, and quarterly report MWSA June 1910, p. 14, quoted in Strom, "Leadership and Tactics," 386.

27 Andrews, box 15 f. 226, Mary Hutcheson Page to Andrews, 3/2/15, trying to raise $15,000 to pay for the work; box 15 f. 225, and on hired canvassers, 11/15/07, Andrews to Fitzgerald.

28 Foley, carton 1 f. 20, 6/17/14, C.I.R to Foley.

29 Foley, carton 1 f. 38; see Andrews, box 15 f. 226, Announcements 1914/15.

30 Foley, carton 1 f. 20, Reitman to Foley, various letters from 7/14/15 to 8/31/16.

31 See, for example, Nichols-Shurtleff Family Papers, box 7 f. 33, Mrs. Ella (Richard) Cabot to Marion Nichols, 12/19/08, Schlesinger Library, Radcliffe College, Cambridge, MA; and Andrews, box 15 f. 232, Evelyn Peverley Coe to Andrews, 2/9/22, at which point the League of Women Voters owed Luscomb $100. During her work for the Margaret Brent Suffrage Guild, Foley received no pay for seven weeks. Foley, carton 2 f. 45, 9/25/19, to members of the executive board; similarly, carton 1 f. 37, on a disputed bill, 3/16/20, Foley to Mrs. Richard A. Lynch.

32 Foley, carton 1 f. 17, Tillinghast to Foley, 1919. On Tillinghast, see Durwood Howes, *American Women: The Official Who's Who Among the Women of the Nation* (Los Angeles: Richard Blank Publishing 1935), 555.

33 Foley, carton 1 f. 17, 2/25/18, Grace Johnson to Foley.

34 Foley, carton 1 f. 37, 2/19/16, Blackwell to Foley, on the national being unable to offer full-time work and Blackwell not wanting Foley tied up in case Massachusetts needed her; 6/15/15 and 8/5/15, Blackwell to Foley, explaining her inadequacies as a fund raiser as why she could not aid Foley; and 1/27/14, Gertrude Halladay Leonard, MWSA to Foley on Alice Paul wanting to hire Foley but the unlikelihood of Mrs. Rossing letting Foley go because Rossing had little sympathy with Paul and her Congressional Union.

35 Foley, carton 1 f. 20 [1914], Reilly to Foley.

36 Andrews, box 15 f. 226, 4/6/17, Eleanor J. O'Brien, secretary and Page; and 3/26/18, where the "War Service Committee" dwarves BESAGG on the masthead.

37 Foley, carton 1 f. 7, 8/23/18, Bagley to Foley.

38 On the transfer to the state see Andrews, box 15 f. 225, 6/13/10 and 9/14/10 minutes; on

friction see Foley, carton 1 f. 39, 7/23/15, Foley to Mrs. Gertrude Halladay Leonard, MWSA; and carton 1 f. 8, resumé.

39 For example, Foley, carton 1 f. 20, Reilly to Foley, Saturday [c. 1914].

40 Foley, carton 1 f. 7, 8/4/19, Blackwell to Foley. Foley, carton 1 f. 15, 10/2/18, Sally Keene to Foley.

41 Foley, carton 1 f. 7, 8/9/18, Foley to Bird.

42 Foley, carton 1 f. 7, 9/4/18, Anna C. Bird to Foley.

43 Foley, carton 1 f. 8, resumé. She had been attending broadening lectures since 1916, including talks on psychology, socialism, mental development, and history. Foley, carton 1 f. 2, diaries.

44 Foley, carton 1 f. 19, 10/2/18, Lucinda W. Prince to Foley.

45 Foley, carton 1 f. 8, 12/2/18, Foley to Mr. Very, Lockwood Green and Co.; and f. 26, 3/29/18, Edwin Mulready to Hon. George Holden Tinckham.

46 Foley, carton 1 f. 7, 7/29/18, Foley to Mrs. Bagley.

47 Foley, carton 2 ff. 44, 45.

48 Foley, carton 2 f. 45, 9/25/19, Foley to members of the executive board; f. 44, 12/10/19, Mrs. Minnie T. Wright to Foley; 3/12/20, M. Foley as secretary reporting on Margaret Brent Suffrage Guild; and 7/21/19, report by Foley.

49 Foley, carton 1 f. 8, 1/10/20 Civil service exam grades Mary Anderson to Foley, 4/8/20; f. 17, 9/16/19, Marian C. Nichols.

50 Foley, carton 1 f. 22, 4/8/20, Anna C. M. Tillinghast to Foley; f. 8 applying for the Democrat's speakers bureau; f. 21 Apr. 20 correspondence with Anna Tillinghast at the Republican State Committee.

51 Foley, carton 1 f. 21, example, 11/29/20, carbon of bill for St. Mary's Catholic Women's Club; also f. 22, for parliamentary law class, and see f. 26, for Americanization classes offered through the WML.

52 Foley, carton 1 f. 7, 10/30/20, Cram to Foley. For the official letter of appointment, see same file, 11/23/20. Foley, carton 1 f. 8, 11/19/20, Cram to Foley.

53 See Norwood, *Flaming Youth*, on Matthews, for example, 143.

54 Henry L. Higginson Collection, case XII–13, 1912, general correspondence, 1912 I-LA, 11/22/12, Lee to Higginson. Baker Library, Harvard Business School, Cambridge. On Curtis, see Joseph Lee, "The Chelsea Fire," *Charities and the Commons*, 20 (May 2, 1908): 149–151; Andrews, box 24 f. 290, vol. 14, April 1928, pp. 8–11; *Boston Globe* 12/12/21, Elizabeth (Lowell) Putnam Collection box 30 f. 489, 11/6/25, to Mrs. Williams, Schlesinger Library, Radcliffe College, Cambridge, MA.

55 Kaufman, *Boston Women*, 394–395. On Curtis's equal pay position, see *Boston Globe* 12/10/23, 7, "Equal Pay."

56 Ethel McLean Johnson Collection, carton 2 f. 25, *Boston Herald* 11/26/31, "Those Appointed," and n.d., "Women in Meehan Fight"; *Boston Evening Transcript* 1/20/32, "Ely Orders," Schlesinger Library, Radcliffe College, Cambridge, MA.

57 Putnam, box 33 f. 570, clipping, *Boston Herald* 3/30/24, "Massachusetts Women Cast Spring. . . ." *Boston Herald* 3/30/21, in Putnam, box 33 f. 570.

58 *Boston Sunday Herald*, Social Life section, "Candidates . . . ," 7; and 11/11/25, 1. Meehan came in tenth.

59 Johnson, carton 2 f. 25, *Boston Evening Globe*, 1/20/32, "Orders a Speaker Out"; n.d., "Women in Meehan Fight."

60 Johnson, box 1 f. 2, resumés, carton 4 f. 100, 8/27/18, June Richardson Donnelly, director of the School of Library Science to Johnson; and see, carton 2 f. 46, "Why Vote? An Anti-

Suffrage Monologue" by Johnson, reprinted in *The New American Woman* in 1918, and in similar vein in carton 3 f. 73, "Miss Christabel Thinkhurst in WHY VOTE? An anti-suffrage monologue."

61 Johnson, box 1 f. 2, resumés.

62 Johnson, box 1 f. 12, 3/8/29, Marion C. Johnson to Ethel M. Johnson; carton 2 f. 52, has the articles by Johnson on her trajectory from the WEIU into politics.

63 Johnson, carton 2 f. 26, "Politics and Public Welfare." Cf. Felice Gordon, *After Winning*, on the range of organized women's attitudes toward party politics after suffrage, in particular her material on the regular and the irregular Republican women.

64 Johnson, carton 2 f. 26, EMJ 1922.

65 Johnson, box 1 f. 4, "Massachusetts Council on Women and Children in Industry." Cf. L. Gordon, "Black and White," 576, on women achieving appointive or elective office continuing to call on their network of private sector welfare leaders, blurring the lines between private and public power.

66 *Boston Herald* 1/21/32, in Johnson, carton 2 f. 25.

67 *Boston Globe* 12/16/31, "Women Republicans Oppose . . . ," in Johnson, carton 2 f. 25.

68 Johnson, carton 2 f. 25 [1932], "No Action Yet"; *Herald* 1/21/32.

69 *Boston Herald* 11/26/31, "Those Appointed"; and n.d., "Defends Herself on Meehan Stand." On Andrews, see *Boston Herald* 11/3/27, 1, "Andrews to be Councillor." Johnson, carton 1 f. 25, 1932, "Mrs. Andrews Charges Deal . . ."

70 *Boston Evening Transcript* 1/20/32, "Ely Orders," in Johnson, carton 1 f. 25. *Boston Globe* 1/20/32, "Orders a Speaker. . . ."

71 Johnson, carton 2 f. 24, Hallowell, Jones and Donald, Wool Merchants, to Lt. Gov. Youngman, 12/15/31.

72 See Paula Baker, "The Moral Framework of Public Life: Gender and Politics in Rural New York, 1870–1930" (Ph.D. diss., Rutgers State University of New Jersey, 1987), 50, 57–68, 83, 113; Kristi Andersen, "No Longer Petitioners: Women's Political Involvement in the 1920s" (paper prepared for presentation at the annual meeting of the Midwest Political Science Association, Chicago, Apr. 14–16, 1988), 20–21; and Jill Kathryn Conway, *The First Generation of American Women Graduates* (New York: Garland Publishing, 1987), 314–318, 373. On politicization, see, for example, National Urban League Papers, group 4 box 28, 1/29/34, Goodman to Hill, Library of Congress.

73 Johnson, carton 2 f. 25, "Women in Meehan Fight"; and see letters in f. 24.

74 Johnson, carton 2 f. 25, *Boston Evening Transcript* 1/20/32, "Ely Orders."

75 *Boston Globe* Evening edition 1/20/32, "Orders a Speaker Out," in Johnson, carton 2 f. 25.

76 Johnson, carton 2 f. 25, *Boston Herald* 11/26/31, "Those Appointed"; and f. 24, Johnson's January 1932 statement on the departmental conflicts. Johnson complained of "a system of espionage and intimidation." Johnson, carton 2 f. 25, *Christian Science Monitor* 1/21/22, "Renaming of Miss Johnson. . . ."

77 For example, *Boston Globe* 11/17/20, 16, a cartoon, "Mrs. Simon Pure."

78 Lorinda Perry, *The Millinery Trade in Boston and Philadelphia: A Study of Women in Industry* (Binghamton, NY: Vail-Ballou, 1916), 16.

79 Frances G. Curtis, "Woman's Widening Sphere," in *Fifty Years of Boston: A Memorial Volume*, ed. Elisabeth M. Herlihy (Boston: n.p., 1930), 626.

80 *Boston Globe* 11/16/20, 12, "Telephone Girls Making Plans for Two Parties"; 11/18/20, 1, "Labor Federation Cuts Out Radicals," and 4, "Prof. Hudson Talks to WTUL"; 11/19/20, 12; 11/20/20, 2, 8, on employee parties. Louis Levine, *The Women's Garment Workers: A History of the ILGWU*

(New York: B. W. Huebsch, 1924), 450 on striking the radical preamble (1918) from the 1924 constitution of cloak-makers; *Boston Globe* 11/2/25, 1, on the new delegates plan of the BCLU.

81 On slave auctions by Urbain J. Ledoux, see Alexander Keyssar, *Out of Work: The First Century of Unemployment in Massachusetts* (New York: Cambridge University Press, 1986), 237–244. On labor fragmentation and business coherence see Trout, 18.

82 Levine, *ILGWU*, 358–359, 385, 395, 428, 490; James R. Green and Hugh Carter Donahue, *Boston's Workers: A Labor History* (Boston: Trustees of the Public Library of the City of Boston, 1979), 102–103.

83 Judith E. Smith, "Our Own Kind: Family and Community Networks in Providence," in *A Heritage of Her Own: Toward a New Social History of American Women*, ed. Nancy F. Cott and Elizabeth H. Pleck (New York: Simon and Schuster, 1979), 393–411, and Smith, *Family Connections: A History of Italian and Jewish Immigrant Lives in Providence, Rhode Island, 1900–1940* (Albany: State University of New York Press, 1985), on choices from declining homework; Linda Gordon, *Heroes of Their Own Lives: The Politics and History of Family Violence* (New York: Viking, 1988), 181–182, for examples of family economies; Dawn M. Saunders, "Class, Gender, and Generation: Mother's Aid in Massachusetts and the Political Economy of Welfare Reform" (Ph.D. diss., University of Massachusetts at Amherst, Economics, 1994), 71–72; Keyssar, *Out of Work*, 169–170; Green and Donahue, *Boston's Workers*, 103. See Baker Chocolate Company records, female payrolls for dichotomy of 119 women in six departments at Baker Chocolate Company in Dorchester in 1928: 57 had been there in 1918 and 1919; on the other hand, the company had severely cut the workforce, and those 119 had been 296 in 1918. Baker Library, Harvard Business School, Cambridge.

84 Norwood, *Flaming Youth*, 259–260, 305.

85 Ibid., 14, 277–279.

86 *Boston Post* 11/3/27. See *Boston Globe* 12/3/23, evening edition, 12, "What Every Flapper Knows."

87 *Boston Post* 11/3/27. See also Murolo, *Working Girls' Clubs*, on working-girls' clubs shifting increasingly to entirely social programming. Barbara Miller Solomon, *Pioneers in Service: The History of the Associated Jewish Philanthropies of Boston* (Boston: Court Square Press, 1956). Even in coverage of actual women on the streets, the paradigm had shifted. In 1920, the *Globe* (11/20/20 and 11/26/20) covered two assaults on women; one headline read, "Girl Puts Up Good Fight with Assailant" (8); the other, (1) "Woman Fights Alleged Footpad at South End." Cf. Joanne J. Meyerowitz, *Women Adrift: Independent Wage Earners in Chicago, 1880–1930* (Chicago: University of Chicago Press, 1988), 127, 130–131, on 1920s plucky heroines, regardless of their prior sexual behavior, winding up with the men they love.

88 Curtis, "Widening Sphere," 635.

89 John L. Rury, *Education and Women's Work; Female Schooling and the Division of Labor in Urban America, 1870–1930* (Albany: State University of New York Press, 1991).

90 Chamber of Commerce Collection, case 72, item 364–62, Boston Forewoman's Council, c. 1922–1925, n.a., 9/14/23, received filing department, "The Forewoman and Her Job," Baker Library, Harvard Business School, By contrast, see Susan Porter Benson, *Counter Cultures: Saleswomen, Managers, and Customers in American Department Stores, 1890–1910* (Urbana: University of Illinois Press, 1986), 24, on New York department store clerks offended by the term "saleswomen," insisting on "salesladies." None of Boston's department stores belong to the forewomen's council, most likely because it was avowedly industrial.

91 WEIU, box 8 f. 64, "The Part-time Worker in Boston Settlements"; and box 11 f. 162, information from the Altrusa Club, Oct. 30. *Boston Globe* 11/217/20, 3, "Association of Women Lawyers has Dinner"; the president was a married woman; and 11/18/20, 17 "New England

Women's Press [Association] Thirty-fifth Anniversary." *Boston Herald* 12/1/21, 13, "Advertising Women Selling Campaign" on the Advertising Women's Club of Boston, Mrs. A. Frances Hanson, president, and "Business Women's Club Chorus Heard" (at its clubhouse, 144 Bowdoin Street).

92 Barron and her husband set up practice together and shared child-tending duties. See *Boston Globe* 11/5/25, 1, "Finds Time to be a Lawyer. . . ." Dr. Joseph V. Lyons, a dentist running for School Committee in 1927, was married to Dr. Marie F. (Gavin) Lyons, also a dentist. *Boston Herald* 11/3/27. (Loitman Barron was Jewish; Lyons was Catholic.) Benson, *Counter Cultures*, 185, found that department stores' employment recruiters in the 1920s focused on married women as well as students. See also James Joseph Keneally, *History of American Catholic Women* (New York: Crossroad, 1990), 137, on Theresa O'Leary Crowley's career.

93 Curtis, "Widening Sphere," 634.

94 Charles H. Trout, *Boston: The Great Depression and the New Deal* (New York: Oxford University Press, 1977), 24.

95 Karen J. Blair, *The Clubwoman as Feminist: True Womanhood Redefined, 1868–1914* (New York: Holmes and Meier Publishers, 1980); Andrews, box 15 f. 226, on parlor meetings at Mrs. Langdon Frothingham's (476 Beacon St.), and "Reconstruction: What Congress Is Doing Now"; and f. 234, a five-week study course on U.S. foreign relations under the BLWV international relational relations committee, at the home of Mrs. Arthur Moors, 171 Beacon Street. *Boston Globe* 12/3/24, p. 11, "Mrs. Turner Heads Fragment Society."

96 WEIU, box 11 f. 129, "Journalism."

97 *Guardian* 1/15/43, 1, "Women and Public Office."

98 Quotation from Eva Whiting White, "Social Agencies in Boston, 1880–1930," in Herlihy, ed., *Fifty Years*, 140—six policewomen were added in 1921; *Boston Globe* 12/3/21, 1. Andrews, box 15 f. 232, 3/25/20, BLWV report of the executive secretary (Pinkham); and [between 12/1 and 12/4/21], "To Endorse. . . ." And see Gordon, *Heroes*, 358 52n.

99 *Boston Herald* 11/25/31, 1–2, "Hub Policewomen Eligible for Post of Sargeant."

100 *Daily Advertiser* 11/5/27, 15 "Girls vs. Boys." WEIU, B-8, box 11, has a number of folders organized by vocation; see, for example, f. 129, journalism, offering many opportunities for editorial assistants and virtually none for managing editors. See also f. 117, chemistry; f. 183, nursing; f. 148, psychiatry.

101 *Guardian* 4/14/34, f. 3, for example, when Mr. and Mrs. Frank Snowden had five Howard University men as guests, and all attended an "elegant soiree" given by the Delta Conclave [sorority] at Dorchester Plaza; or 4/28/34, 3, when Minnie T. Wright, prominent club woman, former suffragist, and civic leader in cross-racial groups, held "a swank seafood dinner party at one of our leading grills" with lobster and champagne for the reception of the Grand Exalted Ruler of her sororal group, Boston University Collection (hereafter BU).

102 For example, *Guardian* 4/14/34, 3, "Here and There" by Paul Jordan. Ruffin Family Papers, 87-2, box 2 f. 89, has the June 1928 edition of the *Saturday Evening Quill*, Moorland Springarn Research Center, Howard University, Washington, D.C. For Boston area black college enrollments, see *Crisis* (August 1928): 260; "Along the Color Line," *Crisis* (January 1929): 14.

103 *Guardian* (BU), 4/21/34, 3, for example.

104 *Guardian* (BU), 7/28/23, 3.

105 Mitchell's husband was a lawyer. Lucy Miller Mitchell in *The Black Women Oral History Project from the Arthur and Elizabeth Schlesinger Library on the History of Women in America, Radcliffe College*, ed. Ruth Edmonds Hill (Westport, CT: Meckler, 1991), vol. 8, pp. 30, 68. See *Guardian* 9/30/39, 5, "Gets Scholarship"; and 10/7/39, 1, "Boarding School Solution to Working Mothers." And see Shaw, *What a Woman Ought*, 124, on Lucy Mitchell.

106 Reprinted in Urban League campaign flyer, 1926, Urban League, series 4 box 28. And see *Boston Globe* 11/17/20, 9, "Pageant Shows Rise of the Colored Race." Bostonians put on a seemingly endless stream of pageants in the 1920s, many of them on the Common, enacting racial and ethnic harmony that was more wished for than present. (See, for example, 7/10/23, Horace Morrison to Eva Whiting White on one in East Boston, Eva Whiting White Papers, box 1 f. 3, Schlesinger Library, Radcliffe College, Cambridge, MA). A black counterpart occurred in 1930 when a group of black girls performed in "The Beacon" on the Boston Common, portraying market scenes from the West Indies, Tripoli, Morocco, and the East Indies. "Along the Color Line," *Crisis* (Feb. 1930): 309. Also representing the race, though with less sugarcoating, were Maud Cuney Hare and her players in a series of plays by black playwrights. See *Crisis* (Feb. 1928): 55; (Apr. 1928): 124–125; (June 1928): 199; (July 1929): 237; (March 1930): 96; (May 1930): 166; and (July 1930): 238.

107 *Globe*, 12/8/21, p. 10; Urban League series 4 box 28 1/15/26; NAACP Papers, I-G-88, 7/29/25, Wilson to J. W. Johnson, Library of Congress. Boston Urban League's 1920 Annual Report, pp. 5–6. See Urban League series 13 box 5; and Boston YWCA Collection, carton 2 f. 46, "History of the Interrace Committee," p. 2, Schlesinger Library, Radcliffe College, Cambridge, MA. On sales work see Benson, *Counter Cultures*, 211–212. "Bridget" was becoming "black." In "Polly," a comic strip in the *Boston Herald*, the white family has quite a staff, all of whom are white, except the Japanese valet and the black cook, "Liza." See, for example, *Boston Herald*, 12/11/21. Even domestic work could be scarce. The *Globe* (12/5/23, 8, "Colored Maid a Suicide . . .") reported of Miss Sadie Johnson, forty, "It is believed she was despondent because she could not find work." In 1919 the Northeastern Federation of [Colored] Women's Clubs applied for affiliation with NAWSA; the latter barred them on the basis of expediency, see Suzanne Lebsock, "Woman Suffrage and White Supremacy: A Virginia Case Study," in *Women's America: Refocusing the Past*, 4th ed., ed. Linda Kerber and Jane Sherron De Hart (New York: Oxford University Press, 1995), 327.

108 NAACP, Group I-G f. 88, 12/22/26, Frances Gunner to Walter White; 8/25/26, Mabel C. Bradley, Farmer's School of Cooking, to Miss Vinson; 5/11/27, Bradley to Miss Thelma Ellen Williams, on Miss Farmer's School of Cooking. NAACP, I-G-88, 4/30/29, Mrs. James S. Tipon to New York NAACP, re: Sargent School in Boston for Physical Education; 11/3/25, Julia M. Stratton to Major Joel E. Springarn, re: Posse Normal School of Gymnastics; and Urban League flyer for 1926 campaign, series 4: box 28 on business colleges. On hospitals, see NAACP I-G-88, 1/23/27, Thelma Pear Perry to NAACP; 1/25/27, Wilson to White; and clipping from *Transcript* 2/17/28, "Divide on Hospital"; Sherlene Voogd Cochrane, " 'And the Pressure Never Let Up': Black Women, White Women, and the Boston YWCA, 1918–1948," in *Women in the Civil Rights Movement: Trailblazers and Torchbearers, 1941–1965*, ed. Vicki L. Crawford, Jacqueline Anne Rouse, Barbara Woods et al. (Brooklyn: Carlson Publishing, 1990), 263; Boston YWCA papers, carton 2 f. 46, "History of the Interrace Committee," p. 2, Schlesinger Library, Radcliffe College, Cambridge, MA; "Along the Color Line," *Crisis* (Dec. 1929): 417. See Urban League series 4 box 28, "The Work of the Boston Urban League," n.d. [approximates an annual report for 1927/28], re: opening new occupations; and 10/20/26, 6/4/26, 2/3/27, 4/26/27, 5/27/27, all Allen to Hill; the jobs opened included, among others, the public library, dress factory pressing and finishing, and elevator operator. See Urban League Series 4 box 28, 5/21/28, Miss Bernice W. Billings, R.N., to Hill. The Boston YWCA Interrace Committee started in the spring of 1924. See BYWCA, History of the Interrace Committee, pp. 3–4.

109 Foley, carton 1 f. 22, Mrs. John B. [Harriet C.] Hall, Mrs. A. H. Casneau, Mrs. Minnie T. Wright, and Mrs. Rose Brown were suffragists; Mrs. E. C. Roundtree was a black realtor. On

black Boston suffragists, see also files at Harriet Tubman House, Boston, MA, on Mrs. Melnea Cass, 1896–1978; Beverly Guy-Sheftall, *Daughters of Sorrow: Attitudes Toward Black Women, 1880–1920* (Brooklyn: Carlson Publishing, 1990), 109, 124; *Guardian* 2/3/40, 1, on Miss Gertrude L. Cromwell.

110 Elisabeth S. Clemens, "Organizational Repertoires and Institutional Change: Women's Groups and the Transformation of U.S. Politics, 1890–1920," *American Journal of Sociology* 98: 4 (January 1993): 756.

111 See Chamber of Commerce, case 53 f. 340, Committee on Municipal and Metropolitan Affairs, discussion of suggested program of that committee for 1921–22.

112 Trout, *Boston*, 16.

113 Ibid., 16. See also, Connolly, *Ethnic Progressivism*, 36, 96.

114 Connolly, *Ethnic Progressivism*, 109–110; Perry R. Duis, *The Saloon: Public Drinking in Chicago and Boston 1880–1920* (Urbana: University of Illinois Press, 1983), 256.

115 Trout, *Boston*, 28–29; Keyssar, *Out of Work*, 272, 279; Peter K. Eisinger, "Ethnic Political Transition in Boston, 1884–1933: Some Lessons for Contemporary Cities," *Political Science Quarterly* 93 (summer 1978): 235–236, from 1884 to 1930 only one Irishman, David Walsh, held the governorship, and then only for two years.

116 *Boston Herald* 12/10/22. Trout, *Boston*, 28–29, and foreward to Trout, by Richard C. Wade, xii. And see *Boston Globe* 11/6/39, 16, "Hendricks Club Fails to Indorse for City Council," for an example of the fragility of Boston's machines.

117 Andrews, box 15 f. 226, special business meeting announcement, Twentieth Century Club, 10/3/19.

118 Mary Williams Dewson Papers, box 1, 11/21/52, Dewson to Dear Hick, Schlesinger Library, Radcliffe College, Cambridge, MA. J. Stanley Lemons, *The Woman Citizen: Social Feminism in the 1920s* (Chicago: University of Illinois Press, 1973), 91–92. See also, John D. Buenker, "The Urban Political Machine and Woman Suffrage: A Study in Political Adaptability," *Historian* 33 (February 1971): 271–272.

119 See, for example, Andrews, box 15 f. 227; and f. 232, 9/13/22, letterhead.

120 See Lemons, *Woman Citizen*, 97–100, and Cott, *Grounding*, 107, on politicians' attacks.

121 *Boston Globe* 11/17/20 evening edition, 1.

122 Andrews, box 15 f. 232, 3/25/20, BLWV report of executive secretary Pinkham. Putnam, box 35 f. 601, Putnam replying to 7/20/20 note from Bagley, the former objecting to endorsement by the Republican State Committee of a letter "written by a partisan body like the League of Women Voters."

123 Andrews, box 15 f. 232, BLWV call to convention to Ward 8 members.

124 *Boston Globe* 12/1/21, 41. *Boston Herald* 12/1/21, 9; 12/5/21, 3, "Most of Council Candidates Unknown"; and 16, "Woman Candidate to Open Her Campaign." And see *Boston Globe* 12/7/21, 8, "Mrs. Chipman opens her campaign"; and 12/12/21, 5.

125 *Boston Globe* 12/7/21, 8, "Mrs. Chipman"; *Boston Herald* 12/5/21, "Most of Council," 3. *Boston Herald* 12/7/21, 3. The BLWV endorsed Thomas Niland, a self-employed East Boston member of house painters local no. 170 with one year of law school, a record as an active Democrat, and a term in the State House of Representatives (1918–1919), whom the GGA deemed honest but of unsound judgment; and Charles Carr, Harvard 1899, Harvard Law 1902, with offices on Beacon Street, a member of the Republican Club of Massachusetts and of the central board of directors of the Family Welfare Society. He had served on the Common Council in 1908, the Board of Alderman in 1909, and the State House of Representatives from 1910 to 1912, as well as on the financial commission that oversaw Boston from 1912 to 1917 and on the Overseers of the Poor from 1919 to 1921.

126 *Boston Globe* 12/1/21, 41.

127 Putnam, box 33 f. 574.

128 Andrews, box 15 f. 232, BLWV Brief Summary of Year's Work; f. 226, BLWV letterhead, 11/10/19 with motto listing good citizenship as "consecration"; on fending off the spoilsmen, see *Boston Herald* 12/1/21, 24, "Women Voters Appeal for Funds"; *Boston Globe* 12/10/21, 16, "Murphy Only Man." Cf. Cott, *Grounding*, 112–113, on politically active women in the 1920s.

129 *Boston Globe* 12/10/21, 16, "Murphy Only Man"; *Boston Herald* 12/9/21, 14, "Murphy to Speak." *Boston Globe* 12/8/21, 10, "Pledges Colored Vote to Murphy"; Keneally, 136. So, too, did labor leaders, *Boston Herald* 12/8/21, 15, "Campaign to Reach. . . ." The Republican Women's City Committee, of course, also endorsed Murphy. *Boston Herald* 12/3/21, 7, "Women of G.O.P. Indorse Murphy." See also Hasia R. Diner, *Erin's Daughters in America: Irish Immigrant Women in the Nineteenth Century* (Baltimore: Johns Hopkins University Press, 1983), 142–148, on Irish women and the woman suffrage movement.

130 *Boston Globe* 12/4/21, 2, feature section.

131 Norwood, *Flaming Youth*, 143; *Boston Globe* 12/4/21, 2, feature section. See also Foley, carton 1 f. 7, 5/29/20, Eliza Daly to Foley.

132 On numbers, see *Boston Globe* 11/25/20, 9, with 131,170 registered men, and 67,473 registered women; in 1921 there were apparently 78,000 registered women. See *Boston Herald* 12/1/21, 24, "Women Voters Appeal for Funds." By the end of the decade, the numbers seem to have evened out. The *Herald* reported on 11/5/29, 25, "Offices to Be Filled," that the registered voters included approximately 152,000 men and 127,000 women.

133 *Boston Globe* 12/11/21, 1, "Vote of Women Expected to be the Deciding Factor Tuesday."*Boston Globe*, evening edition, 12/13/21, 1, 20, "Heavy Voting by Boston Women"; and 12/14/21, 11.

134 *Boston Globe*, 12/14/21, 1; only one GGA candidate won. The only clear elite reform victory was that of Fanny Curtis for School Committee, heavily triumphing (with 78,989 votes—7,769 ahead of her rival) over a less elite male challenger, and benefiting by a large vote from women. *Boston Herald* 12/13/21, Chipman received 17,513 votes; the lowest contender, George Murphy, received 13,967. The council winners garnered over 50,000 votes each.

135 Frank Kent, *The Great Game of Politics*, quoted in Lemons, *Woman Citizen*, 110–111. Norwood, *Flaming Youth*, 276.

136 *Boston Globe*, Sunday feature section, 2, "Boston Women Making. . . ."

137 Cf. Ira Katznelson, "Working-Class Formation and the State: Nineteenth-Century England in American Perspective," 257–284; in Ira Katznelson and Aristide R. Zolberg, *Working-Class Formation: Nineteenth Century Patterns in Europe and the United States* (Princeton: Princeton University Press, 1986).

138 Andrews, box 15 f. 232, 6/22/22, Mrs. Malcolm Forbes to members.

139 Luscomb, box 10 f. 229, 11/29/22, press release from her headquarters; *Traveler* 12/5/22.

140 Norwood, *Flaming Youth*, 139–140. On the advisory council, see Johnson, box 1 f. 4, "Advisory Council on Women in Industry," listing O'Connor on the executive committee.

141 Norwood, *Flaming Youth*, 219, 265 ff. Molloy had been one of the first presidents of the union; O'Connor, having served two terms as vice president, became president in 1918. Molloy represented the toll operators, older and more skilled operators who had initially dominated the union and were threatened by the new dial telephones. O'Connor, according to Henry Wise, "let the ordinary Irish of South Boston know she was above them," in contrast to the earthier Molloy. Ibid., 269, 273, 276–277, 280–282, 292.

142 Luscomb, box 10 f. 229, clippings, *Boston Globe* 11/22/22, "Seven Quality," and *Transcript* 12/2/22, "Two G.G.A. Candidates."

143 Andrews, box 15 f. 232, 3/25/20, on Luscomb sending weekly press notices to Boston papers;

Luscomb, box 10 f. 229, documents on nomination and election expenses. See Andrews, box 15 f. 232, 12/4/22, Pinkham to members BLWV.

144 Luscomb, box 10 f. 229, *Boston Globe* 11/17/22, "Miss Luscomb Enters. . . ."; *American* 12/5/22.

145 Luscomb, box 20 f. 229, *Boston Globe* 11/17/22, "Miss Luscomb Enters. . . ."

146 Andrews, box 15 f. 232, 12/4/22, Pinkham to members with Luscomb's statement.

147 Luscomb, box 10 f. 229, n.d., Pinkham to Mrs. John C. Lee; and mass mailing letter. Luscomb, box 10 f. 229, *Boston Globe* 12/4/22; and *Boston Herald* 12/10/22.

148 Luscomb, box 10 f. 229, *Traveler* 12/5/22.

149 Luscomb, box 10 f. 229, *American* 12/5/22.

150 Luscomb, box 10 f. 229, *Telegram* 12/4/22; and 12/11/22.

151 See, for example, the 1913 masthead of the Massachusetts Association Opposed to the Further Extension of Suffrage to Women in Foley, carton 2 f. 72, which included a Codman, Lowell, Russell, Putnam, and Saltonstall, among others; as opposed to the letterhead of BESAGG in 1918, full of reformers, less elite, if still solidly well off, and college professors, as well as a complement of Brahmins, in Foley, carton 1 f. 7.

152 Luscomb, box 10 f. 229, 11/29/22, press release from her headquarters; and *Traveler* 12/5/22.

153 Luscomb, box 10 f. 229, *Christian Science Monitor* 12/4/22, "Women More Thrifty Buyers." Ironically, Luscomb had become a union organizer among office workers in the 1930s. See Cantarow, *Moving the Mountain*, 5.

154 Luscomb, box 10 f. 229, *Boston Post* 12/13/22.

155 Luscomb, box 10 f. 229, *Boston Herald* 12/13/22.

156 Luscomb, box 10 f. 229, *Post* 12/13/22. The lowest winner (the GGA candidate, Healey) had 19,335 votes; Luscomb had 18,682 and Molloy 8,305. On Luscomb, see Schlesinger Library, OH-2, Twentieth Century Trade Union Women Oral Histories. Florence Luscomb, 4/4/78, interview with Brigid O'Farrell; Cantarow, *Moving the Mountain*, 23, 27; Luscomb, box 10 f. 230, on her 1936 campaign, including the circular, "People's Labor Ticket"; Chamber of Commerce, case 53 f. 340, Committee on Municipal and Metropolitan Affairs, Cornelius A. Parker to Brehaut, secretary of committees, Boston Chamber of Commerce, 8/18/25, on the Massachusetts Civic League.

157 Luscomb, box 10 f. 229, Harriet F. Blake, "The Woman in Politics," *Review* 12/14/22. For alienated BLWV members see, for example, Luscomb, box 10 f. 229, *Telegram* 12/11/22; and *Boston Globe* 12/4/21 Sunday features, 2, "Boston Women Making." See F. Gordon, *After Winning*, on the New Jersey LWV's retreat from partisan politics, shifting to more educational mode at mid-decade, 46, 49; and cf. Chamber of Commerce, case 53 ff. 340, Committee on Municipal and Metropolitan Affairs, Suggested Program for 1924–1925. See *Boston Globe* 11/20/20, evening edition, 5, on the Republicans getting "an infinitely greater number of the new voters on the lists than the Democrats." Susan Fitzgerald was a progressive, reform Democrat. A supporter of the League of Nations in 1917, she was the first woman to nominate a presidential candidate at a Democratic National Convention. As the most prominent Democrat among the Massachusetts suffrage leaders, it is not surprising that the party fingered her in 1922, wooing former suffragists, for a seat in the Massachusetts House of Representatives. Mead, SCPC microfilm publications, Edwin and Lucia Ames Mead 1880–1938, DG 21 box 6 reel 78.3, Swarthmore College Peace Collection, letterhead of the League for Progressive Democracy. Putnam, box 33 f. 570, clipping, *Boston Herald* 3/30/24, "Massachusetts Women Cast Spring . . . ," on Fitzgerald as "easily the foremost woman in the Democratic party." See Lemons, *Woman Citizen*, 86–87, on Democrats and women, 1920–1924. On Fitzgerald at the nominating convention, see *New York Times* 7/1/20, 1, 4. She nominated a progressive

prohibition candidate. Fitzgerald had earlier run for the School Committee (1912) and lost: *Guardian* 1/6/12, 5; and 1/13/12, 1, 4. See Kaufman, *Boston Women*, 390. For a comparison of similar trends among New Jersey women, including the courting of suffragists by both parties, the suffragists opting for offices in party state committees rather than in the LWV, etc., see F. Gordon, *After Winning*, 36, 38, 77, 79, 80, 92. Cf. Cott, *Grounding*, 106, 108–109.

158 Buenker, "Political Machine," 271–272.

159 Luscomb, box 10 f. 229, *American* 12/28/22.

160 For example, Luscomb, box 10 f. 229, *Boston Globe* 12/8/22; *Boston Herald* 12/9/21, 4, 11; *Boston Post* 10/28/29, 1, "4000 Women Hear Curley," on speaking at women's organizations.

161 *Boston Globe* 12/1/23, 8, 9; 12/9/23, 19; 12/10/23, 7; and 12/12/23, 1. On instability see, for example, *Boston Globe* 11/1/33, 10; and 11/2/33, 1, 7; Trout, *Boston*, 42, 62–64.

162 The measure passed narrowly, by about 53,000 to 51,000 votes. *Boston Post* 11/6/24, 1, "City Council by Wards is Favored"; *Boston Herald* 11/1/25, Social Life section, Political Comment, 7. That year 113 candidates ran for twenty-two council places. According to Peter Holloran, *Boston's Wayward Children: Social Services for Homeless Children 1830–1930* (Rutherford, NJ: Associated University Press, 1989), 181–182, from 1924 to 1949 100 city councillors were elected; they included 12 Jews, 9 Yankees, 4 Italians, 1 African American, and 84 Irish.

163 *Boston Post* 10/9/29, has the Democratic Women's headquarters at 20 Beacon Street; the Republicans were at 46 Beacon Street Putnam, box 34 f. 596, George A. Rich, president of the Republican Club of Massachusetts.

164 Putnam, box 30 f. 489, 11/6/25, to Mrs. Williams; and box 20 f. 371, 6/26/26, Putnam to Hyde. See also her conflicts with Anna Tillinghast, the businesswoman, suffragist, and Republican Party leader (chair of the Republican Women's Executive Committee in 1920 and vice president of the Business and Professional Women's Republican Club of Massachusetts): Putnam, box 20 f. 371, 5/14/24, to Hyde; box 34 f. 595, 2/9/20, to Hon. John Weeks, and 7/19/20, Tillinghast to Putnam; box 35 f. 602, 1/14/21, Mabel C. Batchelder to Putnam; box 34 f. 591; box 30 f. 484; 5/22/28, Putnam to Alice Robertson; box 34 f. 589, 3/4/22, Putnam to various against Tillinghast's plan for female representation on the Republican State Committee. See for national comparison Lemons, *Woman Citizen*, 86–87; F. Gordon, *After Winning*, 90. On Putnam, see Putnam, box 34 f. 591, 1/15/21, Putnam to Mr. Hardenbrook, on her election as president of the Massachusetts electoral college, giving a brief bio; box 3 f. 46, 4/4/15, clipping from the *Boston Herald*, "Woman Objects to Peace Party"; box 30 f. 178, on Amy Lowell; box 30 f. 483, 1/9/31 Putnam to Amos Taylor; box 20 f. 371, 3/28/24, Putnam to Mary Hyde; box 30 f. 48, 10/29/26, on her antiradicalism and service during World War I; box 30 f. 503, Boston Centennial Committee, 1921/22; box 34 f. 594, 10/2/26, letterhead of the Republican City Committee; box 16 f. 188, 2/10/24, letter to the editor of the Springfield *Republican* on the Shepard-Towner Act; box 30 f. 483, on her position regarding prohibition; box 4 WML reports; and box 7 f. 128, on her cutting her political eyeteeth trying to get milk reform in Boston.

165 *Boston Globe*, evening edition, 12/13/21, 20, "Heavy Vote by Boston Women"; Lutz, M-105, [c. 1893], Stone to Mrs. Upton. See, also, Andersen, "No Longer Petitioners," 23, citing "Women Who Won," *Woman Citizen*, 11/18/21, on the shift from saloons and pool halls as polling places to churches, schools, and public buildings.

166 *Globe* 12/4/21, Sunday features, 2, "Boston Women Making." On earlier spacial politics, see the thought-provoking piece by Louise L. Stevenson, "Women Anti-Suffragists in the 1915 Massachusetts Campaign," *New England Quarterly* 52 (1979): particularly 181–182.

167 Johnson, carton 2 f. 26, Ethel Johnson [c. 1931], "Mary Jane and the Primaries." See also

F. Gordon, *After Winning*, 85, on women suffrage leaders' sense that office seeking was self-seeking; Cott, *Grounding*, 100.

168 Curtis, "Widening Sphere," 630.

169 Putnam, box 3 f. 46, 4/22/[22], printed with revision in Scrapbook III, p. 134.

170 SCPC Microfilm Publications, Edwin and Lucia Ames Mead 1880–1938, DG 21 box 6 reel 78.3, 9/1/22, Mead to Hurlburt, president of the bar association of the city of Boston in regard to a dispute over George White's will. Cf. Cott, *Grounding*, 101.

171 Unedited transcript of 12/10/34 National Consumers' League Conference on Labor Standards, "Can Industry Police Itself?" courtesy of Landon Storrs. See also in this vein, Mary Dewson in Emily Newell Blair, "What's SHE Up to Now?" *Today*, 6/2/34, in Dewson, box 1. See Roby A. Black, "Mary W. Dewson," *Equal Rights*, 8/8/36, clipping, p. 179, in Dewson, box 1.

172 Cott, *Grounding*, 106, 108–109. See F. Gordon, *After Winning*, 55, 58, 115, for a similar picture in New Jersey and for her term, "moral prodders." And see Consumers League of Massachusetts Papers, box 28 f. 478, Schlesinger Library, Radcliffe College, Cambridge, MA on their 1930s campaign against the resurgence of sweatshops.

173 Dewson, box 1, [1912], to My dear Mr. [Theodore] Roosevelt.

174 *Boston Post* 11/3/27; *Boston Globe* 11/3/27, p. 1, "Woman Rejoices at Council Seat as 'Honor to Sex.' " The Governor's council confirmed expenditures, modified sentences in capital crimes, and inspected state institutions.

175 *Boston Post* 11/3/27; Boston *Globe* 11/3/27, 1, "Woman Rejoices." Contrast to a piece the *Globe* 12/2/23, 5, on the "Little Mother of Chicago."

176 *Daily Advertiser*, 11/3/27, 9; and 11/6/27, 17.

177 Eva Whiting White, box 2 f. 26, Eleanor W. Allen, "Boston WEIU," *New England Galaxy* (spring 1965): 5, on Barron's work with them; *Boston Globe* 11/2/25, evening edition, 17; and 11/5/25, 1; see also Edward T. James, with Janet Wilson James and Paul S. Boyer, eds., *Notable American Women 1607–1950: A Biographical Dictionary* (Cambridge: Harvard University Press, 1971), 55–56.

178 Putnam, box 34 f. 601, Republican State Committee, 1/18/27, showed Pigeon as a delegate from East Boston (second Suffolk district); and box 35 f. 602, 4/30/20, showed her as a delegate from the first Suffolk district. Putnam, box 30, f. 479, to Pigeon, 9/30/29, responds to Pigeon's request for advice on her candidacy.

179 *Boston Herald* 11/3/29, 29, "City Councilmen . . ."; and 11/6/29, 1, 20; *Boston Globe* 11/7/29, 1, "New School Board Member . . ."; *Boston Post* 10/18/29, 24, "Campaigns All Day on Anniversary."

180 See *Boston Globe* 11/5/29, 5; and 11/6/29, 1, when Pigeon and William A. Reilly, also endorsed, ran first and second. *Boston Globe* 11/4/31, 1, banner headlines "P.S.A. Loses Control of Boston School Committee"; *Boston Herald* 11/4/31, 1, "Election Breaks Rule of P.S.A. Control."

181 Barron, the only woman on the committee, was also unable to get through a proposal for appointing career advisers for high school girls; the *Post* ranked it with "other 'frills and fads' which appear in the guise of modern education." *Boston Post* 11/10/27, 8, "Record Vote"; and 10/8/29, p. 22, "Beats Mrs. Barron's Proposal"; Kaufman, *Boston Women*, 182–184—on that 1882 committee there were six Catholics, sixteen Protestants, and one rabbi. Two of the Protestants were women. Andrews, box 15 f. 226, 10/21/14, circular to "fellow member"; Andrews and Mrs. Louis D. Brandeis were both active in BESAGG.

182 *Daily Advertiser*, 11/6/27, section M, 7, "With New England Women's Clubs." On New Hampshire woman, see 11/9/27.

183 *Boston Post* 11/7/27 and 11/9/27, 11. See also Foley, 81-M58, carton 1 f. 39, delegates to the MWSA Annual Convention, 1918.

184 See, for example, *Boston Globe* 11/2/33, 10, 11/4/33, evening edition, 2; and 11/6/33, 4, 11/8/33, 1, 22. Regan ran again in 1935, finishing tenth of twenty-nine; in 1933 she had finished sixth of nine. *Boston Globe* 11/6/35, 1. See also *Boston Post* 11/8/39, 8, on that year's three female candidates for School Committee. *Boston Post* 11/5/39, 7; and 11/2/39 2. Lally had also run in 1937, see, *Boston Globe* 10/20/37, 1. In contrast, in New Jersey, F. Gordon, *After Winning*, 160, found the number of women running for state and county office on major party tickets declined from the 1920s to the 1930s, though more women ran on third party tickets.

185 *Boston Globe* 11/8/33, 1, 22. Ward 1 had eight candidates; Ward 9 had three. For Miller see *Boston City Directory* 1933, p. 1297; Miller worked in East Boston and lived there with her father and brother.

186 *Boston Globe* 10/26/31, 5, "Is Fifth Woman to Seek Council Post." Her picture in the *Boston Globe* 10/31/31, 8, shows a youthful looking woman with long, wavy hair. Portia Law School for women had opened in 1908. Curtis, "Widening Sphere," 632.

Contrast this relatively extensive coverage and even coverage for a candidate as *un*serious as O'Connor (*Boston Globe* 11/1/35, 24, "Candidate to Vindicate") with that given to Mrs. Lena Clark, who ran in Ward 1 in both 1937 and 1939, to whom the *Post* gave the most coverage, which consisted simply of describing her as "a housewife." *Boston Post* 11/1/37, 8, "Hot Fights"; *Boston Globe* 11/7/39, 1, which has a picture of all three women running for City Council that year. The other two were from political families and received more coverage. On Clark see *East Boston Argus* 9/15/39, 4; she was affiliated with the ladies' auxiliary of the Moose Lodge, the Women's Democratic Club, and the Merry Makers Club. "She believes," it reported, "she will get a large vote in the across the tracks precincts where hundreds of voters have signed her nomination papers." According to the 1939 *Boston City Directory*, p. 370, her husband was a watchman.

187 *Boston Globe* 10/31/31, 8.

188 *Boston Herald* 10/21/31, 21; 10/27/31, 8, with the GGA endorsements (six of ninety-three candidates), which were all men; 11/2/31, 2; and 11/4/31;*Boston Post* 11/4/31, 14 (L'Ecuyer garnered 569 votes; Curley candidate Richard Garvey, 2,256; and the winner, Francis Kelley, 5,106). *Boston Globe* 11/1/31, 17, "Interest in Voting. . . ."

189 *Boston Globe* 11/3/37.

190 *Boston City Directory* 1935–1938.

191 *Boston Globe* 3/13/37, evening edition, 1.

192 *Boston Globe* 3/13/37, evening edition, 1; *Boston Globe* 3/13/37, 1, 18.

193 *Boston Globe* 3/13/37, evening edition, p. 1, "Service Rendered Mrs. Harris' Aim," by Dorothy G. Wayman.

194 Lemons, *Woman Citizen*, 103, and James et al., eds., *Notable American Women*, 587–589 (thanks to Pamela Phillips) on Edith Nourse Rogers, the sixth woman elected to the U.S. House of Representatives, who served from Massachusetts from 1925 to her death in 1960. On non-Boston female successful candidates, see, for example, *Boston Post* 11/6/24, 7 (Lynn); *Boston Globe* 11/16/20, 13, re: Wellesley, where they worried "Women Will Crowd Men Out of Town Meeting"; and 11/8/39, 1, "First Woman Mayor in Bay State" (Westfield). On demography, see Putnam, box 34 f. 595, police listing by wards, 1921, and *Boston Post* 10/18/29, 18.

195 *Boston Post* 10/18/29, 18, "Destiny. . . ." In 1937, the *Globe* found women harder to read, 11/2/37, 1, 14.

196 Putnam, box 34 f. 595, police listing by wards, 1921. In Wards 1 through 7, 9, men outnumbered women; in the North End, they did so by 6,000. In Ward 8 (Back Bay), by contrast,

women outnumbered men by just under 5,000. Women also outnumbered men in Wards 10 to 26, usually by little, but in Ward 16 by 1,500 and in Ward 25 by about 2,000.

197 *Boston Post* 10/18/29, 18, "Destiny. . . ." There were 254,268 women and 238,982 men in Boston, but only 127,272 women registered to vote, as opposed to 152,091 men. In the early 1920s, about 78,000 women had registered and about 140,000 men.

198 See Cott, *Grounding*, for example. Lemons, *Woman Citizen*, 103–104, 108–111, on the hostility of male party politicians.

199 DH, box 5 vol. 12, study of the Denison House area, p. 21.

200 *Globe* 11/6/35, 1, 20, "100 IN RACE RIOT IN SOUTH END."

201 *Chronicle* 11/9/35, 1, "Cooke Asks . . ." Gleason had 2,149 and Cooke 1,545 votes; and 5/6/39, 1, "Wyche Out for Council Post," on Gleason's invincibility a decade earlier.

202 See, for example, NAACP Papers, Group I-G f. 90, 8/12/37, Myrtle to Juanita, Library of Congress:

203 [Julian Steele], Robert Gould Shaw House, Annual Report, 1932/33, in the National Federation of Settlements Collection, box 34 f. 341, at the Social Welfare Archives, University of Minnesota. Minneapolis, MN. National Urban League Papers, Series 4, box 28, Library of Congress.

204 NAACP, Group I G f. 90, 1/12/38, executive committee minutes: Met Life said they did not hire colored agents or stenographers; and 10/31/37, Myrtle to Williams. BYWCA, "History of the Interrace Committee," p. 2; Urban League, annual reports and correspondence, series 13 box 5 and series 4 box 28 1919–1939; *Chronicle* 5/28/32, 1, "Negroes Barred at Art School"; box 32 f. 15, Grace Abbott, report on Harriet Tubman House, 10/19/34, Edith and Grace Abbott Papers, Special Collections, Regenstein Library, University of Chicago. Cochrane, "Compelled," 53; *Chronicle* 5/6/39, 1, "NAACP Fights Jim Crow Charges"; *Transcript* 7/14/34 and 7/17/34 on the shooting; *Chronicle* 4/23/32 and 10/28/33. *Guardian* 8/22/42, 1, "Boston Gets First Race Police Lieutenant."

205 *Chronicle* 5/7/32, 1, "Gangsters Insult and Kick Two Women."

206 *Chronicle* 5/7/32, 4, editorial, "To Parents of Girls."

207 *Guardian* (BU) 4/28/34, 1; *Chronicle* 8/28/37, 4, "Hub-Bub"; *Chronicle* 4/9/38, 1, 5, "Citizens Complain. . . ."

208 *Chronicle* 11/12/32; 4/28/33; and 3/11/33. Michael P. Conzen and George K. Lewis, *Boston: A Geographical Portrait* (Cambridge, MA: Bullinger Publishing Co., 1976), 38.

209 Gerald H. Gamm, *The Making of New Deal Democrats: Voting Behavior and Realignment in Boston, 1920–1940* (Chicago: University of Chicago Press, 1986), 91, on the gendered nature of the black voter party switch. On Ruffin's organization see, for example, Darlene Clark Hine, " 'We Specialize in the Wholly Impossible': The Philanthropic Work of Black Women," in *Lady Bountiful Revisited: Women, Philanthropy, and Power*, ed. Kathleen D. McCarthy (New Brunswick, NJ: Rutgers University Press, 1990), 73, 86, and *Guardian* 7/15/39. On a tradition of female antilynching activity in Boston, see, for example, 9/5/16, Wilson to Nash, NAACP, Group II-L f. 43, and the (*Hartford, CT*) *Courant*, 3/5/17.

210 On antilynching, see, for example, the Northeastern Federation of [Colored] Women's Clubs' 1922 delegation to Senator Lodge of Massachusetts to urge passage of the Dyer [antilynching] bill; Rosalyn Terborg-Penn, "Discontented Black Feminists: Prelude and Postscript to the Passage of the Nineteenth Amendment," in *Decades of Discontent: The Women's Movement, 1920–1940*, ed. Lois Scharf and Joan M. Jensen (Westport, CT: Greenwood Press, 1983), 272. On Judge John J. Parker, see, for example, NAACP, Group I-G f. 89, 10/16/30, headquarters to Loud and replies 11/7/30 through 1/7/31.

211 *Chronicle* 6/3/33, 1, "Democratic League Ousts Worthy." See also *Chronicle* 9/9/33 and 10/14/

33. On Rainey's 1925 run, in which he came in second in a field of five, see *Boston Herald*, Social Life section, 11/1/25, 7, "Candidates"; and 11/5/25, 20. *Chronicle* 9/9/33, "Worthy's Democrats Begin to Work." *Chronicle* 12/8/32, 1, "Democrats Plan for Union."

212 *Chronicle* 7/23/32, 1, 8.

213 "Along the Color Line," *Crisis* (April 1930): 133, on Rainey's appointment as assistant corporation counsel for Boston, which carried a $5,000 salary. Jack R. Van Der Sil, *Black Conflict with White America* (Columbus, OH: C. E. Merill Publishing, 1970), 8 (thanks to Jeffrey Sammons). *Globe* 11/2/33, evening edition, 10. Unified or not, by 1934 black Democrats were able to hold a "Monster" rally for Curley. *Guardian* (BU), 11/10/34, 1, "Colored Democrats Hold Monster Curley Rally." The *Chronicle* (11/10/34, 1, "Huge Crowd at Rally") estimated the attendance at 1,500. Earlier that year, for the first time in city history, black men won places on a Democratic ward committee (Ward 4); *Guardian* 5/5/34, 8, "City News." And in 1936, Mrs. Mabel Worthy was named a presidential elector and elected a member of the state committee with Rainey. *Chronicle* 6/13/36, 1, "Convention Sidelights."

214 *Chronicle* 3/19/32, 1, "Women Learn Politics 'Too Fast' says Bullock," and 6/3/33, 4, "Our Girls in Roxbury." Bullock had been appointed by Republican Gov. Alvin T. Fuller as parole board officer in 1927. *Guardian* 7/8/39, 4.

215 John Daniels, *In Freedom's Birthplace* (1914; reprint, New York: Arno Press, 1969), 98–101, on state representatives and patronage, 269–271 and 275, on redistricting, and 275, n1 on the black Company "L" in the state militia.

216 Ibid., 112–116; 130–131.

217 Ibid., 279, 290, 298–304.

218 While Detroit's black population between 1910 and 1930 grew by 1900%, Cleveland's by 800%, and Chicago's by 430%, Boston's grew by only 50%, from 13,564 to 20,574. In 1920, Boston had had 16,350 blacks, and by 1940, it had 23,679. That made them 2% of Boston in 1910, 2.2% in 1920, 2.6% in 1930. Stephan Thernstrom, *The Other Bostonians: Poverty and Progress in the American Metropolis, 1880–1970* (Cambridge: Harvard University Press, 1973), 179; Gamm, *The Making of New Deal Democrats*, 95; Urban League, series 13 box 5, Annual Report of the Boston branch of the National Urban League, 1919/20, p. 4.

219 *Guardian* 6/3/39, 3, and 7/29/39, 1 (on Slade's and Estelle's); and 6/10/39, 1 (on the Charles Street Church); *Chronicle* 9/17/32, 1 (on the South End Co-op, whose officers and directors by this time included two women and several male NAACP officers, Drs. John B. Hall and T.E.A. McCurdy and Rev. David Klugh); Urban League, series 13 box 5 Boston branch Annual Report, 1919/20, p. 5.

220 *Guardian* (BU) 7/28/23, 1; and 7/12/24.

221 *Guardian* 7/27/40, 7, "Civic Leader." For another example of a black female Republican politico, see Mrs. William O. (Edna S.) Goodell, daughter of an original member of the Women's Era Club, a founder and one-time president of LWCS, from 1924 a member of the Ward 4 (South End) Republican Committee, and in 1932 the first black woman named by the Republican State Committeemen as an alternate delegate to the Republican convention. A former teacher in the public schools, she helped organize the Women's Council of Massachusetts to instruct black women in the vote. She was not quite of the status of Hall: her husband was never mentioned, and her son was a member of the auxiliary committee of the Red Caps union. *Guardian* 12/2/39, 8; *Chronicle* 6/18/32; 3/19/32, 1; and 1/7/39 [chairing the community orchestra rehearsals at Harriet Tubman House]. *Guardian* 7/22/39; *Guardian* (BU) 4/28/34. Elizabeth (Lowell) Putnam Papers, box 34 f. 601, 3/1/22, Keniston to Putnam, Schlesinger Library, Radcliffe College, Cambridge, MA; *Chronicle* 3/19/32, 1; and 9/17/32, "Change

Ward Committee," 1. *Guardian* 5/27/39, 4, on multiple black candidates for the ward's City Council spot. *Guardian* (BU), 4, "Political Results"; *Guardian* 2/19/44, 4.

222 On Slade's, see *Chronicle* 9/17/32, 1, On the Ward 9 Civic League, see *Chronicle* 9/3/32, 1 advertisement, "Join the Ward 9 Civic League; 9/10/32, 1; and 9/17/32, 1 "To the Voters of Ward 9."

223 On Hall, see *Chronicle* 3/16/35, on WSC; and 7/6/40, 3; and see profile in *Guardian* 7/27/40, 7, "Civic Leader." *Boston Globe* 12/8/21, p. 10, speaking at a Murphy rally. Her husband, Dr. John B. Hall, a comrade of Trotter with lifelong connections to the Equal Rights League, was also active in fraternal and other organizations (he was examining physician for the Elks). He shared many of her political interests and affiliations and also served with the New England Tennis Association. See *Guardian* 4/14/34; 11/6/43, 1, 4; and 1/9/04, 1. On the elitism of the NAACP, see, for example, NAACP, Group I-G f. 89, 2/10/32 memo, re: conversation with Wilson; and 11/22/12, Wilson to Nerny. On Women's Republican Club, see *Guardian* 1/21/39, 4, "Republican Club Elect Officers"; and 10/26/40, 5. Adelaide M. Cromwell, *The Other Brahmins: Boston's Black Upper Class, 1750–1950* (Fayetteville: University of Arkansas Press, 1994), 143–147.

224 On Worthy, see, for example, *Boston Globe* 11/2/33, 10; *Chronicle* 5/20/33, 4. On Hall, see, for example, *Boston Globe* 12/8/21, 10; *Guardian* 7/27/40, profile. *Chronicle* 11/9/35, 4, "A Sad State of Mind."

225 *Guardian* 10/28/39, 5, "Mildred M. Harris Councillor."

226 *Chronicle* 2/12/38, 1, "City Councillor Speaks to Friendship Club."

227 *Boston Post* 11/8/39, 8; 11/7/39, 6; and 11/4/39, 5. *Guardian* 11/18/39, 4, "Edna Black's Statement." And see *Guardian* 9/23/39, on the controversy over naming part of Madison Park. Craven came in third and Harris last in a field of four. *Boston Post* 11/16/39, 2. *Boston Globe* 11/8/39. Black still bypassed the opportunity to support a black candidate; particularly poignant in this campaign, since David Kenney, the black candidate in question, came in second, even closer to victory than Cooke had been in 1935, with the largest number ever recorded by a black council candidate in the history of the present Ward 9, just 500 votes short of the winner. *Guardian* 11/11/39, 1. The rules of patronage politics may have explained Black's reluctance to support a black candidate. Attorney Ernest D. Cooke, the most promising contender for office, was a Republican. Black's connections in this "distinctly Curley ward" were Democratic. See *Boston Post* 10/27/29, 3, "City Councillors Contact Men," and *Guardian* 7/6/40, 3, "Well Known Republicans . . ." Cooke was attending the GOP national convention that year.

228 *Guardian* 4/26/41, 3, Louis B. Ransom, "Let's Gossip." Also *Guardian* 8/19/39, 1. *Guardian* 8/24/40, 4.

229 On Whiteman, see *Chronicle* 7/20/35, 1, "Roxbury Motorists Hurt in Auto Crash." *Chronicle* 6/6/36, 1, "Mrs. Helen Whiteman . . ." On Worthy, see *Chronicle* 8/5/33, 1, "Four Work for N.R.A." See also *Guardian* 11/18/39, 1, "Miss Cutler gets NYA Job." *Guardian* 11/25/39, 1, "For NYA Jobs."

230 Trout, *Boston*, 149, 155–158, 164, 191, 278.

231 Urban League, series 4 box 28, 1/29/34, Goodman to Hill. See his frustrations, 11/26/38 and 11/29/38, in letters to Hill on trying to get placements, as opposed to 11/28/38 announcing that Miss Oliva Johnson, one of those placed by Worthy in 1933, had been assigned as assistant librarian, Project No. 17579, according to the state WPA administrator. *Chronicle* 8/5/33, 1, "Four Work for N.R.A." Trout, *Boston*, 278. Note that Worthy also protested New Deal injustices in the South when she went job seeking, see *Chronicle* 9/16/33, 1. And at the

same time, there were many complaints of discrimination on New Deal projects in Boston. NAACP, Group I-G f. 90, 2/24/38, minutes of executive committee in the annual report. See also *Guardian* 6/11/38, clipping, in NAACP, Group I-G f. 90, on Luscomb fighting to get black supervisors in the WPA. Urban League, Series 4 box 28 11/29/38. Goodman to Hill.

232 See *Guardian* 10/18/02, 1, which profiles the four black women teaching in greater Boston's public schools; they included Miss Maria L. Baldwin, sister to former councilman Louis F. Baldwin; Miss Hattie Smith, whose father had been prominent in state politics; and Miss Gertrude Mabel Baker, sister-in-law to State Representative W. H. Lewis of Cambridge.

233 *Chronicle* 4/23/32, 1, "Politics Tinge Federation."

234 See, for example, *Chronicle* 3/5/32, 4, and NAACP, Group I-G f. 90, 6/14/38, Goodman to Marshall.

235 *Chronicle* 3/5/32, 4, Random Notes column, by Alvira Hazzard, "Colored Radicals." On organizing, see same issue, "Communist 'Nut' Cracked"; and 8/27/32, 5, City Gossip column, announcing an unemployed council meeting; *Guardian* 4/7/34, 5 "City News," on an ILD dance for Scottsboro.

236 *Guardian* (BU) 4/7/34, 1, 5; and 4/21/34.

237 *Guardian* (BU) 4/7/34, 1, " 'Negro' History Class." *Chronicle* 4/20/35, 1; and 6/22/35, 8. *Chronicle* 2/22/36, 1, "National Negro Congress Makes History." Mrs. M. Cravath Simpson was on the region's executive committee (*Guardian* 5/11/40, 1, "New England Congress Elects Officers"), having been, with William Munroe Trotter, one of its founders; *Chronicle* 3/14/36, 4, editorial, "Communists and the Congress"; and 2/15/36, 1, "N.E. Congress Huge Success." The *Chronicle*'s rather blasé attitude toward communism came amidst continued red baiting in Massachusetts, including the local activity of the Dies Committee. See James R. Green and Hugh Carter Donahue, *Boston's Workers: A Labor History* (Boston: Trustees of the Public Library of the City of Boston, 1979), 106–107, for example, on a 1930 garment strike and Curley's response; *Boston Globe* 10/21/37, evening edition, 2, "Girl Refuses to Tell Names of Communists"; *Guardian* 4/13/40, 1, 5, "Ann Burlak Answers Dies"; and see Trout, *Boston*, 213–215. "Along the Color Line," *Crisis* (January 1929): 14.

238 *Guardian* 4/7/34, 1.

239 *Chronicle* 8/1/36, 1, "Communists Name Leader."

240 On Simpson, see *Guardian* 12/9/39, 5; 8/12/39, 1. For some other black businesswomen who managed to cross these boundaries, see Maud Trotter Steward, *Guardian* (BU) collection; NAACP, Group I-G f. 90, 11/27/39, Mrs. Cora Reid McKerrow; 11/13/39, report on Boston Branch election; 12/11/39, Executive committee minutes. *Chronicle* 3/16/35; 4/22/39; 5/6/39; and 12/23/39. *Guardian* 12/30/39; 1/13/40, 8; 6/8/40; 8/2/41, 1 (versus her sister, Mattie Reid, *Guardian* 3/16/40, 3); *Guardian* 8/5/39, 1, Mrs. Esterene Z. Roundtree, 8/12/39; and 12/7/40, 8.

For an example of black businesswomen's affiliations, see *Chronicle* 6/18/38, 5, in NAACP, Group I-G f. 40, on the Wisteria Charity Club, whose treasurer was dry goods merchant and beautician Mrs. Estella Crosby and which included in its membership Geneva Arrington, also a beautician and frequently an officer in the Progressive Hairdressers' Club and future officer in the Greater Boston Negro Trade Association. When the NAACP began a membership drive in 1937, its organizer urged the branch to create three teams, one for social clubs, one for sororities, and one for women's lodges, mimicking the female social organization of black Boston. NAACP, Group I-G f. 90, Jackson to Dorch, 2/25/37.

While their directories seldom overlapped, their families often did. Black businesswomen numbered among their relatives teachers, nurses, and dentists, and daughters of black attorneys occasionally became beauticians. *Guardian* 7/6/40, 3, "Ruth Bates Back in Hub"; *Chronicle* 3/12/38, 1, "Bronze Boston" on Mrs. Lillian Craig of Craig Nursing Home; *Guardian* (BU) 6/23/34, 8; and 6/30/34, 4.

241 *Chronicle* 8/21/37, 8, "Playground Halted by Legal Quibble."

242 *Chronicle* 9/25/37, 4, editorial.

243 On Moore, see *Chronicle* 10/1/32, 5 (with picture); 4/1/33, 5; 8/21/37, 8; 9/7/35, 5 (with picture); and 1/23/32, 5. In the *Guardian* see 11/9/40, by which time she had become a lecturer for a WPA Community Recreation Project; 7/4/42, 3, and 7/19/19, 1. Almost any edition of either the *Chronicle* or the *Guardian* would demonstrate the importance of black women's enterprises to the papers' advertising revenues. On public/private identity, see, for example, *Chronicle* 2/5/38, 1, "Bronze Boston" by Alvira Hazzard, who referred to restaurant and beauty-shop owner Mary Lee as "in private life" Mrs. Robert Smith, even though the story made clear that Lee's husband's chicken and waffle meal contributed greatly to the restaurant's success.

244 See, for example, *Guardian* 7/29/39, with pictures; 7/16/40, 8; 8/5/39, 1, on the funeral of Mrs. E. Z. Roundtree.

245 *Chronicle* 4/9/38, 1, Mrs. Geneva Arrington, "Beautician Says Growth Rapid."

246 *Chronicle* 4/9/38, 1, Mrs. Geneva Arrington, "Beautician Says Growth Rapid." *Guardian* 9/14/40. The association united practitioners of the two major black hair systems, Apex and Poro, each of which also had their own clubs. *Guardian* 6/15/40 (Apex); *Chronicle* 3/26/38 (Poro). On Arrington, see *Chronicle* 12/9/33, 5, "New Apex Salon Opens"; *Guardian* 1/14/39, 8 (with picture), on her election as head of the Beautician's Club for the third consecutive year; 3/25/39, on her membership in the Wisteria Charity Club; 3/4/39, when she was president of the Progressive Hairdressers Association; 10/19/40, when she was its secretary.

247 The new law made it illegal for beauty-parlor owners to rent booths to independent operators. They now had to pay those operators at minimum wage, at least $16.50 per week, which, she claimed, would force the closing of many black beauty shops. *Guardian* 10/28/39, 4, "To the Hairdressers of Massachusetts"; 11/11/39, 1, 5, "Mrs. Taylor explains"; 11/18/39, 5, "Hair Dressers. . . ." On Bullock, see *Chronicle* 11/11/33, 1 (with picture); *Guardian* 1/14/39; *Crisis* (November 1930); *Globe* 12/8/21, 10. On Taylor, see *Chronicle* 1/25/36, 1 "Hairdressers Hold Meeting"; 1/23/32, ad. *Guardian* 9/23/39, 1 (with picture); 5/25/40, 1.

248 In 1939, the three were elected to offices in the Trade Association: Arrington, vice president; Crosby, recording secretary; Taylor, statistics and director of committee chairmen. *Guardian* 4/1/39, 8; 12/16/39; 12/4/40, 1, "Boston Trade Association Elects"; *Chronicle* 2/11/39, 1, "Housewives Form Group." *Guardian* 2/18/39, 4, "Trade Association Forms Housewives League." The head of the new association was Mrs. Mayme Dandridge, of the Silver Box [photographic] Studio at 522 Columbus Avenue, also active in Ebenezer Baptist and the Resthaven Ladies Auxiliary. On Wisteria Club, see *Chronicle* 6/18/38, 5, when Crosby was treasurer and Arrington was a member. In 1939, the Wisteria Charity Club pledged its support to the Housewives' League. *Guardian* 3/25/39. Dandridge served as president 1939–41; Mrs. Estella Crosby was elected president in 1941. The group met monthly. *Guardian* 3/39/41, 8; and see 3/8/40, 8; 3/23/40, 8; 6/22/40, 8; 10/22/42, 6.

The Housewives League was actually late in coming to Boston. It had its roots in Detroit in 1930. Darlene Clark Hine, "The Housewives' League of Detroit: Black Women and Economic Nationalism," in *Hine Sight: Black Women and the Re-Construction of American History*, ed. Hine (Bloomington: Indiana University Press, 1994), 130, 133, 137–138, 141.

249 *Chronicle* 2/11/39, 1, "Housewives Form Group"; and 5/6/39, 1; *Guardian* 2/18/39, 4, "Trade Association Forms 'Housewives League' "; and see Hine, "Housewives' League," 144. *Chronicle*

4/22/39, 1, "Name Delegates in Fight for More Jobs"; *Guardian* 4/15/39, 1, "Boston to Move on Utilities" and 4/12/41, 1.

250 Cf. Ardis Cameron, *Radicals of the Worst Sort: Laboring Women in Lawrence, Massachusetts, 1860–1912* (Urbana: University of Illinois Press, 1993), 10. And cf. Joanne Meyerowitz, "Beyond the Feminine Mystique: A Reassessment of Postwar Mass Culture, 1946–1958," *Journal of American History* 79 (March 1993): 1459, on the "ethereally pale housewife" who had served in both houses of the state legislature of Oregon before being elected mayor of Portland in 1952. On unemployment, see *Chronicle* 2/4/39, 1.

251 I have minimal evidence as to membership. For example, *Guardian* 3/11/39, 1. On charter member Mrs. Rosa Brown, see *Chronicle* 4/23/32; 4/29/33; and 3/16/35; *Guardian* (BU) 4/21/34. Similarly, on Mrs. Jacqueline (Alexander M.) Gilbert, see *Chronicle* 6/18/32; *Guardian* 5/20/39; and 4/22/41.

252 *Chronicle* 3/26/32, 1, "Home Owners' Protest Heeded."

253 *Chronicle* 3/26/38, 1, "Mothers Determined to Get Home-School Body."

254 *Chronicle* 4/2/38, 1, "Women Fight Sales Taxes."

255 *Chronicle* 1/22/38, 1, "Conference Hears Demand for Better South End Housing"; *Guardian* 4/28/39, 4, on her officership of the Housewives' League; and 4/19/41, 8, on her trade.

256 Urban League, Series 4 box 28, 9/16/38, Goodman to Arnold T. Hill, acting industrial secretary, National Urban League, including a brief to the mayor on housing. Trout, *Boston*, 14–15, 263.

257 National Federation of Settlements, box 34 f. 341, Robert Gould Shaw House, Annual Report, 1932–33, p. 3.

258 *Chronicle* 2/1938, 1 "Public Gets House Plans." Abbott, Report, on what the Joint Planning Committee was.

259 William E. Leuchtenburg, *Franklin D. Roosevelt and the New Deal 1932–1940* (New York: Harper Colophon Books, 1963), 257.

260 Trout, *Boston*, 152–154.

261 *Guardian* 5/27/39, 1, "Housing Authority. . . ." Trout, *Boston*, 14–15, 263.

262 *Guardian* 6/17/39, 1; 6/29/39, 1, "Mass Meeting on Housing" at the Columbus Avenue A.M.E. Zion Church; and 7/8/39, 4, "Women Stage Meet on Housing." See *Guardian* 8/12/39, 4, "Hire Colored on Lenox Street Project: Our Slogan"; 12/16/39, 1, "Starts Drive for Colored Workers on Housing Project"; and 9/7/40, 3, "Let's Gossip."

263 *Chronicle* 8/13/32; and 12/17/32, 4, "Gerrymandering."

264 *Guardian* 9/21/40, "Women and Politics."

265 *Chronicle* 8/24/35, 1, "No Candidate for Council."

266 *Chronicle* 9/25/37, 1.

267 *Guardian* 9/23/39, 1, "Endorse Candidate Wyche."

268 *Guardian* 4/26/41, 3, "Let's Gossip." I have no record, however, that she actually did so.

269 In 1929, fourteen of the twenty-two ward representatives were Irish; in 1939 thirteen were. Over three-quarters of the wards were solidly Democratic. Trout, *Boston*, 41, 278. See also *Boston Post* 11/3/31, Joseph A. Maynard, "Correct Injustice," supporting Henry Sassernoto for School Committee. On alliances between conservative Catholics and conservative Republicans, see Putnam, box 30 f. 488, to Mrs. Trabue, 10/29/26, and f. 189, to Mrs. Clarence Williams, 3/15/29, for examples.

270 In 1939, Susan Donovan won the City Council election by twenty-three votes only to lose in a recount. Her father was Manassah E. Bradley who served in the City Council and the state legislature, and her late husband had done the same, holding the ward seat where she ran. See *East Boston Free Press* 11/4/39, 1. See *Boston Post* 11/17/39, 8, "Wins By 13 Over Woman Foe";

Donovan and her rival were both currently in the Massachusetts House of Representatives. *Boston Post* 11/16/39, 2. The field comprised Donovan, Lena Clark, and seven men, including James F. Coffey, the ultimate victor. See also, *Boston Globe* 11/7/39, 2; 11/8/39, 1, announcing Donovan's victory. Donovan's husband had been a wizard at getting mammoth public works projects for his ward in the 1920s. See *Boston Daily Advertiser* 11/6/27, "Donovan to See Project Rise," for example.

271 Compare with Paula Baker, "The Domestication of Politics: Women and American Political Society, 1780–1920," *American Historical Review* 89 (June 1984): 645.

Conclusion

1 Kate Gannett Wells, "The Transitional American Woman," *Atlantic Monthly* 46 (December 1880): 819.

2 Brown, "Negotiating," 113.

3 See Nan Enstad, "Fashioning Political Identities: Cultural Studies and the Historical Construction of Political Subjects," *American Quarterly* 50 (December 1998): 745–782 for both examples and a theoretical discussion.

INDEX